VIKING FUND PUBLICATIONS IN ANTHROPOLOGY
Number Twenty-Seven

Culture and Conquest
America's Spanish Heritage

By

GEORGE M. FOSTER

QUADRANGLE BOOKS · CHICAGO · 1960

S. L. WASHBURN

UNIVERSITY OF CALIFORNIA

Editor

Published 1960 by
Quadrangle Books, Inc., 119 West Lake Street, Chicago 1, Illinois

Printed in the United States of America

CULTURE AND CONQUEST

America's Spanish Heritage

FOREWORD

THIS is a study of acculturation or, perhaps more accurately, of a series of culture contact problems and hypotheses exemplified by the sixteenth-century Spanish conquest of much of America. I am trying to do two things: to present a solid body of substantive data on Spanish ethnography, as an aid to anthropologists working in the Spanish American field; to use these data, in relation to the New World, to consider aspects of acculturation theory which, it seems to me, have not received the attention they deserve. On pages 7-9 some of the shortcomings in the theoretical framework characterizing contemporary studies of culture contact are discussed. Here it is sufficient to suggest that in recent years most anthropologists have dealt with acculturation as if the problem were largely limited to the reaction of a recipient people to a dominant donor group. This approach, while valid and important, channels thinking towards individuals, and consequently emphasizes psychological and sociological processes, to the neglect of culture. It is frequently stated—in fact, it is axiomatic—that cultures never meet, that only people who carry culture come into contact with each other. Of course in a strict sense this is true. On a different level, however, it is quite justifiable to argue that cultures do meet. If the point of reference is cultures rather than individuals, different types of problems suggest themselves.

In this study my point of reference is culture, and particularly the contact of cultures. The methodological approach further differs from most acculturation studies in that the characteristics of the donor culture, rather than the psychological and sociological reaction of the recipient peoples, receive primary attention. This has led me to ask, "How can we conceptualize and describe the profile of a dominant donor culture that impinges on a less complex society? What are the selective processes that create this profile? How does a dominant culture, as it is manifest in a contact situation, work to develop new hybrid cultures?" To answer the first two questions I suggest the theoretical model of "conquest culture," representing the totality of donor influences brought to bear on a recipient society. To answer the third question I offer the concept of "cultural crystallization" to explain the dynamics of "conquest culture" in the contact situation, and to show how its total potential impact is channeled and limited by the successful efforts of new hybrid cultures to achieve reintegration and stability. These ideas are discussed explicitly in chapters 2 and 17.

The selection of topics to illustrate these problems has been eclectic and arbitrary, reflecting my substantive and theoretical interests, and my personal experiences in Spanish America and Spain. Several bodies of data which logically belong here have been omitted because they have already been discussed in article form. Particularly to be noted are the relationships between *cofradías* and the *compadrazgo* in Spain and America (Foster 1953a), relationships between folk medical practices in both areas (Foster 1953b), and the San Juan fiesta of San Pedro Manrique (Foster 1955).

My desire to work in Spain stemmed from field research in Mexico, and particularly from the study of the mestizo village of Tzintzuntzan (Foster 1948a), in which the mixture of native American and Spanish cultures is so obvious. This work was carried out from 1944 to 1946 under the auspices of the Smithsonian Institution's Institute of Social Anthropology, while I was assigned as visiting professor to the Escuela Nacional de Antropología e Historia in Mexico City. The Spanish study likewise was done during my period of association with the Institute of Social Anthropology.

In October, 1948, I spent three weeks in Spain making official contacts for the proposed research. The Smithsonian Institution sent me as delegate to the centenary celebration of the Royal Academy of Geography in Madrid in the spring of 1949, an event that gave opportunity to my wife Mary and me to spend two months driving through Andalusia and Extremadura making preliminary observations. The greater part of the work, however, was carried out from September 1949 to September 1950. During this time I had the good fortune to be associated with the Spanish ethnographer, Dr. Julio Caro Baroja, then Director of the Museo del Pueblo Español.

Together we worked out a plan for library and field research, designed to promote our mutual interests. This plan involved the systematic selection of geographical areas of Spain which seemed to hold most of interest with respect to the New World. We then examined pertinent literature, marking significant sections for typing on cards, to be filed according to the Human Relations Area Files (HRAF) system. After each literary survey we visited the area concerned, timing our visits to the extent possible to correspond with fiestas of particular importance and with the major agricultural and economic activities of the year. Equipped with questionnaires which emphasized the lacunae in published data, we were able to fill in the more obvious gaps, in addition to taking fairly complete notes on selected aspects of culture. Field notes also were typed on HRAF-size cards, in duplicate, and filed in separate containers. Each of us thus had a complete file of field and reading notes.

Altogether it proved possible to visit and take significant notes in the following provinces: Pontevedra, La Coruña, Lugo, Oviedo (Asturias), Santander, Guipúzcoa, Navarra, Burgos, Soria, Valladolid, Salamanca, Avila, Segovia, Madrid, Guadalajara, Cuenca, Toledo, Ciudad Real, Mallorca and Ibiza, Valencia, Alicante, Murcia, Almería, Granada, Málaga, Cádiz, Jaén, Córdoba, Sevilla, Huelva, Badajoz and Cáceres. The greatest gaps are Catalonia and the Orense–Zamora–León–Palencia area.

In addition to field notes and published and archival sources, a third invaluable source of data became available. In 1901 the Section of Moral and Political Sciences of the Madrid Atheneum drew up a long questionnaire dealing with the ethnography of birth, marriage, and death, and sent it out to schoolteachers and other persons of similar background and interests in several hundred Spanish towns and villages. Two hundred and eighty replies, complete in varying degrees, were received which, when copied on 5-in. by 8-in. cards resulted in the enormous number of 8,500 entries on birth, 20,000 on marriage, and 15,000 on death. An almost complete copy of this questionnaire, which has been only slightly exploited in published sources, is preserved in the library of the Instituto de Antropología "Bernardino de Sahagun" in Madrid. Through the courtesy of the Institute's director, Dr. José Pérez de Barradas, it was possible to consult this mine of information, and to make copies of such parts of the data as appeared useful. A printed outline of this questionnaire, which comprises more than 15 pages, is contained in Hoyos and Aranzadi (1917). This is perhaps the most extensive questionnaire which has been used to date by ethnologists.

A field study cannot be carried out without the help and friendship of many persons. I am indebted to the Wenner-Gren Foundation for Anthropological Research for generous support in the field and for the publication of the finished work. A John Simon Guggenheim Memorial Foundation fellowship materially aided the field research. To the Smithsonian Institution I am indebted for permission to absent myself for so long from my regular work, and for the opportunity to serve as delegate at the centenary celebration of the Royal Academy of Geography in Madrid. It is a pleasant duty to acknowledge the high degree of aid, coöperation, and interest on the part of official Spanish circles. Particularly to be mentioned is Dr. Pablo Merry del Val, at that time Cultural Relations Consul of the Spanish Embassy in Washington, to whom I first presented by plan. He introduced me to individuals and institutions in Spain with corollary interests. Without his enthusiastic support and friendship it is doubtful that the field work would have been undertaken. In Madrid Dr. José María Albareda, Secretary of the Consejo Superior de Investigaciones Científicas, was most helpful in introducing me to Spanish scientists and in facilitating official contacts as needed. All Spaniards with whom I had contact, in official positions, as private scholars, or as field informants, showed the courtesy and friendship for which Spain is famous, and which makes working in Spain one of the most pleasant experiences an anthropologist can have.

Editorial note:—The descriptive data of this monograph apply primarily to Spain. I have found no easy solution to the problem of relating these data to Spanish America. Moderate use has been made of footnotes to call attention to specific similarities. In general, however, I attempt to meet the problem by introducing each descriptive chapter (4 through 16) with a brief synthesis of Spanish American patterns, as background for the

Spanish data, and ending each chapter with several paragraphs of comparisons and comments to tie the two areas together. References to Spanish (but not American) sources used to supplement field observations are appended at the end of each descriptive chapter. Some titles are not specifically quoted; all, however, have been consulted in preparing the chapter in question, and all contain valuable data for further reading.

June 1, 1959   GEORGE M. FOSTER
Berkeley, California

TABLE OF CONTENTS

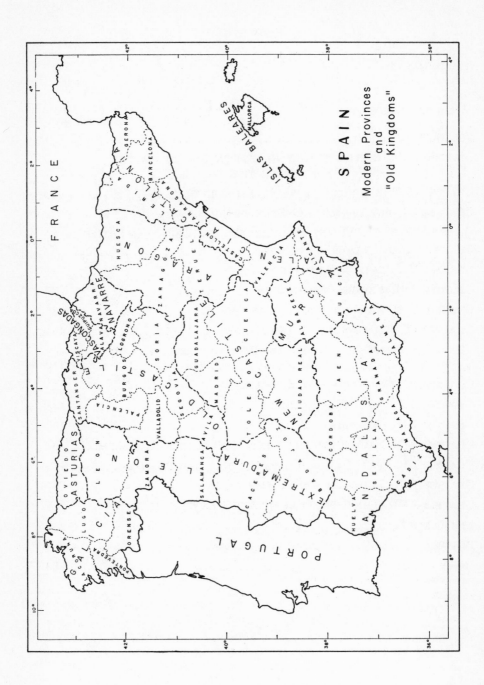

SPAIN

Modern Provinces
and
"Old Kingdoms"

CHAPTER I

CONTEMPORARY HISPANIC AMERICAN CULTURE: THE PRODUCT OF ACCULTURATION

THE native peoples of America at the end of the fifteenth century formed, in terms of cultural complexity, a spectrum or continuum ranging from the simplest hunting-fishing-gathering tribal societies to highly developed civilizations with urban and peasant components. Yet, in spite of these notable differences, they were alike in that they had all developed from the level of pre-bow-and-arrow hunters without significant contact with other regions. From the point of view of culture history they represented one of only two truly independent cultural traditions; the Old World was the other. This tradition had culminated, in Meso-America, in high civilizations based on agricultural and trading economies, with craft specialization, large cities, monumental architecture, elaborate politico-religious organizations, and dense populations. Soft metals were worked, writing was being developed, and the idea of the wheel was present in toys.

The peoples of the Iberian Peninsula until near the end of the fifteenth century were grouped in several politically autonomous units, which reflected significant cultural and social differences. Yet they were alike in that they had shared the same basic culture history through several millenia, during which time they were exposed to the basic innovations of Western Eurasia and North Africa. Neolithic farmers from Africa had been followed by Hallstatt iron workers from Europe, and Phoenicians and Greeks had brought civilization from the Eastern Mediterranean. Six centuries of Roman domination gave the peninsula a common language, unified political control, widespread urbanization, and other forms and values of Rome. The subsequent Moorish invasion brought Graeco-Roman learning of antiquity, as well as notable original contributions in such fields as agriculture, medicine, mathematics, and other forms of science. Finally, with the slow Christian reconquest, the peninsula was again brought within the orbit of Western European culture. No fifteenth-century Old World cultural tradition was richer than that of the Iberian Peninsula.

At this time chance brought Spanish culture into contact with that of a large part of the New World. Within a hundred years, and in most areas much less time, most of the native peoples from northern Mexico southward (Brazil excluded) were conquered and subdued by Spanish force of arms, their native forms of life rudely broken, and great changes brought about in their ways of living. At no other time in history has there been such a significant degree of culture contact between peoples of completely distinct traditions. Within fifty years as many as 150,000 Spaniards of all social classes and occupations (Friede 1952) had swarmed over America, mixing racially and culturally with the conquered native peoples and setting in motion the historical processes that subsequently produced the contemporary hybrid civilizations of Spanish America, civilizations that, in most of the area, draw upon the racially vigorous and culturally varied backgrounds of the Old and New Worlds.

In some parts of America, like southern Argentina and Chile, and northern Mexico, native populations were sparse, and exerted but little influence on the invaders' way of life. But in most of the area populations were moderate to dense, and Spanish ways were profoundly modified by existing cultures. The remarkable thing, however, is not that indigenous culture played such a role in modifying Spanish culture but rather that these powerful native influences should in the long run have been shaped and controlled by even more powerful Iberian forces. In Mexico, Guatemala, Ecuador, Peru, and Bolivia, the visible Indian populations and the elements of Indian culture are impressive, giving to each country many of its distinctive qualities. These Indian elements are now parts of the national culture, shared by educated and elite with the illiterate and lowly. But overriding the Indian-based characteristics are the generic Spanish similarities, stemming from the time of the Conquest and giving Hispanic America a cultural unity which has led anthropologists, historians, and philosophers to think in terms of a common Contemporary Hispanic American culture (e.g., Gillin 1947b, 1955). That is, in anthropological terminology, Hispanic America can be thought of as an enormous culture area, modern in origin, distinct from British America and from all other world areas. To quote Gillin "there is a common pattern of customs, institutions, and ethos that characterizes modern Latin [read Hispanic] American society as a whole . . ." (1955, p. 488).

This common pattern becomes understandable if we conceive it to be the result of the Spanish way of life from the beginning of the sixteenth to the early years of the nineteenth centuries, molding new forms based on Old and New World races and cultures. The "Spanish way of life" was manifest in the character, personality, personal habits, and beliefs of the first conquistadors and the later settlers who went to America. It was manifest, perhaps even more sharply, in a philosophy about God, sovereign, State, and man which was remarkable as much for its effectiveness as a guide to action as for its internal consistency and completeness. This philosophy was instrumental in producing a colonial policy which had as its goal the spiritual and legal conquest of the native peoples of America, the suppression or modification of large parts of their indigenous cultures, and the replacement of aboriginal ways with those characteristics of Spanish culture believed by Church and State to be the most advanced and desirable forms of Spanish life and thought.

So effective was this colonial policy that, by the time of the Wars of Independence in the second decade of the nineteenth century, all of Hispanic America from northern Mexico to southern Argentina and Chile was strongly marked by a common cultural stamp which reflected the drive of Spanish culture and the vitality of the race that carried it. Although, following separation from Spain, a series of independent nations emerged, each with peculiar geographical, economic, and social characteristics and with local traditions and histories, the supranational resemblances even today, a century and a half later, are so pronounced that, in anthropological concept, all countries together constitute a single culture area. The traveler who begins at the Rio Grande and journeys southward will find, all along his route, material forms, habits, and mental attitudes so similar that, after some experience, he can predict a great deal of what he will find in any new area into which he ventures.

Of these common characteristics language is the most striking. Pronunciations and vocabularies vary a bit from country to country—*ll* is pronounced *y* in Mexico while the Castilian *ly* is retained in Colombia, and the Guatemalan *aguacate* (alligator pear) becomes *palta* in the Andes—but if the foreign traveler has learned Spanish well in one of the eighteen countries, he will encounter few difficulties in any of the others. In no other place in the world is it possible to travel so far, through so many countries in which the same language is spoken.

In all of these countries the cities, towns, and villages are laid out in essentially the same fashion. Except in those places where the industrial age is rushing in, destroying the patterns of centuries, the checkerboard streets of the "grid-plan" town surround the central plaza with its cathedral or church, government buildings, and market. Traditionally the homes of the "best" families, of wealth and lineage, are near the center of town; only in the larger and most modern cities does one find a growing tendency to build fine homes in suburban residential areas.

Although the pattern is weakening today, fairly inflexible social classes still characterize much of Hispanic America. History teaches that the Catholic Church in the Middle Ages justified a tight class system in which each social group had its particular social and economic function to fulfill. And anthropology teaches that when a technologically superior or more warlike group conquers a less powerful group and sets itself up as ruler, caste differences tend to result. Both of these historical factors have combined in Hispanic America to perpetuate a class structure that is increasingly strained by the impersonality of growing industrial economies. Other social characteristics of Hispanic America include the large size of the extended family and the importance of the resulting relationships, the legal dominance of the male in family relationships and his freedom to avail himself of a socially sanctioned double sex standard, and the love of and the desire to have many children.

In religion, Catholicism is dominant. From the Rio Grande to Patagonia the cult of the Virgin Mary is the core of religious loyalty; the same saints are honored on the same days and in essentially the same fashion, and the same Mass draws the faithful each Sunday.

In government democratic forms exist in constitutions and law courts, but the functioning of the system demonstrates that by democracy most Hispanic Americans understand something rather different from Anglo-Saxons. *Personalismo*—an effective personal working relationship with the right people—rather than impersonal principle is more often than not the basis on which government, and business as well, functions.

A similar ethos is found in all the area. Life tends to be looked at in the same way, there is common agreement as to the desirable goals, and attitudes toward work, health, and enjoyment betray common historical bonds. The external forms of human relationships are more highly stylized than in more hurried societies, and courtesy for its own sake is elaborately developed. Personal and national pride are great, and dignity and face must be preserved at all cost.

In spite of, or perhaps because of, a long authoritarian tradition in Church and State, laws and regulations often are considered things to be avoided, and satisfaction is taken in an individualism and a freedom of spirit and action which sometimes approach anarchy. Although authority may be flouted, power is respected and desired, power as exercised by the political *caudillo*, the strong man, or the ruthless yet successful military general or business man. Unlike the traditional attitude of predominantly Protestant societies, work is not thought to be a positive value; it is regarded as a necessary evil, something most people must do to live, but something to be avoided when and if one has been born wealthy or has had *suerte*, fortune in financial dealings. Government lotteries are general, and reflect the near-universal hope that good luck will mean freedom from monetary worries and work.

In rural areas the Spanish legacy is equally apparent. Farm tools, and the techniques associated with agricultural production, usually reflect more of Spain than of native America. Old World oxen draw the Mediterranean scratch plow, even to prepare the ground for maize in many places, and the hoofs of horses tramp out grains of wheat, just as is done in Extremadura today. The adobe walls of houses may reflect both Spanish and native techniques, but the common red tile roof is but one of a number of Moorish elements that found their way to the New World. The lake or ocean shore fisherman, whether Indian or mestizo, draws in his catch in a *chinchorro*, *atarraya*, or *trasmallo* net, all of Iberian origin (as far as America is concerned), while the hook-and-line fisherman uses the common peninsular *espinel* or *palangre* trot lines.

Hispanic American arts and crafts, while owing much to Indian developments, reveal profound and far-reaching European influences. The colonial Spanish flat-bed loom long ago replaced simpler native weaving techniques, except in areas of continued dense Indian populations, and heavy fulled woolen cloth quickly became a standard clothing material, even among such Indians as the Tarascans. Spanish carpenters' and masons' tools brought greater mastery of wood and stone, in building and in woodworking, while the primitive circular Mediterranean kiln made possible higher temperatures so that glazed ware could be made, and the introduced potter's wheel encouraged the continuation of fine Talavera-type majolica. The solid-wheeled cart and the pack animal facilitated transportation in America, thereby strengthening preëxisting patterns of commerce, and particularly periodic markets.

In the life of the individual, Spanish influence is apparent at every point. The taboos associated with pregnancy, and with the postnatal *cuarentena*, the beliefs and rhymes about teething, and the games played by children are far more often Spanish than indigenous. Courting patterns and marriage rules, too, reveal Spanish influence, even in those areas of life in which the Church was not particularly interested. The same is true of death rites and beliefs.

Contemporary Hispanic America, and its Indian and Spanish antecedents, has attracted anthropologists for more than a hundred years. Initially, research interest was directed toward the living native peoples and the archaeological remains of their forebears. During the latter half of the nineteenth century and the first quarter of the twentieth the field techniques and general concepts that characterized anthropology in other parts of the world were applied to this area. Tribes were studied largely as the products of their own particular developmental sequences, modified by other native tribes which, although they might be somewhat simpler or more complex, were nonetheless all very different from Western civilization. Attempts were made to reconstruct the "pure" form of tribal culture, before contact with civilization, and the differences between tribes were emphasized, at the expense of the similarities. The goal of most field workers was to find out as much as possible about a tribe, and problem-oriented research was limited to historical reconstructions, presumed early contacts, and the like.

Subsequently, interest expanded to include Hispanicized Indian and mestizo communities. This trend is most clearly marked by Redfield's study of Tepoztlán, Mexico (1930), although there were precursors, particularly Gamio's monumental work on the valley of Teotihuacán (1922). Redfield differed from his predecessors in selecting a small town essentially mestizo in composition, although much Aztec was still spoken there, rather than a tribal people. Here he emphasized, not the unique and the aboriginal, but rather the town and its culture in relation to Mexican national life, and as a part of what he called a generic Mexican "folk" culture. A majority of subsequent ethnographical studies in Hispanic America concentrated on the town or village rather than the tribe. Sometimes the communities were essentially mestizo, such as Gillin's Moche (1947a) or Foster's Tzintzuntzan (1948a). Sometimes the communities were more completely Indian in speech and in many customs, such as Parson's Mitla (1936) or Beals's Cheran (1946).

In all these studies, however, there was a change in much more than field subjects. On the one hand, new research techniques were employed, some sociological in nature, like the use of census materials and questionnaires, others psychological in inspiration, like the application of projective tests coupled with attempts to determine personality types. On the other hand, conceptualization of basic problems broadened enormously. Anthropologists came to realize that most Hispanic American culture, whether rural or urban, of small-community size or national in scope, was a new and distinctive entity with two dominant roots, one embedded in indigenous American culture and the other in Iberian culture, largely of the colonial period.

It became apparent that, to understand contemporary Hispanic American culture in its many aspects, it would be necessary to approach the problem of culture change with a broader perspective than that afforded by traditional anthropological concepts of simple trait diffusion. Acculturation theory (which began to develop in the 1930's), with its emphasis on continuous and prolonged contact between people of different traditions and ethos, appeared to offer the key, and during recent years this theoretical framework has been instrumental in pointing the problems that have occupied the attention of field workers in Hispanic America.

Before the significance of a contemporary Hispanic American culture as a new and distinctive phenomenon was completely understood, acculturation studies in that region were usually marked by a rather severely limiting conception of the nature of the problem. Depending on whether the peoples being studied appeared (on an impressionistic basis) to be more Indian or more mestizo, their culture was looked upon as native American modified by Spanish contact or as essentially a Spanish culture which had taken on many of the material elements and at least some of the ethos of Indian life. Usually the anthropologist placed greater emphasis on the Indian component; his professional inclination to be attracted by exotic culture, and his grounding in basic New World prehistory and ethnography, made the Indian elements he encountered more easily recognizable than the Iberian elements. And not infrequently Spanish traits were erroneously ascribed to native American culture: the frequent classification of foods, herbs, and illnesses into "hot" and "cold" categories, and the division of towns into "upper" and "lower" *barrios* are illustrative.

This tendency to emphasize the native American components in contemporary Latin American culture, at the expense of Iberian elements, is easily understood. The wealth of peninsular documentation left by meticulous chroniclers, Church archivists, and government officials, not to mention the writings of novelists, playwrights, and other literary figures, is overpowering to the student who feels his hands to be full in making a field study. Nevertheless, anthropologists have become aware of Iberian history and culture, and the limited research they have done has been helpful in sorting out Iberian and Indian elements in Spanish American culture and in understanding the processes whereby they have mingled together, been transformed, or been replaced by new forms. At the same time, documented history is silent on many points that are important to anthropological research. A long series of Spanish chroniclers and native American scholars educated by Spaniards have given us superb accounts of much Indian culture as it existed at the time of the Conquest and in subsequent years. Nevertheless, our knowledge of Amerindian culture in Spanish America would be very incomplete without the ethnographic tribal and village studies that have been made by anthropologists. Similarly, in addition to the work of historians in Spain during the past five hundred years, first-hand ethnographic investigations of Spanish culture, particularly rural and folk, will add much to our understanding of the Spanish component in contemporary Hispanic America.

Since the concept of acculturation has provided the major theoretical frame for a majority of anthropological studies in Hispanic America, it is necessary to consider in some detail certain shortcomings in this theory as applied to the field situation.

Acculturation can be thought of as both the processes and results of the contact of cultures. The term "results" implies that changes occur in the contacting cultures. The term "processes" refers to the sociocultural and psychological mechanisms whereby the changes are achieved. This definition is somewhat broader than that of either Herskovits or Kroeber, who discuss the subject in widely used texts. The former thinks of acculturation as "the study of *cultural transmission in process*, as contrasted to diffusion, "the study of *achieved cultural transmission*" (1948, p. 525), whereas the latter emphasizes the results: "Acculturation comprises those changes produced in a culture by the influence of another culture which result in an increased similarity of the two" (1948, p. 425).

Although anthropologists generally recognize that an acculturative process occurs when groups of essentially equal power and cultural complexity meet, in practice most studies have dealt with situations in which a more complex or powerful donor group controls the contact situation and guides at least a part of the transmission of its culture to the weaker, recipient group. This fact recently has led Drucker to suggest that the element of dominance be included in an operational definition of acculturation, a point of view to which I subscribe (1958, p. 4).

In contact situations marked by disparity in power and cultural complexity, the donor group changes its ways in some degree, but the major changes are found in the ways of the recipient group. Perhaps for this reason most acculturation theory centers around the question of what happens to the dominated group. Certainly most of the studies labeled "acculturation" describe single groups and the changes they have undergone as the result of contact; this is as true for Spanish America as for other parts of the world. We find that these accounts deal with process in terms of borrowing, and the selection of elements by the recipient group that leads to acceptance, rejection, integration, syncretism, and the like. Cultural processes are discussed on the basis of compatibility, adaptability, congruence, fundamental fit, or utility, and sequence and nativistic movements. Psychological processes tend to be thought of in terms of the individual, the alternate choices he faces, and his decisions. Perhaps, too, the recent interest in innovation and its linkage to acculturation theory—through the view that, whether a new trait originates from within or without a society, the mode of treatment is the same—strengthen concern with the recipient group.

This interest in recipient groups has led, in practice, to the essential neglect of many problems associated with the nature of the donor culture and its role in bringing about change. I say "in practice" because in theory the problem has been recognized since the early stages of interest in acculturation. In their 1936 "Outline for the Study of Acculturation" Redfield, Linton, and Herskovits repeatedly mention such things as "the elements of culture likely to be made available" by the members of contacting groups, the "types of traits permitted and forbidden to the receiving group," "traits presented by the donor group," and so forth. Four years later Linton stressed the importance of knowing which elements are available for borrowing, and pointed out that, at least in the contacts of Europeans and natives, only specialized representatives of the donor culture normally influenced the recipient group. Moreover, even with an entire band of settlers, only a part of a total culture is presented (1940, pp. 496-498). Finally, he pointed out that members of a donor culture frequently consciously withhold elements of their way of life, for reasons of political control, prestige, and the like (*ibid.*, p. 498).

Among the British, Malinowski has emphasized that the "aggressive or conquering community *in situ*" is by no means a direct replica of its mother country (1945, p. 17). He speaks of the "piecemeal bestowal of cultural benefits on the part of Europeans," of a "selective giving by the Europeans" (*ibid.*, p. 41), and finally of the fact that "selective giving influences the process of change perhaps more than any other element in the situation" (*ibid.*, p. 58).

In spite of these and other similar statements, field anthropologists appear to have thought largely of acculturation situations in terms of total cultural systems in contact, and of the changes that occur in the recipient culture. Monica Hunter illustrates this point when she writes: "I am concerned to discover the reactions of Pondo culture to European culture" (1936, p. 343). It is this tendency that led Julian Steward to remark about Latin American research that "many studies are made of acculturated peoples but few studies are made of their acculturation" (1943, p. 201).

Since most acculturation studies have involved modern Western society in contact with primitive or peasant peoples, the problem of conceptualization of the nature of the donor culture has seemed almost insurmountable. Presumably this first requires thorough description parallel to that attempted for the recipient group. But the anthropologist studies primitive and peasant peoples precisely because their societies are small and their cultures simple; up to a point they can be described. He tends to avoid

Western civilization, simply because his methodological and conceptual techniques are not adequate to tackle the problem. In most acculturation studies, therefore, the anthropologist on page one bows in the direction of the principle that both groups must be understood, that acculturation is a two-way street, and that changes in the donor culture are theoretically as important as those in the recipient culture. Then he goes his own way, analyzing the changes that occur in his primitive or folk community.

The problem of how to handle a dominant and complex culture in a contact situation has received somewhat more attention in recent years. In the 1954 Social Science Research Council statement, "Acculturation: an Explanatory Formulation," the authors state the position that "cultures do not meet, but people who are their carriers do. As carriers of traditions such contacting individuals never know their entire cultures and never convey all they know of them to one another" (p. 980). More precisely:

Two components figure in this complex design [intercultural communication], namely, the range of presented fact and the cross-cultural interpretation of it. That is, *no culture presents its full face to the other*, and to the facade that is presented cross-culturally meanings are attached which may have little or no relation to their intracultural significance (p. 983, my italics).

And again, "acculturation is very much a matter of *range of presentation* and of perceptual reality . . ." (*ibid.*, my italics).

Mason is perhaps alone among American anthropologists in addressing himself to the problem of more precise definition of the donor culture. Recognizing repeated statements about the importance of knowing the donor culture, he nevertheless finds that "a survey of the literature reveals that most students of culture contact have neglected to examine critically the character of the more familiar, dominant group, with a consequent incompleteness of analysis and conclusions about the acculturation of the exotic group" (1955, p. 1264). Speaking specifically about American culture, he concludes that "most anthropologists fail to apply the same critical standards of observation to the donor side of contact situations as they do to the receiving side" (*ibid.*). Summarizing, Mason is struck by the fact that, in spite of early emphasis on the importance of treatment of the donor group (e.g., Redfield, Linton, and Herskovits, 1936, and Linton, 1940), not much has been done in concrete terms along this line.

Since acculturation is a process of culture change which involves more than a native people and its culture, future studies aimed at understanding the nature of this process should include more detailed analyses of the culture of the donor group and the significance of the latter within the total contact situation. It is not enough for observers to characterize the donors as "Americans" [or "Spaniards"] and simply leave the matter there (Mason 1955, p. 1275).

CHAPTER II

THE CONCEPT OF "CONQUEST CULTURE"

C AN we construct a model to facilitate conceptualization of the nature of a dominant donor culture and its mode of presentation to a subordinate recipient culture? If so, such a model, while it must fit all contact situations of similar type, is most efficiently built from a specific case. For many reasons Spain in relation to Hispanic America offers unusual opportunities for this attempt. Although sixteenth-century Spain had a diversified culture, it was generally less complex than a large, modern industrial nation. Its impact on America was more intense, and freer from complicating factors, than that of the Western nations which impinged, in the nineteenth and twentieth centuries, upon colonial areas. Finally, the Spanish conquest was marked by a consistent and logical philosophy of purposeful guided change that extended over a period of three centuries. This philosophy had as goal the extension of an ideal Spanish culture and culture values to all parts of America where it was physically possible, a policy not duplicated elsewhere in modern times. Guided change, too, requires paper work and record keeping; fortunately, the preservation of this documentation has been excellent.

The model I have in mind deals with the general question of the profile of a donor culture and, specifically, of Spanish culture. What is really meant when one speaks of Spanish culture in Latin America? Such people as conquistadors, colonizers, missionaries, government administrators? Ideas? Material culture? The totality of Spanish cultural forms of the sixteenth-to-eighteenth century? In other words, what was the "Spanish way of life" that, reaching America as an acculturating force, produced Hispanic American civilization, and how was it formed?

In constructing this model it is important to note that the transmission of culture from a dominant to a recipient people represents, in simplest terms, a pair of screening processes. Two complete cultural systems never come into full contact. There is always an initial selection that determines which parts of a donor culture will be made available to the recipient group and which parts, consciously or unconsciously, will be withheld. This first of the two screening processes, in which the authority of the donor culture plays a positive part, must be studied with the donor culture as the point of reference.

In the second of the two screening processes the recipient culture selects, or has forced upon it, only a part of the total range of phenomena presented by the dominant group. This is largely unplanned and informal, culture traits being channeled through the personal decision of individuals. In some areas the subordinate group can exercise choice and, depending on how it perceives the new phenomena in these categories, on its ability to resist imposition, or on its economic capacity to possess, it will accept or reject. This second selective process must be studied with the recipient culture as the point of reference.

It must be noted that the form of donor culture presented in a contact situation represents more than a mere selection and synthesis of traditional elements from the mother country; the contact situation itself not only provides the guide to choices, but also brings forth new ideas and items that are not a part of the preëxisting culture, but which significantly influence the recipient peoples.

Traditional United States culture as it is presented to and perceived in tropical America, for example, represents only a small range of the total variety found in the fifty states. But this "small range" is added to and amplified by items—trade goods, commercial policies, and political programs—that are not a part of our customary way of life. Most United States citizens have never seen a Collins machete, and perhaps do not even know the brand name. Yet this artifact, and its trademark, have made an enormous impression as an acculturative force, and as one expression of America, in the areas it has reached. Similarly, African prints from Manchester are not a part of traditional British culture, but these colorful cotton textiles, like machetes, have produced striking results in the areas which gave the original impetus and to which they are exported.

The theoretical model with which I am concerned here deals primarily with the first of the two screening processes. Through this process a choice is made from the totality of forms found in a dominant, conquering donor culture and to these forms are added ideas and items called into being or developed as a result of the contact situation itself. This process results in a new "culture," with a distinctive profile which becomes the acculturative force on the recipient people.

Some time ago, and speaking specifically of Spain, I suggested that this model be called "conquest culture" (Foster 1954). A "conquest culture" can be thought of as "artificial," "standardized," "simplified," or "ideal," in that it is at least partially consciously created and designed to cope with recognized problems. The concept presupposes that the government (or the agent of the government) of the donor culture has some degree of military and political control over the recipient people, and that this control is utilized to bring about planned changes in the way of life of this group. There are other contact situations in which change processes are not unlike those here described, but in which formal political control, and perhaps military control as well, are absent. Missionary enterprises or trading concerns often bring great changes in the traditional cultures of less developed peoples, without formal control; the acculturation of Hawaii can be thought of in this fashion. For such situations the term "contact culture" may more accurately express the idea.

A conquest culture—or a contact culture—can perhaps best be thought of as the totality of donor influences, whatever their origin, that are brought to bear on a recipient culture, the channel whereby the dominant ways, values, and attitudes of the stronger group are transmitted to the weaker. A conquest culture is the result of processes that screen the more dynamic, expanding culture, winnowing out and discarding a high percentage of all traits, complexes, and configurations found in it and determining new contexts and combinations for export. It is the result of a process in which the new face of the donor culture is precipitated out of the infinite variety of original forms and enriched by the elements produced by the contact situation itself.

A conquest culture, obviously, is not the same thing as the culture of the donor group; neither must it be confused with colonial culture. It is a force which may, and usually does, produce a colonial culture, but it also modifies the ways of native peoples who do not participate fully in a colonial culture. A conquest culture likewise is not conterminous with that part of a donor culture that takes root overseas, because it is subject to the second, local screening process, which rejects a part of it. In other words, all the facets of a donor culture presented to a recipient people and a colonial area are not exploited. A greater potential than that actually utilized in any specific situation is present; in spite of the thorough homeland screening, conquest cultures still present more than will be absorbed in a new setting.

Conquest culture characteristically is produced in dichotomous fashion: it is the result of two principal types of selective processes, which can be called "formal" and "informal." The expression "formal process" applies to all those situations in which institutions and individuals in positions of authority play a positive planning role: government administrators, armies, the church, trading companies, and the like. "Formal," in the sense here used, can be equated with the idea of "guided" or "planned" or "directed" culture change, in which specific goals are set and efforts are made to achieve these goals.

The expression "informal process" applies to all those unplanned mechanisms whereby the personal habits of emigrants, their food preferences, superstitions, popular medicine, folklore, music, attitudes, beliefs, hopes, and aspirations are selected and maintained in the new country. In formal processes, groups in authority make the decisions they feel to be desirable, and attempt to enforce these decisions. In informal processes, we are dealing with a multitude of personal decisions, in which each individual, through his pattern of living, is a channel of cultural transmission to the contact area.

The formation of a conquest culture is characterized by a "stripping down" or "reduction" process in which large numbers of elements of the donor culture are eliminated and the complexity and variety of many configurations become simplified. This phenomenon of reduction continues, of course, after the presentation of conquest culture in a colonial setting, and as a result of the second of the two screenings inherent in the acculturation process. Whether the area is Spanish America, Africa, or Oceania, an anthropologist is impressed by the fact that, with respect to almost any institution or trait configuration, the colonial forms are less numerous and less varied than those in the home country.

Now I propose to examine the model of conquest culture in terms of the Spanish domination of America: the selection from an almost infinite variety of peninsular elements, the formal and informal processes involved, and the "stripping" down of Spanish culture in America.

The complexity of this first screening process, and its implications for an understanding of contemporary Hispanic American life, is far greater than American anthropologists customarily have realized. As late as 1949 the authors of a National Research Council subcommittee memorandum, "Research Needs in the Field of Modern Latin American Culture," while fully cognizant of the importance of knowing the Iberian background, misinterpreted the nature of this background by calling for but a single present-day study of a Spanish community. "Purpose: to compare end results of culture development from a common Spanish base in Spain and in America, i.e., what has been added to Spanish culture in America in the course of time which did not develop in Spain?"

The limitation of this conception is apparent when we realize that six-teenth-century Spain consisted of a series of regional nuclei—the Castiles, Aragón, Catalonia, Galicia, Extremadura, Andalusia, for example—each with cities, towns, and villages, and each with marked provincial charac-teristics but all bound together on a national level by political forms, religion, economic activities, history, and some awareness of identity of interest. Each of the traditional major areas of Spain constituted a com-plete sociocultural system, representing roughly the same range in com-plexity from urban-elite to village-peasant as all the other areas. Any one of these nuclei, if it alone had conquered large parts of America, could have supplied a complete culture which would have set off the accul-turation process. In Portugal, of course, this is what happened. A major cultural subarea of the peninsula, which happened also to be politically independent, conquered a major part of America and became the accul-turating force.

Because of this great peninsular diversity, any single Spanish village reflects the reality of only one section of the country. If it is assumed, as has sometimes been done in the past, that a majority of conquistadors and colonists came from Andalusia and Extremadura alone, this embar-rassment of cultural wealth would not be too important: since northern and eastern areas would not have contributed many people, they would not have contributed much culture. But, as we now know (see chapter 3), significant numbers of colonists came from nearly all parts of Spain, so that culture forms from the entire country are potentially significant in America. Moreover, the "single village" approach, which interprets accul-turation in terms of migration of people, overlooks the role of formal processes. Regardless of the place of origin of Spanish emigrants, the formal processes of State and Church alike tend to be based on Castilian models. For these reasons, although the thorough analysis of a single village is enormously interesting, it answers fewer questions, in terms of the basic problems of Spanish culture in America, than we formerly believed it would.

It is apparent that the total cultural resources on which Spaniards in the New World might draw were far greater than the continents could absorb. The potential cultural mixture was too rich. Conquerors and colonizers from different parts of the peninsula had to form new communities and societies, usually in some symbiotic relationship with Indians and Indian culture, and reach levels of integration which ensured viability for the new communities. But there were limits to the complexity of these new societies and communities, particularly in a frontier epoch. In terms of functional analysis there is an optimum number (or level of development) of institutions and traits. Beyond this optimum level replication seems to be impossible. In other words, America could not possibly incorporate all Spanish influences to which it was exposed and combine them in any series of societies with all of native American culture. It is a little like trying to combine two households of furniture in a single dwelling: even with crowding there are limits, and for comfortable living there are optimum combinations. Beyond these combinations, the excess must be discarded.

The mechanisms whereby many traditional Spanish elements were discarded are found in the formal governmental and church decisions involved in selection of desired existing forms and the creation of new ones. Both State and Church believed that not all Spanish traits, however proud the individual might be of them, were good or desirable as parts of a civilizing mission, so by administrative decision many elements of culture were withheld and new elements were devised to take their place. Formal processes, for example, produced standardized municipal organizations, as contrasted to the variety of local Iberian forms, and it produced the grid-plan town in place of the loosely planned or completely unplanned Spanish community of the sixteenth century. Formal processes likewise congregated Indians in villages, governed commerce and trade, and introduced an ideal or theologically purified Catholic dogma and ritual to America.

What appear to be the informal mechanisms of selection and diffusion of culture traits to America are less well understood, and it is here that ethnographical research in the peninsula offers special opportunities. If we assume the informal mechanisms operated particularly in such areas as food, much of family life, the life cycle, music, folklore, medical beliefs and practices, magic and superstitions, which are not well recorded in history, it is apparent that to the extent we can know the Spanish base line, we have grounds for drawing conclusions, or at least advancing hypotheses.

For example, the widespread popular Latin American concept of "hot" and "cold" qualities that characterize food, medicine, and illness have generally been assumed by anthropologists to represent direct diffusion from a similar pattern of belief held by people of a comparable socio-economic type in Spain. So, when the ethnologist discovers that this widespread New World pattern does not exist in Spain, and apparently did not exist on the folk level in earlier centuries either, new explanations must be sought, and culture processes different than those of simple diffusion must be invoked.[1]

The "stripping down" process which characterizes conquest cultures is abundantly apparent in Spanish America in almost every category of culture. Here one is impressed continually by the relative monotony of appearance of Iberian forms. The term monotony is used, not in the sense of dull or boring—quite the contrary, in most cases—but rather with the meaning of limited range, or variety, of phenomena.

The ritual calendar of the Catholic Church well illustrates the process of reduction. The basic observances in America are the same as in Spain: Epiphany, Candlemas, Lent, Holy Week, Corpus Christi, All Saints' and All Souls' Days, Christmas, and so forth. But one looks, usually in vain, for most of the popular or local religious customs which give so much color to Spain. Where, for example, is the pig of San Antón? Santa Agueda and the *alcaldesas*? *Jueves Lardero*? the burial of the sardine? the fiestas of San Blas? the fire walkers of San Pedro Manrique? *Domingo de Piñata*? and a host of other popular fiestas which one finds in Spain today. Catholicism in conquest culture was purified through simplification. In its conquest of Europe primitive Christianity had been forced to incorporate, or at least tolerate, local and widespread customs pagan in origin, which it did by identifying local rites with Christian belief and practice. But in missionizing America the Church had the opportunity to throw off these popular observances, to define Catholicism in terms of rites and observances central to dogma, to produce a theologically ideal religion. To the ethnologist it appears that it was this expurgated Catholicism that took root in America; it is an explanation which accounts for the lack of so many Spanish Catholic customs in America.

Of course, once in America, the Church was again faced with the same problems as fifteen hundred years earlier; in its spiritual conquest of America, as of Europe, certain native religious beliefs and practices were again subsumed under Catholic forms, producing religious variants in Spanish America not found in Spain. But such concessions were nominal. The Catholic ceremonial year in Spanish America owes its form to the fact that the Church knew what it wanted and what it did not want, and that it had the power to encourage the former and discourage the latter. *Autos sacramentales* taught the Christian doctrine, and hence were useful in converting illiterate Indians; carnival observances were recognized as a threat to morality and order, and they were discouraged, but not entirely suppressed, in America as in Spain.

The same type of simplification or "stripping down" of Spanish culture is apparent in political and economic planning. It was possible to draw up for Spanish America what the rulers thought to be an ideal Spanish political and economic system, one which could disregard the rights and privileges acquired over the years in Spain by individual cities or groups or social classes. New World forms could be modeled after those thought to be the best or most useful, and forms which bothered the central government could be largely ignored. Another illustration of the ideal conquest culture is the physical form of cities. The grid-plan which characterized scarcely half-a-dozen pre-Conquest Spanish towns—none of them major— was recognized by the planners as an ideal form for the establishment of new towns. The great variety of plans of Spanish towns and cities is replaced in Spanish America by the one form, a cultural simplification from much variety to little variety.

Similar selective, simplifying processes likewise characterize the informal levels of conquest culture, although it is more difficult to explain why. In almost any aspect of material culture brought from Spain we find that only a small proportion of the totality of Spanish forms has reached America. To illustrate, traditional Spanish plows are characterized by great diversity in form. Some have the "pig-snout" share, others the lance-shaped share. Some have wheels, others have coulters. Often a student of plows can very nearly tell the village from which a specimen comes. But there is only one basic type in Spanish America, the Andalusian *arado dental* (p. 52). A specimen from Chile is nearly identical with one from Mexico. Moreover, the simplifying process which reduced the many Spanish plows to a single form likewise completely eliminated threshing devices. Neither the ancient Roman *tribulum* nor the Andalusian threshing cart *(plostellum)* seem ever to have reached America. In short, Spanish American agricultural tools and techniques are generally based on Spanish forms (except in those areas where indigenous practices survive), but these forms represent a small selection only from the available models.

The story is the same with respect to fishing. Probably no area of comparable size is characterized by more diversity in fishing techniques than Spain. Yet little of this diversity reached America. The *chinchorro, atarraya,* and *trasmallo* nets and the *espinel* hook and line are found from Mexico to Chile. But most of the other common Spanish devices, including the *jábega* and *boliche* (p. 78), seem not to have been generally incorporated in conquest culture, and appear only rarely in America.

A comparison of Spanish folk medicine, superstitions, refrains, and popular birth, marriage, and death rites (as contrasted to those standardized by the Church) with the Spanish American forms reveals the same selective force at work, the simplification of the wide variety of Spanish elements, and the selection of relatively few.

At least a part of the explanation for this simplification of culture, the elimination of many traditional elements, lies in the sheer mechanics of transportation. This is particularly true of items of material culture. A people on the move cannot carry with them many of their home belongings.

Rigorous selection is essential, and those things that can be most easily carried, or which are thought to be of most utility in the new home, are favored. Then, too, a new environment, and often a frontier way of life, makes unnecessary some items of material culture used in the old home, while placing a premium on new items heretofore unknown. In Mexico, for example, lack of sufficient streams of water and of regular winds make it difficult to reproduce the watermills and windmills of Spain. For this reason the Indian metate grinding stone, admirably adapted to the preparation of maize and chocolate, became a standard item of equipment in the homes of all Spaniards in America, and even of many in Spain.

In other cases, particularly the nonmaterial aspects of popular culture—folklore, beliefs, superstitions, folk medicine, folk festivals, and the like—it is hard to say why so much traditional Spanish culture fell by the wayside. One reason may lie in the fact that the conquistadors and settlers were a mixed group, coming from all parts of Spain. The settlers of new communities often shared relatively few local folk customs and beliefs with their new neighbors. With a mixed group it would obviously be impossible to continue every local fiesta and observance known to each settler, and to perpetuate all folktales, refrains, home medical cures, and the like. A society can support only a given amount of belief and ceremonial life, and when there is a superabundance of sources—as in the cases under consideration—a selection must somehow be made. With ritual and ceremonial observances selection was usually made by the Church. The Church in itself had a sufficient number of important religious dates to satisfy the emotional and recreational needs of any community, and the formal organization to plan and carry out such activities.

The concept of conquest culture provides a framework for the study of a number of acculturation problems in Spanish America. For the analysis of cross-cultural regularities in process, and the search for relationships of cause and effect, the situation is perhaps unique: at essentially the same period in history a reasonably homogeneous cultural stimulus was brought to bear upon hundreds of local cultures of the most varied types. This interaction produced results which, for comparative purposes, are particularly interesting since one of the two usual variables in acculturation settings, the donor culture, was relatively standardized. Therefore the differing reactions of many groups to a single stimulus over a long period of time can be observed and compared, and possible regularities in the process of change can be more easily isolated than is usually possible.

This monograph deals primarily with the available background of conquest culture, the "homogeneous stimulus"—and even here the coverage is selective. This need for information about Spain was recognized long ago by anthropologists. In 1912 Boas emphasized the importance of Spanish elements in Spanish American and Indian folklore (1912); this recognition was apparently influential in leading Espinosa to carry out research in Spain in 1920 which resulted in a monumental collection of Spanish folk tales (1921, 1946–1947). Redfield touched upon the problem in Tepoztlán, although this was rather incidental to his main theoretical interest (1930). Parsons more sharply pointed up the problems involved in the study of Hispanic American Indian culture, as influenced by 400 years of Spanish contact, and she was fully cognizant of the need to study Spain (1927, 1930, 1936). In 1943 Steward discussed the shortcomings of acculturation studies in Latin America, and called for more knowledge "about the culture which the Europeans brought to the Indians, that is, a more thorough ethnography of sixteenth and seventeenth century Spain and Portugal" (1943, p. 202).

What kinds of knowledge about sixteenth- and seventeenth-century Spain must we have to construct conquest culture, and to study its impact in America? For a long time anthropologists thought in terms of diffusion, and the sorting into their respective categories of Indian and Spanish elements found in America. This is what Parsons had in mind when, in the final chapter of Mitla, she asked the question, "Indian or Spanish" (1936, pp. 479-544). This approach has proved to be limiting for at least two reasons. First, since it stems from and thereby focuses the main attention on the recipient culture, it conceives of the donor culture as a grab-bag from which a selection of elements somehow has been made. Second, since the anthropologist's point of reference is a recipient culture, he works backward from the particular variant of Hispanic American culture that he happens to know best, to the essential exclusion of other variants that may be significantly different. This again fragments any conception of Spanish culture.

Spanish America is, ethnographically speaking, one of the best described areas of the world. Yet it is astonishing how little synthetic work has been done, how few attempts have been made to sketch distributions and point out basic patterns on any level other than that of generalized "ethos." The anthropologist who has worked primarily in Peru sees Spanish American culture in a fashion somewhat distinct from the one whose major experience has been in Colombia. And the anthropologist who knows Paraguay will have a rather different idea from the one who has made Mexico his principal research area.

Apparently these limitations to the anthropologist's traditional treatment of the Spanish background are paralleled in the field of history. Bishko recently has called for a much broader historical interpretation of the "Iberian Background," to include information on such things as human geography, social structure, the church, economic development, and law and government. We urgently need, he says, greater knowledge on such subjects as the historical forms and techniques of crop-farming and stock raising, the kinds and distributions of land holdings, and the patterns of village and urban settlement. Moreover,

. . . the basic Iberian sectional patterns and diverse cultural traditions in dress, architecture, language, folklore, customs, and techniques that Beiranos, Alentejanos, Andalusians, Basques, Gallegos and Extremadurans contributed to the making of the *patria chica* and criollo society are still quite obscure [so that] . . . a paramount need is more cultural-anthropological studies of the type of Julio Caro Baroja's *Los pueblos del norte de la península ibérica, Los pueblos de España,* and *Los vascos* (1956, p. 64).

Bishko points out that "the Iberian Background [of Latin American history] is by no means identical with, but cannot possibly be understood apart from, Spanish and Portuguese history as a whole" (1956, p. 53), just as conquest culture is by no means identical with Spanish culture, but cannot possibly be understood apart from it. For this reason, he writes:

To limit attention exclusively to the specific ethnic, institutional and cultural elements in Spain and Portugal transplanted across the Atlantic from 1492 on, is to ignore the crucial historical process by which these, and not other, elements were selected for overseas survival or adaptation, and to be unaware of hitherto unenvisaged factors in problems of historical origin.

Finally, a corollary of this "profession of faith" is that the

overworked mechanical formula of tracing Ibero-American ideas or institutions to their metropolitan ancestors should be expanded to include the larger problem of why, how and from what general context these and not other forms were adopted for use in the Indies (pp. 54-55).

The plan of this monograph stems from the kinds of questions anthropologists working in Spanish America have been asking in recent years, as they seemed to me to be meaningful, once I was in Spain. The approach is consistent with the problems Bishko recognizes, and his "profession of faith" about the importance of abandoning the mechanical formula of element tracing is also my profession of faith. Since, however, a complete Spanish ethnography, even in outline form, clearly is beyond the scope of a single study, I have settled on what may be called the "chapter" approach. This involves the selection of a series of problems rooted in those areas of Spanish culture which obviously have been instrumental in shaping Hispanic American culture. The American patterns, to the extent that I know them, are considered briefly, and then the Spanish forms from which presumably they have sprung are examined in some detail, again, to the extent that I know them. Although in a general sense this approach is "Spain as seen from Hispanic America," following Bishko's caution I do not "limit attention exclusively to the specific ethnic, institutional and cultural elements [which] Spain" transplanted across the Atlantic. Since the problem of conquest culture deals equally with the question why some aspects of culture reached America and why others, apparently equally useful, did not, I have found it best to examine a particular Spanish institution in terms of itself, not as seen from a distance, twice screened.

The field data here reported are for the years 1949–1950. Most of the other data are from the years 1880–1958, that is, the modern period. Some readers, particularly those not familiar with ethnographical techniques, may ask whether one may justifiably speculate about the nature of Spanish culture of the sixteenth to eighteenth century on the basis of much more recent information. The anthropologist assumes we may so speculate. For, if this assumption is denied, then it can be argued with equal logic, but entirely erroneously, that the study of contemporary Latin American

Indian culture adds nothing to our knowledge of the nature of Amerindian society during the sixteenth century, and nothing to our knowledge of the culture processes activated by the contact of Spain and America.

Judicious use of contemporary data, tied to historical accounts, is basic anthropological methodology, as important and valid in Spain as in America. No one believes that Spain of today is the Spain of the year 1500, any more than Tarascan Indian culture of today is Tarascan culture of the same year. But Spanish society is conservative: old social forms, customs, techniques, and ideas have survived, particularly in rural areas, making possible a great enriching of published and archival sources which, however complete, customarily leave unsaid many of the things in which the student of culture is interested. I am sure that, through the study of modern Spanish ethnography, in the light of known and recorded history, it is possible to understand many of the forces of traditional Spanish culture as they have shaped the native cultures of half a world, in a way impossible of achievement with any other similar colonizing movement. A study of modern France will tell us very little of the cultural processes at work in the French colonization of the New World; a study of modern England, even less. The cultural conservatism of Spain has given the social sciences a laboratory unrivalled in any other country for the investigation of many acculturation phenomena, and especially that of the model of conquest culture.

NOTE

[1] In this case the process now seems fairly clear, although the details have not been worked out. In sixteenth-century Spain the "hot-cold" concept, in more sophisticated form, represented the best medical practice and belief, as derived from the Hippocratian concept of humoral pathology. Perhaps because there was already a vigorous and satisfactory body of popular medical belief and practice in Spain, it seems not to have spread to the folk level. Presumably this medical knowledge came to America on an elite level, filtered in simplified form to the folk, and with the general receptivity to new elements that characterized the New World, was avidly taken up.

CHAPTER III

THE DIVERSITY OF SPANISH CULTURE

S PAIN is culturally a diversified country, and this variety is particularly striking to visitors from young countries in which industrialization has inhibited the growth of comparable regional forms. For the reasons discussed in Chapter 2, an understanding of this cultural heterogeneity is of the utmost importance in relation to the formation of conquest culture and the acculturation process in Hispanic America. This great variety in a relatively small area is due both to geography, including climate, and to history. Both will be discussed briefly, as they bear particularly on the problems outlined.

On a small-scale map, and in comparison with Europe and America, the Iberian Peninsula does not look large. Its absolute extent, then, comes as a surprise to many visitors. At its most distant points the peninsula stretches nearly 900 kilometers from north to south and 1,100 kilometers from east to west. Spain accounts for five-sixths of the total area of nearly 600,000 square kilometers, and Portugal for the final sixth. With respect to Europe this land mass is an enormous, semidetached promotory, in some ways easier of access to Africa—from which it is separated by a scant 14 kilometers at Tarifa—than to France. The Pyrenees, although not the barrier to communication that romantic writers make out, in a very real sense separate the peninsula from the remainder of the continent. No plain, no broad valley, not even an easy pass joins Spain with France. The two lines of railway cling precariously to steep hillsides on the eastern and western shores respectively, and highway crossings, except at the coast line, are often closed by snow for months at a time. Even migrating birds in their autumnal flight south must beat against fierce winds which whistle through hostile passes, forcing them to fly so low that they are easily captured in great nets suspended in their paths.

Behind this barrier great differences in climate, rainfall, soils, and topography have played their roles in producing a polychrome of subcultures and regional variations. In a few short kilometers a traveler may go from the lofty wastes of the Sierra Nevada to the lush sugar-cane fields of the Joya de Motril, from the verdant uplands of the Montaña de Santander to the steppe land of Burgos, from Lagartera with its folk costume to Madrid with its skyscrapers and broad avenues.

A quick glance at a relief map shows that the gross characteristics of Spain's surface are simple: central tablelands corrugated by the drainage pattern of a half a dozen long rivers, high mountains on three sides, narrow but fertile coastal plains, and two great pie-shaped depressions, the valleys

21

of the Guadalquivir and the Ebro, reaching far inland from the Atlantic and the Mediterranean respectively. The tablelands are the Meseta Central, with an average elevation of 700 meters, which slope gently westward towards the Atlantic Ocean. They are divided at approximately midpoint, and just north of Madrid, by the Central Cordillera. To the north lies Old Castile, slightly higher and colder than New Castile to the south. The Duero and its tributaries drain most of Old Castile, carrying the scant rainfall of the area to the sea at Porto, Portugal. The Tajo, the longest of Spain's rivers, and the Guadiana, drain New Castile.

The northeastern limit of the Meseta Central is marked by the Iberic Cordillera, beyond which lies the Ebro Valley. The eroded southern slopes of the Pyrenees, which lie beyond the Ebro, have been particularly favorable to the development of numerous local cultures and customs, and each valley is notable for its distinct ways. West of the Pyrenees the Cantabric Cordillera cuts across the provinces of Vizcaya, Santander, Oviedo, and Lugo, and the geographical pockets of this jumbled mountain mass have given shelter, like the Pyrenees valleys, to small and isolated human groups which are among the most interesting in the country.

The southern limit of the Meseta Central is defined by the Sierra Morena, a low and broken range separating New Castile from the Guadalquivir Valley and Andalusia. These hills, which hardly show on a relief map, enjoy fame out of all proportion to their size. The traditional land of bandits, of scenes from Don Quijote, of kidnapping and legend, the Sierra Morena has come to be in the minds of Spaniards and foreigners alike a region of enchantment and mystery, romantic and wild, in which the most unlikely adventures are daily happenings.

The gentle meanders of the Guadalquivir have produced a wide plain, the largest low-level area in the country. This broad and fertile *campiña andaluza* was the center of Moorish civilization. Two of the greatest Moorish cities, Sevilla and Córdoba, were built on its banks, and a third, Granada, grew beside its most important tributary, the Genil. The southeastern limits of the Guadalquivir drainage are defined by the Penibetic Cordillera, in which, in the Sierra Nevada, are found Spain's highest peaks, culminating in the snow-covered summits of Mulhacén and Veleta, nearly 3,500 meters high. Where the Sierra Nevada pitches towards the Mediterranean, unequal erosion has produced weird badlands, the Alpujarra, a region only recently penetrated by roads and, like the Sierra Morena, a traditional haunt of bandits and smugglers. Above the port of Málaga and pressing close to the sea rises the brown and green Sierra de Alhama, and farther west one finds the lovely Serranía de Ronda, with scenery spectacular out of all proportion to the modest elevations reached.

Spain's climate, like her land forms, is marked by diversity. Although it is the southernmost country of Europe it is not, contrary to popular opinion, a subtropical region. In latitude it stretches north from 36 degrees to 44 degrees. Madrid, in the center of the country, is parallel to New York. Tarifa, the southernmost city, is on approximately the same parallel

as such American cities as Winston-Salem and Tulsa. Bilbao, San Sebastián, and La Coruña on the north coast are in the same latitude as the
cities of upstate New York, central Michigan, and southern Minnesota.

There are, say Spanish geographers, two Spains, the "wet" and the
"dry." "Wet" Spain includes all of Galicia, Asturias, Santander, the
Basque provinces, and the Pyrenees, where the Atlantic gales strike high
mountains to condense their moisture-laden air and drop the water before
the winds pass to the inland tablelands. Few points in this region experience less than 1,000 mm. of rainfall; the number of rainy days exceeds
half the year, and no month can properly be called dry. Extremes of temperature are not great, and the soft moist months of July and August draw
great numbers of vacationers who find relief from the heat of southern
summers.

The remaining two-thirds are the "dry" Spain, where summers are often
marked by months without water and where, in extreme points in Murcia
and Almería, a year or more will pass without rainfall. Rainfall in dry
Spain ranges from less than 200 mm. along the coasts of Almería and
Murcia to 400–750 mm. in the moister parts of inland areas. But averages
mean very little, because of the great variation from year to year. With an
even distribution of rainfall in dry Spain year after year there would
be just enough moisture to ensure successful dry farming. With unequal
distribution, a year of bumper crops may be followed by five of failures.
Reservoirs run dry, water and electricity in the great cities are rationed
to a few hours a day, and suffering is genuinely great. Even with the most
complete measures for water conservation, chronic shortages of rain will
probably always plague Spain.

Dry Spain has several types of climate. The coastal provinces of Catalonia, the Levante, and Andalusia enjoy a Mediterranean climate, with
short though often raw winters, long and lovely springs, and hot summers
with several months of no rainfall. The inland plateaus have a true con-
tinental climate, with cold and raw winters with snowfall proportionate
to total precipitation and with hot and dry but fairly short summers. The
Guadalquivir basin experiences relatively cold winters. Frost in Sevilla is
by no means uncommon, and subfreezing temperatures occur in the higher
hills. The reverse is true in summer, and here the highest temperatures of
Spain are registered in July and August.

Geographical and climatic diversity have produced a wondrously rich
Spanish flora; it is said that of all the species of Europe more than half
are found in Spain. Rainfall is the most important element in determining
vegetation types. In wet Spain a typical boreal forest exists, with fine
stands of conifers, birch, maple, beech, chestnut, willow, ash, elm, and
oak interspersed with mountain pastures of fern and other fodders. The
central tablelands to the south, with endless treeless prairies, constitute one
of the most characteristic landscapes of Spain. Chronic rain shortages and
man's destructive cutting have limited wooded areas to a few isolated
mountain points, where live oaks, pines, chestnuts, and other varieties are

found. Uncultivated areas here are typically covered by heath and copse of scrub oak and such aromatic plants as the gum cistus, rosemary, and thyme.

In this central granary Spain produces its wheat, barley, oats, and rye, and in the more amenable areas stretch great vineyards. A botanical and cultural division of prime importance cuts across the middle of this region: the northern limit of olive cultivation (which also corresponds in a rough way to that of the fig and almond). This line is culturally and historically significant, for Spain to the north of it seems to have held few attractions for the Moors, and here they quickly relinquished their conquests to the Spaniards. It is interesting to speculate on the history of Spain, and Europe, had all of the peninsula been marked by a Mediterranean climate and the cultivation of the olive.

Andalusia, with its wide river valleys and sea coasts, is characterized by the greatest floral variety in all Spain, and is marked by the most intense cultivation of the olive and grape. Cork oaks are found along the coast, and live oaks producing sweet acorns are common, especially in Huelva. Subtropical conditions prevail in the *hoyas* of the Mediterranean coast, and in those of Motril, Málaga, and Vélez-Málaga one finds the only important sugar-cane stands in Spain. Oranges, lemons, and pomegranates also flourish along the coast, and far up the Guadalquivir basin.

In the driest parts of Murcia, Alicante, and Almería, like the valley of the Río Segura, the aridity is so great that true desert conditions prevail, and only by tapping the river for irrigation is it possible to grow lemons, oranges, and garden produce. Here also are found the only commercial plantings of the African date palm. *Esparto* grass (*Macrochloa tenacissima*)—Spain's principal indigenous source of fibre—is characteristic of the slightly higher and less dry steppe country of these provinces.

Most Mediterranean of all areas is that which includes Catalonia, the old kingdom of Valencia, and the Ebro drainage system. Agriculture here —although by no means to the exclusion of other areas—is marked by the olive, grape, almond, citrus fruits, the algarrobo and, in some specialized areas such as the Albufera of Valencia, by rice. The Ebro Valley from lower Navarra to Teruel is, after the Guadalquivir basin, the most important center of olive culture in Spain.

All the geographical and climatic differences of Spain have played their part in the development of the many regional subcultures of the country. The isolated mountain valleys in the north favored the development of local ways, and particularly of the linguistic forms that gave rise to the historical and modern Romance languages of the peninsula. Here wet winters stimulated the building of great houses to shelter men and animals alike, establishments which in turn may have given rise to communal kinds of family organization, whose traces remain to this day. The arid lands of southern Spain, on the other hand, called for different agricultural crops, different implements to till the thin soil, ingenious irrigation devices, less elaborate houses, and distinct forms of social structure. Again, the shallow salt-water tidal areas of the coasts of Valencia, Alicante, and Murcia—the *albuferas*—offer unusual possibilities for the exploitation of game birds, fish, reeds, and the growing of rice, which have given rise to the specialized subculture described in the novels of Blasco Ibáñez.

Turning briefly to political divisions, we may note that since 1833 Spain has been divided into 47 mainland provinces plus the island provinces of Baleares and Canarias. This provincial division is one result of the Napoleonic conquest and represents a fractioning for administrative purposes of larger historical units which have themselves been divided in many ways at various times throughout history. These larger units are spoken of as the 13 Old Kingdoms, corresponding roughly to the major political units which emerged during the reconquest. "Kingdom" is not always quite the correct word, for Extremadura never was a kingdom, nor was Galicia, except nominally, and the "kingdoms" of Sevilla, Córdoba, Jaén, and Granada lose their identity in the larger Kingdom of Andalusia. Nevertheless Spaniards more often than not refer to the major areas of their country by these terms, and the reader will find it helpful to remember these main divisions and their provincial components:

GALICIA: La Coruña, Pontevedra, Lugo, Orense
ASTURIAS: Oviedo
LAS VASCONGADAS (Basque Provinces): Vizcaya, Guipúzcoa, Alava
NAVARRA (Navarre): Navarra
LEÓN: León, Zamora, Salamanca
CASTILLA LA VIEJA (Old Castile): Santander, Palencia, Burgos, Logroño, Valladolid, Avila, Segovia, Soria
CASTILLA LA NUEVA (New Castile): Madrid, Guadalajara, Cuenca, Toledo, Ciudad Real
EXTREMADURA: Cáceres, Badajoz
ANDALUCÍA (Andalusia): Huelva, Sevilla, Córdoba, Cádiz, Málaga, Granada, Almería, Jaén
MURCIA: Murcia, Albacete
VALENCIA: Castellón de la Plana, Valencia, Alicante
ARAGON: Huesca, Zaragoza, Teruel
CATALUÑA (Catalonia): Gerona, Barcelona, Lérida, Tarragona

The Balearic Islands, recaptured from the Moors by Catalonia and consequently very similar in language and custom, may be considered a part of that major area. The Canary Islands lie so far from Spain that they cannot properly be considered a part of any major area, although in general they show greater similarity to Andalusia than to the other areas.

The modern cultural diversity of Spain—using "modern" in the sense of the last four or five centuries—is a function of its history as well as of its geography. In a culture-historical sense Spain must be viewed as part of a "Circum-Mediterranean" culture area which has existed for several millenia and which even today unites in many ways the countries that border this inland sea. The traits that may be used to define this area are many, and include such things as similar agricultural implements and practices, similar fishing implements and techniques, and a love of and a feeling for town life. Although the initial impetus that gave rise to this culture area was the birth of civilization in the Near East, it must not be thought of, in its modern and historical forms, as African or Near Eastern, to the exclusion of other influences. For essentially European influences, during the past thousand years and more, have been influential in bringing a notable homogeneity—in broad perspective—to all of the countries of southern Europe.

The more obvious African and Near Eastern elements in Spanish culture have led some authors to the careless conclusion that, in the words of Alexander Dumas, "Africa begins at the Pyrenees." Havelock Ellis, who was in many ways remarkably perceptive in relation to Spanish culture, likewise was carried away by this thought when he wrote, "Spain is a great, detached fragment of Africa, and the Spaniard is the first-born child of the ancient white North African" (1908, pp. 29-30). And again, "The land of Spain and the physical traits of Spaniards lead us back to Africa. If we take a more penetrating survey we shall find that there is much in the character of the Spaniard which we may also fairly count as African" (*ibid.*, p. 36).

This kind of thinking is potentially dangerous, quite apart from the question of its validity for Spain, because it leads to misinterpretation of the origin and meaning of many culture elements in Spanish America. The tendency to think of Spain as an African country—or at least as non-European—certainly stems in large part from the Moorish legacy, and this in turn leads to the supposition in Hispanic America that certain traits are ultimately Moorish. Actually, many such traits represent much earlier cultural accretions in the peninsula. The simple agricultural practices of Spanish America, for example (possibly excluding certain irrigation techniques), many fishing methods and implements, and much superstition and folklore are basically pan-Mediterranean, and were brought to Spain by Phoenicians, Greeks, and Romans long before the Moorish invasion.

The full import of Moslem culture, significant as it is, is difficult to assess accurately, and great care must be exercised in explaining the Spanish cultural resurgence of the reconquest period as due in large part to the stimulus of Moslem culture. For, as will be pointed out, Spain was also simultaneously receiving very important influences of another type from France and Italy and, to a lesser extent, other European countries.

With these cautions in mind, the impact of Moorish culture in Spain can be briefly considered. In broad terms, this consists of the introduction of the Graeco-Roman learning of antiquity (including Alexandrian Hellenism) which had been translated and preserved by Arabic scholars in Syria and Persia. But the Arabs did not limit themselves to mere copying; they were original creators in their own right, both in their homeland and in Spain, with a keen sense of scientific and literary values. Córdoba, during the Caliphate, came to be the most advanced city in the western world—

with the possible exception of Constantinople—with a library reputed to number 600,000 volumes. Notable works in medicine, mathematics, astronomy, and botany come from this period.

A study of Hispanicized Arabic words affords many clues to the areas of influence of Moslem culture, as indicated by the following examples.

Military terminology: *atalaya* (watchtower), *alcázar* (castle, fortress), *alférez* (ensign).

Science: *álgebra, cifra* (cipher), *cero* (zero), *cenit* (zenith), *alquimia* (alchemy), *alambique* (still), *alcohol, bórax.*

Municipal government: *aldea* (village), *alcalde* (mayor), *alguacil* (constable).

Commerce: *almacén* (store, warehouse), *bazar, almoneda* (auction), *alhóndiga* (public granary), *aduana* (customs), *barato* (cheap).

Measurement terms: *quilate* (karat), *arroba, quintal, almud, fanega.*

Artisans: *albañil* (mason), *alfarero* (potter).

Buildings: *azulejos* (tiles), *azotea* (flat roof terrace), *zaguán* (house entrance), *alcoba* (bedroom).

Agriculture: *arroz* (rice), *azúcar* (sugar), *azafrán* (saffron), *algarroba* (carob), *berengena* (eggplant), *azahar* (orange blossom), *jasmín* (jasmine), *albaricoque* (apricot), *acequia* (irrigation ditch), *noria* (irrigating well), *aljibe* (cistern), *alberca* (reservoir).

Medicine: *alferecía* (epilepsy), *alfombrilla* (measles).

Games: *ajedrez* (chess), *azar* (chance).

Music: *tambor* (drum).

Use of an Arabic term is not proof of Arabic introduction, but nearly always it indicates strong influence in some way. Other Moorish introductions include the raising of silkworms and the manufacture of paper. The so-called Persian water wheel (p. 63) undoubtedly came with the Moors, as did many other agricultural techniques. Pottery styles were improved, weaving methods bettered, and architecture vastly changed.

Castro suggests still other traditional ways of life, as well as linguistic expressions, that are probably Moorish in origin (1954, pp. 107-120) : the Andalusian custom of women covering their faces (see p, 98), the ceremonial offering to a friend or acquaintance of something he admires, the form of saying "Your house is at such and such a place" in reply to the question where one lives, the *"Usted gusta?"* ("Will you eat?") said by the diner to those who enter the room, and the equally ceremonious *"Buen provecho,"* or *"Que aproveche"* ("May it profit you"), by which the invited gives thanks and declines simultaneously, the expression "to kiss the hand [or the feet]," and the multitudinous blessings and curses that punctuate Spanish conversation.

The later centuries of Moorish hegemony in Spain correspond with the period in which Christian Spanish culture was being crystallized into those forms that were instrumental in shaping Hispanic America. In part this development was autochthonous; in part it was stimulated by extra-Spanish contacts in addition to those with the Moors. The discovery, in the early years of the ninth century, of the sepulcher which, according to tradition, guarded the remains of the Apostle James (Santiago) was of extreme importance to Spain. These remains, which appeared in what is now Padrón (La Coruña), were soon removed farther inland, and churches and other religious buildings began to be built near by. Thus developed Spain's most famous shrine, Santiago de Compostela, which became, in addition to a religious center, a thriving industrial and commercial community to meet the needs of the crowds of pilgrims who came from all parts of Europe.

The numbers of peregrines gradually grew during the ninth to the eleventh centuries, reaching enormous proportions in the twelfth, when this pilgrimage was raised to the level of a major peregrination, in the same category as the trip to Rome and Jerusalem. Pilgrims passed through France by various routes and entered Spain at Roncesvalles on the Navarre frontier, from which point it was considered to be a 13-day trip across northern Spain to the west coast. Along this route hospitals, inns, and monasteries grew up, to cater to the needs of and to aid the pilgrims. Foreigners of all social classes and occupations visited Spain and thus constituted an important force for introducing to the country the developing culture of Medieval and early Modern Europe. Upon their return home they transmitted Spanish and Moorish culture to Europe. Santiago remained an important place of pilgrimage through most of the fifteenth century, before changing interests drew the attention of Europeans to new activities (Castro 1954, pp. 130-170).

Other European influences reached Spain through monasteries and monks, especially those of Cluny—established in Navarre in the eleventh century and subsequently in Castile—and those of the Franciscan Order, founded in 1215. Still other non-Moorish influences came to Spain by way of Catalan and Valencian merchants in the Mediterranean and by Basque seafarers who voyaged in the Atlantic, particularly to Flanders. In later centuries, Spanish students went in large numbers to France and Italy, and foreign teachers were brought by Castilian and Aragonese rulers to help in the establishment of the first universities in the thirteenth century. In the last years of the thirteenth century Sicily and southern Italy were added to the Aragonese throne, thereby making accessible an area that, in later years, was to become a highly important source of new culture elements in Spain.

Thus, during the period of Moorish occupation of southern Spain parallel Christian influences in the north contributed to the forging of a Christian Spanish culture which, in spite of marked regional variation, reflected a basic unity in belief, values, and customs. The ethnologist who today digs trait by trait into Spanish culture, searching for the points that will illuminate Hispanic American culture history, finds that a majority of the questions he asks lead to Europe, and only a minority to the south and east. The content of religion is that of France and Italy: the same Romanesque and Gothic churches, the same religious services, the same annual festivals. The vitality of the Spaniard and of his culture has exalted Catholicism to a point higher than that found in other European countries, but the religion is still basically the same.

Town plans, buildings, house construction, and furnishings often show Mediterranean and African traits which, on superficial examination, seem un-European. But more detailed scrutiny reveals that European influences have been dominant. The sturdy stone houses, slate roofs, enormous fireplaces and chimneys, chairs, tables, beds, knives and forks—all indicate European background.

In matters of social orginization there are elements which suggest the Orient—the traditional seclusion of women, former veiling in the south, and the like—but the basic family pattern, with its rules, regulations, and customs again turns out to be European. Medieval cities in Spain—their guilds, their walls and fortifications, their religious brotherhoods, their nobility and commoners—all reflect European forms and values. And in the centuries of the reconquest, the king was a European king, not a Moorish Emir.

Folk culture and folklore, using the terms in the popular sense, likewise are essentially European. A large part of the stories that are told in France are also told in Spain, and many popular dances turn out to be much like English Morris dances and Pan-European sword dances. When similar stories are found in Spain and Morocco, the Moroccan stories frequently are those of Christian Spain, carried by the Jews when they were expelled from that country.

In utilizing contemporary Spanish ethnographic data better to understand the impact of earlier Spanish culture in America, it is essential to maintain proper historical perspective. Recognize Spain's unique position in Europe and the Near Eastern, African, and Moorish influences which have helped shape her culture, but do not lose sight of the fact that Spain is Europe and Spaniards are Europeans.

One final point is needed to complete this discussion of the factors involved in the development of Spanish culture and subcultures, and particularly with respect to the extension of the new northern Spanish cultures to the southern part of the peninsula. Excluding the Basques there were, during the final centuries of the reconquest, five principal political-cultural-linguistic foci of Spanish Christian culture. These were, from west to east, the Galician, Asturo-Leonese, Castilian, Navarro-Aragonese and Catalan. As the Moors gradually were pushed south and reconquered lands became available for settlement, colonizers migrated south from these foci. Grants of land, towns, castles, and revenues were made by kings to nobles, prelates, military orders, and other individuals and organizations which aided in the reconquest. Some grants were for limited periods of time; others were perpetual. The latter founded the great *latifundios*, particularly in Andalusia, and the pattern for the present large land-holdings was established.

The areas settled by people from each northern kingdom quite naturally reflected the local characteristics of each of these Christian subcultures, and even today political divisions, linguistic forms, and cultural traits in the southern half of the peninsula reveal the broad outlines of these southward movements. The expansive drive of the five foci was not equal. Galicians worked southward in essentially a straight line, to repopulate and give Christian culture to the lands which, in the twelfth century, became an independent Portugal. Castilians swarmed southward, fanning out east and west until they occupied all of what is now Andalusia, southern Extremadura (Badajoz), New Castile, and Murcia. Catalans reconquered Valencia and the Balearic Islands. Colonists from Asturias and León, pinched between the more vigorous Galician and Castilian movements, were able to go no farther than Cáceres. The Navarrese and Aragonese similarly were constricted between the more powerful Catalans and Castilians and although they temporarily reached Murcia they were forced to withdraw subsequently to the north, whence they turned their interest to Sicily and Italy. Hence, cultural diversity in southern Spain is explicable to a significant extent in terms of the areas to the north from which repopulators came. In Extremadura, for example, Cáceres is quite different in many ways from Badajoz, because it was repopulated by Leonese, whereas Badajoz received major forces from Castile. Certain peculiarities in Murcia are explained by the temporary presence of Aragonese, even though Castilian influence ultimately became dominant.

The historical increments that explain the diversity of Spanish subcultures, and the spread of these subcultures southward, are important in understanding the acculturation process as it transmitted Spain to America, because of the question which parts of the peninsula most influenced the New World. Many anthropologists in the United States have shared the belief that a majority of the conquistadors and colonizers came from Andalusia and Extremadura, and that therefore Spanish culture in America primarily represents the sixteenth-century forms of these two regions. This hypothesis rests on two assumptions: that Andalusia and Extremadura were, in fact, the home of a majority of migrants; that culture transmission and change result in direct ratio to numbers of people and their individual cultures. Both assumptions will be dealt with in turn.

The first, that Andalusia and Extremadura contributed most settlers, is found, upon examination of historical records, to be erroneous. In another place (Foster 1952b) I have examined in some detail these sources, and only the conclusions are of importance here. From data in the Archive of the Indies in Sevilla, as reproduced in the *Catálogo de pasajeros a Indias*, it becomes clear that these two Old Kingdoms did not have a monopoly on emigrants. Although in the earliest days of the Conquest they sent a disproportionately large number as compared to other parts of the country, very quickly more northerly provinces, particularly in the Castiles and León, began to be well represented, and we even note significant numbers from Galicia, Asturias, and the Basque provinces. The analysis by Pérez Bustamante (1941) of the first volume of the *Catálogo de pasajeros a Indias (1509-1534)* shows how wide the spread is (see opposite page).

Data comparable to that of the first half of the sixteenth century are not readily available for subsequent centuries. During this time significant

DISTRIBUTION OF EMIGRANTS, 1509-1534

Andalusia:		*Old Castile:*	
Sevilla	1,365	Valladolid	424
Córdoba	231	Burgos	316
Huelva	223	Avila	175
Jaén	151	Segovia	153
Cádiz	146	Palencia	156
Granada	78	Santander	103
Málaga	45	Soria	78
Almería	6	Logroño	71
	2,245		**1,476**
Extremadura:		*New Castile:*	
Badajóz	890	Toledo	425
Cáceres	499	Madrid	192
		Guadalajara	91
	1,389	Ciudad Real	127
		Cuenca	45
León:			
Salamanca	652		**880**
Zamora	166		
León	103	*Catalonia:*	
		Barcelona	17
	921	Gerona	15
		Tarragona	5
Basque provinces:		Lérida	1
Vizcaya	72		
Guipúzcoa	85		**38**
Alava	59		
		Aragón:	
	216	Zaragoza	34
		Teruel	10
Galicia:		Huesca	2
Coruña	50		
Lugo	35		**46**
Orense	27		
Pontevedra	27	*Murcia:*	
		Albacete	31
	139	Murcia	17
Asturias	181		**48**
Valencia:		*Navarra*	23
Valencia	20		
Alicante	4	*Baleares*	11
Castellón	2		
		Canarias	2
	26		

shifts in emigration foci took place. Extremadura rather quickly fell off in importance, as did Andalusia at a somewhat later date. Conversely, Galicia, Navarra, and the Basque provinces became more important.

Thayer Ojeda (1919, p. 59) gives the following picture of three centuries of Spanish emigration to Chile. Comparable tables for other countries, however, have not been worked out.

SPANISH EMIGRATION TO CHILE
(Thayer Ojeda 1919, p. 59)

Ranking of emigrants, (by numbers)	Sixteenth century	Seventeenth century		Eighteenth century	
		First half	Second half	First half	Second half
1	Andalusia	Andalusia	Andalusia	Old Castile	Basque provinces
2	New Castile	Old Castile	Old Castile	Basque provinces	Old Castile
3	Extremadura	New Castile	Basque provinces	Andalusia	Navarra
4	Old Castile	Basque provinces	Navarra	Navarra	America
5	Leon	Navarra	America	America	Andalusia
6	Basque provinces	America	New Castile	Galicia	Galicia
7	Galicia	Extremadura	Leon	Asturias	Asturias
8	Asturias	Leon			Catalonia

The second of the two assumptions—that culture transmission and change result in direct ratio to numbers of people and their individual cultures—is more difficult to test. Obviously emigrants carry with them much of their cultural baggage, but is this fact determinative? It has been pointed out that formal processes of transmission guided by Church and State supplanted in many areas of life the opportunity of the individual to choose from his past experience. Again, it is clear that environment will limit the extent to which many customary ways can be established in a new country. Perhaps we can assume, however, that those parts of culture not guided by Church and State are potentially present in a conquest culture in rough correlation to the frequency with which they characterize individuals and groups of migrants. Carrying the argument further, since nearly all parts of Spain have contributed significant numbers of emigrants to America, we must assume that a representative sample of the culture of these several areas was presented to America. Each "sample," obviously, and all of its constituent elements, must have been in competition with all other samples and, given the infinite variety, only a small percentage of elements could survive. It seems reasonable to assume, therefore, that in the absence of other factors the informally transmitted Spanish culture ought to reflect something of the customs of all parts of Spain, in rough proportion to numbers of emigrants. That is, if we were to trace Spanish culture in America (excluding formally transmitted elements) trait by trait to the mother country, we should find a geographical distribution roughly reflecting the percentages of migrants from each area.

This is the assumption on which I operated while doing research in Spain and it is an assumption which I took for granted during much of the time spent in working up field notes. For reasons explained in the last chapter I have concluded the assumption is incorrect, and I suggest the concept of "cultural crystallization" to explain why such a logical hypothesis apparently is not true. To test the assumption, however, required the description and analysis of data from many parts of Spain and the attempt to give a fairly complete picture of any institution or custom in its many differing forms.

REFERENCES

Geographical: Benito Melero (1947), Carandell (1924, 1934), Dantín Cereceda (1942), Dobby (1936), Florest an Samanes (1951), Gil Muñiz (1926), Jensen (1946), Jiménez de Gregorio (1950 *et seq.*), Martín Echeverría (1940), Madoz (1845-1850), Martín Granizo (1922), Miñano (1826-1829), Rivera (1945), Vergara y Martín (1917).

Historical: Aguado Bleye (1947), Altamira y Crevea (1949), Castro (1954), Ellis (1908), Foster (1952b), Menéndez Pidal (1950), Pérez Bustamante (1941), Thayer Ojeda (1919).

CHAPTER IV

CITIES, TOWNS, AND VILLAGES: THE GRID-PLAN PUZZLE

IN SPANISH AMERICA

MANY characteristics of the traditional Spanish American community are modeled after Iberian prototypes. These include the division into barrios, often called "upper" and "lower," as well as the religious and social aspects of barrio life, the naming of streets on the basis of occupation and guild activities, the intense love of one's natal place, and formalized suspicion of the people of neighboring pueblos.

Other characteristics exemplify the new cultural forms that are not traditional in a donor country, but which are called into being as a result of contact. The "grid-plan" or "chess board" design which marks nearly all Spanish American communities is the most striking example of this. Most Spanish towns are relatively formless. In Spanish America, however, streets radiate from a square or oblong central plaza and intersect at right angles to form rectangular blocks of great neatness, much like small midwestern communities in the United States. Usually the important buildings face the plaza: church or cathedral, municipal hall, homes of important political and religious leaders, and other structures central to the life of the inhabitants. Commercial life takes place in coffee shops or on the benches of the plaza itself, and in the late afternoon and evening people come to stroll and relax, to greet friends or to court. In villages and small towns a periodic market may be held in the plaza, while in larger communities a separate square, often covered, shelters a daily market.

IN SPAIN

Cities, towns, villages, and hamlets characterize Spain. Although in places, especially in the wet parts of the country, isolated farmhouses are found, the average Spaniard cannot imagine himself other than as an immediate and intimate member of a social group much larger than his family. And, as with the family, membership in the local community—the pueblo—stems from birth, and endows the individual with characteristics and prerogatives which time and process of law cannot erase. Membership in an urban or semi-urban settlement implies far more than residential propinquity; the spiritual tie is at least as strong. This Spanish identification with community of birth reflects an ancient Circum-Mediterranean trait, now dignified in anthropological terminology by the Italian word *campanilismo*, the feeling that one's real world extends only within earshot and sight of the village campanile. The love of crowded and busy streets, noisy markets, and cool coffee houses with their opportunities for endless conversation is engrained in the Spaniard. To him the urban way of life, however simple its form may be, is a basic value without which life would be difficult.

The Spaniard's sense of attachment to his community is intense. When he travels within the region where his home is known, he identifies himself in terms of that pueblo. And if for any reason he settles in another pueblo, as likely as not he will be known all his life by the prevailing nickname for individuals from that particular place. Thus, to pick four neighboring towns in Huelva, a person from Cabezas Rubias is a *rubiato*, from El Cerro de Andévalo a *cerreño*, from Alosno an *alosnero*, and from Calaña a *calañés*.

The sizes of Spanish communities vary enormously. Each province has as capital a major city, which may be as large as Madrid and Barcelona, each with about 1,500,000 inhabitants, or as small as Soria, with 13,000. Centralism in government, Church, and commerce is matched by centralism in population. Only occasionally does a province have a city larger than its capital: for example, Vigo with 80,000 as contrasted to Pontevedra with 35,000. Between north and south Spain there are important differences in the size of local communities. In the south big towns—often dusty and ugly, in spite of whitewashed walls—are the rule, with populations of 5,000, 10,000, and more. Settlements of less than 1,000 inhabitants are almost nonexistent, and villages of 1,000 to 3,000 are rare. In the north the opposite is true. Good-sized towns are relatively rare, and the greater part of the population clusters in villages of a few hundred to a couple of thousand. Vera de Bidasoa, a Basque town in northwestern Navarra with 2,500 inhabitants, is considered an important center and is probably known by name to more Spaniards than is Bujalance with its 15,000 dwellers in the Cordobese *campiña*.

But whether one's native town be large or small, the same attachment to, love of, and fierce pride in it are found in each heart. This sense of community is not reflected in a local social structure that functions without major conflict and stress. The opposite is more nearly true: enmities may be strong, and antagonisms are deep and frequently long standing. At the same time against the world there is unity in local patriotism, and a genuinely strong belief that one's community is superior to all others. Strangers, if on obvious business which in no way conflicts with the interests of the community, are welcomed; the Spaniard's sense of hospitality is strong. To treat a stranger well, particularly one of obvious standing in the world, is considered both a pleasure and a duty. On innumerable occasions, sitting in the local casino with new-found Spanish friends, I have been told, when American mores suggested that the next round was on me, that this could not be. "You are our guest; it is our *duty* as Spaniards to see that you lack nothing." And that always settled it. The visitor must reciprocate in some less obvious fashion.

Less affluent visitors, or potential new community members, may be treated less well. Working hands which threaten the livelihood of local *vecinos* are looked upon with suspicion, and beggars, although tolerated, are urged to move on. Courting of local girls by youths from other towns is viewed with disfavor. In much of northern Spain, where youths formerly organized themselves into formal bachelor's clubs, the outsider, in order to visit his girl, had to meet the approval of the local club—an approval obtained, if at all, by treating the members to substantial quantities of drink. Pitt-Rivers describes the varied reactions to "foreign" swains in Alcalá in the south: ducking in the fountain, or even such rough beatings that the young men had to break off their engagements (1954, p. 9).

As in Spanish America, a sometimes real and sometimes feigned enmity exists between neighboring towns, and this often gives rise to tales that ridicule the stupidity of the inhabitants of the "other" community. For example, in Córdoba province the wits of little Cañete make assonance their ally and mock the people from Bujalance as *bujarrones,* "sodomites," while the Bujalanceños strike back with *avetardas,* "bustards." In the same province the inhabitants of Espejo are said by those of Castro del Río to be so stupid that on one occasion when they saw the reflection of the moon in the river they jumped in after it, thinking it was cheese. This old folklore motif appears to be widespread in this context. Davillier tells of two *primos,* cousins from Chiclana (Cádiz), who mistook the moon's reflection in the river for a cheese. But however fast they ran along the bank, the cheese kept its distance. In exasperation one finally said to the other, "Take a shortcut ahead and intercept it [*y atájala, primo*], cousin," and so the Chiclaneros today are dubbed *atajaprimos* by their neighbors (1949, p. 337).

Literary exuberance as a manifestation of civic pride reaches its most developed form in the *dichos,* ubiquitous rhymes and sayings which eulogize the qualities the sons of a pueblo believe should make it the envy of the world and which ridicule all other places. The traveler will not be long in Sevilla before he will be asked if he has not heard that

Quien no ha visto Sevilla,	He who has not seen Sevilla,
No ha visto maravilla.	Has never seen a marvelous thing.

Or in Valladolid:

Quien sale de Valladolid,	He who leaves Valladolid,
¿Adónde irá a vivir?	Where will he go to live?

The small towns are not behind their larger sisters; in the curious round walled town of Madrigal de las Torres Altas (Avila) one hears,

Vino de Madrigal,	The wine of Madrigal,
Me quita todo mal.	Cures me of all.

The possibilities of derogatory couplets rhyming with the name of neighboring communities evoke even more profuse poetic efforts than praise of one's home town. Some sayings reflect the real or imagined niggardliness of neighboring peoples:

A Amayas, sin pan no vayas.	Don't go to Amayas and expect to be fed.

Sometimes understatement effectively does the trick:

Es usted de Bilbao?	You're from Bilbao?
Pues bastante hemos hablao.	Well, enough said.

Again all the scorn for a neighboring place may be wrapped in a single package:

Almazora la vieja,	Almazora la vieja,
Montes sin leña	Woods without firewood
Mar sin pescado	Sea without fish
E hijos mal criados.	And inhabitants without manners.

If Spanish dichos about the qualities of communities were taken at face value, as reflecting commonly held beliefs, it is hard to see how other than perpetual civil war could prevail. But, in spite of real antagonism between paired communities and in spite of derogatory opinions about the inhabitants of specific provinces and pueblos, the dichos appear for the most part to be simply literary forms, puns based on assonance and rhyme which give the Spaniard the opportunity to show his virtuosity either in coining new ones or remembering great numbers of old ones. The surest way to be welcome at a village gathering in the coffee house or bar is to have a ready command of well-known dichos and a facile wit in improvising new ones appropriate to the chance turns of the conversation.

Spanish streets, until relatively recent times, took their names from identifying characteristics, such as a monastery, convent, church, the occupation of the inhabitants, the location, and the like. By studying maps of modern Spanish cities it is possible from street names to learn much about the social and economic life of Medieval society, for many street names are those which date from the time of guilds, when members of the same group tended to live on the same street or in the same neighborhood. To this day, for example, Salamanca has its street of *caleros* (limeburners), *canteros* (stone masons), *caldereros* (tinkers), *carniceros* (butchers), *bordadores* (embroiderers), *padilleros* (bakers), *bodegones* (taverns or wine shops), *libreros* (booksellers, a street near the University), and *pan y carbón* (where bread and charcoal were sold). The list from Valladolid is similar: *panaderos* (bakers), *hosteleros* (keepers of small inns), *ebanistería* (cabinet-making), *platerías* (silversmiths' shops), *guadamacileros* (makers of embossed leather), *mantería* (shops of blanket sellers), *guarnicioneros* (harness-makers), *especiería* (spice shops), *tahonas* (bakeries), and *lecheros* (milkmen). Murcia has its streets of *frenería* (harness shops), *jabonería* (soap-making), *trapería* (rag collectors), *lencería* (linen trade), and *esparteros* (esparto weavers).

Such names as *Calle de los Gallegos, de los Moriscos, de los Mudéjares,* and *de los Judíos* reflect the tendency of members of racial, ethnic, or geographical groups to settle in the same neighborhood. Many Spanish towns still have a street or section called *judería*, the one-time ghetto.

Although many of the old names are continually being replaced officially by those of military and political heroes, as in Hispanic America, the traditional names frequently continue in use for a long time, and through them it is possible to learn much of the physical form, social ecology, and economic patterns of earlier centuries.

Towns and cities vary in their appearance from one part of the country to the next, with respect to house and building types, paint and whitewash, and ground plans. Stone, rather than adobe, is the most common building material, for small houses as well as large buildings. Only in the south is whitewashing general.[1] But to the visitor from Latin America the most striking aspect of the Spanish town is the slight importance, and frequent absence, of the plaza and the lack of the grid-plan form of streets, crossing at right angles at even intervals. To one acquainted with the history of Spanish America it seems natural to expect Spanish towns to resemble their American offspring.

What, if anything, does a study of Spanish towns tell about the possible origin of the grid-plan in America? Scholars such as Wilhelmy, in his thorough study of South American cities (1952, pp. 71-82), and Stanislawski (1947, pp. 102) both point out the unquestionable influence of Vitruvius in the Crown's instructions for the laying out of new towns. At the same time, a more thorough examination of the history of town planning in Spain than is made by either author suggests additional leads.

First, it may be noted that town planning is much more ancient and varied in the peninsula than might be imagined, although it does not have a continuous history. Shifting sociocultural conditions have produced periods of planning alternating with periods of no planning. The usual prerequisites for effective planning—a strong central authority, a concept of planning, and new settlement or extreme rebuilding—first existed in Spain in Roman times. New cities and towns were founded for Roman settlers, particularly for soldiers paid off ofter campaigns (e.g., Itálica and Mérida), or were reconstructed after devastation in the wars of conquest (e.g., Numantia). These planned cities were based on the grid-plan, which the Romans had adapted from earlier Greek designs, and consisted of two main streets crossing at right angles at the center of a quadrangle, terminating at gates in each of the four walls. Four equal quarters thus resulted, which were in turn subdivided by lesser streets into rectangular city blocks. At the central crossing an open space was left as a forum, on which public buildings faced. Roman military encampments were also laid out on the same plan, and some of these developed into cities. With the fall of Roman authority and the division of the land into small administrative units, a process of civic disintegration set in which, in time, destroyed the original regular street patterns. As houses and buildings decayed, fell, and were reconstructed, the once straight streets became increasingly crooked, were blocked off, or shunted in oblique directions, so that after centuries little evidence of the original planning remained. Braga, in north Portugal, is thought by city planners to be the only Iberian city in which the original Roman grid-plan has survived to the present time.

During the Dark Ages following the destruction of Rome settlement patterns changed to meet new social and economic conditions. In Europe the unit of social life was now the rural manor, the lord's castle surrounded by the homes of his tenants. Defensible sites and stout walls became the basic requirements, and from these needs rose the walled towns of the Medieval period. Spain's requirements were similar to those of other western European areas, but more complex. With half of the country, and more, held by the Moors, Oriental attitudes towards city planning prevailed over a wide area. Or perhaps it is more accurate to say that Oriental lack of attitudes prevailed, for the large Moorish cities in Spain, like Sevilla, Córdoba, and Granada, still show today the tortuous passages and narrow streets which interlace the urban area, without apparent plan or thought. In the north and along the advancing frontier, walled fortress towns which afforded protection against warring Moors and Christians alike were essential. Avila remains today, with its complete wall, the most perfect surviving example of a Medieval walled city. But within, the streets ramble at will. Many other cities retain parts of their walls, and in San Pedro Manrique, a village of Soria, the town gates were locked at night until a generation ago.

The twelfth century saw a significant resurgence of commerce and prosperity in western Europe, accompanied by the revival of strong rulers exercising hegemony over more than local areas. Both factors stimulated the founding of new towns, and by early in the thirteenth century, and continuing for a century and a half, a rash of new planned cities appeared from Sicily to England and from Spain to the Baltic. The finest examples of Medieval town planning appeared in southern France. As a result of the Albigensian crusade in the first part of the thirteenth century much of the country lay devastated and underpopulated. The planned *bastide* (Fr. *bastille*) and *villeneuve* arose to meet this challenge. St. Louis, King of France, and his brother Alfonse, Count of Poitiers, were responsible for these constructions. Most were small, and many have disappeared, but others, such as Pau, have survived to become important cities. In each the planning was the same. The new town was plotted into square or oblong blocks, marked by straight streets intersecting at right angles. The main avenues ran from the town gates to cross in the center, thus forming a square, often arcaded, on which public buildings were erected. A smaller adjacent square was dedicated to the church. On and around these squares the important inhabitants had their homes. One of the most noteworthy of these villeneuves is new Carcassonne, planned in 1248 when the confines of the old walled *cité* were outgrown.

During the thirteenth century the British, particularly under Edward I, also founded many new towns in Aquitaine and Guienne, of which the finest example is Montpazier, in the Dordogne, founded 1284. Thus, by the thirteenth century, town planning based on the grid-plan and the central plaza was well known in western Europe. It is difficult to tell to what extent Roman ideas influenced this development, but it may be noted that in northern Italy a few Roman grid towns maintained something of their original form. And later, at least, Vitruvius was rediscovered and strongly influenced ideas of city planning.

The parallel development of town planning in Spain was related to but separate from these movements. From the eleventh century on many new towns were founded in northern Spain. With the pushing back of the Moors and the increased powers of the rulers of León, Castile, and Navarra, conditions propitious to town founding existed. These included underpopulated lands, potential settlers, the need for new strong military positions, and, of course, the central authority with the power to enforce its will. The discovery of the remains of St. James and the lively commerce which sprang up with the increasing importance of the pilgrimage to this shrine also played a significant part in the formation of new Spanish towns. Market concessions were granted, which increased the prosperity of towns. New bridges were built on the main roads, and towns founded or rebuilt to defend such sites. By no means all the new towns were along the several routes followed by pilgrims, but the accounts of pilgrims are among our best sources of Spanish history of this time, and accordingly our data are most complete on towns so situated.

The earliest towns which seem to show some formal planning, or at least an organic concept of the function of the new towns, date from the second half of the eleventh century, although with the vicissitudes of the years it is often difficult to tell to what extent the earliest surviving street plans reflect those of the first settlements. Along the road from Roncesvalles to Burgos, passing through Pamplona, appear such towns as Puente la Reina (Navarra), in existence in the eleventh century and refounded and planned in 1124; Estella (Navarra), 1090; Logroño

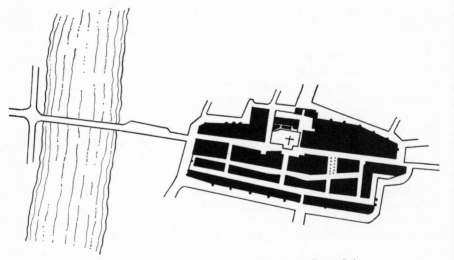

PLAN 1. SANTO DOMINGO DE LA CALZADA (LOGROÑO)

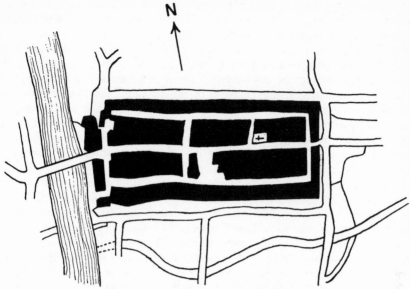

PLAN 2. PUENTE LA REINA (NAVARRA)

(Logroño), refounded at the end of the eleventh century; Nájera (Logroño), dating from the ninth century but reconstructed during the first part of the twelfth; and Santo Domingo de la Calzada (Logroño), dating from the last half of the eleventh century. All these were bridge towns. Santo Domingo (Plan 1) and Puente la Reina (Plan 2) are most interesting, because they show an emergent plan which seems to have been followed in many later towns. The *calzada*, the road, after crossing the river continues in a straight line, along which the first constructions presumably appear. Two flanking streets, parallel to the calzada, accommodate the increasing population, and these are joined to the calzada by short streets crossing at right angles. In Santo Domingo, the flanking streets both lie on the same side. In Puente la Reina, in the more common pattern, a street lies on each side of the calzada to form a rectangle of greater symmetry. From available plans it is impossible to tell whether the plaza of Puente la Reina is a part of the original scheme or the result of the plaza-building process of subsequent years. It does not form an organic part of the plan, and can perhaps best be thought of as a subsequent clearing of old structures. The other towns along this route lie parallel to their respective rivers, and though they show straight streets, the symmetry of plan of those described is absent.

Under the reign of Alfonso VIII the Basque provinces of Alava and Guipúzcoa were incorporated into the Crown of Castile (1200), thus encouraging the opening of a new direct road and pilgrimage route from Bayonne to Burgos. A series of thirteenth-century towns on this route show planning along the style of Santo Domingo and Puente la Reina, of which the most interesting, although somewhat aberrant, is Vitoria, actually founded in 1181 by Sancho el Sabio of Navarra. In 1256 Alfonso X founded three new towns on the new road north from Vitoria. Salvatierra (Alava), within its walls, shows a neat grid plan of oblong blocks grouped on the principle of a main street joining twin plazas, flanked by a single parallel street on both sides. Tolosa (Guipúzcoa) appears to have been almost identical in its original form, although the symmetry is destroyed by constructions towards the river. The original plan of Segura (Guipúzcoa) also appears to have been that of three parallel streets, with a plaza at least at one end. But subsequent changes, including rebuilding after a disastrous fire in 1422, make it hazardous to draw too many conclusions as to its original form.

A similar, and in some ways more startling, planned urban development took place in the Levante, particularly in Castellón, beginning in the second half of the thirteenth century. During and after the reconquests of Jaime I new towns were founded and old towns were relocated. Some of these appear to follow the form of small Roman encampments: a rectangular plan consisting of four quarters formed by two principal streets crossing at right angles at midpoint, where a plaza was left open, on which faced the church, town hall, jail, and other public buildings (Torres Balbás *et al.*, 1954, p. 59). Secondary streets ran parallel to the major streets, dividing the communities into blocks. The city of Castellón, refounded 1251, shows something of this regularity. Nules, Almenara, Soneja, and other settlements of this period likewise reflect conscious planning. But it is Villarreal de Burriana, founded by Jaime I in 1271, that shows this philosophy in most perfect form (*ibid.*, p. 61). To judge by surviving plans, no other Spanish city since Roman times has had such classic design and symmetry in layout (Plan 3).

The first comparable grid-plan town of northern Spain is Briviesca, a short distance north of Burgos on the road to Vitoria and Bayonne

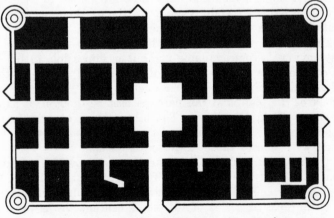

PLAN 3.   VILLARREAL DE BURRIANA (CASTELLÓN)

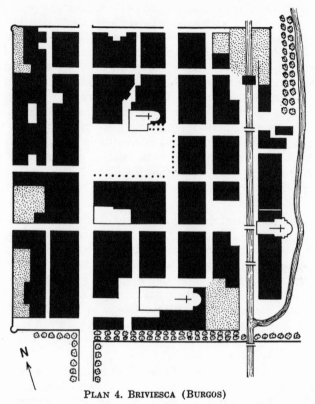

PLAN 4. BRIVIESCA (BURGOS)

(Plan 4). Although all streets are not cut through, Briviesca is essentially composed of five streets crossing five more at right angles, two of the resulting blocks having been omitted in the center of town to form a true plaza. Although the plan of Briviesca is relatively symmetrical, its principal longitudinal thoroughfare, unlike Villarreal de Burriana's, lies to the west of the plaza, and to the west of the central axis of the community. This plaza is noteworthy because it bears the same relationship to adjoining streets (with the exception of one potential street to the west, apparently never cut through) as do Spanish American plazas to their adjoining streets.

Briviesca was a well-known town in Roman times and is mentioned by Pliny and Ptolemy, but subsequently it sank into obscurity, and it seems unlikely that its superb Medieval grid-plan has anything to do with Rome. The town again became an important stopping-place in the early years of the pilgrimages to Santiago, and apparently in 1208 it was relocated from the east to the west bank of the Río Oca, where it now stands (Torres Balbás et al., 1954, p. 66). About the year 1314 scattered barrios of the town were brought within a new wall, and presumably the plan described dates from this period (ibid., p. 66).

These examples indicate that conscious town planning was practiced in Spain at least as early as the twelfth century, quite possibly before the revival of the art in other parts of Western Europe. The earliest form, exemplified by Puente la Reina, seems to have been an indigenous development which arose to meet specific needs. In the thirteenth-century towns of Castellón and in Briviesca, however, it seems very likely that the similarity in plan to the bastides of southern France represents diffusion. Briviesca, which lies on the former pilgrimage highroad from France, has a plan essentially the same as the thirteenth-century French towns with arcaded plaza faced by church and municipal buildings, a plan which is quite different from any other northern Spanish community of the period. Torres Balbás categorically states that the plan of Briviesca, as well as the less rectangular cities of the Basque Provinces, represents French bastide influence (*ibid.*, p. 67).

Certainly by the fifteenth century, as the result of diffused ideas, local experimentation with new designs, and theoretical speculation on the nature of the urban community, Spain had set the stage for the development of the grid-plan town as it was realized in the colonies in America. Torres Balbás tells of the ideas of the Catalan Franciscan, Eximeniç, who, writing from 1381 to 1386, described the ideal city, which was based on the grid-plan with main and subsidiary plazas (*ibid.*, pp. 89-90). Three-quarters of a century later Rodrigo Sánchez de Arévalo, churchman, ambassador, and statesman, speaks in detail of how cities should be planned and built (*ibid.*, pp. 90-91).

The extent to which the ideas of these, and other men, were instrumental in the planning of at least two Andalusian towns that predate by a few years the New World cities is uncertain. The Catholic sovereigns, Isabel and Ferdinand, founded Puerto Real in 1483 on the Bay of Cádiz. Its streets cross at right angles and several entire blocks are omitted to form plazas, on the largest of which front the public buildings. Ponz, three centuries after the founding of Puerto Real, lauds its straight streets and sound construction (1947, p. 1597).

Santa Fe de Granada offers a more intriguing problem. It was founded by Isabel and Ferdinand in 1491 during the final stages of the siege of Granada. At first a military encampment, stone workers and carpenters were brought in to convert it into a permanent city. Its original walled area was a rectangle, 400 by 260 *varas* according to Madoz (13:759) and 400 by 312 varas according to Torres Balbás (1954, p. 73). The plan (Plan 5) is not quite what a model military-encampment-become-permanent should be. The principal longitudinal street lies to the left of the central axis, and there is a secondary longitudinal street to the right, which has the merest hint of a companion to the left. The great plaza lies at the intersection of the two main cross streets that lead to the four original gates, and when built, it was faced by the town hall, public granary, hospital, and jail.

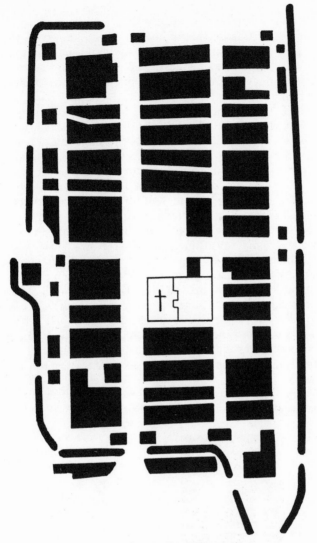

PLAN 5. SANTA FE (GRANADA)

A comparison of the plans of Briviesca and Santa Fe reveals a striking similarity, though not an absolute identity. This apparently is not acci-dental. Torres Balbás quotes Lucio Marineo Sículo, who wrote in 1530, as the first of a long line of writers who state that Santa Fe was copied directly after Briviesca (*ibid.*, p. 74). Ponz (1947, p. 1685) picked up Marineo Sículo's statement towards the end of the eighteenth century, and Madoz (13:760) and Miñano (2:166) repeat it toward the middle of the following century. Apart from the similarity in plan there are historical reasons to believe this may be true. Briviesca had been an important town; in 1388 a session of the Cortes was held there which decreed that the crown prince of Castile should henceforth be known as the Prince of Asturias. Isabel herself, and doubtless Ferdinand, had passed through it many times. So its plan was unquestionably known to the sovereigns, and its advantages both for military and colonizing purposes would have been apparent to them.

After Santa Fe other similarly planned towns appear, like Mancha Real (Jaén) in 1540, the "New Colonies" of Córdoba and Jaén, founded in the latter half of the eighteenth century for German and Flemish Catholic settlers brought by Charles III, and Nueva Carteya (Córdoba), founded in the early years of the nineteenth century. Planned communities also sprang up in other parts of Spain as, for example, Nuevo Baztán (Madrid), founded in the second half of the eighteenth century by a Basque nobleman from Baztán (Navarra).

These later towns, while all built on the grid-plan, do not follow the system with the same faithfulness as most New World Spanish cities. La Carolina (Jaén), the most important of the New Colonies, was laid out in an L-shape, with the main plaza, on which the town hall fronts, at the point of juncture of the two arms (Plan 6). The church stands on a low hill on the far side of a subsidiary plaza three blocks to the north, while to the east lies, first, a hexagonal plaza and then, just within the twin towers of the town entrance, a small round *Plaza de la Aduana*, or toll plaza for collecting customs fees. The hexagonal plaza also appears in several other New Colonies towns, such as Aldea Hermosa and Aldea de los Ríos (Jaén).

It seems very likely that Spanish American grid-plan towns are transplanted bastides, brought via the path of the pilgrimage route of Santiago

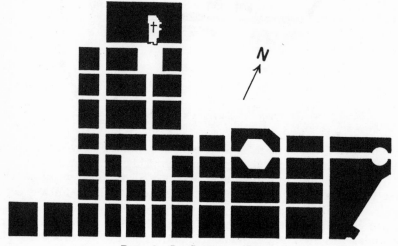

PLAN 6. LA CAROLINA (JAEN)

to Briviesca, then to southern Spain, and subsequently across the Atlantic to America. Although Mexico City, whose Spanish reconstruction began in 1523-1524, is often referred to as the first true grid-plan town in America, Palm has pointed out that Ovando laid out Santo Domingo in 1502 in essentially this form (1951, p. 241).[2] Then, too, Ferdinand, in his 1513 instructions to the conquistador Pedrarias Dávila on town planning, implies but does not spell out the grid-plan. In any event, it is apparent that, from the time of the discovery of America knowledge of the grid-plan town and an understanding of its advantages were common among many Spanish officials, and that almost from the earliest days this design was settled on for permanent New World communities.

The origin and development of the plaza, which became the hub of village, town, and city life in Spanish America, is also germane to the growth of the idea of city planning. In Spain there are actually several types of plazas: market plazas, which developed from the eleventh century onward; "organic" plazas built as integral parts of planned communities; and "monumental" plazas of great cities, which historically are the latest of all. At the time of the beginning of town and city markets in Spain, the cemeteries which surrounded churches were sometimes used as weekly market sites (Torres Balbás *et al.*, 1954, p. 83). Limited space within town walls discouraged the allotment of large open areas for true market plazas. Consequently weekly markets more and more sought open spaces outside the walls, near a principal gate. In time the temporary shelters erected by merchants became permanent buildings, and little by little true market plazas developed in many communities in this fashion. Plazas of this type sometimes are related to surrounding streets, but scarcely ever is this relationship in the precise form of that of communities planned from the beginning.

In the plazas of other small towns, it is difficult, judging by modern appearances, to see an origin in the process just described. For frequently the plaza seems to be little more than a wide spot in a street, the chance opening of irregular paths, without definite form or shape. Often such melancholy plazas are unpaved and otherwise unimproved in any way, lacking even a simple fountain.

The town and village plaza, whatever its origin and whatever its form, characterizes northern rather than southern Spain. In the south the Moorish city plan still predominates, and only when a special effort to carve out an open space has been made, is a real plaza found. In Extremadura the plaza of Garrovillas (Cáceres) is one of the most interesting: a wide, dusty, irregularly-shaped space which seems to separate rather than tie together the town. But the *soportales* (arcades) are extraordinary, and take the form of a two-storied arcade surrounding much of the plaza. Other typical old plazas are those of Arévalo (Avila), Pastrana (Guadalajara), and Medinaceli (Soria) (pl. 1, top). In these, the arcades were built before French influence brought in stone arches, and take the form of covered walks formed by the flat projection of the second story, which is held up by a series of square wooden or stone posts.

The *plaza monumental,* the great city plaza, is a phenomenon of relatively recent times, and is particularly associated with Castile. These plazas, carved out of the center of cities and bearing little or no functional relationship to street patterns (as contrasted to the planned Spanish cities just discussed), began to appear in the late sixteenth century. The reconstructed plaza of Valladolid, finished in 1592, appears to have been the first of the monumental type. That of Madrid followed in 1619, while that of Salamanca—perhaps the finest in Spain—was not completed until the early years of the eighteenth century. The classic plazas of both Madrid and Salamanca are surrounded by fine stone buildings with arcades and are entered by streets passing under arches—not at the corners of the plaza. Ricard rightly describes these plazas as "closed" as contrasted to the "open" New World plaza (1950, pp. 321, 325), consciously formed by the suppression of one or two blocks in the city planning and with the eight principal streets entering two at each corner. These monumental plazas, which rarely are adjacent to the church or cathedral, were designed for public executions, *autos da fe,* bullfights, and other festive occasions. The town hall is found on one side, but the other public buildings are usually lacking.

Sociologically, the Hispanic American plaza is far more important than the Spanish plaza. The former is the geographical as well as the cultural center of a community, where the evening promenades take place, where the major stores front, adjacent to which, or even in which, will be found the open market. Life seems to swing about these central focal points. In Spain, with rare exceptions, plazas almost seem to be avoided. Fashionable promenades follow streets in the cities, and the hub of the community usually lies away from the plaza.[3] In small towns the barren and unimproved plaza is usually little more than a space to be traversed as one makes his way home or out into the country. The Spanish plaza, with rare exceptions, was not planned as an organic part of the community, and it has only occasionally achieved functional success.

COMPARISONS AND COMMENTS

The historical processes that produced the American grid-plan town obviously were distinct from those that introduced many other cultural items. A religious fiesta, a marriage form, a domestic animal and its mode of care, a plow, a fish net—these, and hundreds of other traits, simply replicate traditional Spanish forms. But in the town, the Spanish government was introducing something new, which with rare exceptions did not exist in Spain or in other parts of Europe. The plans of older sections of Spanish cities, especially those of the south, appear as veritable spider webs, with narrow and twisting streets often coming to dead ends. Plazas, when found at all in this region, are either a creation of the past three centuries or simply a wide, and often barren, ground, where several streets chance to intersect.

City planning in Spanish America represents, therefore, not the diffusion of a material trait, but the utilization of an idea in a new context, with specific goals in mind. The process of the founding and growth of cities, towns, and villages in America illustrates particularly well the "formal" side of conquest culture in which careful planning and direction rather than the customs and forms familiar to conquistadors and administrators were instrumental in developing new patterns.

In a sense Spanish city planning in the New World recapitulates earlier Greek and Roman patterns. Greece and Rome, already built up when the grid-and-forum pattern evolved, built their most perfectly aligned cities in their provinces and overseas colonies. By the time the Spaniards had worked out their ideal grid-and-plaza town most of their cities had been built or rebuilt, and only in the New World was it possible to execute the beautifully symmetrical plans so dear to the Spanish bureaucrat of the time.

REFERENCES

Caro Baroja (1949b, 1950a, 1952b, 1954), Coello (1848-1870), Davillier (1949), Madoz (1845-1850), Miñano (1826-1829), Niemeir (1937), Palm (1951), Pitt-Rivers (1954), Ponz (1947), Ricard (1950), Rodríguez Marín (1926), Stanislawski (1946, 1947), Torres Balbás et al (1954), Tout (1934), Vázquez de Parga et al (1949, vol. 2), Vergara y Martín (1936), Wilhelmy (1952).

NOTES

[1] The rich variety of traditional Spanish house types is not discussed in this monograph. For information on this subject the interested reader is referred to the following works: Bouza Brey and Lorenzo (1947), Caro Baroja (1944b, 1946a), Casas Torres (1943, 1944), Giese (1937, 1951), González Iglesias (1945a), Hoyos Sancho (1952), Krüger (1925, 1936a, 1939b, 1944), Lorenzo Fernández (1949), Manrique (1950), Torres Balbás (1946), Violant y Simorra (1949, 1950).

[2] Palm's excellent study, "Los orígenes del urbanismo imperial en América" (1951), came to my attention after this chapter had been written.

[3] Julian Pitt-Rivers has called my attention to several places where the *paseo* takes place in the plaza: Salamanca, Pamplona, and the town of Alcalá, which he describes in *The People of the Sierra*.

CHAPTER V

AGRICULTURAL PRACTICES

In Spanish America

TRADITIONAL Hispanic American agricultural practices, apart from Indian areas, are based to a great extent on Spanish models. Implements, techniques, measures, vocabulary, many crops, and at least some social forms were brought to America by early colonists. From Mexico to Chile fields are prepared with a form of the ancient Mediterranean "scratch" plow drawn by oxen attached to the shaft by a horn yoke. European field crops, especially wheat, are grown in this way, and in most places this is also true of indigenous American crops like maize and beans.

The quality of land is described by terms such as *de pan llevar, tierra de barro,* and *tierra cascajosa,* and individual fields carry identifying names, so that the farmers of a village usually, and without difficulty, can identify any plot of land in the neighborhood of their community. To prepare land with a scratch plow requires several plowings *en cruz,* at right angles to the previous furrows, and each operation, including cultivation of young plants, has an identifying name such as *alzada, cruzada,* or *escarda.* Wheat land is divided into strips called *melgas,* representing the width that can be seeded broadcast. Wheat is threshed in Biblical fashion: horses tramp the stalks on a circular floor.

Until recent years fertilizers have been chiefly limited to animal sources. In Peru, at least, and doubtless other countries, the operation may be accomplished *a tumbo de red:* sheep are enclosed at night in a portable fence, which is moved on succeeding days systematically to cover an entire field. The *fanega,* or *fanegada,* is a dual measure used to calculate both land area and dry measure. Irrigation is important in Andean countries, where the *acequia* ditch brings water to distribute to individual plots. Water-lifting machines are rare. The mule-drawn *noria* is still found in Zacatecas and San Luis Potosí (Mexico) but its use appears not to be widely extended in America. The much more elaborate *aceña,* or Persian water wheel, is even more rare.

This plow-based agriculture is marked by many superstitions. Weather prognostication is accomplished in many places by the *cabañuelas,* in which, in a common form, the farmer observes the first twelve days of January (or the month in which the agricultural year begins), thereby predicting the average weather for each of the following twelve months. The phase of the moon is important in planting certain crops, and in harvesting others, as well as in cutting wood. San Isidro is patron saint

of cultivators in all Spanish America, and on May 15 seed is usually
blessed during Mass.

In contrast to agricultural techniques, which are well covered in accounts
of Spanish America, traditional forms of land ownership and utilization
are little described. We know almost nothing of the operation of the great
haciendas that characterize much of Spanish-speaking America. Sharecropping practices, usually based on "halves" *(a medias)* are known to
occur widely, but descriptions of any other important renting usages are
not to be found in anthropological literature.

IN SPAIN

Spain's varied agricultural forms reflect the accretions from diverse
sources over many centuries, modified by local climatic and soil characteristics. At an early period the agricultural knowledge of the Circum-Mediterranean area reached the peninsula, bringing the wooden
"Egyptian" or "Roman" scratch plow, the *tribulum* threshing board, the
plostellum threshing cart, basic Old World crops, irrigation methods, and
a variety of superstitions. The high state of Spanish agriculture in antiquity, in the south at least, is attested by the famous treatise on Roman
agriculture written by Columella, born in Cádiz in the first century A.D.,
who, although he wrote in Italy, undoubtedly learned much of what he
knew in his homeland (Ash 1941). Agriculture in dry Spain was enormously enriched as a result of the Moorish occupation, which saw the
development of elaborate irrigation techniques, garden technology, and
new crops, probably including rice.

A second classic Spanish agricultural source, the twelfth-century *Libro
de agricultura* of Abu Zacaria (1802), tells us of practices of cultivation
at that time. A third great treatise on Spanish agriculture, the *Agricultura
general* of Alonso de Herrera (1790, first published in 1513), reflects the
knowledge of farmers of the period just before New World crops began
to be important. Alonso, it is interesting to note, believed in far more
agricultural superstitions than did Columella nearly fifteen hundred years
earlier.

The distinct areas of Spain are marked by different crops and different
forms of land exploitation. In a general sense the south is a region of
latifundios, great estates of 500 to 1,000 and more hectares, whereas the
north, especially Galicia, is a region of *minifundios*, small plots often so
broken up as to be of uneconomic size. Associated with the latifundios of
the south are large towns distributed over its region and populated by an
agricultural proletariat, workers who go each day, when work is available,
to labor for wages on the great estates. Small villages, scattered farms,
and widespread individual ownership of small holdings are associated
with the north. But the division is not quite this simple. The aristocracy
comes from all parts of the country, and extensive properties are found
outside Andalusia, Extremadura, and New Castile. Conversely, small
landholdings are found interspersed with large estates all through the

south. For the small landowners, however, one must look to hilly or mountainous areas where the soil is thin and where, in the period of repopulation following the expulsion of the Moors, the nobles found little to interest them.

Large agricultural estates usually are called *cortijos*. In Andalusia the common American term *hacienda*, while known and occasionally used, is not common. The word also appears in limited use in the Levante, in Murcia and Alicante. Other terms are used for smaller holdings. For example, around Grazalema (Cádiz) a *rancho* is a very small plot with a correspondingly small house, while a *finca* is a somewhat larger farm. In the Andévalo region of Huelva isolated houses with their surrounding lands are known as *montes*.

Regardless of the form of land exploitation, the same kinds of implements are used within a given area. These have been quite well studied and illustrated. Plows, particularly, have attracted the attention of travelers and ethnographers: in the late eighteenth century the English agronomist, Townsend, made careful observations and drawings (1791) and more recently the studies of the Aitkens (1935) and Caro Baroja (1949a) have outlined the distinctive types and their distribution. Two main types of plows can be distinguished. The first, called by Spanish students the *arado dental*, is essentially the wooden Mediterranean scratch plow found in most of Latin America. Two variants are illustrated in figure 1. This plow consists of a heavy bottom piece, a bed or "head" *(dental* or *cabeza)* whose forward tip ends in an iron share *(reja)*. The handle *(mancera)* may be set in the head at nearly a right angle (fig. 1, *a*), or it may be shaped to form a continuous piece with the rear of the bed (fig. 1, *b*), as in Tzintzuntzan. The "throat" *(garganta)* is a heavy curved piece which joins the shaft *(timón)* to the body of the plow. This joint is strengthened and control for the depth of furrows is achieved by a short vertical peg *(telera)*, held in place by a wedge *(cuña)*. Spreaders *(orejeras)*, which make a wider furrow than the share alone, project from each side of the bed.[1] This plow today is found in lower Andalusia to the edge of the Sierra Morena, in western Extremadura and León, and in much of Portugal as well. Archaeological remains of shares indicate that its distribution formerly was much greater along the Mediterranean coast.

A variant of this plow type, called *radial* by Spanish ethnographers, is found in parts of Navarra, Upper Aragón and Galicia. The shaft and throat of this plow, unlike the arado dental, are a single straight shaft, and the handle and head form a continuous construction, sometimes of one and sometimes of two joined pieces of wood (fig. 1, *e*). When the position of the shaft is more nearly horizontal, necessitating joining to the handle rather than to the plow bed, the *cuadrangular* plow type results (fig. 1, *d*). Occasionally this plow is provided with a pair of small wheels at the front end of the shaft. The cuadrangular plow is found in the Basque provinces and in parts of Galicia and Asturias. All three types of plows described

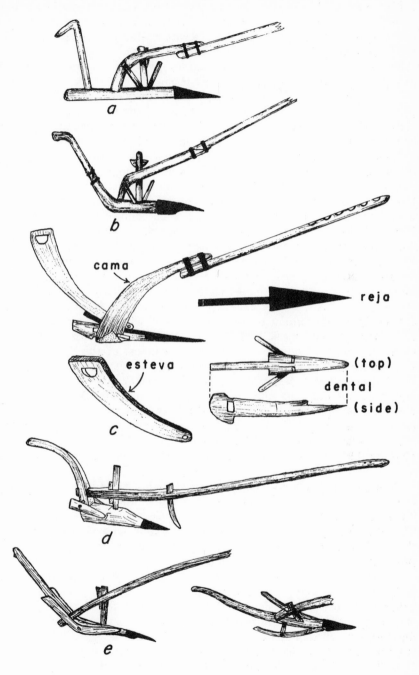

FIG 1. SPANISH PLOW TYPES

resemble each other, and differ from the Castilian type (below) in having a share which is a triangular sheet of iron curved to clamp on the front of the plow bed. This type of share scratches furrows in the ground but does not turn the soil like a mold-board plow.

The share of the Castilian *(castellano)* plow, by contrast, is a lance-shaped section of iron which derives its rigidity from the integration of its shaft with the assemblage of the other main pieces (fig. 1, *c*). In this plow the *cama,* corresponding to the throat of the *dental* plow, is a much heavier piece of wood, and is perforated at the butt so that the rear of the bed, capped by the iron lance of the share, and the bottom of the handle (usually called *esteva*) are wedged together. With this construction no telera peg is necessary, since the resistance of the ground is transmitted directly to the cama. The Castilian plow also scratches but does not turn the soil. The Castilian plow characterizes all of both Castiles, and extends varying distances into adjacent provinces. In point of area of distribution it exceeds that of all other plow types combined, and in recent years it has gained at the expense of the other forms.

Formerly plows were usually drawn by oxen (and cows: cows still commonly serve as draft animals in the north). During the past two hundred years, however, mules have replaced oxen in wide areas, particularly the Castiles, and oxen are seen much less often. This gradual change from one animal to another was not without repercussions, and many agricultural "specialists" of the end of the eighteenth and beginning of the nineteenth centuries lamented the madness of the Spanish farmer in utilizing mules rather than the old reliable ox. It was pointed out that, in addition to lower first cost, the ox was stronger, ate less, and when old and worn out was still valuable for its meat and hide. Many blamed the low state of Spanish agriculture at that time on this inexplicable whim of the countryman.[2] Today oxen are seen principally in Andalusia, although mules also are much used here. They also appear in the north, along with draft cows, and in isolated regions they may be seen almost anywhere in the country.

Both horn and collar yokes are used in Spain. The former is, of course, the older, and is still associated with oxen in the central and southern parts of the country. This is the common yoke found in Spanish America. The collar yoke is found in the east, north, and northwest, and is one of the many items of central European material culture that have penetrated into the northern parts of the country.

Hoe culture is practiced in a number of places in Spain, particularly the irrigated *hoyas* and other coastal areas in the south and east. Hand cultivation, to the exclusion of the plow, is also found in parts of the Basque country where the principal tool is the *laya,* a two-pronged iron digging fork with an off-center handle. Soft earth is worked without foot traction; for harder earth a single implement is used and the flat top bar is pushed with the foot. Hoes and similar tools come in various sizes and shapes but have little unusual about them. The *garabato* is a long-handled instrument with twin curving iron points set at the angle of a hoe blade. It is used in digging root crops and in similar activities. The *almocafre* is a short-handled trowellike tool used in weeding. The short-handled toothed sickle is used to harvest grain crops, while in wet Spain the scythe is used to cut forage crops. In most of Spain it is believed that the scythe, admittedly a more rapid cutting implement, knocks grain from the heads, and food is too scarce to permit such waste.

Spanish threshing practices vary greatly. The threshing floor *(era)* may be in the field, but usually it is on the outskirts of the village. Hence during threshing season the traveler sees great piles of wheat stacked over a large area on the edge of towns, each group of farmers working on a particular floor. In hilly regions threshing floors are carefully terraced and cobbled, to save other flat land for planting (pl. 1, bottom).[3] Good floors are cobbled, but land well trampled by horses is also satisfactory, and in the spring one often sees droves of horses being driven around and around on a bare floor *"para asentar la era,"* to compact the floor.

In some places, particularly in isolated parts of Extremadura and Andalusia (Bierhenke 1929, pp. 26-28) and in valleys in the Pyrenees (Krüger 1939a, pp. 269-301), grain is threshed by the ancient method of running horses around and around to trample out the heads. In most places, however, this method has been replaced by one of two types of primitive threshing machines *(trillo)*, both of which have been known since classical antiquity. In central Spain, in an area roughly corresponding to the Castilian plow, this is the old Roman *tribulum*, a wooden sledge with flints or other cutting stones set in the bottom (pl. 2, top). It is drawn by a team, and the thresher rides to guide the animals. Frequently two movable iron hooks project over the rear. When lowered they catch and turn the straw, so that all sides are progressively exposed to the cutting knives.

The Roman *plostellum poenicum*, which may be called the *trillo andaluz* because of its principal modern area of use, consists of a wooden cart with a series of toothed iron wheels (pl. 2, bottom). This is drawn after the team in the manner of the sledge, the iron teeth doing the work of the flints. This thresher is also found in Badajoz and Caceres, and in some parts of Portugal.

The tribulum is ancient and of widespread use, occurring among other places in the Azores, Madeira, the Canaries, southern France, Italy, Greece, Turkey, the Caucasus, Lebanon, Cyprus, Crete, Mesopotamia, and north Africa. Modern forms, some made in the United States for export under the Point Four program, are of stainless steel.

The plostellum likewise is ancient and widely used. Hamy describes and pictures it as used in Tunisia at the end of the last century (1900), and in the summer of 1957 I encountered it near Teheran, Iran. Caro Baroja (1946a, p. 131), quoting Varro, says that it was introduced into southern Spain by the Phoenicians. Yet it appears not to have been generally known in Spain in modern times until late in the nineteenth century. Townsend, in his remarkably detailed study of Spanish agriculture at the end of the eighteenth century, makes no mention of it, and for the province of Granada he specifically describes the use of cattle to tread out the grain (1791, 3:54). Ford, speaking of Alcalá de Guadaira, near Sevilla, in the late 1830's, mentions only the tribulum (1846, pp. 115-116). Somewhat later Klemm tells of threshing both with animal hoofs and the tribulum, but is silent on the wheeled-cart thresher (1869, p. 114). Giese says that in the Serranía de Ronda threshing was accomplished with animals alone until about 1880; subsequently the threshing cart was introduced, and by the 1930's its use had become general. He speculates that this cart represents a development from the tribulum, but gives no information on how this transformation might have come about (1937, pp. 134-135). The earliest account known to me of the threshing cart in modern times is a 1780 article which describes a "new invention" attributed to one Lucas Vélez of Coronil (Sevilla), a cart with two revolving axles with wooden teeth to dislodge grain (Cordero 1780, pp. 48-51). The evidence suggests, therefore, that in spite of the ancient history of the plostellum in Andalusia, its present use is recent, possibly representing reintroduction from Africa.

Stone or wooden rollers pulled by horses or mules are sometimes used for threshing in Catalonia, the Balearic Islands, and Murcia. The wooden rollers have sharp iron blades embedded in them, so that the action is similar to that of the two more widespread threshing machines (Krüger 1939a, pp. 301-307, 325-326; Bierhenke 1929, pp. 27, 29).

Agricultural lands are divided into two basic categories: irrigated *(de riego, regadío)* and unirrigated *(de secano)*. In addition there are *pastos naturales* and *pastos artificiales*, "natural" meadows being those in which hay grows spontaneously, and "artificial" being those in which alfalfa or some other forage crop is planted. Meadows are sometimes irrigated if there is sufficient water. Besides these distinctions, lands are informally classified according to their quality and their suitability for certain crops, following a system centuries old. The best wheat land is the *tierra de pan* ("land of bread,") or *tierra de pan llevar* ("land from which bread is taken"). Over four centuries ago Alonso de Herrera described lands *buena para llevar pan*. Good land is also called *tierra calma*, and if it is more clay-like, *tierra de barro*. *Tierra cascajosa* is gravelly soil, and *tierra albariza*, or simply *albar*, is a light-colored, chalky soil.

Fields are called *hojas* in some places and *tablas* in others, the latter term usually for irrigated plots. In either case it is customary to name them, so that a farmer in any region knows immediately to what field reference may be made. Names stem from a variety of inspirations: the appearance of a field, its relationship to a town or known natural object, a present or past owner, and the like. A gently undulating low hill in Bujalance, for example, is graphically called *La teta de Teresa*, "Teresa's breast," while an adjoining field is called *La cabaña* after a long-vanished shack which had once been there, and a third field is known as *Er lao de*

Tafarra (i.e., *El lado de Tafarra*), "beside Tafarra," a point called by that name.

Agricultural lands are terraced in many parts of Spain, for almost all kinds of crops and for both irrigated and unirrigated fields. Sometimes stone supporting walls are built, as in the Sierra de Gata in northern Cáceres, but often a sod wall is sufficiently strong to stand unaided. Particularly extensive terracing can be seen in southern Valencia and northern Alicante, in the region of Denia and Jijona.

Organic fertilizers are the traditional Spanish soil enrichers. Chilean nitrates were used in considerable quantities before the Civil War, and formerly good farmers spread lime on their fields every four years. But with the recession of the forests and the high cost of wood for burning lime less of this mineral is used. Today broad beans and lupine are increasingly used for green manuring. In sheep-raising areas, the animals are gathered together at night within a portable net wall *(redil)* so that by morning a considerable amount of fertilizing has occurred. The following night the net is placed in an adjacent plot, and similarly on succeeding nights, until with time a large area has been so treated *a tumbo de red.*

Although the metric system was officially introduced into Spain in 1849, older traditional measurement systems still persist. The common standard of length is the Castilian yard *(vara de Castilla)* of .836 meters, but the "yard" varies in other provinces from less than .8 meters to more than .9 meters. It is subdivided into feet *(pies)* and inches *(pulgadas)*. As in Spanish America the fanega (also called *fanegada, hanega, hanegada)* is the most widespread land measure. The common size of the fanega, in most of Old and New Castile, Extremadura, and parts of Andalusia, is 9,216 square varas (.64 hectares). But the size of the fanega varies from the tiny .08 hectare found in Castellón to .70 hectares in Albacete. The fanega is divided into 12 *celemines* which in turn are quartered into *cuartillos*. The *aranzada* (derived from the Latin *arāre)*, approximately two-thirds of a fanega, is a common land measure in lower Andalusia. The *obrada*, a term used in Valladolid (.47 hectares), Palencia (.53 hectares) and Segovia (.39 hectares) derives from the verb *obrar*, "to work." Historically the fanega, aranzada, and obrada represent, like the English acre (.43 hectares), the theoretical area that can be plowed in a day by an ox team under average conditions. In parts of the Basque area the *yugada* (from *yugo*, "yoke") is a variable area, which likewise represents a day's work for a team of oxen. Because of wet, heavy soils the size of the yugada tends to be less than that of the foregoing measures; in Vera de Bidasoa (Navarra) it is .27 hectares. The *robo* (.09 hectares) and the *ferrado* (which varies from .04 to .06 hectares) are used in Navarra and Galicia respectively, where the tiny parcels associated with minifundio land ownership make the larger measurements impractical. The measure *tahulla*, 1,600 square varas, or .11 hectares, is used in the irrigated lands of the Levante, particularly Murcia, Almería, and Granada.

Dry measure is usually calculated by the *fanega de áridos*, the amount of wheat needed to seed a fanega. Usage has standardized the fanega more than most other traditional measures, and it runs very close to 55 liters. Dry fanegas are subdivided into celemines and cuartillos, just as land is. Often—more so formerly—land areas given in fanegas represent the amount of seed customarily used rather than the result of a careful survey.

The poor quality of most Spanish soils, insufficient and variable rainfall, and inadequate fertilizing have in large measure determined the common methods of land exploitation. In the great grain areas, customarily unirrigated, two systems of rotation are used, depending on these factors and the pressure on the land. Both are referred to as *cultivos extensivos*, as contrasted to *cultivos intensivos* on irrigated and fertilized land where cropping is possible every year. The Spanish version of the classic European three-field system of farming is known as that of *tres hojas, al tercios,* or *asolamiento trienal*. A farm is divided into three approximately equal areas, each of which is sown in successive years in wheat or some other grain. During the second year part of each field may be sown to legumes, and during the third it is prepared for the next grain sowing. The second system of rotation is known as the *bienal,* or *año y vez*. A farm is divided into two equal sections, one of which is sown to grain, the other left fallow or part of it sown to legumes.

Allowing for considerable variation, the cycle for the trienal division is as follows. During the fallow year, in which a field is left in *barbecho,* it is plowed three or four times. Late in the fall, when the first rains have softened the crust of the surface, the soil is broken in the operation known as *alzar* or *romper,* to "raise" or "break" the ground. A couple of months later the field is again plowed, this time at right angles to the first furrows, in the operation known as *cruzar* or *binar,* to "cross" or "second" the field. The third plowing in late spring is again parallel to the first furrows, an activity known as *terciar,* to "third," or work for the third time. A fourth plowing shortly before sowing is called *cortar* or *de cohecho*. If a field is plowed only three times, the final preparation is also often called de cohecho. Since the traditional Spanish plows lack mold boards, it is necessary to plow the field crossways to break up the soil. This action in turn tends to produce the classic Mediterranean square field, as contrasted to the north European strip, the result of plowing in a straight line with a mold-board plow.

Winter wheat is sown from October to December. The workers divide the field in melgas, strips 2.5 to 3 meters wide, by plowing light furrows from one end to the other. In broadcast sowing *(a voleo)* this is the width a man can satisfactorily spread the grain with a sweep of the arm. Not infrequently, and especially when seed is short, grain is planted a *chorrillo,* by dribbling it in furrows from the hand. After the sowing, a grain field is lightly plowed or smoothed with a *grada,* which may be a log, a clump of brush, or a square or triangular wooden frame with spikes. In the spring, weeds are removed with a hoe, or almocafre, in an operation known as the *escarda*.

In the great grain lands of the central plateau reapers traditionally are Galicians or Old Castilians, who travel in groups, each with a leader who contracts for their services *a destajo* (a flat sum for a field) with the owner of the land. Men work from dawn to dusk, with short periods off for rest, and often sleep under the stars. And by beginning in Andalusia in the early summer and working north as fields ripen, reapers obtain a couple of months of steady work before returning home.

After the harvest a grain field becomes *rastrojo* (stubble) or, in Andalusia, *erial* or *eriazo*. Cattle are turned in to graze, and in the late fall or following spring, depending on the legume, a portion of the field, usually from 10 per cent to 35 per cent, will be planted. Algarrobas and broad beans are planted in the fall, with little more than a scratching of the surface to cover the seeds. Chick peas and similar spring crops require a bit more preparation of the land. Then the field again becomes barbecho (fallow) for a year and the cycle begins anew. Usually a small part of a barbecho field is planted to chick peas, broad beans, or similar crop so that an establishment is producing small amounts of crops from the fallow fields, in addition to the grain hoja. Barley, oats, or rye may alternate as the grain crop, although they are relatively less important than wheat. Rye tends to be used on high marginal land, where frost threatens wheat.

A mixture of wheat and rye, known variously as *tranquillón, morcacho* (or *morcajo*), or *mitadenco*, is sown in some high, cold regions in the hope that, depending on the vagaries of weather, one or the other will ripen.

The two-year cycle of año y vez is an intensification of the three-field system. At the other extreme, as often happens in Extremadura, a field may be sown only once in four or five years. True slash-and-burn agriculture has been a part of the traditional Spanish picture under even more inclement conditions. Costa describes this system of *roza ambulante* in Galicia, Burgos, Córdoba, and other provinces (1915, pp. 354-363) and relates that in the early years of the New Colonies in the Sierra Morena, during the final quarter of the eighteenth century, land was allowed to lie idle for as much as twenty years (*ibid.*, p. 264). Often such agriculture was associated with communal efforts, in the sense of joint clearing of the land and either joint working of or the drawing of lots for individual small parcels. In Galicia the section of land to be cut was determined by the community, lots were drawn, and the entire area was enclosed, cleared, and planted on two successive years, first with wheat and then with oats. Then the enclosure was removed and the land was left fallow for twenty or more years while other sections were similarly exploited (*ibid.*, p. 355). Increasing population pressure has constantly reduced the amount of land that can be so utilized; there is a natural tendency to try to keep cleared land, however poor, under a semblance of cultivation.

The cortijo farming of Andalusia is based essentially on the three-field system. The following account is for the system in use around Bujalance (Córdoba). Four classes of country estates are recognized: the cortijo proper, a large establishment of from 700 to 1,000 fanegas of land; the *cortijillo,* a smaller edition of the former; the *casilla,* the house and surrounding land of the small farmer; and the *casería,* the dwelling that goes with a small holding of olive trees. The true cortijo is of two types, corresponding in a general way to size: the larger, of two barrios, and the smaller of a single barrio. That of two barrios has the following arrangement in one building or group of buildings: the *casa del grano,* for grain storage; *cuadras,* the stables for mules and horses (oxen are not much used in this particular region); kitchen for feeding farm hands; and the rooms of the owner, who usually is absent. The other barrio contains: the *tinahón,* the stable for cattle; the *pesebrera,* or room of feed stalls; and the *descansadero* or *zahurda,* for pigs.

The land close to the buildings, and comprising 5 to 10 per cent of the entire holding, is called the *ruedo.*[4] Normally it is divided into two sections, one of which is manured from the production of the stables each year. The freshly manured section is first sown in barley, and the second year with chick peas or broad beans. Then the land is again manured, so that production is continuous. The unfertilized fields—90 to 95 per cent of the total—are divided into the usual three sections. The one in which grain is sown is called *raspa,* the one with stubble (normally called rastrojo) is erial, and the third is the barbecho.

A large cortijo has only a few permanent hands. Most workers are contracted in the plaza of neighboring towns for periods of from one day to two weeks. Apart from administrators the working personnel of cortijos are the *aperador* or *cortijero* (foreman), the *casero* (in charge of the kitchen and meals), the *pensador* (from *pienso,* stall feed of animals, who is in charge of cattle), the *boyeros* or *gañanes* (ox drivers, for plowing), the *yegüero* (who cares for horses), and the *porquero* (who cares for the pigs). These are privileged individuals known as *panzas,* who, at mealtime, are entitled to sit at the head of the long tables where they have first chance at the choice morsels that may be in the food. In addition there are several permanent handy men and their families—today no more than four or five—who live on the cortijo, a couple of *zagales* (boys who help with the pack animals), and a *haterillo* or *chanquero* (a boy who takes food to men working too far to return at noon).[5] A conch-shell trumpet is the traditional instrument for calling field hands to meals in Andalusia.[6] Although its use is dying out, it can still be heard in the fields around Ronda (Málaga).

Owners of cortijos rarely live in the country, although each building has rooms of greater or lesser comfort for the use of the family on their rare visits. But in general the buildings, however imposing from a distance, with their tile roofs and whitewashed walls, are dusty and dirty, often in a poor state of repair and disorder, reflecting the usual lack of attention which results from absentee ownership.

A considerable number of agricultural superstitions continue down to the present time. The most important of these have to do with the time of planting in relationship to the phases of the moon, beliefs which have existed from Roman times and before. Alonso de Herrera, for example, is careful to advise that planting, sowing, and grafting should be done during the first two quarters, and particularly the first, which is "hot and humid," as are healthy young people. The last two quarters, "cold and damp," like old people, are the times for harvesting and cutting of wood. These instructions are often followed by farmers today, although not always in the same way. In Vera de Bidasoa (Navarra) the Basques prefer to sow grain crops with the waning moon, and leaf and forage crops with the waxing. In Yegen (Granada) some men still plant during the waning moon and cut wood only during the fourth quarter. Garlic is the crop which is still most guided by the moon: it is sown during the waning period.[7]

Weather prognostication is accomplished, some believe, by means of the *cabañuelas*. In simplest form the farmer observes the weather for the first twelve days of January, and the weather for each of these days forecasts the general weather for the numerically corresponding month. Thus, if the seventh day is sunny, July, the seventh month, will be fair; if the tenth is rainy, October will be rainy. In parts of Avila the first thirteen days of August are watched. The first day is a general indication for all the next year, the second day for January, the third for February, and so on. Occasionally the first test may be checked by observing the next twelve days, this time in reverse, so that one works backward from December to January. An Andalusian variant of the cabañuelas is to put twelve small piles of salt on the table on the last day of the year. If some become more humid than others the months to which they correspond will be rainy.[8]

Some days have predictive value. In La Mancha and adjacent regions (Villanueva del Río Segura) San Augustín, August 28, is the *llave de dios*, "the key of God." If it rains on this day, the next agricultural year will be bad.

As in Anglo-Saxon countries, Candlemas is a day for predicting the remainder of the winter weather, and, as on Ground Hog Day, rain is a happy omen. *Si la Candelaria plora, invierno fora; y si no plora, ni dentro ni fora* ("If it rains on Candlemas, winter is going out; and if it doesn't rain, neither in nor out") is the proverb known over all the country, and in Galician and Catalán as well as in Old Spanish. Even closer to the Anglo-Saxon reading is the form, *Si la Candelaria rie, invierno sigue* ("If Candlemas laughs, winter continues").

Similar weather couplets may be found widespread over Spain. In Alosno (Huelva) the sayings go, *"Si llueve el día de Santa Viviana, llueve cuarenta días y una semana"* ("If it rains the day of St. Vivian, it will rain for forty days and a week."), and *"Si llueve el día de San Canuto, llueve tres meses justos"* ("If it rains on the day of St. Canute, it will rain for exactly three months"). Pleas for rain usually take the form of prayers to especially venerated local images, such as that of the Virgen del Rocío in Almonte (Huelva), to which thousands of people travel for her fiesta in the spring, or of processions in which an image of the Virgin from the village church is paraded through the streets.

Various other simple agricultural rites and superstitions are found in Spain. In Galicia rude crosses of blessed laurel are placed in fields to ensure better crops. In the Basque provinces the priest blesses the fields on the Day of the Invention of the Cross, May 3. In other places the blessing is given on San Marcos, April 25, San Blas, February 3, or San Isidro, May 15. But in general San Isidro Labrador, patron of Madrid and farmers, does not have the importance for agriculturists that he has in Spanish America. Menstruating women are believed by some to cause growing things to wilt by touching or being near them, and where this belief is common, women in this condition are expected to remain away from fields, gardens, and blossoming orchards.

Without irrigation much of the richest land of Spain would be useless. The Arab origin of such words as *acequia* (irrigation ditch), *aceña* (water wheel), *azud* (water wheel), *noria* (a type of bucket lift in a well), *aljibe* (cistern), *alberca* (reservoir), *alfarda* (tax for irrigation of land), *tahulla* (measurement of irrigated lands) indicates the significant contribution of Moorish culture to Spanish agriculture. In addition to terminology, many of the actual irrigation works of today were first constructed in Moorish times, and have been in constant use ever since. Whenever possible, water is taken from a stream by gravity through the *acequia madre*, the "mother ditch," and distributed through smaller ditches called *brazales*. When ready sources of water at the right level are lacking, recourse is had to a number of devices to obtain a head of water. The most common method is the noria, found in most parts of central and southern Spain; La Mancha is the land par excellence for norias (Caro Baroja, 1955). A well 1.5 to 2 meters in diameter is sunk deep enough so that a meter or more of water collects in the bottom. A chain of buckets, or in older forms clay pots tied with esparto cords, passes over a vertical wheel just above ground level, which with wooden or metal gear pins meshes with a horizontal wheel supported on a crossbar resting on two masonry posts. The axle of the horizontal wheel projects through the crossbar, and is fastened to a horizontal lever, a *malacate*, to which a blindfolded mule is hitched. As the mule walks in an endless circle, the force is transmitted to the vertical wheel which pulls the filled buckets. These empty their contents at the top of their arc into a trough which conducts the water to the canals. This is a slow and inefficient system, but it has the advantage that water tables are not seriously disturbed.[9]

Along the Mediterranean coast the noria has been combined with the windmill to form a very efficient lifting device. It is frequently found in the region adjacent to the Mar Menor, north of Cartagena (Murcia). This mill consists of a circular stone tower with a conical revolving wooden roof. In the most common type eight triangular sails are set in the eight openings formed by crossing four long poles. Several more modern mills, of iron rather than wooden construction, have ten rather than eight sails (pl. 3, left). Through a simple system of gears the motive force is transmitted to the noria wheel over which the chain of buckets passes (Caro Baroja 1952a, p. 333). In addition to the fact that it is used to lift water rather than to grind grain, this mill differs considerably from those of La Mancha, where sails are canvas rolls, usually four in number, which are spread over lattice vanes (pl. 3, right). The Cartagena windmill is normally used in association with a reservoir, so that in periods of good winds large quantities of water can be stored for use as needed.

It is strange that the windmill-noria was never introduced into La Mancha, where both devices have been known for centuries and where the combination would appear to promise great utility. The distance from La Mancha to Cartagena is relatively short, and Manchegan reapers go annually to Murcia to harvest crops, so it is not a question of ignorance of the Murcian form. But in La Mancha the windmill is used for grinding grain, and tradition or some less obvious factor has prevented the adoption of the water windmill.

The hydraulic water wheel, known in English as the Persian water wheel and in Spanish as the aceña or azud, survives in a few places in Spain, notably along the Río Segura in Murcia (pl. 4, top) and along the Guadalquivir. This is a double-frame wooden or iron wheel erected vertically in a swift-flowing stream so that a meter or so of the lower rims is submerged. The two rims are joined by a series of rectangular paddles against which the strength of the current exerts the force necessary to cause the wheel to revolve. Chambers around the rim fill when submerged, and empty their contents when they reach the top of the arc.

Caro Baroja has outlined the cultural history of the Persian water wheel (1954a). The most complex forms of this device are found along the Orontes River in Syria, where some wheels are nearly 30 meters in diameter. They have been known since antiquity in the eastern Mediterranean, whence they spread east to China and west to Europe; their presence in the Iberian Peninsula is certainly due to the Moors. Isolated wheels are found in Latin America: the fine iron "Spanish water wheel" of Falmouth, Jamaica, a crude wheel south of Santiago, Chile, and the wheels of the lower São Francisco River in Brazil reported by Donald Pierson (Caro Baroja 1954a, pp. 147-148). One wonders why, with the abundant waters and adjacent deserts or dry lands of much of America, this ingenious device was not more generally used.

Simpler water wheels, also of very ancient form and operated by manpower, are found in Spain. Near Murcia I noted a wheel of this kind, 2.5 meters in diameter, riveted of sheet metal and divided into wedge-shaped chambers, with wooden cleats across the rim. By climbing continuously on the cleats, a worker causes the wheel to revolve, partly filling the chambers, which empty their contents at a higher level. I have seen more elaborate wheels of this type constructed of bamboo in the Balsas basin of Guerrero, Mexico, but the presence of these wheels on the Acapulco—

Mexico City trade route from which Oriental merchandise reached the West also suggests a Chinese origin.

The *tahona* scoop-bucket is used in southern Valencia and northern Alicante. It consists of a lever, a three-sided wooden trough 2.5 to 3 meters in length, balanced on a masonry wall at the edge of an irrigation ditch. The end which submerges in the water contains the scoop, a wooden chamber open at the top, and on the opposite end a stone is bound as counterweight. The two operators dip the scoop in the water, then pull on the top until the channel is slightly past the horizontal point. The water in the scoop runs down the channel and into the field, and the process is repeated. This is an exhausting means of irrigating, and the minute quantities of water hardly seem worth the effort.[10]

Large-scale irrigation produces elaborate rules and regulations with respect to water rights. In those places where a number of individuals, or several towns and villages, draw from the same network, there is usually a *junta* or *Tribunal de Aguas* with appointed or elected officials who govern distribution of water and settle disputes over rights. The most famous of these is the *Cort de la Seo,* the Tribunal of Valencia, which for centuries has held open session from 11 to 12 o'clock on Thursdays in the plaza of the cathedral, the *seo,* to hear complaints and promulgate regulations. The junta, composed of seven *síndicos* elected in each of seven towns, has no formal powers; its recognized honesty and justice, and lack of legal complications, are sufficient to exact compliance in all save the most unusual cases from the farmers dependent on irrigation water.

Forms of private and communal land ownership and use through share-cropping, renting, and other forms of contracts, have received much attention at the hands of Spanish political economists. The subject is vast and complex, and only a few general points can be sketched here. As has been pointed out, in northern Spain there are proportionately more small landowners who work their holdings, while in the south large estates account for most of the best land. But even in those parts of Spain where small farmers predominate much land is worked by others than the owners, and elaborate systems of tenancy have developed over the years. Here again there is a significant difference between north and south Spain. In south Spain, tenancy traditionally is short term and is accompanied by elaborate legal documents specifying in detail the exact conditions which must be observed. This is particularly true of the renting of cortijos. Conversely, in the north much letting of small holdings is by verbal agreement, and tenants may be succeeded by their sons and grandsons on the same property.

Two basic types of tenancy exist: *aparcería* or sharecropping, and payment of a predetermined amount, either in cash or in kind, regardless of size of harvests. In either type the length of the contract is related to the common system of land usage. Thus, in Andalusia, where cortijos are farmed according to the three-field system and where a cycle lasts three years, traditional contracts have been for six years. Contracts stipulate that only the fallow fields may be sown in grain and that boundaries must be scrupulously observed. However, certain *libertades*, or liberties to sow a legume in a third or a fourth of the field currently fallow and *semillas de raspa* (oats or *escaña* wheat) in a third or fourth of the stubble field, are commonly permitted. All of the fertilizer produced by the cortijo animals must be used on the grounds of the ruedo, the fields immediately adjacent to the estate buildings. Contracts frequently bear the expression *de riesgo y ventura*, meaning that, regardless of weather or acts of God, the rent must be paid. They also stipulate that one must farm according to *uso y costumbre de buen labrador*, according to recognized good farming practices.

In other areas, where the cycle is that of *año y vez*, contracts may be for only four years, allowing two complete cycles of farming for the renter. North Spain, particularly Old Castile and adjacent areas, is the region in which verbal contracts based on mutual confidence between lessee and lessor are the rule and where a man expects to farm land during his whole lifetime, and probably pass it on to his son.

Sharecropping has become increasingly rare, and generally is found in marginal areas where more than usual risk results from the poor quality of the land and uncertain rainfall. Extremadura traditionally has been one of the great areas of sharecropping. Several systems are known, depending on the amount of crop received by the owner. Halving *(aparcería a medias)* is the most common system. Customarily the owner pays taxes and furnishes half the seed and fertilizers. The sharecropper supplies the remainder of the seed and fertilizer, and does the work. On inferior land the shares are *al tercio* or even *al cuarto*, a third or a fourth for the owner, since an equal amount of work on the part of the sharecropper produces less harvest.

Custom dictates different dates in different parts of the country on which the agricultural year is considered to end and on which payment must be made. San Miguel, September 29, is one of the most common days, and if payment is made in kind, it is on this date. If payment is in cash it is later, often November 1, to allow the renter time to sell his crop. La Asunción, August 15, is also a common day on which contracts expire.[11] In times past it was customary for a renter to give *dádivas* or *adehalas* to the owner, in addition to the rent per se. Such presents might consist of fowls, pigs, chick peas, or the like.

In addition to individual forms of land ownership and renting there has existed in Spain, especially in the north, an old theme of communal and coöperative rights and work which has been extremely important in much village life. This stems from the fact that Spanish villages have held communal title to a part or all of the surrounding land, and also to such structures as buildings, grain mills, fulling mills, ovens, and slaughtering floors. Costa (1915, pp. 307-336) divides these holdings into two categories: those legally known as *propios de los pueblos*, the profits of which formerly were customarily sufficient to pay many municipal expenses such as public instruction and police; and the *tierras concejiles*, or *comunes*. Included in the latter are the *ejidos*, which usually are uncultivated lands near the village where threshing floors are located and into which cattle are turned. The two forms of ownership often blend, but in theory title to the proprios de los pueblos was vested in the municipal government as a legal entity, and the income had as its function the support of municipal services and civic undertakings. Title to the tierras concejiles was vested in the citizens themselves, and the purpose of the land was the partial support of all families. This system began to break down in 1855 with the passage of a law requiring the dissolution of such communal holdings. This was only partly carried out, and some of the communal holdings have survived down to the present time. But the backbone of the system was broken, and descriptions of it apply to the nineteenth century.

Proprios de los pueblos lands were exploited both by renting and by communal work of villagers. Renting was more common: the highest bidder or bidders at public auction received the use of the land for two, four, or six years. Sometimes municipal authorities directed the group labors of the heads of families in the community. Tierras concejiles were exploited in three principal ways: communal working of the land and equal division of the produce (parts of Upper Aragón, León, and Zamora); adjudication of land to citizens for their personal use during their lifetimes, based on necessity and availability of land (parts of Segovia, Burgos, León, Valladolid, Salamanca, and Sevilla); distribution of land to citizens for short periods on the basis of drawing of lots.

Costa describes the communal working of consejil lands in the Ribagorza and Sobrarbe (Upper Aragón), the *partido* of Alcañices (Zamora), and in the Cabrera Alta and Baja (León). In Aliste (Alcañices) a group of citizens formed a *cabildo* (municipal council) for the task. Toward January the mayor convened the cabildo, which named four electors, who in turn named two judges, the six men forming the governing body for the year. The land to be cleared was then marked out, and the men ate together. For each day of work in clearing, burning, plowing, sowing, harvesting, and threshing, the judges called all participants (who included widows as well as men). Each contributed the same amount of seed and the same amount of work. After being threshed and winnowed the grain was divided equally among all who had participated, and a community meal was held (*ibid.*, pp. 394-396; also Méndez Plaza, 1900, pp. 17-25). I do not know whether traces of this system still remain, but they appear to have survived at least into the first years of the twentieth century.

In the examples of adjudication of consejil land for an individual's lifetime, the community often divided certain of its lands into *vitas* or *quiñones*, which were given in turn to citizens with the right to participate. Costa describes such grants in Old Castile, León, and Sevilla (1915, pp. 383-389).

But much the most common system of exploitation of such lands—and to a limited extent it exists today—was the drawing of lots for use of the land during one or several years. In most communities such land was an addition to private ownership of fields, but in some villages all land, except houses, house plots, gardens, and orchards, was communal property. At the end of the last century Costa found, in the region of Sayago (Zamora) alone, about fifty villages where this was so (*ibid.*, pp. 340-346). In that region the distribution was for two or three years, according to whether the complete cycle of rotation was two or three years. Each citizen, including the priest, carpenter, schoolteacher, and veterinarian, received two or three plots within the section under cultivation that year, so that good, average, and poor land would be equally distributed. The drawing of lots in Palazuelo, for example, customarily took place on November 1, and on this day the municipal council offered a round of drinks to the assembled men. The names of each group of plots forming a unit were written on slips of paper, along with the names of the men who had last worked them. These slips were mixed in a jar, and a boy of ten or twelve, or the men in turn, drew out their lots for that year (*ibid.*, pp. 342-344).

In past years the custom has been general in Spain of distinguishing between *vuelo y suelo*, the trees and the soil, of public lands. Individuals have had the right in many places to plant trees on ejidos, for the utilization of fruit, nuts, firewood, and lumber, without thereby acquiring title to the land. Chestnuts were the trees most often so exploited, but poplars, ash, oaks, and even olives were planted. Beneath the trees the land remained common, for grazing and gathering firewood. Although this custom has declined with the reduction in area of communal lands, it is still found from time to time. In Yegen in the Alpujarra, for example, chestnut trees on public lands are privately owned, but live oaks are the property of all.

COMPARISONS AND COMMENTS

The introduction into America of Spanish agricultural practices contrasts markedly with the introduction of city planning and building, since informal and unguided processes rather than formal direction explain the selection that was made of elements from the donor culture. Here we are dealing with the simple diffusion of material traits and associated activities. In addition to illustrating the informal processes of conquest culture, agricultural data provide a clear example of the stripping down or reduction that characterizes conquest culture. It is the same story that holds for many other categories of culture: infinite variety in the peninsula and relatively few but widely spread forms overseas. Of the many types of Spanish plows, only the arado dental of Andalusia and Extremadura has diffused. Neither the highly useful threshing cart or sledge appear ever to have reached America, and the noria and aceña water-lifting devices have a very limited distribution.

It is apparent that Andalusian and Extremaduran influences have been more important in America than methods from other parts of the peninsula. Although many sixteenth-century emigrants were familiar with the

Castilian plow and the associated tribulum, neither implement is found in America. A guess can be made why the Andalusian-Extremaduran plow became standard in America, at the expense of more northerly models. Although plows were soon made by immigrants, it is possible that in the earliest days some were imported from Spain. If so, these were certainly made in or near seaports such as Sevilla and Cádiz and not transported to tidewater from more distant Castile. Also, this plow is of simpler construction than the Castilian type and requires less iron—a scarce commodity in the New World—in its share. Once established, a type tends to remain constant unless there is a very obvious advantage in a variant form; this advantage is not apparent in the Castilian plow.

The absence of the plostellum threshing cart in America is understandable if we assume, as the evidence indicates, that it was not reintroduced into southern Spain until recent years: it was simply unknown to sixteenth-century Spaniards. There is no equally logical explanation for the failure of the tribulum to diffuse. It is useful, it was known to many emigrants, it could easily be duplicated with simple tools, and wherever draft animals were available for plowing and threshing by hoof it could have been exploited. Nor is it easy to guess why the noria, widespread both in New Castile and Andalusia, was so little used in America. Like the tribulum, it is useful, easily constructed, and could have been operated by the available draft animals.

With respect to agriculture, it is clear that southwestern Spanish influence predominates in America, out of all proportion to the total number of emigrants from these areas.

REFERENCES

Abu Zacaria (1802), Aitken and Aitken (1935), Alonso de Herrera (1790), Alvar (1955), Aranzadi (1943), Ash (1941), Bergmann (1934), Bierhenke (1929), Caro Baroja (1946a, 1949a, 1952a, 1954, 1955), Casas Gaspar (1950b), Cordero (1780), Costa (1915), Dias (1953), Espejo (1900), Ford (1846), Foster (1952a), García Suárez (1950), Giese (1937), Hamy (1900), Klemm (1869), Krüger (1925, 1939a), Méndez Plaza (1900), Teijón Laso (1948), Thede (1933), Townsend (1791), Vicario de la Peña (1901), Violant y Simorra (1949).

NOTES

[1] This is the Hispanic American plow. The description of its form, as found in Tzintzuntzan, is representative of all examples I have seen. As in Spain the "bed" is called *cabeza*, the iron share *reja*, the handle *mancera*, the shaft *timón*, the vertical peg *telera*, and the spreader *orejera* (Foster 1948a, p. 60).

[2] But the mule goes faster, can pull a heavier plow, and can also be used more effectively as a pack and draft animal.

[3] Julian Pitt-Rivers tells me that in Alcalá the placing of threshing floors depends on the prevalent winds and air currents rather than on the conservation of good land for planting.

[4] The term "ruedo" is also used to describe the area adjacent to a town, where middle-class people have small holdings. Beyond the ruedo lies the *trasruedo*, also an area of small holdings, and then the campiña, where the cortijos themselves are located.

[6] The Mendozas give the following comparable terms for hacienda employees in Zacatecas about the year 1885: *la de la metate* (tortilla-maker), *cocinera* (cook), *las recamareras* (chambermaids, who had other duties as well), *los administradores* (administrators, of various ranks and duties), *los monteros* ("those who took care of the *montes*"), *los vaqueros* (cowboys), *los ordeñadores* (cow-milkers), *las queseras* (cheesemakers), *costureras* (seamstresses), *peones* (hired hands) (1952, pp. 428-429).

[6] Sr. Julio Castañeda, a Cuban, tells me that in the region of Sancti Spíritus (Cuba) the conch shell (and sometimes a cowhorn trumpet) is still used to call field workers to meals.

[7] These beliefs are common in America, and until recent years have enjoyed at least pseudoscientific support, e.g., Balmaseda, in his *Tesoro del agricultor cubano* (Habana, 1885, p. 148), warns against harvesting maize during a waxing moon because then the kernels "have great porosity and humidity and are very susceptible to corn borers." Wood, likewise, should be cut only during the waning moon.

[8] Cabañuelas are widely reported in America (e.g., Colombia, Fals-Borda 1955, p. 191; Bolivia, Rigoberto Paredes 1920, p. 107; Dominican Republic, Emilio Jiménez 1927, pp. 56-57; Mexico, García Icazbalceta 1899, p. 63; Steininger and Van de Velde 1935, p. 91).

[9] The noria appears not to have been common in America. For many years I was unable to find any reference to it whatsoever, but in 1958, while driving through the state of Zacatecas (Mexico) I noted several, including an all-wood model.

[10] West describes a somewhat similar but by no means identical device common in Michoacán, Mexico (West 1948, p. 47 and fig. 4).

[11] There appear to be few Spanish American reports on renting periods. In parts of Venezuela, contracts expire on San Juan and the term of renting is "De San Juan a San Juan" (Olivares Figueroa 1949, p. 159).

CHAPTER VI

DOMESTIC ANIMALS

IN SPANISH AMERICA

ANTHROPOLOGISTS have not made major investigations of livestock practices in Hispanic America. Available studies tend to be historical and literary, often colored by the romance of the gaucho. In part these lacunae in our data are due to the fact that large-scale keeping of animals is a specialized activity, not found in all parts of Spanish America, and in part it stems from the relatively greater difficulties the anthropologist has encountered in working in haciendas—really large businesses—as contrasted to villages. Anthropologists have studied primarily small-scale livestock practices: horses for riding and prestige, oxen for plowing, burros and mules for packing, chickens and hogs for food and lard, sheep for food and clothing, and bees for honey.

IN SPAIN

The generic name *ganado* is applied to cattle, sheep, goats, pigs, horses, mules, and burros, and it may even be extended to include bees. The term comprises *ganado mayor* and *ganada menor*—the former being large animals like horses, mules, oxen, the latter the smaller sheep, goats, and pigs. Species are indicated by the addition of a qualifying adjective; thus, *ganado lanar* (or *ovejuno*) for sheep (*lana*, "wool"), *cabrío* for goats, *vacuno* for cattle, *de cerda* (or *porcuno*) for hogs, and *caballar* for horses, mules, and burros.

Historically, sheep have been the great source of Spanish animal wealth. At certain periods, notably the fourteenth to sixteenth centuries, national agrarian policies were predicated on a strong sheep industry and all other internal economic activities were subordinated, when necessary, to the needs of the sheepmen. This industry, which reached its high point about 1560, was based on large-scale transhumance governed by a royally chartered institution, the *Mesta*. Klein has described the origin and the legal, social, and technical aspects of the institution (1920).

It is interesting to note that, although transhumance today is of far less importance than during the high years of the Mesta, it continues to be a noteworthy aspect of the sheep industry. The old *cañadas* and *cordeles* are still recognized and used, and in the fall and spring one may see great flocks of sheep making their way alongside highways, which often parallel old routes. The *mayoral* is in charge of the *cabañas*, and he is assisted by *pastores*, *rabadanes*, and *zagales*. Flocks are led by billy goats wearing *cencerros* (bells) and are followed by rams similarly marked.

Shepherds are viewed romantically by modern city dwellers as simple, unspoiled beings who lead a healthy life in the out-of-doors. Certainly it is a rough life, and one which provides time for contemplation. Shepherds are contracted for by owners of great flocks, or often small owners will band together to pay for shepherds. Contracts run for a year, traditionally from San Juan to San Juan (June 24) or San Pedro to San Pedro (June 29). In addition to payment in kind and cash shepherds are allowed to run a certain number of their own sheep with the owner's flocks. A strict accounting must be made for each animal, and if one dies, the skin must be preserved to show to the owner, a practice that comes down at least from the time of the Mesta. Shepherds today often carry canvas tents, but especially in Extremadura one still sees straw hovels, often simple windbreaks in the form of a half-sphere, known as *chabolas*. At other times somewhat larger grass huts are used, but always the comforts of the shepherd's life are few. Near the hut one usually sees a portable enclosure of esparto ropes or cane, the redil, where sheep are enclosed at night so that the ground will be fertilized by them.

In the Pyrenees of Aragón, if a ewe will not nurse its offspring, it is tied to a post with the lamb beside it. The shepherds take turns at night watching it, singing *jotas* and playing the *gaita*, the flute, to soothe the ewe's nerves. If a lamb dies, it is skinned, and the skin is placed over another lamb which has lost its mother or otherwise needs a foster mother. Thus fooled or attracted by the familiar scent, the bereaved ewe nurses the foundling (Violant 1949, p. 416). In Gistain (Huesca) shepherds sometimes serenade ewes on the guitar to induce them to give milk.

Mutton is relatively less important as meat than goat or pork, but ewe's milk, particularly for cheese, constitutes a major dairy product. The cheese-making season corresponds to the months following the weaning of lambs, and the work is usually done on a small, nonindustrial basis. Some cheeses, like the *queso manchego* from La Mancha, attain considerable renown and are sent to markets in all parts of the country. A curious survival in the cheese-making process is the continued use by the Basques of stone-boiling in wooden receptacles to heat the milk in the first step of coagulation.

Transhumance of cattle, as contrasted to sheep, is largely limited to the rainy mountainous areas of the north, especially Galicia and Oviedo. In western Oviedo the *vaqueiros de alzada* are cattle people who migrate from winter quarters on the seacoast to their *brañas* in the high mountains of the Cantabric coast, and who, because of relative historic isolation, have been looked upon by Spaniards as a distinctive ethnic group. In northern Spain cows, as contrasted to oxen, are often used for draft purposes, as well as for reproduction and milking. My notes are deficient on cattle husbandry, but one primitive survival, known at least in Huelva, occurs: in order to milk recalcitrant cows the calf is first given suck, and then removed when the flow has started.

Goats are tended in all parts of Spain, particularly in barren and marginal areas where other livestock would have difficulty in finding forage. Besides furnishing milk, goats, and particularly kids, are favored for their meat, and are the indispensable basic ingredient of the *caldareta* stew of fiestas and rural banquets.

Thanks to the great acorn groves of Andalusia and Extremadura and the chestnuts of Galicia, hog-raising is a highly successful occupation. Swineherds are referred to as *porqueros* or, when hogs are feeding in acorn groves, *vareadores*, from the use of a flail or *vara* to knock down the acorns. Hogs remain in or near their villages most of the year, but may be driven considerable distances for special feeding purposes. After the grains are cut, the hogs are turned into the stubble fields for the *espigadero* or *rastrojera* feeding period. In the fall they are driven to the acorn grounds for the *montanera* feeding, an operation which may require journeys of as much as 100 kilometers. Hogs from Bujalance (Córdoba), for example, are driven as far as Pozoblanco, in the Sierra Morena, a distance of 80 kilometers. Renting of acorn rights may be on a basis of so much per animal, but a common method consists of weighing each animal upon arrival and departure and charging a given rate per *arroba* of increased weight. In Bujalance we were told in the fall of 1949 that this rate, in the Pozoblanco region, was 120 pesetas per arroba. In the Basque area we noted small canoe-like troughs hollowed from logs, used for swill in hog-feeding.

To facilitate fattening of animals to be slaughtered castration of males and removal of ovaries are common practices. The first operation is performed, usually by the swineherd himself, when the animals reach the age of two months. Sterilization of the females requires the services of itinerant specialists, and is usually done just before the montanera.

Frequently horses are kept by well-to-do villagers and small townsmen as prestige items, for an occasional ride during the year and particularly for *romerías* and other fiestas. In Andalusia, where the shrine housing a miraculous image may be a number of kilometers from the village, gaily bedecked horses are essential to carry their owners and families out and back, and for the formal processions which mark the beginning and end of such fiestas. Mules and burros are the utilitarian *ganado caballar*, charged with the drudgery of hard pulling and heavy loads. But even with these animals owners may show affection and pride, in the elaborate bridles and packs and in the artistic shaving of animal backs. Gypsy shearers do this shaving, which is often marked by a high degree of imagination and skill, especially in the elaborate geometrical designs cut into the long hair of rumps. The explanation given for this practice is that the longer hair of burros and mules often causes pack and saddle sores, the frequency of which is diminished by short cropping. But the time and care taken in working out designs indicate that, in part at least, it is a question of taste and amusement (pl. 4, bottom).

Horses frequently have no names. Oxen are named, so that they may be called to while pulling plows or carts. Cows may be named, or they may be distinguished by color terms. Mules usually are addressed as *mulo* and *mula*, according to sex, but in La Mancha, as in Latin American countries, a male mule is called a *macho*.

In spite of the traditional enmity between sheepmen and farmers, grazing is intimately tied in with the prevailing agricultural system of two or three "fields." Stubble fields constitute an important source of summer and fall fodder for both migrant and nonmigrant livestock, but particularly the latter. A number of ways have developed in which stubble is utilized. Some owners simply graze their own animals in their fields or, if they have fewer animals than the land will sustain, they rent to neighbors. In those places in which an "open field" system of rotation is or was practiced— in which individual parcels were not fenced or in which, through communal ownership, individual plots shifted from man to man over the years— communal renting of stubble rights was essential. Or, if each participant had livestock, he was allowed to turn in a number proportional to the ability of the land to carry them and to the number to be grazed by his associates. Rights to graze in stubble fields, however obtained, are commonly called *derrota a mieses*. Communal grazing lands, usually called *dehesas boyales*, are pastures to which title is held by the community and in which each individual has the right to run a certain number of animals. Or the dehesa may be auctioned for the year to the highest bidder, and the payments divided among the citizens or utilized otherwise as community funds. In Yegen (Granada) there is *monte comunal*, for grazing and wood gathering. Each family head pays a small amount for the privilege of running animals and gathering fuel.

Bees are kept in many Spanish villages. A variety of hives are used, the most novel of which is the *corcho*, or "cork," made from the bark of the cork oak. Several slabs of bark are pinned together with wooden pegs to form a cylindrical container a meter high and 40 cm. in diameter. A roughly rounded cork slab is then pieced to the top to form the roof. Several small, wooden crossbars are placed diagonally across the interior, on which the combs are built. A small notch may be cut on a bottom edge to serve as entrance, or the hive may rest on slightly raised stones, so that the bees enter from beneath. Plate 9 (left) shows an itinerant corcho seller from Badajoz, passing through Puebla de Guzmán (Huelva). The term "corcho" is applied to hives made of other materials in much of southern Spain, some of which are conical in form, made of sewn rolls of esparto grass, or mud-daubed conical cane constructions, of the size of true corchos. Among the Basques and in northwest Spain the most primitive hives are sections of bee trees found in the woods, cut down and brought to the village, to be hung under house eaves in a horizontal position or stood on end on prepared resting places, a practice suggestive of some Indian areas of America. Sometimes logs are especially hollowed to make cylindrical hives a meter high, covered with flagstones, planks, or tiles. Brinkmann has made an exhaustive study of the distribution of Iberian hive types (1938).

A type of bee transhumance in which in the summer hives are moved farther and farther up hillsides to take advantage of successive blossoming of flowers, is practiced in many Spanish villages. Sometimes hives are moved on burro back or, if facilities permit, on carts. Honey is removed once a year, usually during the summer months. Success in starting new colonies depends on identifying and capturing the queen, variously known as *reina, madre, maesa* (old Castilian *maestra*), and *machiega.* In Yegen (Granada), when a hive swarms, handfuls of dirt are thrown at it, a practice which, if successful, causes the bees to alight in a tree. The keeper then holds the new hive under the tree and beats the trunk, and this usually causes the bees to enter the hive. Among the Basques a cowbell is rung or a metal pan is beaten to stop swarms and cause bees to enter the new hive, a practice found in Mexico today (Beals, 1946, p. 32; Foster, 1948a, p. 118).

Bees are considered to be "delicate," in a somewhat mystic sense, and must always be treated with respect. *"Esta gente no quiere mal,"* said Domingo Márquez, mayor of El Cerro de Andévalo (Huelva). But the greatest variety of superstitions is found among the Basques. Generally, if the bee owner dies, a survivor must knock on the hive informing the bees of the event, a custom known in North Africa, Germany, Switzerland, and other parts of Central Europe as well. One rationalization is that the bees must know in order to make more wax for candles to be placed on the sepulcher of the deceased; another is that the bees will die if they are not informed. Sometimes a sign of mourning, such as a bit of black cloth, is attached to the hive. It is generally believed in Basque villages that bees can never be purchased; they must be exchanged for something else, for instance, sheep, or even stolen, although in some villages stolen bees are said not to produce. Generally it is considered a grave matter to kill bees. Some newly wed Basques present themselves at their hives to inform the bees of what has transpired. Bees also are thought to know when a storm is coming, and to so indicate by remaining in their hives.

Chickens are kept in all parts of Spain, both for eggs and meat, and dovecotes are an important part of most cortijos.

Various ills affect livestock, and traditionally veterinarians have been more numerous in the country than medical doctors. A family might survive the loss of a child or even an adult, but loss of an ox or mule might well spell financial ruin and poverty. Especially in southern Spain belief in the evil eye afflicting domestic animals is strong, and not infrequently one sees animals, especially mules and burros, with a bit of antler hung from their necks, a protective amulet believed to counteract the danger. In the Basque area the same *evangelio* charms hung from children's necks are tied to sheep's bells to protect them from the evil eye and, in addition, when a shepherd fears bewitchment, he may spit at the offending party. In

Oviedo *bayeta*-cloth necklaces sometimes are placed around cows as protection against the evil eye (Cabal 1928, p. 241).

Religious beliefs and superstitions surround domestic animals. In some places cattle are taken to bathe for their health at dawn on the Day of San Juan, June 24, a day on which humans likewise may recover or maintain their health by the same act. In many Spanish towns and villages animals are scrubbed and decorated with ribbons on January 17, the Day of San Antón Abad, and taken to the church door, where they are blessed by the priest. Madrid itself sees a special Mass at the Church of San Antón in the Calle de Hortaleza, after which animals are blessed. The municipal government organizes a great afternoon parade in which one may see horsemen in fiesta garb, girls in provincial costumes riding in two-wheeled *calesa* carts drawn by smart horses, Austrian milk-maids driving freshly washed cows, oxen with painted yokes pulling plows, and clowns riding on small burros in imitation of Sancho Panza. As each animal passes the door of the church, a priest blesses it, sometimes handing a small bag of blessed barley to the owner. Great quantities of barley blessed at the morning Mass are also sold through a small window in the chapel adjacent to the church, to be taken to animals not fortunate enough to receive the direct blessing.

Although the custom is on the wane, some small Spanish villages still observe the practice of the *cerdo de San Antón* as a device for raising money for the fiesta of that day. A small piglet is donated by someone, and its ears and tail are cut to distinguish it. This privileged piglet is free to wander the streets, and is fed at the houses at which it stops. By the day of San Antón the pig, now a great fat animal, is raffled or auctioned, and the proceeds are used for the fiesta expenses.

Certainly the most dramatic of all animal fiestas was the *Toro de San Marcos*, the Bull of St. Mark, observed in Castile and Extremadura as late as the eighteenth century. San Marcos, April 25, is the patron of shepherds and his day is associated with cattle in various ways—major cattle fairs, the conclusion of the renting of winter pastures, and special blessings of the animals. On the eve of April 25 in the towns observing the custom, the mayordomo of the fiesta went to the fields and, selecting the fiercest bull, addressed it: "Mark, my friend, come with me, for St. Mark sends me to call you to his fiesta." According to surviving accounts, the bull would tamely follow the mayordomo, enter the church, and assist at vespers, allowing women to adorn his horns with garlands of flowers and bread. Next day he joined in the procession, without being told, and stood before the altar during Mass. After the services, his natural fierceness returned, he would run off to rejoin his companions in the fields. The most famous of the Toro de San Marcos fiestas was that of Brozas (Cáceres) (Caro Baroja 1944a; García Matos 1948).

Because of the symbolism of the Nativity, Christmas is a day of special importance to shepherds. Formerly in the Catalan Pyrenees they attended the *Misa de Gallo*, the midnight Christmas Eve Mass, dressed in their best clothing and accompanied by a sheep draped with ribbons and other decorations. In other communities shepherds return to their homes for the day, often leaving their flocks tended only by their dogs. In San Pedro Manrique (Soria) those shepherds who have not migrated to Extremadura return to the village to be fed by their employers. Then they roam the village, playing their flutes, strumming their *zambombas* (friction drums used at Christmastime), and singing carols. Formerly they attended the midnight Mass wearing cowbells on their backs, while two of their number, with crooks and field sacks, assisted at Mass. After the services pastries and candies were drawn from the sacks to be given to the village children.

COMPARISONS AND COMMENTS

The introduction to America of Spanish domestic animals and associated methods of exploitation resembles that of agriculture and new crops, in that the most important processes appear to have been those of simple diffusion. New World domesticated animals were restricted to a handful of forms like the turkey, guinea pig, and llama, which were found only in limited areas and which were tended in a fashion rather different from European livestock practices. It is therefore not surprising that European animals brought with them a whole complex of superstitions and of methods of care. But again, as in agriculture, New World forms are less varied than those of Spain. Sheep and cattle transhumance is little known in America, and there are no reports of bee or hog movements similar to those of Andalusia. Shaving of animal rumps is unreported in America; apparently gypsies must diffuse if this custom is to be found. The Bull of St. Mark fiesta is not found in the New World, nor is the Pig of St. Anthony. Religious customs, however, like the blessing of animals on the day of St. Anthony, and superstitions, like the belief in the evil eye affecting livestock, flourish in America as in Spain.

REFERENCES

Aitken (1945), Alvar (1955), Barandiarán (1935), Brinkmann (1938), Cabal (1928), Caro Baroja (1944a), Cortés y Vázquez (1952a), Costa y Martínez (1918), Fontavella (1951), García Matos (1948), Giese (1949), Hoyos Sancho (1948b), Klein (1920), Krüger (1925, 1939a), Manrique (1952), María de Azkue (1935), Miralbes Bedera (1954), Teijón Laso (1948), Vela Espilla (1935), Violant y Simorra (1949).

CHAPTER VII

FISHING TECHNIQUES

IN SPANISH AMERICA

THE fishing techniques of native America included the use of nets, hooks and line, poisoning with a variety of plants generically called "barbasco," shooting with bow and arrow, and setting of traps. All these techniques continue to be used, particularly by subsistence fishermen. Commercial fishing, however, is based on Spanish artifacts and methods. It is possible that all sea and beach fishing is Spanish in origin, and much lake and river fishing likewise reveals Iberian ancestry. Nontribal fishing methods have been little studied in America. From scattered reports, however, it is clear that the basic pocket seine is called *chinchorro*, the principal gill net is the *trasmallo*, the most widespread net for home use is the circular hand-thrown *atarraya*, and the common hook-and-line techniques are the *espinel* and *palangre* trot lines, all of Spanish derivation.

IN SPAIN

The importance of fishing in Spanish economy, and the variety of means of exploiting sea life, are reflections of long shore lines with markedly different climatic and marine conditions. Rodríguez Santamaría, in the most complete study of Spanish fishing made in the present century, lists 233 seaports on mainland coasts where fishing is done. Of these, 133 lie on the north Atlantic coast between France and Portugal, 19 on the south Atlantic coast between Portugal and Gibraltar, and the remainder are found on the Mediterranean beaches. The fjordlike northwestern coasts are washed by cold waters with a different fish population than the warmer Mediterranean Sea, and tides, currents, and storms follow distinct patterns. Each section of Spanish coast line has peculiarities which call for special means of working and the setting, with a history of thousands of years of fishing and a series of invasions bringing new techniques, has been ideal for cultural proliferation through borrowing and local development.

Spanish fishing is a particularly rich field for research because, in addition to the variety found today, unusual historical control is possible through the *Diccionario histórico de las artes de la pesca nacional* of Antonio Sáñez Reguart, published in five enormous volumes, 1791-1795. This monumental work which, regrettably, reached only to the letter Q, is in many respects the finest study of material culture ever made and is far superior to any study of fishing made by modern ethnologists. Not only are drawings of nets, boats, and equipment made with meticulous detail, but the sociology of fishing receives equally careful attention.

Emphasis in the present chapter is placed principally on nets and lines and on customary group fishing practices as they were observed along the Mediterranean and south Atlantic coasts. Terminology has proved difficult to handle. Literally thousands of fishing terms are in common use, and confusion is inevitable because the same piece of equipment may be called by ten or twenty different words in as many different places and, conversely, the same nomenclature may be applied to entirely different objects or operations. The Spanish words used here are those which seem to be most widespread or most commonly known.

Fish nets are usually referred to as *artes*. They include pocket or sleeve seines (*jábega, boliche, chinchorro*), haul seines (*agujera, galeón*), purse seines (*cerco de jareta, traiña*), simple otter trawls traditionally pulled by sail boats *(bou, vaca, pareja)*, gill nets (such as the anchored *cazonal* and the drifting *corredera*, also called *bonitera*), and traps, of which the most spectacular is the tuna *almadraba*.

Some form of pocket seine shot from small boats and drawn in by men on the beach is found on most Spanish coasts. Most often these are called *jábega*; the boliche and the chinchorro, which is the common word in Spanish America, are similar but smaller. Nevertheless there is overlapping in terminology and the boliche of one port may become the jábega of the next and the chinchorro of still another. All three consist of three main sections: two long wings (*bandas* or *alares*), and a pocket (*copo*) in the center in which the fish are trapped. Both pocket and wings are composed of a number of different named sections, which differ primarily in size of mesh and weight of the line used in the net. The names of the sections vary considerably from port to port, and from historic periods to the present. Figure 2 shows the jábega of Conil de la Frontera (Cádiz), an ancient port and fishing village midway between Gibraltar and the city of Cádiz, sketched in November, 1949 (author's field notes). This net is rigged with heavy ropes which run along the two edges of each wing. The upper one, to which are attached cork floats, is the *tralla de corcho*, and the lower, for lead sinkers, the *tralla de plomo*. These ropes are fastened to wooden spreaders (*calones*) at the ends of the wings, to which the hauling cables are attached. A cork float (*calimote*) is fastened with a short line to the closed end of the pocket, so that the fishermen can know exactly where the copo lies in the water.

A small pocket seine is shot from a boat which carries nine or ten men. Eleven remain on shore to draw in the net, to be joined by the boat crew as the pocket approaches the beach. Larger nets require twice as many fishermen. The picturesque yokes of oxen used on Portuguese beaches to haul enormous pocket seines and boats to shore are rare in Spain; they may be seen in Finisterre and other ports of the Galician fjords (Rodríguez Santamaría 1923, p. 483) and at the harbor of Valencia (Christiansen 1928, p. 140).

The haul seine is simpler in form and more ancient in point of development. It consists of a rectangular or nearly rectangular flat section of net

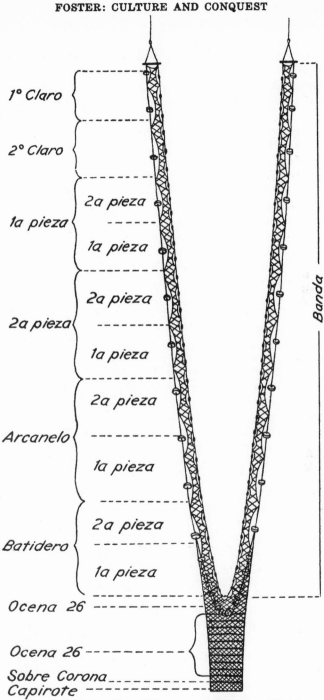

FIG. 2. JÁBEGA NET, CONIL DE LA FRONTERA (CÁDIZ)

with spreaders at each end, to which are fastened the hauling ropes. Some nets of this type (e.g., the agujera) are wider in the center than at the ends, so a semipocket automatically results as the seine is drawn in. Haul seines are shot from small boats in the same fashion as pocket seines.

Purse seines utilize a distinct construction to accomplish the same end as the pocket and haul seines, to surround the catch and draw it to shore or a boat. A typical *cerco de jareta* is more than 300 meters long and from 85 to 100 meters wide. It carries cork floats on the upper rope and lead sinkers on the lower. Suspended beneath the lower edge of the net is a series of rings through which a drawstring cable, the *jareta*, passes. After the net has been shot around a school of sardines, the principal quarry, and as it is being drawn in, the jareta is tightened so that the underside of the net pulls together forming a floor through which the fish cannot pass.

The otter trawl drawn by a steam trawler dates only from about the year 1900 in Spain. Simpler and more ancient forms have, however, been used for centuries, and in some places, particularly the Levante, they are still of great economic importance. The terms "bou," "pareja," and "vaca" are most commonly used for any drag net consisting of a deep pocket and side wings of roughly the same length as the pocket. In general construction these nets are similar to pocket seines, but their smaller size, much heavier construction, smaller meshes, and entirely different mode of use distinguishes them quite clearly.

The trammel (*trasmallo: tres malla,* "three mesh") consists of three separate nets superimposed one on the other. In a typical trammel the central section is of relatively fine thread with a 3-cm. mesh, while the two flanking outside nets are of coarser thread woven into a 10-cm. mesh. A fish coming from either side clears the first large mesh and pushes part of the small mesh through the opposite large mesh, thus forming a small pocket in which it is trapped. Trammels are anchored in a vertical position, with cork floats and lead sinkers to keep them erect.

Gill nets, used on all Spanish coasts, are of flat, rectangular construction of varying length, height, and mesh. A number of sections are usually fastened end to end to obtain greater length. Gill nets may be either anchored, marked with a buoy, and left or set to drift freely, one end fastened to the boat. The cazonal illustrates the former type. Those in use on the southern Atlantic and Mediterranean coasts vary from 300 to 600 meters in length, average about 3 meters in width, and have meshes from 8 to 10 cm. Thread is relatively heavy, because of the weight of the *cazón* (dogfish shark), the principal quarry, which gives the net its name. Each net is composed of a series of sections fastened end to end, so that the length may be varied at will. Round cork floats fastened to the upper rope and lead sinkers to the bottom one maintain the net upright in the water. The corredera, or bonitera, a drifting gill net, common in southern Spain, consists of ten or more separate sections of net, each about 50 meters long and of variable diameters, with meshes similar to those of the cazonal.

The almadraba, an enormous trap made of net sections, is the most spectacular of Spanish fishing devices. Since the time of the Phoenicians Spaniards have set these traps at strategic spots on the southern Iberian coasts to take tuna as they migrate annually in and out of the Mediterranean from the Atlantic. Formerly the choice sites were the property of the king, granted by him to those nobles who contributed most heavily to the reconquest of southern Spain from the Moors. In 1817 these privileges were abolished and the right to exploit the almadrabas was turned over to fishermen themselves, usually to be handled by fishermen's guilds. Today the right to place an almadraba is gained at public auction.

The atarraya—generally abbreviated to "tarraya" by fishermen—is widespread in Spain. This is a conico-circular net about 1.6 meters high with a maximum radius of about 10 meters. It is cast in a wide arc by a single fisherman who stands on a rock, the beach, or in the shallow water of a river or ocean inlet. The lower edge of the net is weighted with lead sinkers so that when the net is thrown it quickly closes at the bottom. By drawing on lines fastened to the lower edge and passing through an iron ring at the apex of the cone the fisherman produces pockets from which the fish cannot escape.

Dip nets take many forms. The cuchara ("spoon"), for example, used primarily in the rivers of western Andalusia, consists of a simple net suspended between two crossed poles 4 or 5 meters long. A transverse bar on the stern of a rowboat serves as fulcrum on which the poles are balanced. The net is gently lowered into the water until it reaches a sharp angle, where it is left until the fisherman feels a sufficient number of shrimp have entered. Then it is slowly raised out of the water, the boat is rowed to shore, and the contents are dumped on dry land. Although the form is different, the name "cuchara" and the mode of use are the same as those of the beautiful "butterfly" nets used by the Tarascan Indians on Lake Pátzcuaro in Mexico.

The term "palangre" is applied to a variety of types of trot line, which have in common a long, strong line known as the "mother," to which shorter, lighter lines with hooks at their ends are fastened at intervals. The palangres examined in Conil de la Frontera (Cádiz) consisted of 75 small hooks, each fastened by a line 80 cm. long to the "mother" at intervals of 3 brazas (2.3 m.) The "mother" is therefore about 180 meters long. This line, when stored, is coiled in a basket with the hooks carefully set in the rim to avoid entanglement. The contents of five to seven baskets may be joined together, to form a single long line. With each basket goes a pandero, a cork float, to mark the joints with the next section.

The espinel is usually a simplified, smaller palangre, set from smaller boats or even cast from the shore. In Conil it consists of a single basket of line with 75 hooks, smaller and lighter than those of the palangre. The fisherman walks through the water at low tide, sets his line, and waits for the tide to rise and fall before retrieving it.

The term caña ("cane") is applied to pole fishing, which is mostly a sport rather than an economic enterprise. Hooks both for the pole and other forms of line fishing follow standard forms. The barb seems to be invariable, but often hooks have no eyes. Small traps are called *nasa*. These come in an infinite variety of shapes and materials and are used in equally varied fashions.

Except for the simplest types of apparatus, fishing is a coöperative enterprise requiring the efforts of a fairly large number of men. Women, too, help in such ways as mending nets (pl. 5, right). Today in the major ports most fishing is an industrial enterprise carried out by corporations which provide and equip vessels and hire fishermen at fixed wages. But even in the large ports and above all in the smaller villages, customary law and tradition set the rules for fishing. In general, each man is reimbursed according to a carefully devised formula, which takes into account his contribution of capital equipment (if any) and the relative danger or difficulty connected with his job. This provides for the division of the catch in proportional shares and subshares, which are then handed out to each participant according to the local rules.

One hundred and sixty years ago Sáñez Reguart (1:279) described the aparcería, or "sharecropping," which characterized a large boliche. This net required 23 men and 2 boys, as follows: the *patrón*, or boss, to guide the work, 11 men hauling on each of the two ropes, and a boy on each rope to coil it as it was drawn in. The patrón, presumably also the owner of the boat and net, took one-third of the value of the catch before deducting any costs. Then costs were deducted for carrying the fish to market, line to repair the net, and rice and oil (for the fishermen's food; each man brought his own bread), and for any other expenses. The oarsmen received an additional undescribed compensation, since they also hauled in the line, and there were other lesser additional grants to some of the other men. Then the remaining profit was divided in equal parts among all who participated.

A common, simple division still used today is also described by Sáñez (1:281). A small *boliche de lisa* required nine men, including the chief. All incidental costs were paid, the chief took one-third of the profits, and the other two-thirds were divided equally among the fishermen. The modern variant in Conil is also based on thirds: the "net" receives one third, the "boat" one third, and the 20 men who draw the jábega divide the remaining third. In this case the chief is the owner of the boat and net, and his share is included with his capital equipment. The oarsmen, here too, usually receive some extra compensation. On the Mar Menor (Murcia), the owner of boats and nets may be an entrepreneur rather than a fisherman. He gives a boat and nets to a master fisherman, who in turn forms a crew. The proceeds of sales are divided in three parts: one each for boat and net and one for the crew, including the master, who takes half of this third and divides the remainder among the *peones*, usually three in number.

The traditional way of disposing of a catch is by auction, the master setting the offering prices for each basket of fish and the price being lowered until a buyer takes it. Normally the auctioning takes place at the wharfside, just after the return of the vessel, or after the jábega has been drawn in. In Conil a conch trumpet is part of the equipment of each boat. If fish have been taken, the conch is sounded while the boat is still beyond hailing distance from the shore to alert women buyers to rush to the wharf to be ready for the auction. When fishing is good, crew members take home enough for *gastos*, household use. When the catch is small and cash is short, all the fish are sold. In Ibiza the conch is used in similar fashion (N. Lewis 1956, pp. 94, 96).

Like most aspects of Spanish economy and society, the fishing industry has been closely regulated for many hundreds of years. A correlate of this condition has been the organizing of Spanish fishermen in brotherhoods or unions, known variously as *cofradías, gremios,* or *comunidades*. In fishing, as in other trades, the thirteenth century saw the beginning of social-religious-economic organizations for the purpose of special religious devotion to a saint, as a form of mutual security for members and their families, and for the purpose of regulating the conditions under which fishing was to be carried on.

One of the best documented of the brotherhoods is that of *San Martín de Hijosdalgo* of the town of Laredo, Santander, which in the year 1200 received its charter from King Alfonso VIII (Sanfeliu 1944). In 1255 Alfonso the Wise extended to fishermen and sailors of this port the privilege of salting fish and, subsequently, to fish and trade in all parts of the kingdom. Although nearly all the inhabitants of Laredo were mariners from an early time, it is difficult to determine the exact date of the formation of the brotherhood which took San Martín as patron. The official title, *Cabildo de San Martín de Mareantes y Navegantes,* does not appear until 1306, but Sanfeliu thinks it not unlikely that the formal beginnings reach back to the ninth or tenth centuries. If this is true, it is much earlier than the formation of other Spanish cofradías. Membership in the organization was open to all inhabitants of the town, with the sole stricture that they be *hijosdalgo (hidalgos),* i.e., of known ancestry and purity of blood, unsullied by Moorish, Jewish, or other infidel strains.

The brotherhood was governed by a mayor *(alcalde)* aided by an administrator *(procurador general)* who guarded the archive with the charter, all documents, and account books in his house. Four deputies completed the top level of management. Subordinate officials included two *mayordomos,* one *linternero,* six *atalayeros,* and two *vendedores.* The mayordomos aided the mayor; the linternero carried a lantern in his boat to guide the other ships at night; the atalayeros—"honest and prudent men"—had the authority to recall all boats when bad weather threatened, to avoid loss of life through excessive risks in staying out in bad weather; and the vendedores auctioned the fish of all members.

The brotherhood had the power to control in great detail the rights of all members, to force them to obey common instructions with respect to fishing regulations, and to punish those who disobeyed. It extended economic aid to all members and their relatives who needed it: the aged, the sick, widows, orphans, and others were cared for, generally by means of *soldadas,* or beneficiary shares. Each vessel carried on its rolls one or more of these beneficiaries, dividing with them the proceeds of the catch as if they were crew members. Care of souls was equally important: each fishing vessel was obliged to detail a crew member to attend the funeral of a deceased brother "even though it be a day when the *besugo* are running" (Sanfeliu 1944, p. 28).

The freedom of the cofradía from governmental intervention, not only in Laredo but on all the Spanish coasts, began to disappear in the mid-eighteenth century, but it was not until 1865 that the formal organization in Laredo was dissolved, by royal order. In 1873 fishing was made completely free in all the country, requiring nothing more than formal registration with the government. Nevertheless, cofradías in attenuated form continue to this day because of their usefulness for a number of purposes. In Conil in 1950, for example, the fishermen's brotherhood had about four hundred members, directed by an elected president, secretary, and governing council. This group has a large warehouselike building for the storage and repair of nets, for meetings, and other activities. But it is largely subject to the municipal and provincial government in all matters beyond those of immediate and technical interest to its members.

An important modern function of the fishing brotherhood, in Conil and elsewhere, is to control and apportion the fishing grounds. In Conil, for example, there are seven recognized *lances,* or grounds where jábegas may be cast. These are picturesquely named: *Las Cuevas* ("the caves"), *Levante* ("levant"), *No te creo* ("I don't believe you"), *Poniente* ("west"), *Espesura* ("thickness"), *Gallarín,* and *Mojoso* (the last two names have no translation). Lots are cast annually, at the end of June, to determine the order in which each crew may fish in each site, and elaborate rules govern all possible points of disagreement and rights.

COMPARISONS AND COMMENTS

Spanish fishing practices illustrate particularly well the manner in which a rich and heterogeneous category of culture becomes reduced, in the New World, to relatively few forms found over wide areas. For its size, perhaps no other region in the world displays so much variety in fishing techniques as does Spain. Seines, drag nets, gill nets, circular throw nets, traps, trot lines, all are found in enormous profusion and wealth of variation. But only a tiny fraction of the traditional fishing knowledge and material apparatus of the peninsula was taken to America. A few of the basic types of each class of fishing equipment took hold in the New World and became the prototypes for the relatively limited forms found today from Mexico south to Chile. Not only is the number of types greatly reduced; the nets themselves seem greatly simplified in construction. Certain specific similarities and differences may be pointed out.

To the extent that fishing techniques and equipment have been studied in Hispanic America, it is clear that Spanish forms predominate, even among some Indian groups. The pocket seine is found on most ocean beaches, and on inland lakes such as Pátzcuaro, Mexico. It usually is called chinchorro, rather than by the more common Spanish names of jábega or boliche. Flores mentions a boliche used in Cartagena, Colombia (1959, p. 134), but gives no details. A Peruvian boliche (Callao; *bolinche* in Concón, Chile) is a cerco de jareta. The Cuban chinchorro duplicates peninsular terminology more nearly than any other New World forms known to me: wings with *calones, batidores, claros, cazaretes* (common in Spain, although not in Conil), and a purse with both *corona* and *copo* sections (Sánchez Roig and Gómez de la Maza 1952, p. 92). In Tzintzuntzan and Coatzacoalcos (Mexico) and on the coasts of Peru and Chile the pocket includes a piece called *cuchillo,* undoubtedly of Spanish origin, but for which I have no specific counterpart. Wing sections in these places usually are called by the general term *paño,* although in Tzintzuntzan the sections next to the pocket are "batidores," as in Conil; in Coatzacoalcos and Peru wings are called "alares," a common Andalusian term for parts or all of the wings; and in Peru some sections are named "claros," again as in Conil.

The trasmallo and atarraya (frequently abbreviated to tarraya) are the two other Spanish nets widely used in America. Gill nets are found, but appear to be less varied in form and name than those of Spain. Frequently they are called after the principal quarry. For example, some Cuban trasmallos (which are gill nets) are called *liseras,* after the *lisa* (Sánchez Roig and Gómez de la Masa 1952, p. 94). The drifting Peruvian bonitera, named after the bonito, appears to be the same net as the south Spanish bonitera. The *cazonera* of Peru is the Andalusian cazonal which is, however, called "cazonera" in the Levante, a fact suggesting a more easterly origin for this than for most other Spanish American nets. Net-weaving techniques appear to be the same as those of Spain. The basic knot, the pointed needle, and the *mallero* mesh-spacer are all identical in both areas. For trot-line fishing the Spanish terms "espinel" and "palangre" are commonly used.[1]

The processes that brought Spanish fishing techniques to America seem to fall largely in the "informal" category, in which fishermen emigrants continued their calling in their new homes. It is not impossible, for example, that the fishing techniques of the Tarascan fishermen of Lake Pátzcuaro derive from the introduction of better methods by Don Vasco de Quiroga, along with the other improvements in arts and crafts that are attributed to him. Similar instances in other parts of America must be rare. To judge by American net terminology, Spanish influences from Andalusia predominate over those both of Galicia and the north coast, and of Catalonia and Valencia.

REFERENCES

Artiñano (1946), Christiansen (1928), Costa (1915), Krüger (1929, 1936c), Pla Cargol (1947, pp. 387-394), N. Lewis (1956), Rodríguez Santamaría (1923), Sanfeliu (1944), Sáñez Reguart (1791-1795), Schroeder (1937), Thede (1933).

NOTE

[1] Data from Tzintzuntzan and Lake Pátzcuaro are drawn from Foster 1948a, pp. 102-110. The Coatzacoalcos observations are from my July, 1958, field notes. Some Peruvian data are from my March, 1951, notes from Cerro Azul at the mouth of the Cañete Valley. Chilean data are from my January, 1952, notes from Concón, a short distance north of Valparaiso. I am indebted to Eugene Hammel for additional Peruvian data from Callao, Constante, and Pisco.

CHAPTER VIII

ARTS, CRAFTS, AND COSTUME

IN SPANISH AMERICA

ARTS, crafts, and costume constitute an important exception to the general rule that, with respect to any major cultural category, Spanish America tends to show less variety than Spain. Here the reverse is true: Spanish American forms are more diverse than those of Spain. Whatever the item may be—pottery, toys, weaving, dress, popular art—the amalgam of Indian and Spanish traditions has produced vigorous forms which, on the folk level at least, make research in Spanish America more interesting than in Spain.

IN SPAIN

Fine pottery has a long history of manufacture in the peninsula, and it has been well described in a number of studies. "Golden" ware first appears in Medina Azahra, on the outskirts of Córdoba, during the latter half of the tenth century, and subsequently manufacture spread to many centers, including Toledo, Málaga, Granada, Paterna, and Manises. Superb lustrous polychrome ware was made in the last two cities from the twelfth to fifteenth centuries, and in other centers in the Levante. True majolica (polychrome painting before firing on a tin enamel background) first appears in Spain in Sevilla in 1503, introduced from Italy. Subsequently majolica was made in Talavera de la Reina and Puente del Arzobispo, both in Toledo.

Spanish majolica is the fine pottery of greatest interest for students of Hispanic American, particularly Mexican, culture, for it was transported to Mexico during the sixteenth century and reproduced in Aguascalientes, Guadalajara, and other cities, notably Puebla de los Angeles. Since the ware in this last city is known as *Loza de Talavera*, it has been assumed by many that the Spanish town of this name was the point of origin of the Mexican style. Cervantes, the author of the basic work on Puebla ceramics, questions the accuracy of this supposition, pointing out the similarity of the ware with that of Triana barrio in Sevilla, a city with which Mexico had, of course, far more intimate contact than with the Toledo cities (1939, 1:x). In either case the Mexican inspiration is from these western Spanish centers, and influence from the eastern centers appears to be limited to design motifs which have been reworked and reinterpreted by the Spanish majolica potters. Today in Talavera, Puente del Arzobispo, and La Triana colorful polychrome pottery in a wide variety of pleasing styles continues to be produced on a large scale.

In contrast to the attention that has been lavished on the fine pottery of Spain, relatively little research has been carried out on the everyday utilitarian ware, which continues a manufacture beginning in the Neolithic. Utilitarian pottery is less important in Spain than in Hispanic America, and in kitchens one finds relatively greater use of metal implements and containers for cooking and water carrying. Presumably this reflects different cultural traditions, one that of a "high" culture which entered the iron age three thousand years ago, the other, one in which the iron-less Indian tradition continues to this day as an effective force in many countries.

This is not to say, however, that great quantities of common ware are no longer made in Spain. The Museo del Pueblo Español in Madrid has specimens from more than forty places. Violant y Simorra lists nearly fifty towns in Aragón, Catalonia, Valencia, and Mallorca alone where pottery is made (1953) and at least an equal number of centers is found in other parts of the country. In some regions this ware is the product of workshops or small factories with hired hands, of which Bailén and Andújar (Jaén) are illustrative. In others, entire towns are devoted to the industry, but on a family basis, as in the New World, rather than as an entrepreneurial system; Salvatierra de los Barros (Badajoz) is typical of this system. In still other, and perhaps in a majority of, places a few families in a town not primarily composed of potters manufacture the ware locally needed, and for a limited trade area. The products of the first two systems achieve considerable renown, and are distributed over a wide area in Spain; in fact, before the Spanish Civil War muleteers from Salvatierra were not uncommon sights in France and other European countries, vending their typical red-burnished water bottles, which have an ideal porosity to keep drinking water at an agreeable temperature.

In spite of this considerable production, there is a relative lack of variety of form and decoration, and the archaeological record suggests this has been true for centuries. Such standardization contrasts strikingly to the rich variety of simple ceramic products which characterizes Hispanic American folk pottery, both Indian and mestizo. To one who has wandered through the markets of Mexico, Guatemala, Ecuador, and Peru, a Spanish pottery stall is an uninspiring experience. Monotonous shapes, monotonous finishes, monotonous colors are the chief impressions one carries away.

At least a part of the explanation for this historical stability and lack of variety seems to lie in the early introduction of the potter's wheel in Spain, in the later phases of the Iron Age. The motor patterns associated with the wheel, and the nature of the wheel itself, place severe limits on the potter's ability to experiment with his medium, to vary significantly the standard forms which emerge from the unending revolving motion, to break away from the force of tradition. When the potter wishes to rise above the pedestrian level of the artisan, when he wishes to become an artist, two principal opportunities present themselves: the basic forms may be modified by adding by hand additional design elements in clay; and the use of glazes of different colors and compositions, and techniques of application produce complex design elements. Except in the simplest forms, both of these methods are too demanding and time-consuming to be used in the production of utilitarian ware. Mediterranean potters, including Spanish, apparently quickly realized the artistic limitations inherent in the use of the wheel. To simplify the laborious task of adding design elements in clay by hand the use of small molds was resorted to, and subsequently, in Roman times, there appeared chalk molds, consisting of two vertical halves which contained the decorations in hollow relief on the inner sides. But this technique, successfully used today by many Mexican folk potters, was so time-consuming for artisans accustomed to the wheel that for household ware it was impracticable. Chalk molds, basically little changed from this time, are used today in Spain in factories in Manises, Talavera, La Triana, and other cities in Spain where fine wares are made, but they are generally not a part of the equipment of the workshops of Salvatierra de los Barros, Bailén, and other towns which supply the kitchens of Spain.

The most primitive pottery technique of Spain is found in Pereruela (Zamora), where women coil casseroles on a simple (single) wheel which is, in fact, sufficiently heavy to make thrown ware possible (Cortés y Vázquez, 1954a). The same implement is used by the female potters of Moveros (also Zamora) to throw *cántaros* and other water jars (Cortés y Vázquez, 1958). This simple wheel, which might be used to advantage by some Mexican potters who used an unpivoted turntable on which to coil vessels, seems never to have reached the New World. Both the primitive kiln of Pereruela—a hole in the ground without a grate, and a firebox pit to one side—and the more sophisticated above-ground circular kiln of Moveros, with a grate, have reached America, and in much of Mexico, at least, the latter is the common form.

The coiling method is also used for large wine jars, in Colmenar de Oreja (Madrid) (García Fernández 1948), Villarrobledo (Albacete), and Mota del Cuervo (Cuenca) (Jensen 1946, p. 514). Most Spanish folk pottery, however, is made on the simple kick wheel of the type that was introduced to the New World early during the Conquest. It consists of a solid disc mounted on the upper end of a vertical axle, supported by a bearing just beneath the head, and a thrust bearing on the bottom. A large disc, the flywheel, is fastened just above the thrust bearing. This apparatus is set in a wooden frame, beside which the potter sits in such position that he can kick and brake the flywheel with his right foot.

The work in Bailén, which has about forty factories, the largest with twenty or more employees, may be described as typical. The whitish gray clay is cut from the ground near the outskirts of town and brought on mule and burro back to the workshops, where it is dumped into outdoor mixing tanks filled with water. The clay dissolves, and as the water evaporates it leaves a soupy paste which, at the end of fifteen to twenty days, is removed, spread in the sun 15 cm. deep to dry further, and then cut in square forms to make *pellas*, pellets of a convenient size for storing and working on the wheel. No temper is added, and the very concept seems to be unknown. (But temper is added in other parts of Spain.)

Two principal forms of pottery are made in Bailén: the *lebrillo*, a heavy casserole with widely flaring sides, and the *orza*, a tall water jar. After a vessel has been formed it is placed outside to dry, preferably in strong sunlight, and then it is bathed in a lead sulfide glaze, which comes in powdered form from Linares. A simple yellow-glaze decoration is added in a curious fashion: the color, mixed with *tierra blanca*, a white chalklike binder, is suspended in a thin solution placed in a tin can with two long thin parallel spouts, which serve as applicators. Simple double lines are thus added around the edges of the pots, and usually a large initial, also double, is placed in the bottom of each lebrillo. Glazing and painting are done before firing. The glaze is purple after application, and transparent, of a reddish cast, after firing.

Kilns are of large size, and take many tons of pottery for a single firing. Like most Spanish kilns they have domed roofs, with an inside height of more than two meters, from which smoke escapes through a series of vents. After the kiln is loaded, the door is sealed with bricks. *Ramón*, olive branches with the leaves, is the principal fuel. This makes an intense heat, but of short duration, so for a period of six or seven hours the fire must be continually stoked. Then the firebox door is closed and the load left to bake for another twenty-four hours.

All work is done by men except for the painting, which is always done by women. Lebrillos and orzas are made in a variety of sizes and in several shapes, because the towns to which the ware is sent are known to have their own local preferences in these matters, and an effort is made to meet these specifications. The sizes are measured in terms of cuartillos. The largest is 2 cuartillos, followed by 1 cuartillo, 2 en cuartillo, 3 en cuartillo, 4 en cuartillo, and 6 en cuartillo, the smallest.

At first glance it looks as if size is based on capacity, but since the liquid cuartillo is only a half-liter, this is obviously not so, since the largest vessel would then have a capacity of only 1 liter, and the smallest the twelfth part of a liter. The term "cuartillo" also means "fourth part of a *real*," the real being a unit of the peso (formerly eight to a peso; the modern real is the fourth part of the *peseta*), and comparative evidence from both Mexico and other parts of Spain indicates that the measure is ancient monetary, not liquid. In Tzintzuntzan (Mexico) size of pots is based on the number which formerly could be purchased for 1 real: de a 2 reales (at two reales) for the largest, de a medio real (at half a real) for a smaller size, de a cuartilla (read "cuartillo"?), a pot at a quarter of a real, de a 3, de a 4, de a 6, and so on down (three for a real, 4 for a real, 6 for a real) (Foster 1948a, p. 84).

In Ugijar (Granada) the measuring system is nearly identical to that of Tzintzuntzan: sizes are named according to the number of pots *en 1 real*, that is, the number which formerly could be purchased for 1 real. For the three most common vessels, the *puchero* (cooking pot), cántaro (water jug), and lebrillo (large casserole for washing), sizes range from de a 2 reales down through five intermediate measures to the small de a 6.

It is interesting to note that the largest size made is denoted in exactly the same way as the largest Tzintzuntzan size, a fact which indicates essential similarity in the value of money in the two countries when the Spanish techniques were introduced into Michoacán. Variants of these folk measurements for pottery survive in a number of Spanish towns, although the tendency seems to be for them to degenerate into simpler systems or to give way entirely to measures based on metric liquid content.

In other ways the eight or nine potter families of Ugijar use techniques reminiscent of Mexico. Particularly to be mentioned is the use of two separate clays, called "red" and "white," mixed in approximately equal quantities. But whereas in Mexico the clays are pulverized and mixed dry before water is added, in Ugijar the raw lumps are levigated in a settling tank to produce a fine paste. The wheel is similar to that used in other parts of Spain, except that it is mounted in an excavation in the floor, so that the potter sits on the edge of a small pit. As in Bailén, glazing is done before the single firing. The potters recognize that superior ware results when the unglazed ware is first fired, but fuel is so scarce that this luxury is not economically feasible.

Several special types of pottery are worthy of mention. Apparently black reduced-fired ware was at one time fairly common in the Iberian Peninsula, and today in Portugal it is made in a number of villages. But in Spain it is a dying art: Quinta Redonda (Soria), Quart (Gerona), and Faro (Oviedo) were the only villages which came to our attention.

The kiln of Faro is of double interest, because of its use for the black pottery, and because it is one of very few surviving prototypes of the simple kilns introduced into the New World by the Spaniards. It is circular, about 2 meters in diameter, built of crudely cut stones, about 1.5 meters in depth from the rim to the grate. A low door about 30 cm. square on one side facilitates loading. The firebox is stoked from a lower level on the right-hand side, an operation made possible by constructing the kiln on the edge of a low bank. To distribute the heat evenly throughout the kiln a number of small round tiles 25 cm. long and 5 cm. in diameter are placed over holes in the grate as loading proceeds. A loaded kiln is covered in primitive fashion with old tiles and potsherds, just as in Mexico today. Other firing techniques also resemble Mexico, particularly the custom of doing the job at night so that the temperature can be judged by noting the blue iridescent flame which rises through the covering potsherds, and the custom of lifting a white-hot vessel and tapping it with a stick, to see whether a bell-like ring indicates that

the heat has completed its task. For the black ware both kiln chamber
and firebox door are sealed up after the period of intense heat, to produce the chemical reactions which result in the penetration of black
color through the walls of the vessels.

Probably the single most interesting pottery town in all Spain is
Salvatierra de los Barros, a village of 4,300 inhabitants in the hills of
western Badajoz. One's entrance into the village is truly astonishing.
A visitor does not have to stop and ask the usual "Can you tell me who
makes pottery here?", for the evidence of the work is on all sides:
piles of clay against house walls on the street, thousands of unfired vessels drying in the sun on sidewalks, burros and mules standing patiently,
their *angarilla* carrying frames filled with straw, ready to receive the
muleteer's load. For Salvatierra is literally a town of potters, a unique
phenomenon in Spain and, in this respect only, comparable to some of
the craft villages of Mexico. In fact, Salvatierra made us think more of
Mexico than perhaps any other place in Spain, and particularly of Tzintzuntzan, which is also a village in which a majority of the families make
pottery. But the similarity lies in much more than the numbers of potters.
In both places the work is done on a family rather than a workshop
basis. In both places the typical ware is made by slipping the dry vessel
with a red liquid paste, which is then burnished in a variety of flowered
designs. And in both places the finished pots are hawked over a wide
area by muleteers who are either part-time potters themselves or are
almost exclusively dedicated to selling. Only in the use of the wheel in
Salvatierra, and the relatively more sophisticated kiln, is there a significant difference in techniques between the two towns.

Although a wide variety of forms is made in Salvatierra, the vessel
which predominates, and which gives the town its fame, is a burnished
water cooler, a *cacharro* with a nipple spout for drinking and a ring
handle. As in other parts of Spain the wheel work is that of men, but
in almost all other tasks, particularly the decoration, women assist. The
prolonged absence of many men, for periods up to several months, means
that the women must accept more responsibility than in those other
places where selling is accomplished through middlemen. In the spring,
and at intervals throughout the summer, the burros are loaded and groups
of men start together, fanning out in all directions as they get farther
and farther east.

It seems likely that there has been historical influence from Salvatierra
on some of the modern Hispanic American potteries, but the amount is
difficult to gauge. The Mexican *botellón* appears to be Spanish in origin,
even though today in Spain it is a relatively uncommon form. And the
similarity in general feel of Tzintzuntzan and Salvatierra design elements
seems almost too much to explain by chance, even though the Mexican
work artistically is superior to the Spanish. At the same time it must be
noted that the red burnished slip of much of Mexico today has a respectable
archaeological antiquity, just as it does in the Old World. As with many

Spanish and New World arts and crafts, similar but independent traditions have blended in America to produce the folk pottery found today.

Similarities between New World and Spanish pottery are also evident
in the *siurell* figurine whistles of the island of Mallorca. These are all
made by a single family in the village of Sa Cabaneta, 12 kilometers
inland from Palma. The most common figures are a turkeylike bird with
spreading wings, men on horseback, men holding rough canes, women
with long loaves of bread, and the hooded figures of Easter Week processions. These are modeled free-hand, today by a single woman, and fired
in the usual kiln by men. Subsequently they are whitewashed and daubed
with red and green commercial enamel in the crudest of designs. Usually
they are called *pitos de San Marsal*, and are sold in greatest quantities
at the time of the *verbena* or street carnival which accompanies the June
30 fiesta of San Marcial in Sa Cabaneta. But they are also produced
the year around, and sold at verbenas over all the island. The appearance
of these figures is suggestive, at one and the same time, of Phoenician
images of pre-Christian times, and of modern and archeological whistles
of Mexico. The similarity to the crude white whistles of Juchitán in the
Isthmus of Tehuantepec, which are made in greatest quantities in the
months before Christmas for the Christmas fiestas in Mexico, is so
striking that some contact between the two places seems to be an almost
essential postulation. But no information elicited from informants gave
any clues about this possibility.

Another New World pottery motif, the bull, is more obviously of
Spanish origin. The magnificent bulls of Pucará (Peru) and simpler forms
in Mexico illustrate this culture transfer. Without discussing the ancient
occurrence in the Mediterranean of clay bulls, mention may be made of
rather sophisticated examples from the Celtiberian site of Numancia,
near Soria, and their modern counterparts, made in Cuenca, which may
be found in museums in various parts of Spain and for sale in at least
one store in Madrid. But to the Indian potters of Pucará must go the
credit for the greatest imagination and artistic virtousity. Although the
Cuenca specimens are of considerable interest, one has the feeling that
the conceptual and technological limitations of a wheel-tradition prevent
the Spanish potters from realizing the full potentiality of artistic expression on a folk level in the modeling of forms. For it is only in the field
of decoration that the true genius of the Spanish potter, today at least,
becomes apparent; the lighthearted, gay, frolicsome bulls painted on
Talavera and Puente del Arzobispo plates show a degree of artistic
sophistication that, in its own way, is equal to the plastic perfection of
the Peruvian bulls.

One searches the literature in vain for detailed descriptions of folk
basketry, cordage, and other similar objects. Museums likewise have
little to offer. Yet visits to any of the markets of southern and eastern
Spain reveal a lively trade in such items, and skill and imagination in

the manufacture of the various styles is apparent. A good account of Spanish folk weaving (exclusive of cloth) would require detailed study and travel; here it is possible only to note some of the gross characteristics that one observes in traveling about.

The region of most intensive basketry work appears to extend from Sevilla east around the coast, through Almería, Murcia, Alicante, Valencia, Tarragona, and Mallorca. A small region in the northeasternmost part of Alicante, and particularly the little towns of Gata de Gorgos, Jesús Pobre, Pedreguer, Teulada, and Benitachell, furnishes much of the finest ware that is found on sale in markets as far away as Sevilla. Several towns on Mallorca are particularly noteworthy. Cap de Pera produces a superb plaited work of dyed palm, and near-by Artá is perhaps the most important weaving center on the island. Fine straw hats come from Lluch Mayor, and in Pollensa raffia, imported from Madagascar, is dyed and woven into beautiful small bags. Adequate utilitarian ware is made near many large cities. La Algaba, for example, supplies the city of Sevilla with a variety of palm products and Alcalá de Guadaira, only a short distance farther away, produces a wickerwork basket of cane. Nerva supplies the city of Huelva, and Málaga, Granada, and other centers have their satellite basketry and cordage communities.

The basketry materials most commonly used are a small palm called *palmera*, esparto grass (*Macrochloa tenacissima*), and to a much lesser extent cane splints, willow, wheat and rye straw, inner bark of trees, and even wood strips. Objects most frequently seen are simple fire fans, to blow life into the ubiquitous charcoal braziers, market baskets of many forms, grain-storage baskets, small objects to hold trinkets, "straw" hats, and the like. As in pottery, relatively few techniques of manufacture and style and design are found as compared to the New World.

Palm is worked by plaiting herringbone strips many meters long, which are then sewn in the style of a rag rug by lacing the edges together with a steel needle drawing a strip of the same palm. Depending on its size and shape, the resulting mat may then be pressed over a mold to form a hat or be doubled, handles added, and ends sewn to produce a convenient carrying basket. Coil techniques also are important. In the southeast a multiple-rod foundation is wrapped with dyed palm, and the successive coils are separated by twisting the sewing strands so that the baskets are open, not unlike much Mexican work, especially types from Tuxtla Gutierrez (Chiapas) rather than the more tightly coiled ware best known from Toluca (Mexico).

The similarity in appearance of Spanish and Hispanic American basketry can probably be explained on the basis of the principle of limited possibilities: the relatively few possible basketry techniques and materials tend to produce similar forms independently.

As in Mexico the sociology and culture history of baskets is intimately associated with jails. This is one of the activities in which prisoners are allowed to engage, nonweavers learning to weave, and weavers often acquiring new techniques. We encountered a young man in Denia (Alicante), an artist in palm weaving, who acquired his skill as the result of a period of incarceration in a provincial jail. Women also diffuse basketry techniques as a result of brushes with the law. This process of acculturation has generally been overlooked by anthropologists.

Cordage is made with esparto, hemp, and the Mexican agave, which grows in much of south and east Spain. Most rope today, of course, is made in factories, but not infrequently one sees the old rope walk in use. In its most common form this consists of a wooden wheel 1 to 2 meters in diameter, with three groves in the rim. Each groove guides a cord, which also goes around a spindle on an adjacent post. Fibers are fastened to each of the three spindles, the wheel is turned, and the three-strand cord is formed as the fibers tighten up. The ancient *tarabilla* (or *taravilla*) for hand spinning is now rarely used, although we did see a three-man team using this instrument in Grazalema, near Ronda (Cádiz). This simple device, which found its way to America in colonial days, consists of a short wooden handle which passes through a hole in a wooden spinner. Fibers are fastened to the knob on one end of the spinner, which is caused to revolve by a short, chopping hand motion. A trio of tarabillas worked simultaneously is all one needs to turn out passable cordage, in lengths up to 100 or more meters.

Unlike pottery and basketry, Spanish folk costume is fairly well documented, and the reader with special interests will find many excellent and lavishly illustrated works. There are, however, several points of a general nature worth noting here in the context of Spain in America. First, the diverse cultural traditions of Spain, with continuous influences from Africa and Europe, and the geographical isolation of many areas within the country, provided people with ample opportunity both to observe and borrow, and to develop along individual lines. Consequently, Spanish traditional costume shows enormous variety and richness, to a degree paralleled in few if any other parts of the world. Second, traditional dress is almost completely a thing of the past.

A gradual leveling of regional costume differences, and the adoption of pan-European clothing, have been going on for many years, but as late as 1935 it was possible to see a good deal of peasant dress. The Civil War, however, effectively erased most local forms: to meet a desperate shortage of clothing, treasured old garments were hauled from storage chests and worn, cut for children, then recut for infants, and finally used as scraps for patches. Consequently, genuine Spanish folk costumes of the elaborate festival types are difficult to find, even as museum pieces. It is only at occasional fiestas and romerías that a few surviving examples of the real thing are found.

The study of regional and folk dress requires an understanding of the organic relationship of costume to culture and of village to city. It is sometimes thought that folk culture, including costume, is something that springs from the soil and represents the creative vitality of sturdy peasant stock. Such culture, according to this point of view, is strongly conservative in the sense of changing little from century to century. In another place I have pointed out that this approach to folk and peasant culture ignores historical reality, and gives an utterly false picture of traditional rural ways of life (1953c). For it is apparent that peasant peoples, in those aspects of life not immediately connected with the mechanics and material equipment of earning a living, are strongly motivated to change by influences which emanate from the city. When we examine the content of a particular folk culture, we find much that is a reflection of the styles of city and court, of the elite and the intelligentsia of earlier years. That is, the modes and customs of the upper classes and the nobility little by little filter down to the level of the proletariat and the countryman where, in spite of being reworked to conform to local patterns, enough of the original form usually remains so that their origin is readily apparent. The motivation is prestige; the process of transmission is imitation.

Clothing—as a visible symbol—is one of the most important cultural categories in which this process works. Folk costume does not spring from the soil in some miraculous fashion and it does not remain unchanged century after century. Amades, for example, points out (1939, p. 22) that the costume of the Catalan countryman of the first years of this century was of relatively recent origin, owing in all probability to French influence in the latter half of the eighteenth century.

It appears that male dress strongly resembles the French mode of Louis XVI of the middle of the 18th century, which must have been imported to our country stimulated by the universal current of imitation of foreign styles. Country people, who always have liked to imitate city people, adopted the current dress which, like so many passing styles, soon was lost in the city and fossilized in the country . . . where it persisted until the almost universal disappearance of typical [folk] garb.

Anderson describes a cloak from Cáceres and Salamanca called *anguarina* (from *Úngaro*, Hungarian), which is a modern peasant survival of the light Hungarian cavalry uniform copied by Spain and other nations in the seventeenth century (1951, p. 64). The list of examples could be extended indefinitely, but the point is clear. The countryman imitates the city elite in a great many ways, and clothing is one of the easiest aspects of culture to ape. Consequently, quite apart from local spontaneous evolution, there is constant outside pressure on folk costume which produces continuous changes in styles. Men's hat brims contract or expand, and crowns rise and fall. Skirts acquire extra pleats, and may change from wrap-around to tubular forms. Head cloths grow from simple coverings to shawls or shrink from sizes and weights affording warmth to mere ornaments.

Spanish folk costume today may be studied from the superb collection in the Museo del Pueblo Español in Madrid, from paintings and pictures of earlier years, and from diligent research in out-of-the-way villages. Anderson, for example, as late as 1949 found a rich harvest in Extremadura, especially in the villages of Cabezavellosa, Malpartida de Plasencia, and Montehermoso in Cáceres. In 1949 in Huelva, particularly in Alosno, Puebla de Guzmán, and Cerro de Andévalo, we encountered superb old garments and willing models. In the valleys of the Pyrenees, such as Hecho and Ansó, and above all in Salamanca, with the *traje charro* of La Armuña, and the beautiful garments of La Alberca and Candelario, the persistent inquirer will find rich rewards.

In the last-named village women still wear, to a certain extent, the traditional dress. The only other village I know where this is done is Lagartera (Toledo). But here the reason is not reverence for old ways; it is a matter of hard-headed business. Lagartera is one of the few towns where hand-weaving is still an important occupation, and Lagartereña women may be found in all parts of Spain, selling their embroideries and tablecloths. Tourists in great numbers, both Spanish and foreign, likewise visit the village, conveniently situated just off the main highway west from Madrid to Portugal. The Lagartera costume is a trademark of such value that it cannot be allowed to lapse. Parts of Old Castile, like Zamarramala near Segovia, the province of Zamora, and León with its Maragatos, are also productive regions in which to search out traditional costumes. In general, then, a western strip in Spain, including the region from Huelva north through Extremadura and the old kingdom of León, and adjacent regions in Toledo, Old Castile, and to a lesser extent in Oviedo and Galicia, and selected valleys in the Pyrenees, are the places the traveler should go to find old costumes. But except for the two villages named and for an occasional shepherd, he will have to search out the garments, cajoling elderly women to bring them out of family chests and young girls or housewives to model them.

As far as one can say that there are standard traditional items of female dress in Spain, these are a full skirt, often pleated, voluminous petticoats called *enaguas* and *refajos*, frequently of bayeta cloth, an apron, a blouse, a *jubón*, or laced bodice, and a shawl. Sleeves sometimes are separate from blouses. Skirts are usually long but not infrequently, as in Lagartera and many villages of Cáceres and Salamanca, they are quite short, reaching only to the knee. When they are short, they are worn with decorated stockings, usually of wool, in which a design is either knitted into the stocking itself, or subsequently embroidered on it. Stockings not infrequently have no feet, emphasizing their decorative rather than utilitarian nature. A variety of head coverings are used by women. Some type of handkerchief or shawl is usual, but hats are also found, of which the most famous are the saucy bonnets of rye straw of Montehermoso, with their bright embroidery and ribbons (Anderson 1951, pp. 119-127).

Much more frequently women wear head cloths, which vary in size from the large *mantón*, often of wool and used as a defense against cold weather, through the polychrome silk *mantón de manila*, to the much smaller mantillas of black lace. Among the most interesting of all head cloths are the famous *tapadas* of *merina negra*, black merino wool, which survived until recent years in a few towns along the Atlantic coast, especially in Cádiz. Davillier describes how women of Tarifa, "famous for their beauty," wore tapadas Arab style when he passed through the town in 1862 (1949, p. 337). He does not explain how, with the tapada, it was possible to pass such sure judgment on the charms of the local women. Ford remarks that these tapadas, which he saw in Tarifa and Marchena, were such effective disguises that cases were known in which philandering husbands had found themselves making love to their own wives (1845, vol. 1, p. 197). Conil, likewise, is still remembered as a town where the tapada, or *cobija*, was the custom, but only in Vejer de la Frontera, an ancient hill town perched high on a bare eminence overlooking the ocean and across to Africa, did we find a surviving, if moth-eaten, specimen. This tapada was semicircular in shape, and was tied around the waist with a string so that it hung down like a skirt, open at the front. When the wearer went outdoors she lifted the tapada from the rear so that head and face, except for a peephole for an eye, were covered.

The principle of the tapada, as a waist-tied garment to cover the head, is also found in parts of Old Castile, Guadalajara, and Navarra, where women wore, over their regular dress, a heavy dark wool skirt, an *aunayas*, which in rainy or cold weather was pulled up from behind to protect the head. And in parts of the Pyrenees separate head cloths, either white or black, were so effectively used that little more face was revealed than those of the Tarifa beauties.

The Mexican *rebozo* raises the question of the Spanish antecedents of this garment. Today, at least, there is nothing in Spain which directly resembles the all-purpose Mexican shawl and head-covering, blanket, and baby carrier. The Spanish rebozo, more often called *rebociño* or *rebocillo*, is usually more nearly a *pañuelo*, or head cloth, small in size and totally unsuited to serve in the Mexican fashion. Even the term itself is not common, although neither is it entirely unknown. In the Andévalo region of Huelva we found the word "rebozo" applied to a small cloth used to cover the face and head, often as an extra protection against the sun, and worn under a straw hat. Palencia briefly mentions a rebociño in León, a type of head cloth used in inclement weather (1926, p. 33). A rebozo or rebocillo also is a traditional part of costume in Salamanca and Cáceres, especially the Sierra de Gata, but here it is also small, barely more than a handerchief. Davillier describes the rebocillo of the Salamanca *charra* as an embroidered cloth which went around the shoulders and crossed on the breast (1949, p. 805), and he also noted its presence in Mallorca, the other main area in Spain where the term is used (*ibid.*, p. 964). Unlike the Salamanca type the Mallorcan garment was a head cloth which women "customarily wore" and which "framed the face." Amades, quoting Francisco Hernández Sanz *(Compendio de geografía e historia de la isla de Menorca*, Mahón, 1908), describes the *rebosillo* as the most characteristic note of Menorquín costume, a semicircular cloth 1.30 meters in diameter, made of cloths ranging from inexpensive muslins to silk embroidered in gold. It was fastened tightly under the chin, with the surplus cloth falling over the shoulders halfway to the waist so that the face, like the faces of Davillier's Mallorcan women, did indeed look as if it were framed (1939, pp. 91-94). To judge by pictures, the appearance was much like the face-framing *huipil grande* of Tehuantepec. There is no indication that Mallorcan *icat*, the tie-dye *lengua de gato* (or *tela de lengua*) cloth was used in the rebosillo whereas, as is well known, the use of icat is the most distinctive feature of fine Mexican rebozos.

The widespread common elements in male costume are the tight knee-length breeches, a shirt, often pleated, with a high collar, not turned over, and a tight-fitting waist-length jacket. Ornamented stockings, sometimes without feet, frequently go with this garb. Usually a sash, often red and nearly always very wide, is used in place of a belt. The long black cape was, and is, a ceremonial garment, for weddings, funerals, Mass, and other important events. Not infrequently a village counted only a few capes, which would be loaned around among relatives and passed on from father to son, an important item in the list of property bequeathed to survivors. In much of Spain, particularly the Levante, Catalonia, and Aragón, but also in Castile, León, and Extremadura, a striped gaily colored rectangular blanket or saddle bag, a *manta* or *alforja*, was worn over one shoulder, to be used as protection against the elements, as blanket, or as knapsack. In the Levante, in Murcia and Valencia, it is most at home, and has survived as an essential decorative part of male costume, just as the Saltillo serape is worn by the modern Mexican *charro*.

The channels by which the alforja came to be the ornamental and gaudy serape of the Mexican charro on parade are uncertain, but the ancestry seems unquestionable. On the other hand, the American poncho, in any of its forms, seems to be entirely lacking in Spain.

Traditional Spanish respect for a man's hat should delight the Freudian psychologist. More than a hundred years ago Ford described with gay amusement the solemn respect shown the visitor's "beaver," which was carefully placed on a chair pulled up beside those on which host and guest chatted (1845, 1:155), and even today a man rarely if ever emerges from his home without head covering.

The Galician *caroza*, a wheat or rye-straw rain cape, is of unusual interest because of the presence of similar garments (of palm) in western Mexico, where they are called *capotes*. Anderson gives the best description of this item of dress: straws laid lengthwise and tied in parallel rows 10 to 15 cm. apart, with ends projecting shinglelike to shed water. There are several styles, including one conical form coming to a peak worn over the head, another which wraps around the shoulders, and a third, leggings, which can be worn with either of the preceding types (1939, pp. 108-109).

The sociological ramifications of dress are multifarious, and can scarcely be mentioned here. As illustration of the types of data found, in parts of Catalonia youths wore a rolled handkerchief on one shoulder and married men wore it on the other (Amades 1939, p. 34). In the same region the color and form of *corbatas,* neckerchiefs, indicated professions: *arrieros* and other muleteers, for example, could be spotted by a special knot that only they used. Hair dress and forms of shaving likewise indicated such things as rank and profession, a practice which still remains in the hair *coleta* of bullfighters.

Space does not permit a discussion of jewelry and ornaments, which display the same variety as clothing. Salamanca again seems to show the greatest richness in style and quantity. Coral necklaces are popular both for their beauty and as charms against the evil eye, and silver and gold work is beautifully made. Articulated silver fishes with individual scales, with heads that open for caches of aromatic herbs, appear to be the ancestral forms of the silver fish earrings and necklaces made today in Peru and Mexico.

Cottage weaving underlies folk costume. In Spain the traditional woven stuffs are wool (all parts of the country), linen (especially Extremadura, Galicia, Oviedo, León, and the Pyrenees), and to a lesser extent, hemp (Aragón, and adjacent regions of the Pyrenees) (Bergmann 1934, pp. 179-180). Home weavers have been fighting a losing battle against waterpowered machinery and mechanical looms for well over a hundred years, and today it is only in occasional out-of-the-way places that the old flatbed loom may be seen in operation. A generation ago Pedroche (Córdoba) was famous for its *colchas de Pedroche* used as bedspreads; in 1949 we found a single aged woman still working. In near-by Villaneuva de Córdoba a few looms still functioned, but the mechanized industry of Pozoblanco (Córdoba) has over the years killed the hand trade. Pozoblanco itself at one time had primitive animal-powered factories that produced a famous fulled bayeta cloth, while her *paños veintecuatreños* (warp of 2400 threads) were so important to the army that her young men were excused from military service if they worked at weaving (Gil Muñiz 1926, p. 62).

Navalvillar de Pela, in the "Siberia Extremeña" region of Badajoz, is far and away the most important weaving center that came to our attention. This importance is not entirely due to a continuation of an old industry: before the Civil War the occupation was dying out, but with the war-borne shortage of cloth and with old and nearly forgotten looms stored away, it was possible to revive the work, which continued strongly in 1949, when both cotton and wool were being woven, mostly for local use. Colored bedspreads, sheets, towels, tablecloths, napkins (further elaborated as *deshilados,* drawn-work), striped skirts, and bright alforjas were being made, as were rough cloths used by women in gathering olives.

Although the spinning wheel, in both the common horizontal Iberian form, which diffused to America, and the vertical central European type found among the Basques, has long been used in Spain, the distaff *(rueca)* and spindle *(huso)* continue to be used in northwest Spain and in the Pyrenees (Krüger 1947, p. 129; Violant 1949, pp. 243-248). Well into the nineteenth century many Spanish fabrics were fulled in water-powered *batanes,* a few of which survived into the present century (Krüger 1936c, pp. 16-24), a process which gave origin to the term *batanada* for such material. The term still survives in America as, for example, in Tzintzuntzan (Foster 1948a, p. 44). Human urine formerly was used in fulling the heavy cloths of Torrejoncillo (Cáceres) (Anderson 1939, p. 104), and in Pontevedra and other parts of Galicia skeins of linen are called meadas after being soaked in human urine *(meado)* for twenty-four hours before bleaching *(ibid.,* pp. 234, 472).

Moorish influence is apparent in the famous blue and white tela de lengua or lengua de gato ("tongue," or "cat tongue") linen cloths of Mallorca, not woven since the middle of the nineteenth century. This tie-dye technique differed from the icat process of Mexico and Guatemala in that, according to Stapley, the warp skein was firmly grasped in the middle and the ends dipped in ultramarine dye (1924, p. 8). This produced a larger, less fine jagged pattern than does the American technique in which the warp, after being strung, is tied according to the design plan, and then dipped. Lengua cloth was used as a canopy over four-poster beds, as bedspreads, curtains, and furniture upholstering.

COMPARISON AND COMMENTS

In the introduction to this chapter it was suggested that in the field of arts, crafts, and costume Spanish America shows more diversity than Spain. The reasons are not difficult to deduce. With metal tools, domestic animals, new agricultural crops, and the plow, the Spanish forms encountered little competition in existing indigenous forms. In most cases the superiority of the Spanish product was quite apparent. But native American pottery, weaving, and basketry techniques represented a vigorous and well-developed tradition, and the undoubted superiority of some associated Spanish techniques, such as the flat-bed loom and the kiln, was not necessarily immediately recognized. Spanish artisans, naturally, continued to work as at home, and it is to them that we doubtless owe the introduction of Spanish colonial weaving and pottery techniques. But Indian craftsmen accepted Spanish techniques on a differential basis. Many recognized the utility—and the ease of construction and operation— of the simple Spanish kiln that permitted temperatures sufficiently higher than open firing so that pottery glazing was feasible. On the other hand, the potter's wheel attracted few Indian artisans, and even today there is much resistance to it. In those centers where much ware is produced for market, as in central Mexico, simpler molding techniques are as efficient except for the most skilled of wheel-users.

Arts and crafts in Hispanic America, therefore, represent a real amalgam of Spanish and Indian traits, to an extent not generally characteristic of other categories of culture. This is less true of costume. Although such indigenous garments as the poncho, in one form or another, continue to be important, by and large Spanish costume early replaced most native forms in the intensively acculturated areas. This in part was due to

"formal" processes of culture transfer, the specific orders of the Crown for
modifications in the costume of Indians. Quite apart from decree, however, many Indians must have had a considerable urge to acquire Spanish
items of clothing. Heavy fulled woolen cloth for skirts surely attracted
women in cold areas where previously only cotton garments were known,
and the Andean poncho principle translated into the Mexican woolen serape
must have appealed to men in the highlands of that country.

A few speculations about Spanish geographical areas of greatest influence in America may be ventured, and several other relationships can be
pointed out. Speaking first of pottery, it is clear that Talavera ware in
America stems from the Sevilla-Toledo area. The influence of folk potteries
is less easily localized. The widespread primitive Hispanic American kiln
has more surviving Spanish examples in the Zamora-Salamanca-Asturias
region than in any other, but this is a primitive Mediterranean type, and
it is not unlikely that at the time of the Conquest it was widespread in
much of Spain. The contemporary mode of designating vessel size found
in such villages as Tzintzuntzan obviously reflects a previously widespread
Spanish custom, which survives still in southern Spain in Ugijar and
Bailén. The presence of reduced-fired black ware in both continents is
doubtless due to independent origin, in spite of the fact that the famous
pottery of Coyotepec, Oaxaca (Mexico), is fired in a simple Spanish kiln.

Spanish pottery techniques in America result from both formal
and informal processes of diffusion. The Hispanization of a previous vigorous Tarascan industry around Lake Pátzcuaro, which brought a simple
kiln and glazing but not the wheel, is due to the planned changes of Don
Vasco de Quiroga. Large workshops utilizing the wheel, and duplicating
Spanish forms, also represent planned introduction into a new colonial
culture. Informal processes must also have been at work, when village
potters of the type still found in Salvatierra migrated with their families.

Spanish basketry techniques appear to have had little influence in America, since there are only a few real possibilities, and these were already
known to the Indians. Except for such things as a steel needle and perhaps
some kinds of dyes, Spanish techniques showed no superiority over American ones. With respect to cordage, however, the simple tarabilla and the
more elaborate wheel were obviously superior to rolling fibre on the thigh,
so they quickly found their place in the new hybrid cultures.

Spanish cloth-weaving and costumes have obviously had enormous influence in America. Although the indigenous backstrap loom and spindle
whorl continue to be used among some Indian groups, and particularly in
Guatemala, the spinning wheel and flat-bed loom are obviously far superior,
and were long ago taken up by Indian as well as by mestizo weavers. At
one time, too, the fulled batanada technique was important in America,
where the term still survives to denote a type of cloth. With respect to
specific garments, tracing of origins is not always easy. The serape is of
Spanish derivation and, as pointed out, appears to descend from the
alforja and manta. Since hats were rare if not absent in pre-Conquest

America, the common Mexican affection for this garment (e.g., Beals 1946, p. 39) must reflect Spanish values. The southern Spanish tapada reached Peru, where it served the women of all social classes above slaves, not dying out completely until the middle of the last century (Pursche 1944, pp. 108-110, figs. 47-51).

The rebozo is more puzzling, although ultimately it must derive from Spain; perhaps it is one of these modifications or reworkings of a diffused idea that characterize acculturation situations. There appears to be no connection between the icat of Mexico and Guatemala, and the tie-dye tela de lengua of Mallorca. The Galician rain capes, likewise, look to me to have no generic relationship with the Mexican capotes. Since the north Spanish upright spinning wheel—similar to the colonial American wheel—appears to be lacking in Hispanic America, it seems safe to assume that weaving practices are based on those of the Castiles, Extremadura, and Andalusia. A detailed comparative analysis of Spanish and Hispanic American looms probably would enable us to pinpoint much more precisely points of origin in Spain, just as a detailed analysis of fish nets permits us to say, beyond reasonable doubt, that the shores of Andalusia supplied the forms that reached America.

With respect to jewelry and ornaments, contemporary evidence suggests that the region of Salamanca has been particularly important in supplying prototypes for America, although here again—as in the kiln—it is difficult to say to what extent these resemblances represent survivals in a conservative Spanish area of traits formerly more widespread.

REFERENCES

Pottery and basketry: Alvar (1955), Anderson (1951), Arenas (1934), Bierhenke (1932), Cervantes (1939), Cortés y Vázquez (1953, 1954a, 1954b, 1958), Davillier (1949), Frothingham (1944, 1951), García Fernández (1948), Giese (1934, pp. 25-41, 1937, pp. 194-203), González Martí (1933, 1944), Hispanic Society (1930, 1931b), Jensen (1946), Krüger (1927, pp. 125-127), Milián (1948), Rackham (1927), Vaca González and Ruíz de Luna (1943), Van de Put (1927, 1938), Violant y Simorra (1953), Voigt (1937).

Costume and weaving: Aguilera (1948), Almela y Vives (1946), Altamira y Crevea (1949), Amades (1939), Anderson (1939, 1951), Arco y Garay (1924), Bergmann (1934), Castro (1954), Davillier (1949), Diego y González and León Salmerón (1915), Ford (1845), García Boiza and Domínguez Berrueta (1940), García Sanz (1951), Giese (1934, 1955), Gil Muñíz (1926), Gómez-Tabanera (1950), González Iglesias (1945b), Hispanic Society (1931a, n.d.a., n.d.b.), Hoyos Sáinz and Hoyos Sancho (1953), Hoyos Sancho (1935, 1945, 1954, 1955), Krüger (1925, 1935b, 1936c, 1947), Palencia (1926), Rincón Ramos (1945), Stapley (1924), Vela Espilla (1935), Violant y Simorra (1949).

CHAPTER IX

TRANSPORTATION AND MARKETS

In Spanish America

PRE-CONQUEST New World transportation techniques were relatively undeveloped. Because of the absence of the wheel (except as a toy), of a draft animal, and of a pack animal (except in the Andean area), goods usually moved on the human back. In most of the area under consideration, even water transportation was relatively unimportant. The introduction of the primitive Spanish solid-wheeled cart, and the horse, mule, and burro, therefore caused a major revolution in the moving of people and goods. Carts, yokes, packing techniques, the mule train and its management, all are direct transplantings from Spain.

With respect to markets, the practice of periodic assemblies for exchange of produce was well established in centers of high culture in America. The formalization of these markets within cycles of seven days, and some of the rules governing them, represent Spanish directives, but the basic pattern of all sellers of the same merchandise displaying their wares in one area characterized both Spain and America.

In Spain

In surveying pre-industrial Spanish transportation, one is impressed by the fact that even today there is a great deal of backpacking. Curiously, really efficient carrying aids, such as tump lines, backframes, yokes, and the like are little used. The usual method of carrying a load is to wrap it securely with a rope, lift it to the back, pass the two ends of the rope over one shoulder, and grasp them with the hands. This is an inefficient, cumbersome, and often uncomfortable method, as contrasted with a tump line. A somewhat improved technique is found among the *pasiego* rustics of the Montaña de Santander: a *cuévano* basket, usually conical but occasionally rectangular, is provided with two adjustable shoulder straps and carried knapsack-fashion (García-Lomas 1949, pls. 7-10).

The forehead tump line is common in Galicia, and has spread to other parts of the country for specialized uses, as by railway station porters. Galician water and lemonade vendors also use a carrying strap which passes over one shoulder and across the chest and back to support, under the opposite arm, a large container, from which the liquid is poured into glasses (Anderson 1939, pp. 400-401). Basques transport firewood in a rude carrying frame *(astoa)*, which resembles an inverted short-legged sawhorse held by a short handle inserted in the center of the bottom of the main piece (Aranzadi 1943, p. 318).

To facilitate head-carrying, especially of water jars, women use a *rodete* (less frequently *rodilla* or *rodillo*), usually formed by rolling a shawl into a temporary ring. In western Spain, however, from Huelva north to Galicia, this becomes a specific bit of material culture, especially made for the task and decorated with colored yarn in such fashion that each village has its own recognizable design. Since most water jars have narrow, flat bottoms, they ride on rodetes at a 45° angle.

I have not encountered a true carrying yoke in Spain, but a shoulder-carrying pole is used in the Pyrenees, usually to support water buckets (Violant 1949, pp. 221-223; Krüger 1929, pp. 162-163, 180). Farther west heavy objects are slung from a shoulder pole carried by two bearers (Krüger 1939b, p. 319).

Pack animals are widely used in south and east Spain to carry not only water, but pottery, field produce, merchandise—anything the owner may wish to move. The most common form of pack equipment is the *angarilla*, a square wooden frame balanced across the back of the animal, from which is hung on each side an esparto or hemp net, in which merchandise is placed. Other esparto pack fittings are made with three hemispherical hollows on each side, in which conical-bottomed water jars may be carried. In Andalusia the jábega (the same term used for a seine) is an enormous net bag, which is filled with straw or wheat and then dropped over the back of the animal so that it projects on each side. In mountainous regions, like the Alpujarra, large pack trains are still commonly used, and the *recua*, the pack string with the belled lead animal, is often seen. Pack bridles, saddle blankets, and saddles are often elaborate far beyond utilitarian needs, and colorful designs in wool are woven into headgear and blinders.

In most of wet Spain a primitive ox- or cow-drawn sledge is used to transport hay, grain, stones, and other loads, particularly in places too steep or rough for wheeled vehicles. Various names are used to designate these sledges: in Galicia they are the *rastra, zorra,* or *corza;* in parts of León the *forcada;* in Asturias, the *abasón;* and in the Vascongadas, the *lera* and the *narria,* the last being the generic Spanish word which, however, is taken from Basque. In simplest form the sledge consists of a heavy forked tree trunk, rudely worked, covered with two or three sticks to form a rough bed, pulled from the single trunk end. Basque narrias are often well made sledges with parallel runners (Aranzadi 1943, pp. 316-319; Caro Baroja 1943, pp. 146-148; 1949b, pp. 215-216; Krüger 1947, pp. 43-46; Violant 1949, pp. 446-447).

The use of the sledge is roughly paralleled geographically by that of the *carro chirrión* (or *chillón*), a primitive two-wheeled cart in which wooden axles and wheels are a solid assemblage. Consequently, friction created by the unlubricated axle rubbing in a dry slot on the cart bottom produces a continuous squealing which is balm to the ears of the drivers and solace—say country people—to the draft cows.

The "squealing" cart has long intrigued Spanish ethnographers and consequently its forms and distributions have been well studied. The principal

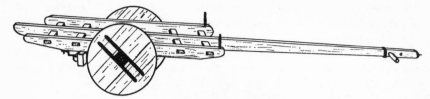

Fig. 3.   Carro chirrión

differences relate to the shape of the cart bed and to wheel type. The most primitive cart appears to have developed from a forked-tree-trunk sledge, and has a pointed front like a ship's prow. In Pola de Gordón (León) the simplest cart bed is still formed around a partly split beam, the split end of which is forced apart and covered with planks, while the unsplit end continues to form the cart shaft (Dantín Cereceda 1935, pp. 139-145). In the oft-studied cart of Reinosa (Santander) the split beam—if such is the origin—has become two separate curved beams joined at the shaft (Aranzadi 1943, p. 326; García-Lomas 1949, pl. 14; Hoyos Sáinz 1922) More often the cart is rectangular with the long shaft forming the central support of the under-frame, as in the Basque carts. The flat bed usually is provided with holes along the edges so that temporary vertical sticks may be placed if necessary for some types of loads (fig. 3). At other times a permanent (but detachable, like an old fashioned auto "winter" top) wickerwork boat-shaped structure is erected on the bed. Such forms are found at least in the Montaña de Santander (García-Lomas 1949, pls. 13, 14) and Galicia (Anderson 1939, p. 218), and represent extensions of the widespread Portuguese custom.

Wheel styles show great variety (fig. 4). The Basque wheel is solid, built up from a series of pieces of wood, and not, as it looks from a distance, made from a single block. It is thickest at the axle, and in cross section tapers toward the rim, which is surprisingly narrow—3 or 4 centimeters at most. Westward from the Basque area different styles appear, all marked by at least two holes, one on each side of a central spoke, and in some, the construction, strengthened by metal bands, is remarkably light and graceful. An informant in Oviedo volunteered that the two types of wheels used in his neighborhood (near Nava) were distinguished as *macho* and *hembra*, male and female (fig. 4, *b, c*). He could give no explanation for the terminology, and the symbolism, if any, is not apparent.

Some form of squealing cart is found from the Basque area westward through Santander, Oviedo, Galicia, and southward into Portugal, including adjacent areas of Burgos, Palencia, León, Salamanca, and Zamora. That is, excluding the eastern Pyrenees, the squealing cart is found in a general sense in wet Iberia.

In other parts of Spain some form of spoked-wheel cart has replaced the more primitive form. The true spoked-wheel seems always to be associated with the rigid axle, and each wheel turns independently of the other. The Andalusian carts are of this type. The most characteristic form has

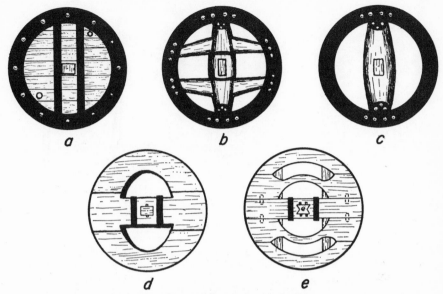

Fig. 4. North Spanish wheel types

enormous wheels, often higher than a man, which have a marked outward camber from the axle. The cart body, which usually has a permanent wooden frame forming the sides, is placed over the axle, but often a wickerwork mat or basketlike hammock is swung beneath the axle, in which passengers may lounge or sleep. These carts are usually pulled by one or more oxen or mules in tandem, rather than side by side, as is the squealing cart. Although they are designed primarily for freight, including grain and straw, peasants ride in them to market and, for fiestas and romerías, the carts are scrubbed clean and gaily decorated with colored paper and flowers.

The form of yoke used depends in part on the draft animal and in part on regional preferences. Horses and mules, of course, require a collar or yoke which places pressure on the shoulders (fig. 5, a, b). Cows and oxen, on the other hand, draw well either with the collar yoke or with the horn yoke (fig. 5, c) which is lashed on the neck behind the horns. Distributions of the two basic yoke forms in the peninsula are well known: the collar yoke characterizes Catalonia and part of Aragón, and most of Galicia and Portugal. The rest of the peninsula is marked by the horn yoke, which extends across the Pyrenees into France.

A major function of carts of all kinds, of yokes and of draft animals is to get regional produce to the periodic markets of the countryside. The contemporary Spanish pattern of town (as contrasted to city) markets and fairs is found in recognizable form at least as early as the Middle Ages. Two basic forms exist: the market, or *mercado*, which is held at least once a month, and the fair, or *feria*, held once or twice a year, usually in con-

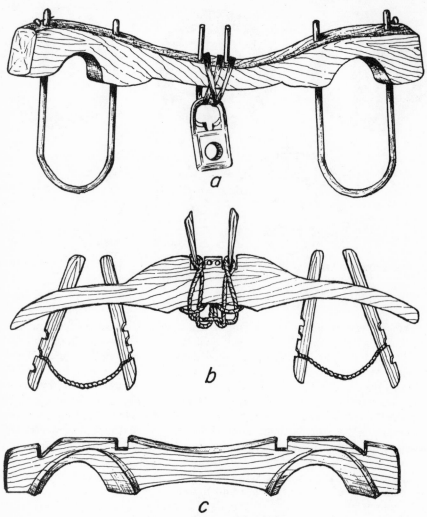

FIG. 5. SPANISH YOKE TYPES

junction with the fiesta of the town's patron saint. The market deals primarily in foodstuffs, clothing, kitchen implements, baskets, pots, and similar articles for which there is continuing need of replacement, while the fair exists particularly for the buying and selling of livestock.

Historically, fairs and markets required a privilege or permission conceded by the ruling king but, as Casas Torres and Garayoa point out, it is logical to assume that no fair or market prospered unless there was a legitimate economic reason for its being (1948, p. 12). In northern Spain the first major markets began to develop near the end of the eleventh century around the new towns that sprang up along the pilgrims' road to Santiago, especially in such "bridge" towns as Estella, Nájera, Logroño, Pamplona, Tafalla, Puente la Reina, and the like. Since the chief merchants were usually Frenchmen and Jews, the protection of the king was especially important, a protection usually granted because of the monarch's desire to stimulate trade and also because of taxation revenues which accrued to him. With the advance of the reconquest the modern pattern spread southward to cover the entire country.

Periodic markets are held in different parts of a town, depending on local custom. In northern Spain and in Old Castile sellers not infrequently take over the main plaza and adjacent side streets. With equal frequency in other parts of the country markets are held in secondary plazas, along streets, or in any other available large open space. Depending on the size of surrounding populations and the importance of trade these markets are held at intervals ranging from twice a week to once a month. The most common pattern is once a week. In Totona (Murcia) we visited the Wednesday market, held in a great, barren, dry creekbed, or *rambla,* overlapping to near-by streets and alleys. Some products, such as pottery from local ceramists and from Lorca, Nijar, and Agost, were spread in the sun, while other goods, and their vendors as well, were protected from the February sun, already hot at midday, by white awnings or umbrellas (*toldos*). Other markets are more neatly concentrated in major plazas. Casas Torres and Garayoa diagram the great market of Estella (Navarra), in which fruits, vegetables, mercery, pots and pans, pottery, *baratijas* ("notions"), fowl, baskets, and cordage all occupy special places in the square, facing the church, in what might be called the classic Latin American market pattern (1948, p. 41).

Thrice-monthly markets, held, for example, on the 10th, 20th, and 30th of each month as in Irurzun (Navarra), are not uncommon, although the twice-monthly market seems to be more frequent. These may be held on a given day every second week or on fixed dates of the month. If on a fixed date, the market day may fall on any day of the week. In some places— we noted it in Ugijar (Granada)—a Sunday market then takes on added importance and animation, while in other towns, such as Navalmoral (Toledo), dates falling on a Sunday automatically postpone the market until the following Monday. Much less frequent are the monthly markets, a number of which are listed by Casas Torres and Garayoa in Navarra (*ibid.* pp. 186-188).

In Ugijar the size of the crowds necessitates four locales. In the main plaza, nicknamed *de la Verdura* ("the vegetable plaza") the visitor will see—in addition to vegetables—fish, pottery both local and imported, cloth and clothing, cheese, hardware, gardening and farming tools, brooms, and the like (pl. 6, left). Pigs are sold in a second plaza, which therefore takes the nickname of "sow plaza" (*Plaza de las Marranas*), while in the *Plaza de las Bestias* burros, mules, horses, plows, yokes, and esparto products are sold. Finally, in an open lot on the edge of town, the *Plaza del Gando,* one finds sheep and goats. All vendors, except those of pack animals, pay a plaza tax to the town.

Major cities, because of their size, have daily markets in permanent buildings as do cities in Hispanic America.

Fairs exist especially for the buying and selling of cattle, although they are also marked by transactions in general merchandise. Itinerant traders make their yearly rounds, traveling from one fair to the other, to take advantage of the loosened pursestrings of countrymen who, come on a social as well as a business outing, find the cheap baubles of these hucksters almost irresistible after the threshold of their will power is knocked down by much wine and cheap brandy consumed in the pleasant company of good friends. Printed guides to the principal fiestas and fairs of the country, listing dates, size of town, size of surrounding trade areas, routes of communication, and the like, are indispensable handbooks for these traders and, although it is doubtful that the publisher foresaw the market, they are equally useful to the working ethnologist. The gay animation of a famous fair, that of September 8-9 in Ronda (Cádiz) is well described by Giese (1937, pp. 213-216).

COMPARISONS AND COMMENTS

Transportation and market practices in Hispanic America reflect both formal and informal modes of transportation to the New World. The simplicity of the weekly or biweekly market pattern contrasts with greater Spanish variety of intervals. I know of no examples in America, for example, of thrice-monthly markets, with the variable day of the week depending on the calendar. The Hispanic American plaza pattern of market appears to be based on Old Castilian practices: at the time of the Conquest there were few plazas in southern Spain that could have served as prototypes. In Hispanic America the distinction between the feria and the mercado is less marked than in Spain, although there are notable animal fairs in some places, like the one at San Juan de los Lagos, Jalisco (Mexico), associated with the fiesta of the famous Virgen de la Candelaria (Toor 1947, p. 184).

It is difficult to tell whether the solid-wheeled cart in America derives from north Spanish forms, or whether only northern forms survive in the peninsula. Regardless of source, the American carts I have seen show much less variety in wheel and body style, and are less carefully constructed. The Spanish animal-drawn sledge appears to have been much less successful in America than the cart, but Fals-Borda describes a Colombian type "very similar to the *narrias* of Austurias" (1955, p. 76). He also speaks of *carretas,* "descendants of the colonial *carros chillones*" (*ibid.*, p. 77). American ox yokes are of the horn type, whether associated with cart or plow, and hence must have been modeled after Spanish ones of similar type. These may have been, as has been pointed out, from any part of Spain except Galicia, Aragón, and Catalonia, if it is assumed that the modern distribution is essentially the same as that of four hundred years ago.

REFERENCES

Anderson (1939), Aranzadi (1897, 1943), Aranzadi and Hoyos Sáinz (1917), Bergmann (1934), Caro Baroja (1943, 1944b, 1949b), Casas Torres and Araus Azlor (1945), Casas Torres and Floristán Samanes (1945), Casas Torres and Garayoa (1948), Casas Torres and Pardo Cajal (1945), Dantín Cereceda (1935), Ebeling (1932), Echagüe (1947), Ford (1846), Fuente Arrimadas (1925, pp. 131-136), G., E. (1839), García Lomas (1949), García Suárez (1950), Giese (1937), Hoyos Sáinz (1922), Hoyos Sáinz and Hoyos Sancho (1947), Krüger (1925, 1929, 1939b, 1947), Lorenzo Fernández (1938), Violant y Simorra (1949).

CHAPTER X

PREGNANCY, BIRTH, AND INFANCY: FOLKLORE AND CUSTOM

IN SPANISH AMERICA

THE customs and beliefs associated with pregnancy, birth, and infancy show a high degree of similarity in all Spanish America. Ethnographic accounts, for example, speak of the importance of satisfying a pregnant woman's *antojos*, her food cravings, so the child will not have birthmarks, and in many places it is believed that the expectant mother must not wind yarn or string around her neck, lest the umbilical cord strangle the infant at the moment of birth. Except in cities, a midwife, usually called *partera* or *comadrona*, guides the mother through pregnancy and birth. Often labor is speeded, or the afterbirth expelled, by such rough techniques as having the woman blow into a bottle or gag on her braids or drink her husband's urine to provoke vomiting and contraction of abdominal muscles. Sometimes the husband's hat or jacket is placed on the woman or under her bed, in the belief that this will facilitate delivery. Frequently the umbilical cord is tied to the parturient's thigh to prevent reëntry into her body. A ritual placenta disposal is common, and frequently the umbilical stump is guarded as an amulet. Infants born with a caul may expect wealth and luck in later life. Ideally the mother observes *cuarentena*, a forty-day period of rest following delivery, before emerging from her house. Diet restrictions are severe: many foods are prohibited and, conversely, nourishing dishes such as chicken and broth are almost ritual. Infants are baptized early, and the selection of godparents is carefully made; unbaptized infants are called *moros*, Moors, and, since they are thought to go to limbo if they die in this state, the ceremony of baptism usually is performed before the mother can leave her house.

IN SPAIN

Spanish society is organized to a large extent around the family, and it is taken for granted that each new married couple will lose little time in contributing its share of offspring to maintain the social and economic position of the group. The newly married girl wishes pregnancy, and long delays may make her position within the family uncomfortable. She is not, it will be felt, living up to her part of the implied contractual obligations incurred in marriage, and criticism mixed with pity may be her lot if pregnancy does not ensue within a year or less. Under such circumstances it is not surprising that an enormous body of folklore has developed dealing with ways in which conception may be hastened. Some practices are based on folk interpretations of physiological conditions, others follow the common religious pattern of appeals to saints and the Virgin, and still others are magical and pagan, undoubtedly survivals from pre-Christian times.

The most widespread belief as to the cause of sterility is that the woman suffers from "open kidneys." This condition is thought often to yield to a poultice placed over the small of the back. Frequently, as in Santander, a still-warm sheepskin from a recently slaughtered animal is placed moist on the woman's back and left until it hardens and falls off. The vital juices of the sheep are believed to soak into the kidneys and bring fertility. Although Hispanic Americans often are preoccupied with the condition of their kidneys, I have encountered no direct parallel to this practice.

In many parts of the country couples desiring children make pilgrimages to shrines, sometimes to bathe or drop pebbles in wells, at other times to leave votive offerings or simply to pray.[1]

Lack of love and affection between spouses is sometimes said to inhabit conception and, conversely, pleasure from the act of coitus and simultaneous orgasms are believed to increase its likelihood. Special forms of coitus, intercourse in unusual places or at special times are all variously believed to influence conception. In Setados (Pontevedra) coitus may be carried out beneath a bridge; in Santa Fe (Granada) in the trough in which bread dough is mixed; in Lérida in a carriage in which a trip is being made; in Junquera de Ambía (Orense) with the head of the bed towards the west; in Argamasilla de Alba (Ciudad Real) with the feet toward the north, in Guijo de Santa Bárbara (Cáceres) the man may press against the wall alcove with his left foot during intercourse—all of these forms are thought, in the places indicated, to increase the likelihood of pregnancy. Occasional mention is made of the moon's influence: the waxing quarter generally is considered the most favorable to ensure pregnancy.

Any change in the usual positions of partners during intercourse, such as the woman taking the superior position, is often said to engender pregnancy. In a few places one encounters the belief that if coitus is carried out in a particular fashion or at a particular time it is possible to conceive a male or female child at will. Thus, conception during a waxing moon is sometimes said to form a male foetus, and during a waning moon, a female foetus. In Huete (Cuenca) it is said that if the mother copulates with her head pointing north, the child will be male; in any other direction, there is no control. In Granada it is reported that if the man reaches the climax first, the child will be male; if the woman first, female. In Ricla (Zaragoza) the man-superior position is thought to produce a female child, and the woman-superior position a male. In Santa María de Oya (Pontevedra) if the male partner keeps his head on the right side of the woman, it is said that a male child results, and if on the left side, a female. This is a manifestation of the widespread Old World belief that the right side of the body somehow is connected with the male principle. Although beliefs about conception are legion in Spanish America, in my experience they do not show the variety (or ingenuity) of those reported for Spain.

Once pregnant, a woman finds her life to some extent marked by certain restrictions and changes in regime. Restrictions, however, appear to be less onerous than might be expected, in view of the generally high level of superstition found among the lower classes and rural peoples. Food restrictions are few: in Vizcaya and Santander, it is believed the mother should not drink milk during pregnancy for fear of developing an abnormally large foetus which would make delivery difficult; in Galicia, squid and other seafoods are avoided in the belief that birthmarks in the outline of the offending food will result if the taboo is violated; in Orense and La Coruña, it is said that if the mother eats hare, the child will be born with a hare lip. Hare is also on the taboo list in Huelva.

Among the lower classes the belief in antojos is almost universal: the food cravings of a pregnant woman must be satisfied, whatever the cost. If these cravings are not met, it is thought the child will be born with birthmarks in the form of the wanted food. Unsatisfied food cravings are also thought to induce miscarriages, to result in the death of the infant after a normal term, or to cause the foetus to be born dead with its mouth open. It is reasoned that since such cravings come principally during pregnancy, it is the child, and not the mother, who is demanding, and that denial to the mother means, in fact, denial to the unborn child. Almost as widespread as the superstition about antojos is the conviction that a pregnant woman should not wind yarn or thread, lest the umbilical cord, through sympathetic magic, wind itself around the foetus, causing strangulation at the moment of birth.

Miscarriages are feared, and various precautions are taken to prevent them. Ankles may be bled, usually in the seventh month, in the belief that this prevents an excess of blood which might asphyxiate the foetus. Or poultices of the type thought efficacious in aiding conception are applied. In Galicia, a woman who has suffered several miscarriages, when again pregnant, goes with her husband to a bridge at midnight, where she asks the first person who passes to baptize her unborn child by pouring water from a shell over her head, shoulders, and abdomen. The passerby is morally obligated to do this, and to be godfather to the child if it is successfully delivered.

If we may judge by the number of forms of divination, interest in foretelling the sex of unborn children is keen. Some predictions are based on simple experiments or tests, and others stem from the appearance or actions of the expectant mother. Scapulimancy is practiced with hare (Ciudad Real, Cuenca, Córdoba), and less frequently beef shoulder blades (Huesca). A scapula is cleaned of flesh and placed on live coals. If it splits open, a female child is foretold; if it burns without cracking, a male child may be expected.

Most divinatory forms are read in contradictory ways depending on local custom. In towns in Salamanca, Valladolid, Badajoz, and Ciudad Real a coin dropped through a woman's dress from neck to floor foretells a girl if it falls "tails," a boy if "heads." In other towns in Cádiz, Badajoz, and

Murcia the prognostication is just the opposite. Similarly, when a spoon or slipper is thrown into the air, a top-side-up fall may mean either girl or boy, depending on local tradition.

Predictions of sex based on a woman's actions or appearance, while subject to varying interpretations, seem to be more constant than those based on such props as spoons, slippers, or coins. Thus, male offspring most frequently are thought to be indicated by the following tests or appearances: a woman who, after a period of rest, takes her first step with the right foot; a woman who has a large and pointed abdomen;[2] a woman whose abdomen bulks more to the right than the left. Female offspring are interpreted from these: a woman who, if suddenly asked to show her hands, extends them palms up; a woman who develops livid spots *(paños)* on her face; a small and flat abdomen during pregnancy; frequent and copious urination during pregnancy.

The moon is widely held to influence sex. We found no exceptions to the interpretation that, if the preceding birth to an expectant mother occurred during the waning moon, the next child would be of the same sex, whereas if it occurred during the waxing moon, the following child would be of the opposite sex.

The midwife (partera or comadrona) traditionally assists at birth, particularly in rural areas. In addition to reliance on the practical knowledge and equipment of this practitioner, the mother and her family place great faith in magical and religious observances believed to facilitate parturition. Almost always a religious picture or image is present in the home, and candles are burned before it during labor; this equipment lacking, candles and prayers are placed before an image in the church. San Pascual Bailón, San Antonio, Santa Rita, and Santa Ana are among the saints often petitioned, but far and away the most delightful is San Ramón Nonato, a thirteenth-century Catalan saint and patron of midwives. Ramón's mother, a woman of noble family, died suddenly at the onset of labor, and amid the consternation of this unexpected event, the unborn child was forgotten. According to legend, a relative, Ramón, Viscount of Cardona, against the advice of others who pointed out that several hours had elapsed since the mother died, ripped open her belly with his dagger. At the first incision the tiny hand of the future saint emerged, in sign of supplication and hope, and upon completion of the operation, a beautiful child appeared. He was named Ramón, after his savior (and godfather), and *Nonat*, "not born," in memory of his entrance into this world.

The mode of his burial reflects a highly stylized bit of Spanish folk literature. His relatives sought divine mediation in selection of his burial place. The coffin was lashed to the back of a blind mule and set free. When it arrived at Portell (Lérida), the birthplace of the saint, it circled the hermitage of San Nicolás three times and dropped dead. Here, where San Ramón was buried, a convent was built, and to this day, on August 31, the legend of the mule is reënacted when at the fiesta a group of horsemen make three circuits of the shrine.[3]

Scapularies, medals, and amulets of many types are placed around the neck of a woman in labor, and objects thought locally to be especially efficacious are passed around town from mother to mother. Sometimes the cape of an image of the Virgin *(manto de la Virgen)* or the sash *(cordón)* from the image of a saint is placed over a parturient. Occasionally written prayers, pulverized in water or rolled up like a pill, are given to the woman to swallow. When images of saints are brought to the house, they may be hung upside down during labor, in a quaint form of sympathetic magic, to be righted at the instant of delivery.

Although it is increasingly common in Spain for delivery to take place in bed, older traditional forms continue in many rural areas. A standing position has been common in Old Castile, León, and northern Extremadura, with the woman sometimes clinging to her husband's neck. An alternate kneeling position was also known in parts of this area, and in Valladolid and Guipúzcoa the parturient might sit on her husband's knees. Delivery from a seated position on two chairs, or in a special *paridera* chair, is generally known, and was more common in earlier times, especially in the east. An eighteenth-century Basque paridera is preserved in the Municipal Museum of San Sebastián. It has a triangular seat, three legs, and arms and back so that the parturient might more easily brace herself.[4]

The *rosa de Jérico* is probably the most common of all magical aids to childbirth. The "rose," a dry herbaceous crucifer said to come from Syria, is placed in water at the onset of labor, and gradually its "petals" open. Finally, it is believed, when the "flower" is completely open, delivery will take place. A similar custom is known in the eastern Pyrenees where a candle called *de la Mare de Deu,* with a medallion of the Virgin at the bottom, is sold in sanctuaries. This is lighted when a woman enters labor, and it is believed that delivery will occur before the flame reaches the medallion "because the Virgin does not wish to be burned" (Violant 1949, p. 270.)[5]

Various articles of men's clothing, and particularly the hat, may be used to aid childbirth. In the Canary Islands the parturient's husband's hat is placed on her head during delivery, and sometimes that of a second man, "one who is known as Juan," is added. In Guijo de Santa Bárbara (Cáceres) a man's old hat is placed on the head of a woman in childbirth before she is forced to vomit in the ways described in the following paragraph. Formerly, in Salamanca villages, the midwife might seat herself at the door of the house when the placenta was slow in descending, to seize by surprise and place on the woman's head the hat of the first male passerby. A Salamanca parturient may also wear her husband's shirt, and in Cariño (La Coruña) a man's waistcoat is placed on the woman. In both cases it appears that the garment is thought magically to communicate to the laboring woman the greater physical strength of the male.

Physical means likewise are used to aid in the expulsion of the foetus and the placenta. Infusions of herbs, lard, wine, and stronger alcoholic drinks are thought to give strength to the mother. Vomiting, to contract abdominal muscles, is provoked by giving the poor woman noxious drinks, such as her husband's urine, by gagging her on her own braids thrust far down her throat, or by forcing her to blow into a bottle or small-mouthed jar. As late as the turn of the present century an ancient Spanish custom, the *manteo*—well known to readers of Don Quijote for the rude treatment given Sancho Panza in an inn—was still in use in Tineo (Asturias). The laboring woman was placed in a blanket, the four corners of which were grasped by four stout girls, who proceeded to toss her repeatedly high in the air.[6]

A common house key is believed to have both magical and mechanical utility in facilitating birth. In Galicia a key may be placed under the pillow or at the head of the bed to hasten delivery, and in Zamora, Palencia, and Vizcaya one is tied to the end of the freshly cut umbilical cord to prevent its possible withdrawal into the body. Such a complication is terribly feared and to guard against it the cord may also be tied to a slipper or to the woman's thigh. In contrast to these fears, the actual method of cutting a cord is of little importance: small kitchen or agricultural implements are the rule. The distance from the navel at which the cut is made is sometimes thought to be important. In Segurilla (Toledo) a long stump for a boy baby is favored, because this is said to ensure a long life and an eloquent speaking voice; a short stump for a girl, on the contrary, will make her slim and flat-bellied.

The stump of an umbilical cord is sometimes saved as an amulet. In Basque villages it is wrapped with absinthe and tied around the infant's neck to guard against the evil eye. In Badajoz it is soaked in water for twenty-four hours and then brushed over the inflamed eyes of the infant. The cord of a twin is thought to have special virtue: in Andalusia it is placed on the stomach to relieve pain and in Huesca, if hidden in a person's clothing without his knowledge, it is thought to protect him from accidents.

At one time the belief that the placenta requires special disposition was probably universal in Spain, and even today remnants of this trait are found. Burial of the afterbirth is still not uncommon in rural areas, because of the superstition that, if an animal licks or eats it, the child will take on whatever undesirable characteristics the animal may have. In Palencia and Valladolid disposition is in a river or lake "so that the new mother will not suffer thirst."

Immediately after birth an infant is washed and clothed, often with the arms bound tightly to the body. At least in northwest Spain garlic is placed in the bath water, the body of the newborn infant is rubbed with garlic, or a clove of it is tied around its neck to guard against intestinal worms. If the child is slow in breathing, the beak of a chick or chicken, preferably black, may be thrust into its anus. The infant is supposed to absorb the breath of the bird, which dies of suffocation.[7]

Circumstances surrounding birth are generally believed to foretell something of an individual's future. The marks of a future *saludador* or *zahorí*, a person born with "grace" to cure, are noted at this time. Other common beliefs are that it is good luck to be born feet first, that people born in leap years have a natural immunity against smallpox, and that being born on Tuesday (less frequently Thursday or Friday) is bad luck. Tuesday the thirteenth replaces the Anglo-Saxon Friday the thirteenth as an especially inauspicious combination. In eastern Spain it is thought to be great good fortune to be born with a caul, because persons so born are impervious to gunshot. Hence, cauls are often preserved, and when a young man goes away to fight he carries a bit as an amulet.

A new mother is tightly swathed immediately after she has given birth and placed in bed if she is not already there. Frequently it is said that changing bedclothes and personal garments is prejudicial to her health, so she lies in soiled linen for several days or a week. As in Spanish America water, in almost any form, is considered dangerous, so she may not be bathed for several weeks. The length of time a woman remains in bed depends in part on her social and economic position and in part on custom. Among the lower classes it occasionally happens that a new mother will be up the day following delivery, but more frequently one to two weeks is the rule. Post-partum diets are restricted for some time. There are both positive and negative aspects to these restrictions: avoid foods believed to be dangerous, and take foods that are nourishing and socially desirable. Almost all foods except those specifically considered good are avoided during the first several days following a delivery, and particularly acid foods and milk. In all parts of Spain chicken broth and hot chocolate are the common first foods, and soon white wine, chicken meat, and eggs are added.

Infants sometimes are not suckled by the mother for two to three days, in which case recourse is had to another nursing woman, a *tetera*. In Serradilla (Cáceres) this gives rise to a special affectionate relationship or pseudokinship form between the child and woman which endures for life *por haber hecho las entrañas a la pequeña*, "for having given of one's substance to the little one." The institution of the tetera seems particularly common in Old Castile. In other places if a mother's milk is slow in rising, the new babe is given a bit of chocolate wrapped in a rag to suck, or broth sweetened with honey or sugar. In Orense, when nursing mothers add solid foods to the infant's diet, they sometimes premasticate it to make it more digestible.

To stimulate lactation nursing mothers are given such rich foods as chocolate, eggs, and cod broth, and particularly *horchata* drinks of the *chufa* root and of piñon nuts and almonds. Amulets and charms are also widely used, the most common of which are the *cuentas* or *gotas de leche*, milk-colored stone beads worn around the neck. These amulets are by no means limited to the lower classes, and women of the highest social position often believe in their efficacy.

Among the lower classes it is commonly thought that a nursing mother must be on her guard against involuntary loss of milk. Usually this occurs if the remains of food left on her plate are eaten by any other nursing female, human or animal; the milk of the first mother passes to and augments the supply of the second. Still other dangers threaten the careless lactating woman. It is widely believed, as in Spanish America, that a snake may enter a house at night, suck milk from the sleeping mother's breast, and place its tail in the infant's mouth to pacify it. In the Pyrenees when a mother inexplicably has insufficient milk, she may strew ashes around her bed, looking the next morning for the telltale marks of the snake's passage. In Andalusia it is commonly believed that if the swaddling clothes of a new babe are touched by moonlight, the mother's milk dries up.

The most common device used by a weaning mother to cut her milk is to hang a *llave macho*, a "male" key (i.e., one without a hollow interior, in contrast to the hollow "female" key) on the nape of her neck. To extract milk manually and dispose of it in special ways, such as over a fire or a candle, is also thought to dry up the supply.[8]

When economic factors permit, a new mother remains in her home for the 40-day period of the cuarentena, as is done in Hispanic America. This is both for her own health and the child's and because it is felt that she is ceremonially unclean and that by confinement she reduces the risk of contaminating others. In the Basque provinces and Catalonia if a new mother were forced to leave her home during this period, she carried a roof tile on her head, thereby maintaining the fiction of staying indoors (Caro Baroja 1949b, p. 315). A new mother reëstablishes her normal contacts with others by attending a Purification Mass. This *Misa de Purificación* is a more or less elaborate ceremony which takes place shortly after the end of the cuarentena, in which the mother, usually accompanied by the midwife who carries the infant, goes to Mass or takes the child to the church to be blessed by the priest.

The much discussed question of the couvade in northern Spain has been thoroughly treated by Caro Baroja (1943, pp. 171-181). The history of the Basque couvade is largely the familiar tale of uncritical repetition of ill-founded statements, until the numerical weight of "sources" gives the impression of scientific certainty. Caro Baroja concludes that the couvade may have at one time been known to the Basques, possibly as late as the eighteenth century, but that there is no trustworthy evidence for its subsequent existence. He also believes that the evidence from other parts of the north is sufficiently positive to assume that in former times there were couvade or couvade-like practices.

The Asturian folklorist Cabal believes a couvade formerly was observed in some places in his province, and Martín Granizo categorically affirms that in León among the isolated and somewhat backward Maragatos the classical couvade was observed as late as 1929 (1929, p. 49). This seems unlikely, to judge by other evidence. The Atheneum questionnaire mentions the couvade only in Ibiza and the Canaries. "In Ibiza the husband gets in bed with his wife immediately following delivery, drinks cups of broth with her, and places the new-born infant between the two of them." In the Canaries husbands remained in bed as long as their wives did, and received the same attention and services. The Atheneum data indicate the custom was common until about 1830. At the time the questionnaire was filled out (1900) husbands no longer went to bed, but were said to remain at home receiving the same gifts and eating much of the same food as their recently delivered wives. Serra Ráfols recently reported the discovery in San Juan de la Rambla, Tenerife, of an old man whose father had told him of the custom of observing the *sorrocloro*, the traditional word for the couvade, and had said that the practice had died out about 1850 (1950, pp. 388-390).

A newborn infant's participation in the life of his family and community begins with baptism. With this ritual act he gains formal access to Christian society; he is no longer a pagan, a "Moor" or a "Jew." Now he can be kissed with impunity, and if he dies, he will be spared limbo. Should his breath of life appear weak, he will be baptized on the day of his birth. Otherwise the ceremony takes place several days later.

Baptism is the first of many ceremonial occasions in which the child will participate. Godparents must be chosen for him with care, for they will be his spiritual parents, with obligations toward him which continue through childhood and adolescence into early maturity. Then the formal obligations are relaxed, but the bond they have created will continue until death.

Before the child is carried to the church a decision on the name must be made. Methods of selection vary a great deal according to geographical area and social status of the family. Among poorer people in small villages, particularly in Old Castile and northern Spain, a single given name is common. Here, with great frequency, the name is that of one of the saints of the day of birth, often the least common of them so that this infant will not be confused with any other.

As a rule, in all Spain the higher the social category of the family the more names with which the infant will be burdened. Of most multiple names, which are by no means limited to the upper classes, one will be that of a saint of the day of birth. Names of relatives or godparents form the second major category. Only rarely are the names of parents given to their children; conversely, the names of grandparents are given with frequency, especially in Andalusia and parts of eastern Spain. Often a rigorous order is followed in the naming of successive children; paternal grandfather (or grandmother) for first son (or daughter), then the maternal grandparents, then siblings of the father and last of the mother. The order may sometimes be reversed to start first with the maternal line. Godparents often also give their names to their godchildren. Sometimes this means names from outside the family, but in view of the regularity with which godparents are grandparents or other close relatives, family names are more common.

Baptism is usually a gala affair for the family. It may take place at any time of day, although early afternoon is the favored time. The mother, since she is normally still in bed and has not attended her Purification Mass, is not present. The father usually, but not always, goes. In small villages in León and Old Castile especially, there is some feeling that he should remain away from the church, or at least not cross the threshold. The godparents, of course, attend, and the godmother usually holds the child, although among the wealthier classes status may be upheld by having a servant girl carry the child. In small villages the midwife is expected to be there, as is the tetera, if there is one (p. 118). In northern Spain, and perhaps generally in the country, a small girl holds a tray upon which salt, bread, a candle or candles, a pitcher of water, and a towel have been placed. The priest places the salt on the infant's lips during the baptismal ceremony, and uses the water and towel to wash his hands afterwards. The candles and bread are offered to him in addition to the normal baptismal fee.

The events of baptism are closely watched by the participants, for through them much may be foretold about the child's future. If he is quiet when the Holy Water is placed on him, it is thought that he will grow up to be a patient and self-restrained adult, whereas if he cries, he will have an impetuous character, following a stormy path through life. If the priest uses an abundance of salt, the child will be handsome and charming. In Andalusia the mother anxiously awaits the return of the baptismal party to learn whether the priest who officiated was ugly or handsome, friendly or abrupt, for she firmly believes that his appearance and character will later be reflected in her child.

If the baptism is preceded or followed by certain practices, the future of the child is also thought to be affected. In parts of Navarra, formerly at least, if older siblings had died, the newborn infant was taken out of the house through a window to be baptized, to free it of the evil influences which plagued the household. In the Basque provinces the same contingency is met with *bautismo a la ventura*. Two or more people carry the child to a near-by shrine. The first person encountered on the road dares not refuse the request to serve as godparent, and joins the party, which continues to the shrine where the baptism is carried out.

Interest in a baptism is by no means limited to family and friends. When it becomes known that a child is being carried to the church, all the children of the village gather at the door to await the emergence of the group; in this they often enjoy the connivance of the schoolteacher, who obligingly dismisses school for the occasion. The wise godfather is prepared for this *bateo*, and when the chant begins *"Aquí, aquí, échalo padrino, no lo gastes en vino"* ("Here, here, throw it, godfather, don't spend it on wine"), he scatters handfuls of *perras chicas* (5-céntimo pieces) and candies among the outstretched palms. If the godfather appears generous, the calls of the children are encouraging: *"Caigan, caigan, anises y confitura, y que viva la criatura"* ("Let fall, let fall licorice and candies, and may the infant live"), but woe to the godfather who hopes to escape lightly, for the calls quickly become pointed and obscene: *"Si no me da confitura, que muere la criatura"* ("If you don't give me candy, may the child die"); *"Viruta, viruta, la madrina es una puta"* ("Viruta, viruta, the godmother is a prostitute") ; and *"Virutón, virutón, el padrino es un cabrón"* ("Virutón, virutón, the godfather is a cuckold").[9]

These are only a small part of the expenses of the godparents. They are expected to provide the white baptismal garments for the child, to pay the church fees, and to provide refreshments, a *convite*, for family and friends assembled after the ceremony in the house of the parents. The convite usually takes the form of offering cigarettes or cigars to the men and light refreshments and drink to all. In addition the godfather sometimes formally presents the mother with gifts, usually a chicken, a pound of chocolate, and perhaps bread, as well as, sometimes, a small quantity of money. Frequently the convite ends in an animated dance, in which the godfather is expected to dance with the godmother; failure to do so is an inexcusable insult.

Godparents are considered to be spiritual parents, and in most places they are expected to care for the child if the parents die. The indoctrination duties implied in the relationship, however, are probably more apparent than real. In many parts of Spain a godfather must bless a dying child "so that it may expire easily." Funeral costs for a minor child are usually paid by godparents, and in the Sierra de Béjar, between Salamanca and Cáceres, the godfather formerly carried the corpse to the cemetery in his arms.[10]

COMPARISONS AND COMMENTS

Except for the sacrament of baptism, customs and beliefs regarding pregnancy and birth appear to fall in the category of informally transmitted elements. Since this is an area of "female" culture, in which native women as wives and concubines of conquistadors might be expected to continue aboriginal customs, thereby perpetuating native ways in the growing mestizo population, it is surprising that Spanish forms predominate not only in middle and lower class mestizo circles, but in acculturated Indian groups as well. The diffusion of such beliefs and customs presumably is a part of the phenomenon of diffusion of so much Spanish medical belief and practice, a process that is but poorly understood at present.

I omit detailed discussion of the *compadrazgo* institution, since it has been dealt with in a previous article (Foster 1953a). It may be of interest, however, to point out several major points of contrast between Spain and Spanish America, since the institutions in the two regions differ more than might be expected. Particularly to be noted is that the cohesion which rural Hispanic American society obtains from the institution generally is not duplicated in Spain. In Spain, unlike Spanish America, relatives rather than friends are usually selected as godparents, so that, rather than extending kinlike relationships, the system folds back upon itself, reëmphasizing existing ties rather than establishing new ones. Moreover, in Spain the primary relationship usually lies between godchild and godparents, rather than between godparents and parents of the child, as in America.

Most anthropologists feel that the forms of the compadrazgo in Spanish America represent reworkings of the Iberian institution to meet a variety of local needs. To the extent that a Spanish variant can be called ancestral to the American forms, it would appear to be in Andalusia, where Pitt-Rivers' description sounds more like New World patterns than any other Spanish forms known to me, particularly in the bond between *compadres*.

Far more important [than the relationship between child and godparent] is the relationship which it [the compadrazgo] creates between the parents and the godparents. . . . It is a bond of formal friendship more sacred than any personal tie outside the immediate family. . . . Its seriousness is stressed by . . . the mode of speech which *compadres* are obliged to adopt in talking with one another. Save when they belong to the same elementary family they must use the third person, even though they have spoken to one another in the second person all their lives. The explanation given for this is that "*compadres* respect one another." This respect does not involve a stiff or formal attitude, on the contrary, they speak to each other with great ease, but each is under the obligation to do for the other whatever he asks of him. . . . In the changing kaleidoscope of friendship the *compadrazgo* is an irrevocable tie of mutual trust, stronger than that of kinship because it owes its existence to the free consent of both parties (1954, pp. 107-108).

In Alcalá, as in all Spain, relatives are the preferred godparents, but Pitt-Rivers points out that, among the poor, sponsors are also sought, in Latin American fashion, from powerful families, in which case the compadre relationship of co-equals is played down and the relationship of the "munificent" *padrino* is stressed.

The compadrazgo, however, appears also to have fulfilled an important functional role in Galicia. Speaking specifically of Orense, and generally of all Galicia, Risco says that "spiritual kinship is, or was, of great importance." Compadres used the compadre-comadre terminology in speaking to each other and even though, before the ceremony establishing the relationship, they had used the informal second person "tu" in direct address, forever afterwards they addressed each other with the formal "usted." Risco is also one of the few Spanish authors who uses the term "compadrazgo" in an institutional sense, assuming the reader will know what is meant (1948, pp. 167-168). However, in view of the fact that Galician influence in America was appreciably less than that of Andalusia, I favor a southern origin of the institution, in as far as the highly developed Hispanic American forms can be said to have a specific peninsular origin.

REFERENCES

All specific references to communities not otherwise noted are drawn from the Atheneum Questionnaire.

Agustín Sánchez (1932), Altamira (1905), Bautista Merino (1949), Cabal (1925a, 1928), Caro Baroja (1943, 1949b), Casas Gaspar (1947), Castillo de Lucas (1943), Diego Cuscoy (1943), Fuente Arrimadas (1925), García Ramos (1912), Giner Arivau (1886), Guichot y Sierra (1882-1883), Lis Quibén (1945, 1949a), María de Azkue

(1935), Martín Granizo (1922, 1929), Morán (1931), Navarro (1901), Olavarría y Huarte (1884), Pitt-Rivers (1954), Prieto Rodríguez (1947), Ramón y Fernández (1945a), Risco (1948), Rodríguez López (1948), Royo Villanova (1936), Ruiz-Funes García (1916), Serra Ráfols (1950), Taboada (1947), Vergara y Martín (1909), Violant y Simorra (1949).

NOTES

[1] The pilgrimage pattern to aid conception is found in Mexico (O. Lewis 1951, p. 355). But the data suggest fewer magical rites to facilitate conception in Spanish America than in Spain.

[2] This and the preceding superstitions are reported by Valdizán and Maldonado in Peru (1922, p. 332).

[3] San Ramón is patron of parturients in America; e.g., Cardona 1954, p. 81 (in Venezuela); Service and Service 1954, p. 244 (in Paraguay); Velásquez 1957, pp. 214 and 220 (in Colombia); in Tzintzuntzan (Mexico); and in the Spanish American villages of New Mexico. But the saint appears to be appealed to here much less frequently than in Spain.

[4] The paridera was known in America (e.g., Mendoza 1955, p. 88, silla de parir for Mexico), but apparently never was common.

[5] A variant of the candle custom is described by Lewis for Tepoztlán: "In cases of difficult or delayed births, the family, at the suggestion of the midwife, may buy a candle for the Virgen de Monserrat, the guardian of pregnant women. The patient measures four fingers on the candle, a mark is made at that point with a centavo, and the candle is put before the image. If delivery does not occur before the flame reaches the mark on the candle, the case is considered very grave" (1951, p. 358). I have, however, encountered no instances of the rosa de Jérico in Hispanic America.

[6] The manteo has also been described for America (e.g., Gutierrez de Pineda 1955, p. 48 in Colombia; O. Lewis 1951, p. 366, in Mexico.

[7] This curious custom is reported by Kelly, García, and Gárate in Mexico (1956, p. 109), and by Gillin in Peru (1947a, p. 137).

[8] Valdizán and Maldonado report both the llave macho and extraction of milk over a fire as Peruvian techniques to stop the flow of milk (1922, pp. 345-346).

[9] In Tzintzuntzan the bateo is known as bolo. It is much less boisterous than the Spanish counterpart (Foster 1948a, p. 263). In most of Spanish America godparents' obligations at baptism are similar to those of Spain.

[10] Spanish American baptismal godparental obligations in case of the death of the child follow those described, including, often, blessing the child to aid it to die.

CHAPTER XI

COURTSHIP AND MARRIAGE

IN SPANISH AMERICA

C OURTSHIP and marriage patterns are rather well described in anthropological accounts, and they show a marked degree of homogeneity from one country to another. Today, of course, traditional ways are rapidly changing, but the customs of earlier years are well known. In towns and cities separation of the sexes and elaborate chaperonage was the rule. In villages the degree of separation was less marked, but opportunities for young people of opposite sex to meet and talk were sufficiently few so that village fountains, where girls come to fill water jars, have been favored places to meet. Formal engagements often were, and are, established utilizing the services of a go-between.

Since the wedding ritual is set by the Catholic Church, it is natural to find essentially the same pattern in all Spanish American countries and in Spain as well. This includes the reading of the banns, the naming of godparents, confession and communion, the use of *arras,* and the "yoke" stole across the backs of the kneeling people.

IN SPAIN

In a country characterized by rather rigid separation of the sexes from adolescence to marriage, there must be mechanisms to bring together and reintroduce young people. In village Spain informal mechanisms associated with agricultural events offer the most opportunities: harvesting and threshing grain, gathering olives and fruits, and particularly the *vendimia,* the grape harvest. As in Hispanic America, visits to public fountains to fill water jars offer opportunities to exchange a few words, as do arrival at and departure from Mass. Fairs, fiestas, and romerías— religious pilgrimages—especially favor the individual interested in broadening his or her horizon by meeting young people from other villages.

In villages of the Pyrenees fairs are such important marriage mechanisms that they are often known as *ferias de novias.* Marriageable girls, dressed in their richest clothing, ride with their fathers to these fairs, where they may view and be viewed by eligible young men who, also accompanied by their fathers, have come with similar ideas. Conversations are easily struck up in the gay and informal atmosphere of such gatherings, new friendships are quickly formed, and the bases of future marriages are established. When all goes well and the talks prosper, the fathers of both make arrangements for future visits, and occasionally details of dowry and weddings may be worked out on the spot (Violant 1949, p. 283).

Other occasions on which marriageable young people come together may be arranged with equal formality. *Jueves de Comadres* and *Jueves de Compadres* are typical of the many small, simple fiestas which have special devices for the furthering of relationships between the sexes. In many parts of the country the Thursday before Carnival (in some places the second Thursday) is called Thursday of Comadres. Young people from six to sixteen or so gather in parties and draw lots to determine who will be compadres and comadres. In Alosno (Huelva) for example, the parties are organized on the basis of streets or neighborhoods. Names of the participants are written on slips of paper, those of the girls deposited in one container and those of the boys in another. A slip is drawn from each urn, and the resulting pairs are named compadres, until all are paired off. The rest of the day is a fiesta, with the girls often preparing rice pudding for their compadres, who in turn may give small presents to their comadres. The drawing of lots is, as might be supposed, not always left purely to chance. Less frequently, Thursday of Compadres, a week earlier than Thursday of Comadres, is celebrated in this fashion.[1]

Similar drawings are held in homes, cafes, and other places of reunion in the parties held on the day of San Silvestre, the last day of the year (p. 167). Next day the youth must call at the home of the girl whose name he drew to escort her to the village dance and, perhaps, to go begging with her the *aguinaldo* of Epiphany.

In much of north-central Spain boys and unmarried young men are grouped in formal clubs or societies, with an elected mayor *(alcalde)* or king *(rey)*, and a secretary and treasurer. Each youth in the village, upon reaching the age of sixteen or so, must formally solicit membership in the society, paying his initiation by treating the older members to drinks in a local tavern. With this formal entrance into the *cofradía de solteros* the young man has license to roam the streets at night with his fellows, to serenade girls, and to attend spinning-bees and dances.

These societies—they are now largely a thing of the past—often observed Epiphany with a special banquet. In Segovia, as described by Vergara y Martín at the turn of the century, all village youths met on Christmas night to elect their *alcalde de mozos*, their "mayor" who would preside at their meetings during the coming year. Following Mass on Epiphany the youths went singing to each house, where they were presented with an aguinaldo, a gift of bread, chick peas, eggs, smoked meats, and the like. The food collected was brought back to the town hall where a banquet was prepared, and all eligible girls were invited, first to season the food and then to join in the feasting. After the feast, which was also attended by the priest, civic authorities, and families of the girls, tables were cleared away, the older people danced a round or two, and then left the young people on their own, confident that the boy "mayor" would be accorded the respect necessary to prevent rowdyism (1909, pp. 15-16).

Even in Andalusia, where girls traditionally are most carefully guarded, there are similar if less frequent occasions for the sexes to mingle. The most interesting we saw was in Alosno (Huelva) on May 3, The Invention of the Cross. In Alosno this day has lost most sacred connotations, and its activities are purely social. For each sector or barrio an older woman, the *encargada de la Cruz*, obtains a room opening directly onto the street and, assisted by others, she decorates a cross, which remains the property of the same group year after year. Room decorations follow a rigid style: lace, drawn work, and fine bedspreads cover walls and ceiling, and on the walls are hung pictures of saints, of flowers, of ladies in large hats, French lithographs, and the like. The crosses, one placed near the back of each room, are about two meters high, covered with gold and silver artificial leaves and flowers, red medallions, *manguitos* (tiny red capes), paper heads of angels, cameos—almost anything the decorators like or have. Benches and chairs are arranged around the room so that an open space for dancing is left in the center.

By midevening the women of the neighborhood have gathered, the grandmothers, mothers with babes in arms, children of four or five, schoolchildren, and, of course, the marriageable girls. The latter are dressed in their finest clothing, many of them still in the traditional costume of fifty or more years ago. Other girls wear the striking *sevillana* costume, a dress of red or blue calico with large white dots, puffed shoulders, and long, flaring skirts, a Manila shawl, and a high comb. Presently, to the sound of castanets and tambourines, the singing begins. *"De la flor la violeta,"* sings a girl, by way of introduction and to give the key to the others, who repeat the line and continue the verse.

De la flor la violeta,	Of flowers, the violet,
De los emblemas la Cruz,	Of symbols, the cross,
De capitales mi Huelva,	Of capitals, my Huelva,
De mujer me gustas tu.	Of women, you.

Attracted by the singing, the men begin to arrive, youths of fourteen attending the dance for the first time, old hands of sixteen, younger married men, older men, miners who work in near-by Tharsis, and even the town fool. No woman can refuse an invitation to dance, no matter how ridiculous it may seem, and each couple is the momentary center of interest, since only one dances at a time. A dance consists of four verses, with a brief pause between each two, and at the end the girl calls the stylized phrase *"Una perrita para la Cruz de mayo"* ("Five céntimos for the May Cross"), a sum which each dancer is expected to contribute to expenses of the evening. In Alosno in 1950 there were thirteen crosses.

Not unnaturally, a Spanish girl is curious who her husband will be. Will he be named Juan? Or Pedro or Antonio? Will he be rich or poor? A sailor or a farmer? Is there danger that she may die young? Or that through some quirk of fate she will not acquire a husband? A variety of divinatory techniques, most of which are carried out on the eve or day of San Juan, give the answers to these questions. To know the name of her future spouse a maiden may throw a jar of water onto the street from her balcony at midnight of San Juan eve, and ask the name of the first man who treads on the damp spot. His name will be that of her husband.[2]

To know whether she will marry well a girl may place three broadbeans under her bed or pillow, one shelled, one half-shelled, and the third unshelled. The following morning she withdraws a bean without looking. If it is unshelled, her husband will be wealthy, if half shelled, in moderate circumstances, and if shelled, she must expect poverty.[3]

Another series of trials performed on the eve of San Juan gives a clue to the occupation of one's future husband. At midnight a girl may break an egg into a glass of water. By the following morning it will have assumed a shape symbolic of the profession of the man she is to marry. The egg white often produces a stringy and membranous mass suggestive of the sails and rigging of a ship; if so, her suitor will be a fisherman or sailor. In another test, the mechanics of which appear difficult, a girl is said to pour molten lead into a container of water, where it hardens in a form recognizable as an agricultural implement, an animal, an artisan's tool, or some other symbol of a profession.[4]

In another eve-of-San Juan act a maiden stands nude in her room and sifts flour upon the floor. The flour may take a form suggestive of a male occupation, and if so, all is well; but it may also resemble a coffin, signifying that she is to die unwed. Or, in her darkened room, she may peer into a mirror or a basin of water. If lucky, she will see the face of her future sweetheart, if unlucky, her own reflection or a skull, in which event she will die within the year.[5]

The ancient Greek coscinomancy, sieve divination, survives in both Spain and America, to give yes-and-no answers to such questions as "Will I have a sweetheart?" as well as who stole what. As reported in Andalusia, two girls on the eve of San Juan impale a circular wooden sieve on the points of a pair of scissors. Then they lift the sieve by simultaneously placing their index fingers through the finger holds. As it dangles they pray to San Antonio, the special patron of girls wishing a husband, and ask "Little sieve, tell me yes or no." If the sieve remains motionless, the answer is yes, but if it moves, no sweetheart will be forthcoming (Coves 1935).[6]

San Antonio may also be prayed to on any other occasion, and in southern Spain, at least, there is often a certain unceremoniousness in dealing with him. If prayers go unanswered, his image, or that of the Christ child customarily held in his arms, may be suspended upside down in a well until he brings success in the love suit.[7]

Courting relationships may be initiated through any one of a number of rather formalized procedures. The cigarette offers one of the simplest advances and permits a graceful and face-saving refusal if the girl is uninterested. A would-be suitor knocks at her door and asks a light for his cigarette. If it is given, he enters the house and takes a seat beside her in the kitchen, knowing that his suit has been successful. If she informs him there are no coals to light his cigarette, he thanks her and departs.

The custom of pressing one's suit by snatching a handkerchief from the girl—a handkerchief which, needless to say, has many times been left carelessly dangling or even allowed to fall to the ground—is widespread. Should the youth's attention be undesired, the girl may request the return of the handkerchief; otherwise he keeps it several days as a sign of victory, and upon returning it, talks with the girl and formalizes his new status. In the Castiles, Extremadura, and Andalusia the lass who hears the cry *"Porra fuera o porra dentro,"* followed by a loud thud inside her front door, is not surprised or taken aback. She knows that some earnest though timid young man has summoned his courage to declare his love for her. In effect, he has thrown the porra, a heavy club, through the open door or into the patio, while shouting "Does it remain inside or outside?" If his attentions are unwanted, the club quickly emerges. Otherwise he is accepted. Sometimes in Granada the porra, as a symbol of acceptance, is adorned with flowers and hung in the most conspicuous part of the house.

A father is not eager to have a marriageable daughter living at home for long and formerly, in Asturias at least, he took every reasonable precaution to avoid such a calamity. By whitewashing the facade of his house, painting the balcony, and repairing the doors he gave notice to the youths of the village that the daughter of the house might now be considered a matrimonial prospect. He even sometimes went so far as to frame the window of the girl's room with fresh plaster so that there should be no doubt concerning the target for future serenading (Cabal 1925a, p. 226).

For marriageable girls all over Spain the morning of San Juan may be a crisis. Wondering if her sweetheart is constant, if some bashful youth aspires to her affections, or if she has offended someone in the village, a girl brings herself to the door to examine the house facade. For this is the day of the placing of the *ramo,* which may be a spray from a tree, a wreath of flowers, fruit, candy, or even an entire treelet transplanted to her door. In Alpedrete del Enebral (Madrid) the suitorless girl who finds the ramo knows that she will be serenaded that night and that among those who serenade will be her aspiring swain. She waits breathlessly, dressed in her best and, at the close of the serenade, steps to the window to thank the singers. One of them breaks ranks, steps forward, and in a matter-of-fact way asks her to light his cigarette. If she accedes, it is recognition that she approves of him, and henceforth he may court her in more formal fashion.

But, although the morning usually brings happiness, it may also bring shame and anger. In Salamanca the girl who finds a ramo of fig,[8] plum, pear, or mugwort *(artemisia)* knows her disdained suitor is calling her crazy, immoral, or dirty. Hence, if one is in doubt it is wise to keep a sharp eye open, to remove before dawn any ramo which casts doubt on one's good character. And, to avoid the humiliation of finding nothing at all at the door, the cautious maid is up early to place the ramo herself, if necessary, a precaution matched only by that of the youth who, fearing rivalry, stands guard all night to make sure his offering is not replaced by that of another.

The serenade and the *ronda*, the rounds of youths who, with guitar and voice, by turns serenade their sweethearts, are to this day important parts of courting. The art of composition of couplets is one which brings fame to the gifted, but most youths, not so endowed, fall back on stock verses. Love letters, too, play a part in courtship in many places, and bashful or inarticulate swains may purchase paper-backed booklets in markets with sample love letters, imagined conversations, and similar guide-lines to successful courtship, just as is done in Hispanic America.

The formal petition for a girl's hand is presented in various ways. Not infrequently, even among the lower classes, decisions are made by parents. Among the upper classes this is, of course, more frequent. One purpose of parental decisions is to select members of the family, so that land and money will not be dissipated through division and redivision. But with greater frequency young people decide for themselves, and then the question remains of gaining parental consent, traditionally more difficult from the girl's father. In many places a go-between, a *pedidor*, is used, who is thought, through position or eloquence, to plead the suitor's case more effectively than the boy himself. Among the working class, the go-between may be the employer of the youth, whose position and opinion of the lad may be expected to carry weight with the parents.

In the regions of Quiroga and Becerreá (Lugo) the encounter with the girl's father is highly stylized. The youth, either because he knows the girl or because his parents suggest she is a likely match, visits her house with a friend called *chufón*. Both wear long capes. The suitor seats himself dangerously near the fire, and says nothing. The girl's parents warn him of the danger of burning the cape, but the chufón tells them not to worry, that it makes not a whit of difference, that the boy is well off. He then launches into a panegyric praising not only the boy's financial prospects, but his moral character, good habits, and general qualifications as a prospective son-in-law. If the girl's parents agree, plans are then made for a subsequent meeting with the boy's parents, at which time dowry and other arrangements are discussed (García Ramos 1909, p. 51).

More often a boy's father serves as go-between, sometimes accompanying the boy, without ceremony, and sometimes participating in a ritual of public recognition to which friends of both young people have been invited. Naturally, when this is done there has been a previous informal understanding. In Orellana La Vieja (Badajoz) on a previously determined night, friends and relatives of both families gather at the girl's house, the boy's father in the kitchen with the girl and her parents, the others outside. When all are assembled the boy's father begins:

> You know for what reason we are here; were it not so we would not have come. You must decide. I say that the young people are in love, and that they have been keeping company for some time. I have said nothing to you, because I want either to do things properly or not at all, because my boy merits whatever sacrifice is necessary. He has been a fine worker since he was a child, and in truth I have decided to help him so that he can get married.

Then the girl's father takes up:

> Man, for my part I see no reason why they should not, and for the girl, I doubt that she does, for she has been forewarned and has already invited these other girls. My wife has taught my daughter to be like herself, to know that a woman's place is in her house, and beside her family.

When the subject of the good qualities of both children has been exhausted, the other guests are invited in for wine and sweets. First comes the boy's mother, accompanied by the girl's. She carries a roll of linen which she presents to the future bride, to be made by her into a sheet, kisses her, and then returns home. Next the groom enters, accompanied by his friends. He gives his fiancee a small gift of money saying *"Toma para alfileres,"* "Take this for pin money." Then the rest of the evening is spent in drinking, eating, and dancing in the kitchen (Santa María 1925, pp. 3-4). Traditionally the asking for a girl has taken place with the *salida de quintas*, the youth's release from obligatory military service.

The marriage contract (usually *capitulaciones*, but also *conciertos, ajustes, hacer la carta, compostura de la boda, tomarse los dichos,* or simply *el contrato*) follows the formal petition. In small villages the arrangements are verbal or, occasionally, informally written. In cities and among upper classes they tend to be notarized. The contract covers both property settlement and such things as where the new couple will live. With respect to residence the most important problem is whether the marriage will be *para en casa* or not, that is, whether the newlyweds will continue to live for some time with one of the two families. Sometimes it is desired that the couple remain with one of the two sets of parents because of the help that the older people need. At other times it is a favor on the part of parents, to help the young people save money, and again it is a device whereby the principal inheritor begins to take over the family property. Giese found in northeast Cádiz that not infrequently a new couple lived the first year in the girl's parents' home, and the second in the groom's parents' home; only in the third year was a separate house established. Here the reasons were economic: an earlier marriage was possible if the youth did not have to bear the full expense of setting up a new home immediately (1937, p. 211). By 1950 Pitt-Rivers found this custom was largely abandoned (1954, p. 100). In other parts of Spain (the custom may be noted in León, Salamanca, Cáceres, both

Castiles, Murcia, and Valencia) part of the expenses of a new home are postponed by an arrangement whereby, for a year or so or until a child is born, each of the young people continues to live and eat in the house of his or her parents, the husband visiting his wife in her house only at night. In such arrangements husband and wife continue to work for his and her parents respectively.

The size of the dowry depends upon the relative wealth of both families. In the contract the exact quantity of dowry, its nature, whether in property or money, and the time of delivery, are carefully spelled out. Likewise enumerated are the aids which the groom's father will offer. The essentially economic role of marriage is nowhere more clearly indicated than in the parrying and sparring which accompanies determination of the dowry, and not infrequently inability to agree on minor sums will result in the whole affair being called off. It must be emphasized that among Spanish villagers, the word dowry refers not only to the wealth which accompanies the girl, but also to the property of the boy.

Vergara lists typical decisions made among well-to-do peasants in Segovia at the beginning of this century. Generally bride and groom continued to live with their respective parents for one year, the new matrimonial bed being placed in the home of the bride. The groom spent the first week with his bride, but then returned to eat and work with his parents, going to the wife's home only to sleep. The groom's parents gave 250 pesetas to those of the bride, and promised to plant a certain amount of land in wheat or barley for their son, ceding the land to him to cultivate for himself in subsequent years. In addition, they settled on their son one or two cows, and a pair of young burros or a horse. The bride's parents agreed to sow for her from a half to one fanega of chick peas, with the same understanding as for the groom's land, and to give her a team of mules or a cow, so that the monetary value of the contributions of the two sides would be equal (1909, pp. 21-22).

The weight given to the monetary aspects of the dowry is reflected in the answers given in the Atheneum questionnaire to the question of the importance of the bride's virginity. Surprisingly typical of many answers is that from Pola de Allende (Oviedo): "It doesn't matter much, especially if the girl has a good dowry." Unmarried mothers of Asturias, until recent years, had fame in Spain as being the most desirable wet nurses: they were young, healthy, and brimming with vitality, and they were brought to Madrid in large numbers. Returned to their villages, they were especially sought after in marriage, both because of their proved fertility and because they had earned for themselves a tidy dowry. Relative lack of concern about the bride's virginity characterizes north and west Spain, but not the south.

After the contract and before the reading of the first banns marriage godparents usually are selected. The institution of marriage sponsors, although not required by Canon Law, has long been customary in most of the country, and definite geographical patterning, as in the choice of

baptismal godparents, characterizes rules of selection. In general one
of two groups of people is turned to: baptismal godparents of one or
the other of the couple, or one of each; or the parents of the couple, in the
formula "groom's mother and bride's father" or vice versa. Only among
the lower classes of Catalonia are marriage godparents usually lacking.

Obligations of marriage godparents are social and economic rather
than spiritual. Usually they pay church fees, and frequently they furnish
the arras, the thirteen pieces of silver which the groom gives the bride.
Either immediately after the church service, or at a later time, such as
the *tornaboda* on the following day (p. 138), they offer a wedding break-
fast or banquet in their home. Often they visit the newlyweds on the
morning following the ceremony and serve them hot chocolate or other
foods in bed. In addition to these widespread general customs there
are countless local customs: in Tineo (Oviedo) the godmother gives two
sheets to the bride; in Laguna de Negrillos (León) the godfather gives
a hat to the groom; in the province of Segovia both godparents give the
new couple half a fanega of wheat; in Marmolejo (Jaén) and in rural
Badajoz the godmother takes the bride to confession the day before the
wedding, and undresses her on the wedding night.

Specific obligations on the part of the couple towards marriage godparents, unlike those towards baptismal godparents, appear to be lacking, as does the compadrazgo relationship between godparents and the
couple's parents. Since most godparents are family members, customary
behavior patterns already exist which, though they may be intensified,
do not change in nature. Serving as marriage godparent does not imply
spiritual relationship to bride or groom, or to their parents, and is not
in itself an impediment to subsequent marriage to any of them, although
this alliance might well be impossible because of consanguinity.

In León, Salamanca, and Cáceres the bride and groom name, in addition to godparents, two age mates to accompany them to the wedding
and to participate in other activities. In the Margatería of León they are
called *mozo* and *moza del caldo*, presumably because they are expected to
give broth *(caldo)* to the bride and groom upon their return from the
church. In the regions of Astorga and La Bañeza the moza carries a
bread doll to church and the mozo places the stole *(yugo)* over the
kneeling couple. Here both mozo and moza are close relatives of the
bride.

Various prenuptial observances characterize the period of the banns.
In north-central Spain, particularly where there are youths' societies, it
is customary for the groom to offer a *convite* to his erstwhile associates.
At the very least, wine is served, and usually sweets, bread, cookies, or
even a full meal will be provided. Occasionally a *tamborilero* is hired
to play his flute and drum so that the girls can be invited in for a dance.
Less frequently, the bride has a formal *despedida* or goodbye for her
friends. In Sayago (Zamora) the day of the second reading of the banns

the bride's girl friends go to her home and are given a wooden spoonful of candies.

Although each village and area of Spain has its own special forms and variations in weddings, the basic patterns over the country are quite similar. They involve elaborate preparations such as the scrubbing of houses and, in the south, their whitewashing, the assembling of great quantities of food, and particularly bread, the arranging of a series of meals at the homes of bride, groom, and godparents, and the like. Saturday is the most popular day for a wedding, followed by Sunday and Monday; Tuesdays and Fridays are the only days which are entirely avoided for, as is well known, *En martes ni te cases ni te embarques* ("On Tuesdays don't marry or set out on a trip").[9] In addition to the convenience of a weekend for a wedding, economics enter into the choice of day. Since the quantity of wedding gifts determines in considerable measure the economic future of the new couple, a collection is most advantageously held on a day when most of the townspeople are at home and have no good excuse to dodge their obligations.

Exchange of gifts, not only between bride and groom but also between other members of the family, is an important part of a marriage. Often the groom gives the bride a part or all of her wedding trousseau, including a black silk dress, mantilla, shoes, and perhaps the handkerchief in which the arras will be placed. The bride reciprocates by presenting him with a shirt which she has carefully embroidered, and sometimes *calzoncillos* or other undergarments. Handkerchiefs serve on many occasions during engagement and marriage as tokens of love and esteem: often the bride gives them to female relatives of her husband, the godmother may give them to the bride, or the mother-in-law to the daughter-in-law. In León the godfather traditionally presents the groom with a new hat, and in Galicia hats are included among the groom's presents to the men in his wife's family.

Wedding presents, particularly monetary, are called *dádivas*, and they are usually delivered in a formalized fashion. In the village of Añora (Córdoba) on the day before the marriage ceremony all guests eat at the home of the groom. Then the bride seats herself on a bench in her kitchen, her baptismal godmother on her right and a close relative on her left. The wedding guests arrive from the groom's feast and enter the kitchen to *llevar el dao*, to "bring the dádiva." The bride solemnly stands and extends her right hand, palm upward; silently, and with great seriousness, the guests advance and place money in her hand, the men a silver peseta, the women two silver reales. When her hand is full, the bride places the money in a basket and then extends it again to continue until all visitors have contributed. Then furniture is moved back and the "dance of the daos" follows (Porras Márques 1916, pp. 43-45).

In other places the presentation of the dádivas is even more colorful. In a west-central area including Salamanca, Zamora, Badajoz, Segovia, and Toledo, receiving is contingent upon the bride dancing a few steps with the donor, to the tunes of the *gaitero* who, with his simple flutelike *gaita* and small drum hanging from his left arm, lends gaiety to the occasion. In some Salamancan villages guests of both sexes dance a few whirls with the bride, holding a coin in their teeth. When the music pauses, the dancer, if a man, passes the coin to the bride, who must take it in her teeth, receiving simultaneously her partner's kiss. Since male dancers often show reluctance to let go, a tug-of-war sometimes ensues. This form of delivering the gift, with or without the kiss, is variously known as *espigar, respigar,* or as the *respiguijo* or the *baile de abrazo,* "dance of the embrace."

In western Toledo, and especially in Oropesa and nearby Lagartera, dávidas are presented in the "apple dance," the *baile de la manzana* (Mendizábal 1905, p. 15; Rincón Ramos 1958, pp. 191-192). After the wedding feast everyone follows the orchestra to the plaza. Bride and godmother stand together, the latter with an enormous silk handkerchief, with the four corners tied to make a sort of bag. The bride carries a knife on the end of which is stuck an enormous apple with many incisions in it. When the music strikes up, the godfather asks the bride to dance, places a gold coin in an incision, and the two dance a few steps of the jota. When they finish another male guest steps up and asks to dance, also placing a coin—but this time of silver—in the apple. And then another and another. When the apple will hold no more, the money is removed and placed in the silk handkerchief, and the process is repeated until all who wish to dance have done so. In subsequent dances, sometimes on later days, copper money is used, and even no money at all, the right to dance being purchased with pots and pans and other kitchen objects. A similar apple dance is, or was, found in Villalpondo (Zamora) (Bedate 1928), and in Salamanca (Arias Girón 1839).

In rural Navarra, presents may be delivered before the wedding, in rituals marked by good-humored horseplay. The godfather seats himself on a bed in the bride's home, and relatives and friends cover him with their presents until he must be pulled out, half-asphyxiated, to shouts of, "Now what's lacking?" to which he weakly replies, "A hope chest with its lock and a bride with her jewel" (i.e., virginity).

Formal display of wedding gifts and of the new house furnishings assembled by the couple—particularly the bed and bedding—is common in many places. In the Sierra de Béjar (southern Salamanca), for example, on the day before the wedding, guests bent on horseplay seize the gifts and house furnishings and parade the streets of the village in a grand procession, while villagers at their doors or windows watch the passersby, comment on the gifts, and otherwise enjoy the show. When the future home of the couple is reached the bed is assembled, chests are placed in order, and the gifts are spread out. On this and the following day anyone may enter to observe at close hand the amount and quality of the goods represented.

In northern Spain from Asturias to Catalonia carts and pack animals were used in such processions. In Basque villages in Navarra the procession, which took place on the day of the final reading of the banns, was led by a ram whose horns were adorned with ribbons. Next came a solid-wheeled squeaking cart loaded with bed, sheets, blankets, spinning wheel, carved wooden chest, and other domestic equipment. Perhaps behind this came a mule loaded with a wine skin and a sack of wheat to provide food and drink for the wedding banquet. Then came a female relative of the bride mounted on another mule, garlanded with baskets of chicken and holding in her lap the carefully washed and pressed wedding shirt of the groom. When the procession arrived at the bride's home or the couple's new house, the participants were invited to refreshments (Violant 1949, p. 288; Caro Baroja 1949b, p. 323).

In west-central Spain public display of the marriage bed is an important ritual. In Oropesa (Toledo) on the day before the wedding, the bride and godmother seat themselves in a bedroom in the midst of goods and presents to await the guests, who are received at the door by the godfather. As the visitors enter, the two women, with great gravity and in utter silence, display the bedquilts, blankets, sheets, and spreads.

The blessing of bride and groom by the former's father just before the party leaves for the church is important in Old Castile and other northern areas. The ceremony in Riaño (Oviedo) has a light but touching air. The groom, with the godfather and his friends, arrives at the bride's home, and when the father asks what is wanted, the godfather replies, "We have come to your home in search of a jewel which we hope you will not deny us." If the father is in a good humor, he hands out various trinkets and baubles, but each time the godfather refuses them, saying "The jewel we have come for is much more highly esteemed." Finally he must name the bride, and remind the father that an agreement was previously made at the time of the marriage contract. The father then calls his daughter, tells her why the visitors have come, and she and the groom silently kneel on a cushion placed just inside the house door.

The traditional spot for the marriage ceremony is just outside or just inside the church door. In former times, and even today to some extent, the bridal party's progress to and from the church was punctuated by the discharge of firearms, which gave an animated and joyous air to the occasion. Rockets and firecrackers today are more common. At the church door priest, sacristan, and acolytes await the wedding party. The ceremony is simple. After the exchange of rings the groom takes the arras, 13 silver coins, from a tray held by an acolyte and presents them to the bride. Then all enter the church for Mass *(misa de velación)*. While the couple kneel at the altar, either just before communion or at the time of the offering, the godfather or another participant, such as the mozo del caldo, places the yugo ("yoke"), a stole of fine drawn work or embroidery, across the necks of the pair, where it remains until Mass ends. In Salamanca the symbolism of yoking the couple is carried to such a point that cattle feed troughs are sometimes placed before the kneeling bride and groom. The *besamanos* or kissing of the priest's hand is a part of the ceremony in Cáceres and the Sierra de Béjar. The priest advances to the first step of the altar, an acolyte holding a silver tray beside him. Each guest advances, kneels, kisses the outstretched hand, and deposits a small coin in the tray. The money may be kept by the priest or shared with the acolyte.

Frequently the bride's mother does not go to the church ceremony, and occasionally the father does not go either. The throwing of rice, wheat, or other grains or objects as the newlyweds emerge from the church is an ancient custom in Spain, although, because of the expense involved, it is always done with moderation and sometimes dispensed with entirely. After the return to the bride's, groom's, or godparent's house, as the case may be, felicitations on the part of the guests are expected. These usually take standardized forms, such as *"Que sea para bien y para muchos años,"* "May [the marriage] be happy, and may it last many years," to which the bride and groom respond to the well-wisher with "May you live to see it."

Buffoonery of varying degrees of taste characterizes wedding ceremonies. In the pueblos surrounding Riaño and Valdelugueros (León) a youth approaches the bride as the bridal party emerges from the church, slips his arm around her, swings her off her feet, and separates her a short distance from the remainder of the party. *"Quién me la fía?"* he shouts in a loud voice, "Who will ransom her?" to which the godfather, with complete gravity, responds, *"Yo la fío,"* "I'll ransom her." He takes several coins out of his pocket, hands them over to the captor, who returns the girl, and the procession continues on its way.

Nearly everywhere the more raucous male guests try to keep bride and groom from retiring after the wedding feast. At times in Old Castile the revelers lock the bride in the bedchamber and carry off the groom to round with them for the entire night, or even for two or three days. If the couple is lucky enough to escape such torment, they may find, unless they have arranged to sleep in some unknown hiding place, that their bed has been "frenched" with salt or wheat grains, with cowbells tied to the mattress, or fixed in such manner that it collapses when weight is placed on it. In Salamanca, where the gustiness of wedding horseplay surpasses that of the rest of the country, revelers who discover a secret hideout may force entry, remove the couple from bed, carry them outside, and place them on a painted and festooned burro, forcing them to ride through the streets to the sound of flute, drum, castanets, and other noisemakers. At the home of each guest they are offered wine, and still more wine, while behind them rowdy youths burn pepper, hair, and even more odiferous substances in censors.

In other villages in Salamanca the new couple, after being left in peace for the night, may be pulled from bed at dawn to be paraded through the streets in a cart or mounted backward on a burro. Or the newlyweds will be yoked to a plow and forced to plow a symbolic furrow or two before their release. Still in Salamanca, the lucky groom will be asked by his "friends" for *la sangría,* a monetary contribution—a form of blackmail—for wine, almonds, or cigars which may buy off the tormentors. If the celebrating youths are unsatisfied with the gift, they accost the bride next morning with a blood-smeared cow horn, and try to touch her stockings or petticoat so that some of the blood will rub off.

A celebration which continues on the day after a wedding is known as a tornaboda. Although the custom is now dying out, principally because of the cost, this has been a traditional part of weddings in all Spain. In Valladolid province weddings often lasted three days: the second day was the tornaboda and the third the *abuela* ("grandmother"). In Alcobendas (Madrid) the second day was the *postboda* and the third the *bodilla.* Feasting and dancing were the principle activities of these days.

Tornaboda or not, in much of northern Spain bride and groom carry candles and bread offerings to a Mass of the dead on the day following their marriage. Weddings are a family affair and the dead, who are not forgotten, are included in the only way possible. And in all rural Spain godparents or relatives and friends may enter the bridal chamber early the following morning bringing hot chocolate, chicken broth, brandy, or ham and eggs for the couple to partake of before arising.

A charivari *(cencerrada)* formerly was the universal rule for second marriages and for unions of disproportionate ages. The revelers serenaded the newlyweds with cowbells *(cencerros)* and other noisemakers, or paraded *monigotes* or *peleles,* straw-stuffed manikins representing the couple, through the streets, incensing them with foul-smelling substances.[10]

Bread, which is of great ceremonial and religious importance in many aspects of Spanish life, plays a full role in marriage rites. Its ceremonial usages are legion: in parts of Old Castile small loaves are placed on the altar during the wedding Mass, to serve as candlesticks, and at the following feast the godfather offers bread and wine to anyone who comes to congratulate the new couple; in Carbia (Pontevedra) after the church ceremony the godmother distributes bread from her apron to all who stop her and request some; in Oviedo and León the bride invites guests to her wedding by leaving bread at their homes.

The *bollo* (or *rosca*) is the equivalent of a wedding cake, a doughnut-shaped loaf elaborately decorated with pastry sugar, fruit, leaves, and unshelled eggs. The bride may keep a small piece of this, secure in the belief that as long as it lasts she and her husband will enjoy conjugal felicity. Sometimes the rosca is the object of a competition among the youths, such as a race, a dance, or a singing contest. López Morán describes the *corrida de la rosca* in León (1900, pp. 80-82). The moza del caldo carries the bread, shaped like a doll, to the church ceremony. After Mass the bride and her godmother sit on a wheat-strewn bench outside the girl's home, and pass out biscuit-sized loaves from a basket on the bride's lap to all women who come. Then the moza del caldo gives the bread doll to the godfather who, with the groom and other youths, journey to a near-by field where they race. The winner receives the doll's head as prize, and the body is broken in small pieces and distributed among the others.

Wedding garments have few noteworthy aspects. In most of Spain, however warm the weather may be, the long black cape is the proper dress both for groom and male guests. Black likewise is the dominant note of the bride's outfit, which usually includes a heavy pleated woolen skirt and a long-sleeved jacket. Often a shawl or mantilla is worn over the head or shoulders.

In Largartera, when the bride returns from the church, her mother meets her at the door and removes her mantilla, replacing it with a handkerchief, which she will henceforth wear on her head to mark her as a married woman (Díaz Morales 1928, p. 6). In the Basque provinces until recent times married women always wore handkerchiefs on their heads as a sign of their status. Only unmarried girls would go bareheaded (María de Azkue 1935, p. 281).

Elopement *(rapto)* as a recognized preliminary to marriage is not uncommon in some parts of Spain. It is, in the first place, one fairly sure way to overcome parental objections to a match when other entreaties have failed. But sometimes elopments occur with the full consent and knowledge of parents: it is a way to avoid many expenses of the traditional wedding which often may mean near-bankruptcy for a family. In other cases, as in Ibiza and Murcia (particularly the Huerta and the Campo of Cartagena), long-established custom, as well as romantic and economic reasons, plays a part, and people of good family elope without attracting undue attention (Navarro 1901, pp. 125-129).

Courting and marriage customs in Spain are better described than many other aspects of culture, so that it is possible to map several major "marriage" culture areas. One such area embraces Galicia, Asturias, the old kingdom of León, Old Castile, and to a lesser extent New Castile, and Cáceres, which divides rather sharply from Badajoz, the southern province of Extremadura. This north-central and northwest area may be called that of "maximum intensity" of courting and marriage customs in the sense of wide variety of practices, popular interest in marriage, family and neighbor participation, and the like. This is the region in which unmarried youths are organized into more or less formal associations, and in which suitors from neighboring villages must pay an "entrance" to court a local girl. This is the region in which grooms formally say goodbye to their bachelor days by means of a banquet tendered the other bachelors, and in which brides similarly entertain their girl friends. The paternal benediction is nearly universal here, as contrasted to the more casual attitude toward it in other parts of the country. The "yoke" over the shoulders of the kneeling couple is common, and bread in one form or another plays an important ceremonial role. A Mass of the dead in this area is a frequent part of the total church ritual.

A subarea within this area appears to have its epicenter in Salamanca and to include with greater or lesser intensity Cáceres, Zamora, León, and adjacent parts of Castile. Traits characteristic of this region include the custom of having baptismal godparents serve as wedding godparents (this also is true of Asturias, Galicia, and Valencia), of having the bride dance with each person who offers a gift (e.g., the apple dance, and the passing of money with teeth), of the utilization of mozos del caldo, who accompany bride and groom, of a race or dancing competition for the wedding bread (rosca), of the custom of maximum horseplay and abuse of bride and groom, such as keeping them apart during the first night, of yoking them to a plow and forcing them to plow a furrow, and of the crude sangría; and of the besamanos in which the priest's hands are kissed during the wedding service.

Catalonia and Aragón, in contrast to the regions just described, constitute an area of "low intensity" of marriage customs. Here, marriage godparents usually are lacking or are of slight importance, wedding banquets are simpler, celebrations last less time, and in general less interest is shown in the formal manifestations of weddings. These remarks are less true of the Pyrenees valleys which, from the Basque provinces to the Mediterranean, have many colorful wedding customs, like that of the ceremonial moving of the household goods to the new home.

Andalusia and near-by areas in Badajoz, New Castile, and Murcia, constitute a third major area, with less well defined characteristics. This seems to be a region of "medium intensity" of customs. Celebrations are more elaborate than in the east, but generally less so than in the north and west. Parents, and less often siblings, predominate as marriage godparents (this is likewise true of much of Old Castile and Navarra), and the "general" Spanish wedding characteristics sketched above are more frequent than in the northeastern area.

COMPARISONS AND COMMENTS

Spanish courting and marriage customs in America reflect both informal and formal aspects of conquest culture. Forms of divination to determine who a girl's spouse will be, the prayers to San Antonio, the custom of serenades, and the use of guide-books to successful courtship in all probability represent informally transmitted culture brought by conquistadors and later colonists. These customs presumably were of no concern to the Church and were allowed to flourish as harmless diversions. On the other hand, the more exuberant Spanish forms of horseplay, like the sangría, must have seemed excessive to the Church, and the slight degree of such activity in America may reflect a successful campaign to discourage broad humor.

The Spanish American wedding ceremony itself, of course, represents a part of the Church's obvious policy of propagating the sacraments in the New World, and hence represents formally transmitted culture. Conversion of the Indians required acceptance of the sacraments, and after baptism no activity preoccupied the clergy more than legalizing preëxisting unions and establishing new ones according to Church doctrine.

The patterns of elopement and the use of go-betweens, common both in Spain and America, probably represent independent solutions to common problems, reinforced in many cases by actual diffusion of custom from the Old World to the New.

Spanish courtship and marriage customs described in this chapter show much greater diversity than is found in Hispanic America, again reflecting the reduction process that characterizes conquest culture. Among the Spanish customs that appear to be rare, or entirely lacking in America, may be mentioned the cofradías de solteros and their associated activities, the mozo and moza del caldo, the ramo of San Juan, highly stylized "asking" ceremonies, the dádivas, the apple dance, the badgering of bride and groom on the wedding night, the sangría, and the tornaboda. If these traits are plotted on a map, it is found that they cluster in the northern and western areas of the country. From this it is reasonable to assume that this region has had little to do with determining courtship and marriage customs in America. On the other hand, the paucity of forms in eastern Spain indicates that that region, too, has not been instrumental in setting American patterns.

Thus, through a process of elimination, it becomes apparent that the region of "medium intensity" of custom—Andalusia and near-by parts of Badajoz, New Castile, and Murcia—have been most influential in America in the informally transmitted cultural categories. On the positive side, dowry patterns also support this conclusion. Although the dowry pattern has not been described in detail in America (except by the Biesanz for colonial times in Costa Rica, 1944, p. 47), it appears to have been an upper-class phenomenon, largely to the exclusion of the lower classes. Since in Alcalá (Cádiz) dowries are only rarely given and little property changes hands until the parents' death (Pitt-Rivers 1954, p. 99), it looks as if America follows Andalusia with respect to this trait.

REFERENCES

All specific references to communities not otherwise noted are drawn from the Atheneum Questionnaire.

Arco y Garay (1930), Arias Girón (1839), Benavides (1932), Cabal (1925a), Caro Baroja (1949b), Carral (1929, 1935), Casas Gaspar (1947), Coloma y Santana (1930), Coves (1935), Días Morales (1928), Fernández-Núñez (1931), Fornet (1935), Fuente Arrimadas (1925, pp. 259-269), García Ramos (1909, 1912), Giese (1937), Gil Muñiz (1926), Hoyos Sancho (1948a), Iribarren (1948), N. Lewis (1956), López Morán (1900), María de Azkue (1935, pp. 269-284), Martín Granizo (1929), Méndez Plaza (1900), Mendizábal (1905), Monge (1847), Montoto (1883), Morán (1945, 1950), Naranjo Porras (1948), Navarro (1901), Pitt-Rivers (1954), Porras Márquez (1916), Prieto Rodríguez (1947), Puente (1935), Quiléz Vicente (1935), Ramos (1935), Rincón Ramos (1958), Ruiz-Funes García (1916), Sánchez (1935), Santa María (1925), Vergara y Martín (1909), Violant y Simorra (1949, pp. 278-283), Yaben y Yaben (1916).

NOTES

[1] Jueves de Comadres and Compadres is celebrated in Peru, Bolivia, Argentina, Venezuela, and perhaps other countries as well (e.g., Toor 1949, p. 214; Rigoberto

Paredes 1920, p. 208; Ambrosetti 1917, p. 189; Erminy Arismendi [n.d.] pp. 149-150). I have not encountered this celebration in Mexico.

[2] Similar divinatory techniques, on the same occasion, are found in Spanish America. In Venezuela a girl throws flowers to a passerby; in Puerto Rico, a slipper on the end of a string. In either case, the name of the man involved is that of the future spouse (Olivares Figueroa 1949, p. 156).

[3] This technique also is known in America. Three lemons are used in Venezuela, and three potatoes in Chile and Cuba (ibid., p. 154).

[4] These forms of divination likewise are common in Hispanic America, as in Peru (Toor 1949, p. 217) and Bolivia (Rigoberto Paredes 1920, p. 207).

[5] Mirror divination is reported for Venezuela by Olivares Figueroa (1949, p. 156). In Temuco (Chile) in 1952 informants told me of similar water-and-mirror divination.

[6] Starr describes coscinomancy in Guadalajara (Mexico) to answer love questions and find stolen objects (1899, pp. 104-105).

[7] The same lack of ceremony is found in Mexico; the Mendozas describe how, when questions are unanswered, the saint may be hung upside down, often in a well (1952, p. 466).

[8] According to the Gospel of Mark (11:13-14, 20-22) Christ cursed a fig tree which he found without fruit when he wished to eat, whereupon it withered away at its roots. Also, in Spain it is popularly believed that Christ's cross was made of fig wood and that Judas hanged himself from a fig tree. For any or all of these reasons, the fig tree is considered in Spain to be nefasto, "cursed," its shade dangerous and its wood useless. (Yet the fruit, of course, is eaten). The San Juan fig ramo is common in many parts of the country as a sign of disdain.

[9] This advice carries over to America: in Tzintzuntzan, although the saying is unknown, Tuesday is considered a poor day to marry, for the couple will be martyrs all their lives (from Martes) (Foster 1948a, p. 251).

[10] Emilio Jiménez (1927, pp. 220-224) describes the cencerrada in the Dominican Republic; it probably has been common in well hispanicized areas in Spanish America

CHAPTER XII

THE RITUAL OF DEATH
In Spanish America

THE basic social and spiritual patterns for coping with death stem from Catholic dogma and ritual, and for this reason they show a high degree of homogeneity in all the area. The sacrament of extreme unction is administered whenever possible to a dying person. A *velorio* ("wake") is held the night of a death, and usually on the next day the body is buried in a locally made wooden casket. A *novena*, or prayer meeting, is held at the home of the deceased on the nine following evenings. Children are believed to die without sin, and hence go straight to heaven without passing through purgatory. They are therefore called *angelitos* ("little angels"). Formerly their death was the occasion for rejoicing, and singing and dancing occurred at their wake. In village Spanish America, at least, formal testaments are rare, and property is passed from one generation to the next following death according to local customary as well as national law.

In Spain

As in Spanish America, of course, the Church has set the basic outlines of funerary procedures. Within these limits there are many local variations and customs, some of which are superstitious and folkloric, deriving from earlier pagan European rites rather than being Catholic in origin.

When death is foreseen but not imminent, arrangements are made for communion and extreme unction. The former is administered to the sick who, it is feared, may not recover. Then, if there is a turn for the worse, a rush call is sent to the priest to administer extreme unction, as is also done when a person is gravely injured or struck with sudden serious illness. A crucifix is placed in the hands of the dying person, and a candle—frequently called *de Jueves Santo* because it was lighted at the altar on Maundy Thursday—is set at the bedside. In some villages impending death is announced by the *toque de agonía* tolling of church bells; in others the bells do not toll until death has occurred. Customarily the pattern of tolling indicates whether the deceased was male or female.

Members of the family are spared the pain of preparing the body for the wake and interment. Friends or fellow-members of burial societies wash the corpse, clothe it in its best garments, close the eyes, fold the hands on the chest, and place candles at the four corners of the bier. After a wake, which lasts part or all of the night, the funeral procession assembles. The priest comes to the house, responses are chanted, and the cortege sets off.

Usually the path includes a stop at the church door for a brief ceremony, and sometimes it includes a Mass known as *del cuerpo presente,* i.e., with the body lying at the church door, in contrast to a subsequent Mass of the Dead when the body is not present. Women often do not accompany the procession to the cemetery. Burial customarily occurs within twenty-four hours, except in large cities where embalming is possible.

Formerly, except for the wealthy, bodies frequently were wrapped in a sheet for burial, but during the past fifty years it has become customary to bury in a wooden coffin. After the interment the party returns to the home of the deceased, where the priest says a few final responses before he departs. Friends and relatives remain, often to be fed, and at this time or during the procession alms may be given to the poor. During each of the nine following nights friends and relatives drop by to pray for the soul of the departed, and on the ninth the novena, or final period of prayer, is held.

Surviving relatives pass through a period of mourning, which is more severe for women, and especially for widows, than for men. Masses for the soul of the deceased are arranged with the priest, and on the first anniversary of the death a final service may be held. Family participation in the traditional rites of All Souls' Day are more marked in the year following the death of a member.

Such, in outline, are the patterns which emerge from a comparison of traditional Spanish funerary customs. The variations around this theme are numerous; when viewed historically, they show evolutionary tendencies, generally toward greater simplicity. The elaborate funeral banquets of northern Spain (described below) and the lavish distribution of bread are now almost entirely things of the past. Mourning is less rigorous, and the paid weepers, the *lloronas,* and the singing and dancing at children's funerals, have now disappeared. All Soul's Day observances are more restrained than formerly. The customs here described are, for the most part, characteristic of the rural Spanish village of about the year 1900, a time when a richness of custom still prevailed which no longer exists. Of course, many of the individual customs and beliefs continue to be found today, especially in small and isolated communities.

Although a decision to call the priest to administer extreme unction or communion to a sick person is based largely on obvious physiological symptoms, popular belief recognizes a number of signs of impending death. The importance attached to these presages varies according to whether all members of the family are in good health, or whether someone is already seriously ill. Omens most widely known, and taken as a sign of impending death, include the nocturnal hooting of an owl or the croaking of other birds, the crowing of a hen in the fashion of a cock, howling of dogs at night, the breaking of mirrors or the falling of pictures from walls, inexplicable taps or poundings on walls or furniture, or the mysterious opening and closing of doors. In Andalusia it is believed that San Pascual Bailón will warn people of approaching death if they previously have entrusted their souls to him and prayed to him every day. Thus, when a person who has made this compact hears three knocks on the family storage chest, he knows the time has come to make such personal arrangements for death as seem indicated.

A death room is usually crowded with weeping relatives, friends, members of the burial society to which the dying person belongs, and even curious passersby. Many people believe that the soul must struggle to leave the body and that bystanders may help the sufferer "to die easily" by praying and aspersing holy water. The blessing of the godmother or godfather is particularly important to alleviate the suffering of a child and to speed the tiny soul on its way.[1] The conception of the soul as having material substance is indicated by the occasional custom of facilitating its departure from the room by mechanical means. Among the Basques a roof tile is often removed from the room of the dying person (Barandiarán 1949, p. 443) and in many places windows and doors are opened wide (Thalamas 1931, p. 43). Cabal reports that in Asturias lighted candles may be placed in open windows so the departing soul will be sure of the exit (1928, p. 72). Since a high proportion of rural deaths were unattended by doctors, it was customary to determine whether breathing had stopped by holding a mirror or lighted candle close to the face of the corpse. If the mirror failed to cloud and the flame burned steadily, it was taken as a sign that life had indeed departed.

In small villages the death of an adult is a matter of importance to everyone. The old-fashioned toque de agonía tolling of church bells to announce impending death has largely died out, but the *toque de muerte* death tolling continues. In both, the number and combination of strokes indicate the sex of the dead or dying. Usually groups of three quick strokes announce male deaths and pairs of strokes female deaths. But common patterns for men and women respectively are groups of 15 and 13, 13 and 11, 11 and 9, 9 and 7, or 7 and 5, and still other combinations are known. Death of a priest is announced by adding several strokes to the normal male pattern.

The *amortajamiento* ("shrouding") of a corpse is carried out as quickly as possible after death so that stiffening limbs will not make it unduly difficult to arrange the body. Formerly corpses were shrouded in a large white *mortaja*. Today, more commonly, a married person is dressed in his best clothing, which is usually black and often may have been his wedding garments. In parts of Catalonia shoes are left off the corpse in the belief that the deceased, if shod, would return to its home to annoy the survivors (Violant 1949, p. 305). Children and teenagers are dressed in white, a sign of purity, and a palm frond, the symbol of virginity, is placed in the coffin beside unmarried youths. The hands of the corpse are usually crossed on the chest, and a crucifix, rosary, or a copy of the *bula de las cruzades*, a small booklet in which are set forth the indulgences conceded by the Popes to those who undertoook the crusades, is placed in them. Not infrequently the lower jaw is tied with a handkerchief, in the stereotyped fashion of a sufferer from mumps, so the mouth will not gape open. Almost always the eyes are closed, if death has not already done this, because of the near-universal belief that the open eye of a corpse calls to death another member of the family.

Since embalming is not customary in villages, hot weather may cause the corpse to bloat. Several magical or mechanical devices are believed to arrest this process, of which the most common is the placing of a heavy flatiron on the stomach. In Santander wax is placed in the navel, and in various places a plate of unground salt is placed on the stomach. Open scissors, crossed swords, or sharp objects on the stomach are also used in many villages.

A house in which death has occurred is given visible evidence of the event through a customary symbol or symbols. Often this symbolism involves keeping one of the double front doors (found on most Spanish houses) tightly closed, while its companion is left slightly ajar. If the deceased belonged to a burial society, the standard of the organization will be placed beside the door. Occasionally black curtains are hung at balconies and windows.

Specific acts are sometimes thought necessary for the well-being of survivors. Formerly among the Basques the straw mattress on which death took place was burned at a crossroad. In Navas del Madroño (Cáceres) all the water in a house is thrown into the street as soon as a person dies. It is thought that the departing soul bathes in this water to appear before God in a clean and pure state and that if a survivor drinks the water he will inadvertently acquire the sins of the departed.

The wake may be held either in the room where the corpse lies or in an adjoining room. In earlier years the body was extended on the floor or on a table, but today it is more common to leave it in bed or to place it in the coffin. The nature and intensity of the wake depend in part on geographical area. In southern and southeastern Spain it is "Irish" in style, being a social event where liquor flows freely. In the north the wake is more restrained, with prayers and eulogies of the departed. If the deceased belonged to a burial society, two members are named to stand guard all night, while the other members will come for only a part of the time. In some villages paid women specialists lead prayers at wakes. For mourners who remain any length of time it is customary to serve such refreshments as bread, chocolate, and coffee, in addition to liquor. Although ostentation is not particularly a part of wakes there is an amusing custom in the mountains of Palencia where the bones of a chicken—presumably those of the fowl that nourished the deceased in his last hours—are placed in a conspicuous place in the room, so that visitors will know that death did not occur because of lack of attention on the part of the family.

The wakes of young children differ considerably from those of adults. According to Catholic dogma they die without mortal sin, and so go directly to heaven to become angels without passing through purgatory. Hence, the death of an angelito, in spite of the personal and selfish grief of the parents, is an occasion for rejoicing. Formerly to show their happiness friends and relatives, and particularly young people, gathered with guitars and castanets, to sing and dance through the night. This *baile de los an- gelitos* was particularly characteristic, at least in recent historic times, of the Mediterranean littoral, from Castellón south to Murcia, of Extre- madura, and of the Canary Islands (Altamira 1905, p. 22). Earlier it probably existed in more of southern and central Spain, as remnants of customs indicate. For example, at the turn of the century in many villages in Segovia the body of a child of less than seven years of age was accom- panied in the funeral procession with the gay music of drum and flute (Vergara 1909, p. 44), and in Perelló (Tarragona) upon the return from the cemetery the mourners went to the town plaza where they danced with members of the bereaved family (Casas Gaspar 1947, p. 351).

In *Viaje por España* the great French Hispanist Baron Charles Davil- lier describes a dance of a "little angel" he witnessed, in company with Gustave Doré, in Jijona (Alicante) in the 1860's.

One day we witnessed a funeral ceremony in Jijona in which, to our great astonish- ment, the visitors danced the jota. We were passing along a deserted street when we heard the *fron fron* of a guitar accompanied by the sharp tone of the bandurria and the clicking of castanets. We pushed back the half-open door of a house of workers, expecting to fall into the midst of a wedding.

. . . It was a funeral. In the back of the room we made out, stretched on a table covered with a robe, a girl of five or six years dressed as if for a fiesta. Her head, adorned with a crown of orange blossoms, rested on a pillow. We thought at first that she was sleeping, but upon seeing a glass full of Holy Water beside her and the four great tapers which burned at the corners of the table, we understood that the poor creature was dead. A young woman—the mother, they told us—was seated beside her daughter, weeping unrestrainedly.

But the remainder of the picture contrasted singularly with this scene of sorrow. A young man and a young woman, dressed in the festive costume of Valencian workers, danced the gayest jota imaginable, accompanying themselves with castanets, while the musicians and guests formed a chorus around them, animating them by singing and clapping their hands.

It was difficult to comprehend this rejoicing alongside the grief (1949, p. 484).

Doré's accompanying drawing shows the child wrapped in a sheet on the table, illuminated by four enormous candles. The mother sits with bowed head, while the musicians in a corner play for the dancers and chorus.

The baile de los angelitos has almost, if not entirely, died out in modern Spain, although we were told that in El Viso del Alcor (Sevilla) it did not disappear until about 1915 and that in Alhama (Murcia) it occurred oc- casionally up to the time of the Civil War of 1936-39.[2]

The morning after the wake the priest goes to the home of the deceased and the funeral cortege forms. Responses are said and the group sets out on its short journey. When it was customary to bury in a shroud rather than a coffin, a communal litter, maintained by the church or a burial society, was used to carry corpses to the graveyard. Sometimes also a body was carried in a communal coffin, loaned to the family for the event and recov- ered at the edge of the grave, where the body was removed and interred in its shroud alone. Communal litters and coffins particularly characterized Old Castile and the Old Kingdom of León.

Married adults normally are buried in black wooden coffins, which are sealed before the departure from the house. Children, unmarried youths, and priests are carried in white coffins, usually left uncovered until the moment of lowering into the grave. Almost always a corpse is removed from the house feet first and carried in this position to the cemetery, except for priests, who travel head first. In southern Spain and in towns and cities women customarily do not go to the cemetery. In central and northern Spain they are much more apt to accompany the cortege. Black clothing is expected of all mourners: the cape for men and a black dress and mantilla for women. Men usually walk bareheaded in the procession, except in the north and northwest, where they wear hats. In all Spain when a funeral procession passes, it is customary for men to remove their hats and for women to kneel.

Paid professional mourners, called *lloronas* or *plañideras,* were found in conservative parts of Galicia, Cáceres, Old Castile, and the Pyrenees valleys until the beginning of the present century. These women, dressed in old and dirty clothing, accompanied the burial procession, loudly lamenting the departure of the deceased, eulogizing his good qualities, overlooking his not-so-good characteristics, and otherwise lending éclat to the occasion. In Galicia the number of plañideras indicated social position.[3]

Formerly it was customary to carry a corpse to the church for the Mass of the Dead, but the introduction of the body inside the edifice proper was prohibited by law in the latter half of the nineteenth century. Today for more ostentatious "first-class" funerals the corpse remains at the church door for the Mass (misa del cuerpo presente), and for simpler "second-class" and "third-class" ceremonies it is simply rested briefly at the door for responses before the group continues to the cemetery.[4] All processions pause for *pozas.* A poza is any spot where a stop is made for the priest to pray, and is also the act of stopping itself. Stone or wooden crosses sometimes mark pozas along well-traveled routes to graveyards, but an improvised stop may be made by resting the coffin on a table, covered with a black cloth, which has been set up for the purpose. Since the priest must be paid for each such stop, the number of pozas is a mark of the economic position of the family and of the number and generosity of the deceased's friends.

Customary usage determines the orientation of the grave. In north and northwest Spain the body is usually interred with the feet toward the church, so that the corpse may "look" at the temporal focus of salvation. Less commonly, feet are toward the east, toward the cemetery gate, or away from the village. Whatever the local pattern, priests are buried in the opposite direction so that they "face" their parishioners. Rites in the cemetery are simple. The priest chants a few responses, the assembled group murmurs the replies, and the body is lowered into the grave. Mourners often throw a handful of earth on the coffin, first kissing the dirt or making the sign of the cross with it.

In early times graveyards were adjacent to the church, and in some small villages where population growth has been slight they continue to be. In the Basque provinces villagers were buried inside the church well into the eighteenth century; the custom was prohibited by law in 1787. This practice led to the current custom in which the head woman of each family has a particular spot on the floor where she and her small children go for Mass. This *tumba* in a real sense is the family tomb, for beneath it lie earlier generations of her or her husband's family. At her "tomb" she keeps one or more *tableros,* small wooden boards with short legs on each side around which are wrapped yard-long tapers, which may be slowly unwound as they are burned in honor of the dead or at other religious observances.

After a burial, villagers return to the home of the deceased to extend sympathy to the survivors. The bereaved family thanks its friends and repays them for their services by offering them a repast of bread and wine. Coloma describes this act as it was carried out in Palencia a generation ago. Two candles, an image of Christ, a jar of wine, and loaves of bread were placed on a table set in front of the house. As the priest led responses and said prayers, the guests paid him by depositing small coins on the table. Then a member of the family gave the priest a piece of bread, and afterwards passed bread to all the guests, while another member went with the wine from guest to guest, each of whom offered a simple toast such as "May we all reunite in heaven," "To the health of the deceased," or "I say the same" (Coloma 1930).

In extreme northern Spain, from Galicia to the Mediterranean, this simple repast at one time became a gluttonous banquet, often served in the church sacristy and attended by priests from neighboring villages as well as by local mourners. A description from the mountains of Santander, presumably during the second half of the eighteenth century, describes such a reunion. Following the burial of an important person twenty or thirty priests assembled around a large catafalque. After the religious ceremony priests and important mourners passed to the sacristy where they ate cheese, bread, cake, and wine. A table was set up at the door of the church and simpler refreshments were passed out to people of lesser category (Lasaga y Larreta 1934).

Bread and wine may also be offered to guests at other times besides the return from the cemetery. In the mountainous region of Becerreá (Lugo) a woman emerges from the house of death just before the cortege sets out and gives bread and wine to all guests, who are expected to respond by paying the priest for pozas on the way to the graveyard. In Forcarey (Pontevedra) several women march ahead of the coffin, carrying baskets of bread and skins of wine. After the interment, the paid mourners seat themselves around the grave to enjoy the provender, which is their payment (García Ramos 1912, p. 24). Sometimes the statutes of burial societies specify that each member who attends a funeral is entitled to receive a certain quantity of bread and wine from the family.

The custom of offering bread and wine to friends who come to a funeral is closely associated with that of offering alms to the poor of the village. Whether the recipient is a friend or beggar, he is being repaid for services. The former pays the priest for responses, and the latter offers, at the very least, prayers for the soul of the dead. Marcos de Sande gives an example from Casar de Cáceres), where a wealthy family will ask fifty poor people to march in the cortege, each carrying a candle. At the close of the ceremony each of these *veleros* is given two pesetas (1950, p. 140). In San Felíu de Guixols (Gerona) food was carried to the cemetery in baskets and was distributed to the assembled poor after the interment. The custom of giving food or money to the poor appears to be, and to have been, more important in northern Spain than in the south.

Traditionally, during funeral services and sometimes at subsequent Masses offerings of bread and food, and usually of wine also, were made in the church. Regardless of how they were made, these offerings were considered a contribution to the priest, who might keep all, divide with other church personnel, or give to the poor. In León and Old Castile it was common to place the offering on the catafalque at the misa del cuerpo presente. In other places each person attending the service, as he advanced to kiss the stole during the offering, deposited his bread in a basket beside the priest. Food offerings were probably at one time common in all Spain, not only for funerals but for church services in general. But the custom seems to have persisted longest in the north. Few traces remain in Andalusia and the south, and we found none at all in the Levante.

Usually during each of the nine nights following the burial relatives and a few friends gather in the home of the deceased for prayers, and on the ninth day a novena is held or a Mass is said.

Subsequent remembrances of the dead are observed, in many places, on the anniversary of the death, and, of course, in all Spain on the days of All Souls and All Saints. Vergara describes how in small villages in Segovia during the first year a member of the family each day came to the spot on the floor corresponding to the ancient family tomb and covered it with a black cloth, on which were placed lighted candles and a piece of bread. After Mass the priest went to the tomb to pray a response, and the relative then gave him the bread and a small coin (1909, p. 49). In parts of Salamanca at the end of a year a bereaved family placed a white cloth on the floor of the church and on it a smaller black one. A candle was placed at each of the four corners, and on the cloth a loaf of bread and a jar of wine were laid; or, if the family was wealthy, a fanega or two of wheat was substituted for the bread.

The length and intensity of the mourning period vary with the relationships involved, with the part of the country, and perhaps also with the social classes concerned. A state of mourning is indicated publicly by signs in the house, by dress, and by actions. In southern Spain, where it is customary periodically to whitewash the exterior of the house, this is not done, and the facade becomes dirty and streaked. Pictures and mirrors are draped with black or turned face against the wall, and flowers and other decorations are removed from their customary places. Brilliant objects are thought to show poor taste, so polished copper kettles and other bright ornaments are removed or allowed to be blackened by kitchen smoke.

Widows must follow much stricter rules than others. Often their period of intense mourning lasts four or five years, during the first of which they do not leave the house. Their costume is black, and even in the hottest weather they cover their head with a heavy cloth. In some places they wear a second heavy skirt, reversed, in such fashion that it may be thrown up behind over their heads and faces in the manner of a shawl, almost completely hiding their features. In the Cerro de Andévalo region (Huelva) restrictions were particularly severe. Widows were expected to keep their hair cut short, for life, if they were middle-aged or over, or for three years, if they were younger. For a year they could not sit on chairs, and made use of small round cane stools known as *redondeles*. They were not supposed to think of eating. To show their disdain for food they cooked in tiny pots which, however, must have been filled to the brim, for a common saying in the area, to describe something filled to overflowing, is *está como olla de viuda*, "that's like a widow's pot." Widows were supposed to make no noise, a custom carried to the point where, when kitchen duties required the use of the mortar for grinding, the woman was expected to disappear under the bed to execute the task.

Particularly among the Basques death and mourning rites involve domestic animals. When a farm owner dies, a survivor knocks on the bee-hives and says, "Little bees, little bees, make wax; your master has died and needs light in the church." Cattle are also informed of a death, and if they are lying down, they are forced to stand up in respect (María de Askue 1935, p. 222). In Tarragona and Huesca bells worn by animals are removed when the owner dies (Casas Gaspar 1947, p. 368). In parts of eastern Spain mules and burros sometimes have black silk ornaments added to their trappings to indicate death in the owner's family.

Various superstitions are associated with the soul and with death. From Galicia and Asturias comes a particularly rich harvest of such beliefs. Here shooting stars are said to be the souls of persons who are dying. Souls of the dead are thought to travel in whirlwinds, and to guard against harm the person who sees one crosses himself. It is believed that souls return to their homes to warm themselves by the fire at night; therefore, to avoid pushing them unceremoniously into the fire or out the door, one never sweeps at night. A child should not sleep while a corpse is being removed from the house; otherwise it may not wake up. In parts of Galicia the first chick of a brood is offered to the priest, for the souls of the dead of the family. The custom is general in Spain of erecting a cross at the site of a violent death, and traditionally the passerby is expected to throw a pebble at its foot, murmuring a short prayer as he does so.

Burial societies or religious brotherhoods known as *cofradías* or *herman-dades* continue to play important religious, social, and economic roles in the rites of death. Modern burial societies, although descended from the Medieval sodality system, appear to have their immediate roots in the seventeenth and eighteenth centuries. A burial society, to which a member makes small weekly or monthly payments, underwrites all or part of the costs of the funeral and pays for one or more Masses of the Dead. Surviving members help with the burial and the arranging of the body, accompany the funeral procession to the grave, and attend the wake and novena. The cofradía is thus economic, in that it is a mutual aid society; it is social, in that in time of grief and trial the friends of the survivors help to relieve them of as much work as possible; and it is religious, in that provision is made for the well-being of the dead in after life.

These societies are characteristic of all Spain, though perhaps their intensity is somewhat less in the east and south, and their activities are most marked north of the Guadarramas. The names most commonly found today are *de la Vera Cruz* ("of the True Cross") and *de las Animas* ("of the Souls"), although other names are often encountered, such as *de la Paz* ("of the Peace") and *del Sagrado Corazón de Jesus* ("of the Sacred Heart of Jesus").[5]

Spanish cemeteries vary in form, particularly between the north and the south. Traditionally, in cities and towns, and in villages in the south, people are buried in wall niches or, if they are wealthy, in pantheons. By paying a large sum a family may buy a niche permanently, but with greater frequency a niche is bought for five years, after which the bones are removed and deposited on the bone pile or, if the family wishes and is able to continue small payments, the corpse will be left unmolested. Because of the great age of many cemeteries it is almost impossible to dig a new grave without turning up skulls and long bones of previous interments. Little feeling seems to be attached to these, and they are tossed back into the grave when it is filled up. Since most graves are marked only by a wooden cross—or at best an iron one—the exact site is covered over and lost after a few years. And, since cemeteries are almost invariably walled, it is difficult to expand beyond these limits.

In northwestern Spain as far south as Old Castile skulls and long bones were often embedded in cemetery walls or over the gate, on which inscriptions not infrequently were placed. Thus, in Tudanca (Santander) the passerby was reminded that "Thus far, vanity; from here on, eternity," while in Liérganes, in the same province, one was asked to ponder that "From nothing we have come, and to nothing we return; God will sentence us, according to what we merit." Among the folk, cemeteries are considered good places to avoid at night. Will-o'-the-wisp lights, said to be particularly common in cemeteries, are popularly referred to as *almas en pena*, "souls in purgatory."

On the death of adults, provision must be made for the inheritance of property. The legal and popular rules that govern the distribution of private property following the death of the owner reflect marked geographical differences in concepts of family structure and relationships. The biggest differences are those between the northernmost tier of old kingdoms, from Galicia to Catalonia, as contrasted to Old Castile and the lands to the south, repopulated by Castilians, where Castilian law prevailed. In these latter areas equal division of property between all children, including daughters, is the rule. This tends toward a fractioning of land into uneconomic units which, however, as Pitt-Rivers recently has pointed out for a part of Andalusia, is counterbalanced by a process of agglomeration in which the more successful farmers buy up the small, uneconomic plots of others. Since a real love of the land as such is lacking in these town-life-oriented people, there appears to be no strong desire to keep a particular piece of land in the family generation after generation (1954, p. 46).

Fractioning of land is in reality not so pronounced as the inheritance system would seem to indicate. Among the upper classes, marked generally by fewer children, careful marriages, including those between cousins, facilitate the maintenance of family properties over the generations, and promote the *latifundismo* which characterizes Andalusia (Pitt-Rivers 1954, pp. 79, 102-104). Consequently, at best the lower-class family has little permanency as a property-owning institution, and most of these families are landless. Local values favor the nuclear family, and property laws and mores are not sufficiently strong to place a premium on larger functional units.

In Andalusia property is usually not transferred until the owner's death. In other parts of the country some or all of the father's holdings may be divided while he still lives. In Segovia formerly it was common for an aging father to distribute his property among his children in equal shares, following Castilian law. Vergara says that by the beginning of the twentieth century this system was being modified, primarily because of the failure of the heirs to recognize the traditional responsibility of looking after old and landless parents (1909, pp. 38-39). Altamira found a similar situation in Alicante: custom dictated that the father, when old, divide the land among his children, reserving a small pension or proportion for his maintenance, but frequently filial obligations were ignored, with consequent suffering for the parents (1905, pp. 20-22).

An interesting variation of the usual inheritance patterns occurs in the Huerta de Murcia: the youngest son inherits the family home and such property as may still remain with the parents. Ruiz-Funes explains this as a function of the father's having given dowries and additional property to the older children as they married and moved away, while the youngest son, remaining to care for the old people, is rewarded in this way (1916, pp. 66-68).

The traditional family communal or corporate concept of property in northern Spain is in marked contrast to the patterns just described. Various Spanish writers, stimulated by LePlay, have described the *compañia gallega* and the similar families of Navarra, Aragón, and Catalonia (e.g.,

Aguilera y Arjona 1916; García Ramos 1909, 1912; Lezón 1903). The ostensible function of such an arrangement, even though the results suggest it is not very effective, is to maintain the family property in units of a size that can be effectively exploited. In the Galician compañía one son, or occasionally a daughter, is elected by the father to receive the home and the major share of the properties. The passing of the estate to the heir, the *petrucio*, is accomplished in one of two ways: by testament at the death of the donor, and by *capitulaciones matrimoniales*, at the time of the marriage contract. In the latter case it is agreed that, following marriage of the heir, the father will gradually withdraw from the active management of home and farm, and the petrucio will assume corresponding responsibilities. The heir is obligated to care for his parents during their lifetimes, eating with them at *una misma mesa y manteles*, i.e., at the same table.

All unmarried siblings live in the paternal home, and siblings of both sexes receive a dowry from the family holdings when they marry. In parts of Galicia the petrucio is required to take back and maintain any of his sisters who, for any reason, finds herself without means of support. In more rigid forms of the compañía married sons with their children continue to live in the family home and to work for the common good in forms that have been compared to the Slavic *zadruga* (Lezón 1903, p. 67).

The passing of an estate to a favored heir at the time of the marriage contract is also traditional in Navarra. Following marriage the principal heir and his wife live in the home of the father who, although no longer legal owner, has the right to manage the property and enjoy the usufruct as long as he wishes. Then, as in Galicia, as the parents grow older, they little by little pass the responsibility and decision-making on to the heir and his wife. Unmarried siblings continue to live in the family home and to work for the economic good of the group (Yaben 1916, pp. 1-42). The heir, the *hereu*, by virtue of his position enjoys special consideration; he is expected to work less than the more unfortunate children and is allowed to spend more time in hunting and other diversions. The unmarried brothers who continue working in the family home never enjoy full social adulthood until and unless they marry and set up their own homes. They do not attend village council meetings, are never elected to public office, and do not represent the family upon any important occasions (Violant 1949, pp. 319-320). Although the heir usually is the eldest son, the father has complete freedom in making a choice, and may even select a daughter.

In Upper Aragón and much of Catalonia similar inheritance systems prevail. The hereu or *pubilla* is named in the marriage contract, but the parents retain control of the land and its profits for as long as they wish. The remaining sons and daughters are entitled by law to a dowry, but the estate remains essentially intact when passed along to the principal heir (de la Fuente 1921, pp. 27-28, 42-44, 58-60). In the Upper Ampurdán (Gerona) when, because of the lack of a son, a daughter was named heir, her husband assumed the family name in order to maintain the line, publicly stating in the written marriage agreement that he would do so (Violant 1949, p. 325).

In the Balearic Islands the heir is usually but not always the eldest son. He remains in the family home, gradually taking over rights and duties from his father, who continues to live in the same house. Younger brothers consciously or unconsciously attribute a certain superiority and respect to the heir although, according to Navarro, dishonesty and quarreling about the family patrimony are by no means uncommon (1901, pp. 142-146).

The use of written or verbal forms in disposing of property, either in marriage contracts or testaments, is a function of the degree of sophistication of the testator. Often in small villages the priest traditionally listens to the donor as he expresses his will and is the final judge in carrying out its provisions. On other occasions notaries prepare elaborate statements. López Morán describes the proceedings in La Cabrera (León). The elderly or sick man called for the priest, schoolteacher, or whoever "best understood the pen" to record his verbal wishes. Once the will was written, five neighbors were called in, and in a loud voice the writer read the conditions, to which the testator indicated his approval. Then the witnesses signed the document, were given a glass of wine, excused themselves, and withdrew, to return only at the time of the execution of the will (1900, pp. 204-206).

Hoyos Sáinz and Hoyos Sancho (1947, p. 366) suggest that three major areas of death practices may be marked out in Spain, and my observations confirm theirs. These three areas generally correlate with those pointed out for courtship and marriage customs (pp. 139-140). In the north, in a region extending from Galicia through the Old Kingdom of León, Old Castile, the Basque Provinces, and along the Pyrenees, one finds the greatest intensity of funerary practices: the opening of windows or removal of roof tiles for the soul to escape, the restrained wake, professional mourners, the symbolic distribution of bread, the gluttonous banquet served in the church sacristy, and the importance of burial cofradías. In contrast, the area of least intensity—with certain noteworthy exceptions such as the baile del angelito—is that of the Mediterranean littoral, from Barcelona south to Andalusia. The remaining central part of Spain forms an intermediate area, which retains many of the northern customs, but which in general does not show the same degree of intensity. In this area, however, the region facing Portugal—Cáceres, Badajoz, and Huelva—in the more remote parts, at least, there is a marked retention of old custom.

COMPARISONS AND COMMENTS

Since in Catholic countries the basic social and spiritual patterns for meeting death are based on Church dogma and ritual, the more important Hispanic American funeral practices must be explained as the result of formal processes of culture transmission. Fals-Borda, for example, points out that in Saució (Colombia) burial rules were laid down by the archbishop in 1556 (1955, p. 211, fn. 10). On the other hand, some of the superstitions and practices associated with death and funerals presumably owe their presence in America to chance; individual colonists perpetuated them, without the aid of formal Church mechanisms. Among these may be noted the Dominican belief paralleling that of Navas de Madroño (Cáceres), where all water in a house is thrown out when there is a death because it is thought the departing soul bathes itself (Emilio Jiménez 1927, p. 27), and the custom of closing the eyes of a corpse so it will not call to death other members of the family (Rigoberto Paredes 1920, p. 150, in Bolivia; Valdizán and Maldonado 1922, p. 15, in Peru).

Village inheritance patterns are not well described in Hispanic America, but in general the south Spanish rule of equal inheritance—or at least the absence of rigid primogeniture—seems to prevail. In Tzintzuntzan, for example, a common practice is for a widow to receive half, and the children, male and female, to divide equally the remainder. When the widow dies, the surviving children again divide equally (Foster 1948a, p. 176). In Tzintzuntzan, as in Murcia, the youngest son often ends up with the family house, since older brothers and sisters have already married and established their homes (*ibid.*, p. 176). In Spanish America the disposition of property in marriage contracts, at least in rural circles, is not found, and I know of nothing resembling the pattern of the compañia gallega.

Although we may recognize that the basic outlines of funerary procedures in Spanish America are formally introduced, it appears that informally introduced elements are drawn particularly from Extremadura, western Andalusia, and perhaps New Castile, to a much greater extent than other areas. The exaggerated death customs described for northwestern Spain are generally absent in America while, at the same time, except for the baile del angelito, east Spanish observances appear to have little specific similarity to America. New World inheritance patterns, too, suggest the influence of south Spain rather than other areas.

REFERENCES

All specific references to communities not otherwise noted are drawn from the Atheneum Questionnaire.

Aguilera y Arjona (1916), Altamira y Crevea (1905), Arco y Garay (1930), Barandiarán (1949), Cabal (1925b, 1928), Caro Baroja (1943, 1949b), Casas Gaspar (1947), Coloma y Santana (1930), Davillier (1949), Ford (1846), García Ramos (1909, 1912), Giner Arivau (1886), Hoyos Sáinz (1945), Hoyos Sáinz and Hoyos Sancho (1947), de la Fuente y Pertegaz (1921), Lasaga y Larreta (1934), Lezón (1903), López Morán (1900), Llano Rosa (1922), Marcos de Sande (1950), María de Azkue (1935), Méndez Plaza (1900), Montoto (1883), Navarro (1901), Pitt-Rivers (1954), Porras Márquez (1916), Répide (1914), Risco (1946), Ruiz-Funes (1916), Thalamas Labandíbar (1931), Valladares (1884), Vergara y Martín (1909), Violant y Simorra (1949), Yaben y Yaben (1916).

NOTES

[1] This is a common practice in Spanish America (e.g., Velásquez 1957, p. 218, in Colombia).

[2] The baile del angelito was once widespread in Hispanic America, and has been described for most countries. I witnessed it among the Popoluca Indians in Mexico in 1941.

[3] Exaggerated wailing at funerals and wakes often occurs in Hispanic American villages, but professional lloronas seem to have been rare in America. Valdizán and Maldonado report them in Peru (1922, p. 35). In the Dominican Republic there are women of wide fame as competent weepers, whom Emilio Jiménez compares to las plañideras griegas y romanas, but they are not paid for their services (1927, p. 27).

[4] Gillin describes first- and second-class funerals in Moche (1947, p. 150), although in many Hispanic American villages this Spanish class distinction has disappeared. I do not know how widespread in America the cuerpo presente funeral is. It is recorded in Putla, Oaxaca (Mexico) (Galván del Rio 1942, p. 150), and Peru (Toor 1949, p. 52).

[5] Burial cofradías apparently are not uncommon in America, but they are not generally described in ethnographical literature. Some may be modern in origin.

CHAPTER XIII

RELIGION

In Spanish America

CATHOLICISM in America represents one of the important Spanish categories of planned or formally transmitted culture. In dogma and doctrine the religion is the same in the Old World and the New. It could not be otherwise. Next to physical conquest, the primary concern of the Crown as well as the Church was the spiritual conquest of the natives of America and the establishment and maintenance of the faith in the new lands. For this reason we find a high degree of homogeneity in religious practices in all countries. Mass is said each day in churches where there is a resident priest, infants are baptized, couples are married in the church, and the dead are buried with the blessing of the priest. The yearly round of feast days is standardized and is essentially uniform from one community to the next. Each town or village has its patron saint, whose day is usually the occasion for the major fiesta of the community. Religion plays an important role in nearly all aspects of life, and through the pattern of brotherhoods, or *mayordomías*, social status, as well as religious merit, is achieved.

In Spain

An examination of religious practices in Spain reveals many things familiar to those who know Hispanic America, some things known to the inhabitants of specific areas, others perhaps known to very few or not at all. For purposes of investigation, Spanish religious manifestations may be grouped under two major headings: the basic cult, as expressed in the regular observance of the seven sacraments of baptism, confirmation, matrimony, extreme unction, the Eucharist, penance, and Holy Orders; and the specialized cults of Christ, Mary, and the saints, which give rise to the annual cycle of feast days, the fiestas of patron saints of towns and cities, pilgrimages great and small, folk drama, pious legends, miracle stories, and a host of superstitions and minor beliefs.

Churches are the first thing that catch the visitor's eye. As the focal point of a majority of religious activities they reflect in construction and furnishings the uses to which they are put, as well as, perhaps, personal whims and idiosyncracies of parishioners. In spite of regional variation there is, in village Spain, a certain harmony in the plan and fitting of churches. Usually they are solidly built of well cut and trimmed stone and are provided with a single bell tower. In Andalusia churches are sometimes whitewashed, particularly the hermitages which house miraculous images of saints and the Virgin. It is in Andalusia also that one often finds, instead of the solid square tower, the graceful whitewashed open-arch construction which carries several bells silhouetted against a blue sky. Occasionally, but not often, separate church towers carry bells. Many churches have covered porches, either across the front or along the right-hand side; perhaps more often than not, an entrance on the right side rather than on the front facade is the rule. In the Castiles the two-shed slate roofs of many churches are higher over the altar than over the rest of the nave, a construction which, when balanced by a tower, produces a peculiar "sway-back" effect.[1]

Numbers of bells in a church range from two or three in the most humble structures, to twenty-four in the *giralda* tower of the cathedral of Sevilla, and perhaps more in others. Regardless of importance, each bell has been baptized and named, and is a member of the Christian community. A few bells are very old, but most have a tendency to crack with time and use, so that it is uncommon to find one with a date much earlier than the eighteenth century. The four bells in the Puente Genil (Córdoba) parish church are typical of many. The smallest, familiarly known as *La Chica* ("The Little One"), carries the legend (in translation): "I am the voice of the Angel, that sounds on high, Ave María, gratia plena, 1789. This bell was made and paid for at the instigation of Excmo. Señor Duque de Medinaceli, Marqués de Priego." The *Doce* bell is so known because it is sounded at noon, and its legend reads, "S. Luis Obispo, ora pro nobis, 1826. We were cast by order of S. E., los Maestros Villas." Around the rim of *Las Animas* bell ("The Souls"), so named because of its use by the confraternity of Souls, one may read, "San Rafael ora pro nobis. Me facit los Villas, 1826." And finally *La Gorda* ("The Fat One") reveals that it is "Our Lady of los Remedios, ora pro nobis, 1789. Francisco de Otero made me. This bell was made and paid for at the instigation of Excmo. Sor. Duque de Medinaceli, Marqués de Priego."

In addition to bells many church towers also have a *matraca*, a hollow wooden cross or similar construction on which hammers are made to sound when the cross is revolved. The matraca is used to call people to Mass from Maundy Thursday to Easter Saturday, a period in which the bells are mute, following the crucifixion of Christ.

The interiors of village churches are marked by a paucity of furnishings. Pews and chairs are found in a few, but more often than not they are lacking, except for parallel benches facing each other on each side and in front of the altar, reserved for members of the town council, whose ceremonial presence at Mass emphasizes the union between Church and State. Women and children in some places occupy the section behind these pews, kneeling on the flagstone floor or on low prayer stools, while men stand in the rear of the building, with the older boys and youths relegated to the choir loft. In other places, as in Latin America, women occupy the right-hand side of the nave and men the left-hand side. Pictures of the Fourteen Stations of the Cross hang from the walls, and images of Christ, the Virgin, and saints stand on side altars or recline (as doeŕ the image of Christ) on biers or in glass cases. Music is provided by harmoniums. In larger churches and cathedrals the great organs are marked by a series of trumpet pipes which project horizontally from the foot of the tall pipes, a Spanish peculiarity noted by Davillier nearly a century ago (1949, p. 14).

Votive or ex-voto offerings may be seen on or near images which are thought to have particular wonder-working powers, although the custom today is less intense than in Spanish America. Ex-votos of silver, tin, or wax are made in the form of arms, legs, eyes, female breasts, heads, and entire human figures, usually in bas-relief. A sufferer hangs the figure appropriately symbolic of his ailment on the image of his special devotion, at the same time lighting a candle and offering a prayer, hopeful that this token of faith will bring relief. Ex-votos for animals are also hung.

Other ex-votos are similar to Mexican *milagros:* painted wood or tin sheets which depict, in crude folk art, an accident or illness from which the supplicant was rescued by his appeal to the Virgin or a saint. Subías Galter reproduces two, one showing a workman falling from the roof of a three-storied building, the other a *peón* being gored by a bull in a country bullfight (1948, pls. 470, 471). But this type of ex-voto is no longer common, for many of the old ones were destroyed during the Civil War.

The custom of ex-votos, Christian for centuries, goes back at least to the Greek temples of Asklēpios, and in Spain it is nearly as old as civilization itself. Tiny clay feet, presumably votive offerings, were turned up in the excavation of the pre-Roman city of Numancia (Soria), and today may be seen in the museum in Soria.

Much of the basic cult—and particularly the rites associated with the sacraments of baptism, confirmation, marriage, and death—has already been described. Mass is said according to the regular rules of the Church, with special offices for the many feast days of the year. The playing of the Marcha Real, the "Royal March," on feast days at the elevation of the Host is a characteristic note not found, for obvious reasons, in Hispanic America. In small villages, where there is no organ, a stringed orchestra may provide this music, while in Galicia bagpipe players produce a reverberating din within the stone walls of the church. In keeping with Catholic custom the consecrated Host alone, without wine, is given to laymen when they take communion. Spanish priests wear the tonsure, a shaved spot the size of a silver dollar on the crown of the head.

The cults of God and Christ, the Virgin Mary, and the saints take many visible forms: the annual cycle of feast days with the special offices for Mass, often marked by folk-religious dramas and other simpler popular customs; pious legends and miracle stories which are frequently associated with pilgrimages; the town and village fiestas of local importance, honoring patron saints and other religious characters who have played important roles in the past, and the like. The most important of the feast days and special seasons of the cult of God are The Circumcision of our Lord Jesus Christ (January 1), Epiphany (January 6), Candlemas (Presentation of

Christ in the Temple, February 2), Lent, Holy Week, Ascension Day, The Invention of the Cross (May 3), Corpus Christi, and The Feast of the Nativity on Christmas. The most important feast days that give outward recognition to the Mariana cult are Candlemas (Feast of the Purification, February 2), The Annunciation (March 25), St. Anne's Day, honoring the mother of Mary (July 26), The Assumption (August 15), The Nativity of the Blessed Virgin (September 8), and The Feast of the Immaculate Conception of the Blessed Virgin Mary (December 8). The rites associated with most of these occasions are described in the following two chapters.

Spanish pious legends belong to the cults of Christ, Mary, and the saints. In or near hundreds of towns and villages the traveler may see, usually at the outskirts of the settlement and frequently on a hilltop, a hermitage *(hermita)*, a small chapel erected in honor of an image of the Virgin or a saint which, found under miraculous circumstances, is accorded special homage as patron and for its wonder-working powers. Usually this homage takes the form of an annual pilgrimage or town fiesta commemorating the discovery of the image.

Miracle legends which account for the finding of images of the Virgin are highly stylized and constitute one of the most important forms of Spanish folk-religious literature. The common tradition is that during the Visigothic era a multitude of images were paid homage by the Goths and that, with the rapid Moorish advance, these images were quickly hidden in caves, canyons, and other out-of-the-way places, to be lost and forgotten for hundreds of years. Then, as the reconquest rolled back the Moors, the images were rediscovered, one by one. Almost invariably the image appears and speaks to a humble person, usually a shepherd but occasionally a shepherdess, who advises the unbelieving townspeople. At last they come and, convinced of the authenticity of the miracle, carry the image to their village, where they immediately set about erecting a chapel. But next day the image has disappeared, and after long search it is found at the spot where it first appeared. Often the image is carried a second and a third time to the village before the villagers realize that the Virgin has taken this way to show that she wishes her chapel to be built where she was found. In other stories, the image floats to shore in a box which, when the Christians try to carry it beyond a certain point, becomes so heavy that it cannot be moved. Thus the people know where the chapel is to be built.

These legends of the Virgin relate the discovery or rediscovery of the sacred image. Miracle legends about images of Christ or the saints differ; these explain how the image came to a certain place. In a stock tale an image has been ordered by the community from a famous sculptor and, drawn in a cart by oxen or lashed to the back of a mule, it is being delivered. But at some unexpected point along the route the mule drops dead or the oxen refuse to budge, and it is found that the weight of the image is so great that it cannot be moved. A dispute arises between the inhabitants of the community that has ordered and paid for the image, and those of the place where the image rests. Eventually it is recognized that the image, through this device, has expressed its desire to remain where it is. Then a church or chapel is built in which to house it, a celebration is held, and the custom is repeated on subsequent years until the tradition of the annual fiesta is established.[2]

"Miraculous" images are graded in importance. Some, like Our Lady of Monserrat, atop wild crags in the province of Barcelona, are internationally famous. Others are known throughout the country: the Virgin of Pilar in Zaragoza, Our Lady of Rocío in Almonte (Huelva), the Macarena Virgin in the Triana barrio of Sevilla, and Our Lady of Guadalupe in the great Franciscan monastery in the hills of Cáceres, to name a few. The tiny, almost black-faced, richly robed image of Guadalupe is not that of the Mexican image of the same name (which is, of course, a painting), but the connection between the two seems indisputable. In the choir wall of the Spanish Monastery there is a figure now known as "Guadalupe de México," reputedly carved in 1499, thirty-two years before the appearance of the Virgin of Tepeyac (Rubio 1926, pp. 228-229). The image is by no means the same as the one in Mexico: the Spanish image wears a crown, added at a later date; the Virgin holds an infant Jesus and looks to the left rather than to the right. Still, there is an undeniable similarity in "feel" between the two images, perhaps due, more than anything else, to the wavy lines or rays of light which illuminate both figures and, to a lesser extent, to the rather general features of the crescent moon base above a single Cherub's head. Certainly, in view of the fact that Franciscan friars were the first missionaries to arrive in Mexico, less than ten years before the appearance of the Mexican Virgin, it is not surprising that the two places should be associated in name and legend.

Still other images are of provincial or local importance, the object of the most animated devotion for a few thousand persons but relatively unknown beyond regional boundaries. Such is that of the *Virgen de la Peña* of Puebla de Guzmán (Huelva), whose fiesta and romería are described in chapter 15.

The saints, as intercessors between man and God second only in importance to the Virgin Mary, are the object of universal veneration. Each individual, depending on his name, home town, occupation, and personal choice feels a particular bond with several saints and a special and personal obligation to venerate them. Baptism confers upon an infant the protection of the saint whose name is bestowed on him, and the obligation, usually pleasurable, to honor the saint on the "name" day. As a member of a community, every individual also owes allegiance to the patron of the city, town, or village: the Madrileño to San Isidro, the Barcelonese to Santa Eulalia, the Pamplonese to San Fermín, and so forth. Each community patron is honored with special observances on the saint's day, and often this is the principal fiesta of the year. Then, as a worker, a member of a craft or profession, every individual has still another patron: farmers, San Isidro; masons and bricklayers, San Antonio

de Padua; carpenters, San José; midwives, San Ramón Nonato; silversmiths, San Eloy; doctors, San Cosme and San Damián; and on through an
enormous list.

Still other saints are appealed to in time of special need or trial, particularly illness, but also by the lovelorn, the would-be diviner, and even
the thief. Thus, the sufferer from throat ailments appeals to San Blas;
from toothache, to Santa Apolonia; from eye trouble, to Santa Lucía;
from epilepsy, to San Pablo. San Antonio de Padua, with whose images
one always seems to feel particularly at ease, will aid one in finding lost
or desired objects, and should the good saint be slow, he may expect
to find himself hung upside down in a well until he delivers the goods.
And of the tormentors of the good saint, the most demanding are young
maidens who, it seems, are forever plagued with the problem of sweethearts. The thief, who finds himself in a tight spot and momentarily
decides the honest life is after all the best, appeals to San Dimas, the good
thief on the cross beside Christ. Sterile women may appeal to Santa Ana,
the mother of Mary, and those who fear they have been bewitched ask
the intercession of Santa Cecilia.

Devotion to saints is shown by prayers, by the lighting of candles
before the images and altars, by votive offerings, by participation in the
confraternities which are charged with major fiestas as well as minor
devotions, by participation in dramas, such as the *autos sacramentales*
and the *Moros y Cristianos*, and by pilgrimages. Of all the pilgrimages in
Spain the one to Santiago de Compostela, to pay homage to Spain's patron
saint, James, was historically the most important. July 25, the anniversary
of his discovery, is a major feast day in Spain, and pilgrims come from
many parts of the country to participate in the rites in Santiago. But,
rather surprisingly, popular manifestations outside Galicia are rare, and
observances are for the most part limited to church services.

The pattern of major pilgrimages is of little importance today in Spain,
although religiously motivated visits to the shrines of wonder-working
images are still exceedingly common. Institutionalized pilgrimages now
usually take the form of the romería [3] in which people join together, often
as members of religious sodalities, in making a gay outing to visit and
participate in the annual fiesta in honor of a saint or image of the Virgin.

The ancient system of cofradías and hermandades, of confraternities,
sodalities, and religious brotherhoods, underlies and activates almost all
popular religious fiestas. The modern organizations are largely sacramental in nature. Hermandades, as they are most often called (the term
"cofradía" is, however, still common), are devices for the individual
reaffirmation of religious faith and for the collective sponsorship of
fiestas or of images which are a part of fiestas. They also often have
important social aspects, sometimes approaching the function of men's
clubs in other cultures.

Hermandades differ from place to place in organization, members, and
officers, and terminology, but basic patterns are much the same. An

hermandad usually is headed by an *hermano mayor*, an "elder brother," normally elected for a specific period but sometimes serving for life. Members are known as *hermanos*, "brothers." When a sodality is known as a cofradía, participants usually are referred to as *cofrades*, and sometimes simply as *socios*, "members." The variation in organization can perhaps best be illustrated by examples, most of which are taken from field notes.

The Hermandad de San Benito, which is charged with the annual fiesta and romería to the shrine of the patron saint of Cerro de Andévalo (Huelva), is headed by a near-hereditary governing board of twelve hermanos mayores ("elder brothers") who elect their successors, usually sons of the deceased. Any other man in the town may become an *hermano menor* ("younger brother") upon request and payment of a small annual sum. Other officials are elected biennially from among the elder brothers: *prioste* (chief administrator, sometimes called "president"), *secretario* ("secretary"), and *depositario* ("treasurer"). Formerly there was an alcalde ("mayor") as well, but the position was dropped for lack of duties, although other hermandades in the town still have their alcaldes. A mayordomo is named annually to manage the fiesta itself. Often he is one of the twelve elder brothers, but any man in town may ask this *cargo* of the town mayor, who in turn advises the priest, who then informs the elder brothers. If the solicitant is acceptable to all persons, he is officially named. The mayordomo must pay for food and wine for the hermandad and its guests, for *la musica* (a single musician who plays the three-holed gaita and *tamboril* drum), and the Mass. Serving as mayordomo is a considerable honor, probably the greatest the town offers, and every successful man is expected to validate his position by serving at least once. Sometimes several men will simultaneously share the cargo of mayordomo.

In Belinchón (Cuenca) the fiesta in honor of the village patron, Jesús Nazareno, is sponsored by a mayordomía which differs considerably from the usual Spanish cofradía. Three mayordomos, a secretary, and a treasurer are elected in open town meeting on Easter Sunday, to serve three years, and they together constitute the mayordomía. There are no other types of members. Belinchón is also unusual in the use of the term "mayordomía" (as in Spanish America) rather than the more common "hermandad" or "cofradía."

Comparisons and Comments

Since Catholicism in America represents, both in basic outline and much detail, planned introduction of ritually pure Spanish forms, it might appear that religion would not be an especially rewarding topic with which to study the acculturation process. Imposition is an effective way in which to change culture, but often we feel that more is to be learned from situations in which there is also a significant degree of choice on the part of the peoples affected.

On closer examination religion turns out to be a particularly fruitful subject in the acculturation process. For not only does a proselytizing religion have an elaborate and institutionalized theology which must be transmitted without major change, but it is also marked by an associated body of beliefs and practices representing informal accretions over the centuries. These beliefs and practices are of diverse origins—pagan, superstitious—and for one reason or another they have received approval, or at least tolerance, on the part of the clergy, who feel that they do not constitute a threat to the central cult. Apparently any proselytizing religion must make certain compromises in the mass conversion of peoples of different faiths. This was true in the conquest of Europe by primitive Christianity, and it was equally true in the Catholic conquest of Hispanic America. Some pagan images in the Mediterranean have survived to this day in the guise of saints or the Virgin, just as in Indian America the phrase "idols behind altars" has come to symbolize the synthesis of certain pre-Conquest beliefs with the dominant religion.

A major missionizing effort gives a Church an unusual opportunity. Since the people toward whom the campaign is directed are presumably unacquainted with the tolerated "fringe" practices of the country from which the missionaries come, and therefore cannot have the emotional associations with them that make them so difficult to extirpate, the undesirable aspects of a religion can simply be withheld. The peoples towards whom the effort is directed can be exposed only to the expurgated or theologically ideal religion. In Spain "devils" dance in churches in some fiestas, devotees walk barefoot over live coals, maidens stick pins into images of the Virgin, a representation of a saint may be hung upside down in a well or stones may be thrown at his bare navel—all in the name of religion. These, and other practices, must represent survivals from pre-Christian times, customs which the Church "captured" and brought within its own body of belief, as the most effective way of coping with the problems of conversions. It is apparent that sixteenth-century missionizers felt that such customs were better left at home and not included in export Catholicism.

If we look at the basic pattern of fiestas in Hispanic America, as manifest in all countries, the picture is surprisingly similar: Epiphany, Candlemas, Lent, Holy Week, Corpus Christi, All Saints' and All Souls' days, and Christmas, plus a fiesta, usually for the patron saint of the community. Presumably these are the feast days the Church considered central to dogma, and the activities of each were thought best calculated to educate Indians in the new faith, as well as to maintain the faith of Iberian settlers. In one part or another of America other customs occur. Devils do dance in some places, but apparently not inside churches, the "sardine" is buried, San Juan fires are lit, the *piñata* appears, San Antonio is hung upside down, and there are even suggestions of fire-walking. But these activities lack the universality of the major activities, and where they occur it seems safe to assume that individuals or groups with particular interest—sometimes clergy, sometimes settlers—introduced them, and for one reason or another they took hold in limited areas only. They are, in contrast to the central dogma and the annual fiesta cycle, best thought of as resulting from informal transmission processes. Church concessions in America to these Spanish fringe religious manifestations are nominal.

In America the Church again was faced with a situation similar to that of a thousand years earlier—the accommodation of approved doctrine and practice to vigorous (and in the eyes of the conquerors, heathen) practices. So again compromises were made. The Virgin of Guadalupe, the patron of America, and especially of Mexico, appeared on the site of the temple of the Aztec maize goddess Tonantzin, conch-shell trumpets are used in at least one famous Mass, and pre-Conquest drums are found in a few out-of-the-way churches. But, much more impressive than such manifestations is the fact that the Church knew what it wanted in America and with remarkable success achieved its goal. The Catholic ceremonial year owes its form to the fact that the Church could encourage the ideal religion and discourage the "fringes," both Spanish and Indian, to produce a basic pattern of striking homogeneity from Mexico to Chile.

REFERENCES

Amades (1955), Davillier (1949), Elen (1950), Izquierdo Moya (1946), Rubio (1926), Subías Galter (1941, 1943, 1948).

NOTES

[1] I have seen this construction in Guatemala and in Izalco (El Salvador). I have not noted it in Mexico.

[2] Morote Best (1953) has made a superb analysis of similar themes in Peru, listing 18 motifs. The Peruvian themes are all obviously based on Spanish origin legends.

[3] In the Middle Ages pilgrims to Rome were known as romeros, after the name of the city, and the pilgrimage itself was called a romería. The terms are universally used in Spain today. In Spanish America the term "romería" is known (e.g., Fals-Borda 1955, p. 216), but in Mexico, where the custom is very widespread, perigrinación is the word most commonly used.

CHAPTER XIV

FEAST DAYS AND FIESTAS: NEW YEARS TO EASTER

IN SPANISH AMERICA

FIESTAS and religious practices are ethnographically the best described of all categories of culture. As one would expect, the principal feast days observed, their organization, and the specific content of celebrations owe their origin to Spanish influence. In all countries there is a rather standard sequence of feast days, the most important of which are Epiphany, Candlemas, Lent, Holy Week and Easter, San Isidro, Corpus Christi, San Juan, All Saints' and All Souls' days, and Christmas. With few exceptions fiestas are organized and financed by religious brotherhoods, and often the obligation to fulfill a vow motivates an individual to undertake costly and time-consuming fiesta responsibilities. Fiesta Masses and processions usually follow standard Church practice, and secular activities, too, such as the *cucaña* greased pole, masked dancers, fireworks, bullfights and horse races stem from common Spanish patterns.

At the same time, the Spanish American fiesta pattern differs from that of Spain in a number of ways. Important peninsular celebrations, such as those of May Day, and of San Blas and Santa Agueda, are rarely if ever found in America. Other occasions, such as the Invention of the Cross and the Assumption, are observed with special Masses, but the dramas found in parts of Spain appear not to have reached the New World. This reduction in feast days in America does not mean that Spain is more varied overall, for native American elements, such as the spectacular Mexican *volador* "dance" have been added to the content of fiestas introduced by the Church, and devout Indians may go directly from Mass to pagan idols in the hills, where food offerings are buried and copal incense is burned.

IN SPAIN

Although much of the traditional yearly round of fiestas has disappeared during the past fifty years, in the smaller towns and villages there are still many things to be seen that probably are not so very different from the time of the Conquest of America and which, certainly, clearly reveal forms ancestral to the activities anthropologists have recorded in Spanish America. In this and the next chapter, which are treated as a unit, the Spanish yearly cycle is described, and many similarities to American fiestas are pointed out in footnotes.

New Year's festivities.—December 31, the day of San Silvestre, is called *año viejo*, the old year, and January 1 is welcomed as *año nuevo*, the new year. Except for the Mass celebrating the circumcision of Christ, New Year celebrations are secular and social rather than religious. The traditional Spanish custom, characteristic of small villages and high society alike, is the New Year's Eve lottery, the "marriage" by lot of partygoers. In the country and among humbler people the custom is known as *echar los años* ("to cast the years") or *echar los estrechos* ("to cast the bonds") while, in more elevated circles, it is grandly called *sorteo de damas y galanes* ("raffle of ladies and lovers"). In both, the form is the same. Names of unmarried partygoers are written on slips of paper, placed in separate containers, mixed, and then drawn two at a time to pair off everyone. These "marriages" last for the evening, or until Epiphany six days later, when another party may be held.

French influence has made itself felt in the cities where, at midnight, each reveler provides himself with a packet of twelve grapes. As the clock begins to strike, grapes are popped in mouths and furiously chewed and swallowed; if any are left at the sound of the stroke of twelve, bad luck will follow in the year. Madrid's main square, the Puerta del Sol, is jammed with crowds on New Year's Eve, waiting so to greet the new year.[1]

January 1 is also a day of popular auguries. The wind which blows on this day, the superstition goes, will be that which will predominate during the year, and the cabañuelas, the 12-day reading of the year's weather also begins in many places on this day (p. 61). The money in one's pocket foretells the money that will be there throughout the year: gold brings gold, silver silver, and copper copper. The characteristics of the first person encountered during the new year also foreshadow luck. A wealthy man brings fortune, a beggar or priest bad luck. But worst of all, in Andalusia at least, is the meeting with a hunchback or a *tuerto*, a one-eyed person. No amount of good fortune can counteract such an inauspicious start to the year.

Epiphany, January 6.—Children receive presents, not on Christmas, but on *el día de los Reyes Magos,* in commemoration of the visit of the Three Kings to the Christ child. According to Spanish legend the kings— Melchor, Gaspar, and Baltasar—go every year to Bethlehem again to pay homage to the infant Jesus, and on their return they visit all children, leaving candies, fruits, and presents with those that have been good throughout the year. Children leave their shoes on an outside balcony, and often place a bit of straw and a dish of water for the horses that bring the Kings. Next morning, shoes are filled with the good things brought by the Kings.

Older children and youths traditionally went to await the Kings, *a esperar a los Reyes Magos,* on the night of January 5. Sometimes these night rambles were organized by parents, one of whom obligingly dressed up as a King for the children to see from afar. But often they were all-night revels which degenerated into street brawls, a development which, if we can believe the constant prohibitions against many Spanish fiestas, characterized the ending of many traditional street celebrations. Nevertheless, in spite of sporadic prohibitions the night parades to look for the Kings was common Spanish practice. Revelers carried cowbells, *almireces* (the old-fashioned druggist's brass mortar and pestle), conch-shell trumpets, whistles, and other noisemakers. Some carried ladders, on which youths would mount to search, as from a crow's nest, the Kings in the distance. At other times the youngest and most credulous were helped into trees with ladders, the better to discern the Kings, and as the youngsters strained their eyes toward the horizon, ladders were surreptitiously removed, a trick which American instigators of "snipe hunts" would look upon with professional admiration.

In small towns in northern Spain the carousing took the form of a "trick or treat" evening: the group sang outside windows, and householders who contributed to the provisions for a picnic were spared the indignities of allusive couplets, of which the singers were masters. Especially characteristic of the north was the custom of making a special occasion of the cake with the hidden *haba*. Not only was the person who found the haba to have good. fortune throughout the year, but he was named *Rey de la Faba*, king of the broad beans. Iribarren cites documents showing that as far back as the fourteenth century the Court of Navarra joined in the fun, and one year fate nominated the son of the royal barber as boy king (1946, p. 116).

Miracle plays also are associated with Epiphany. In simplest form these are little more than processions in which three men dressed as the Kings ride through the streets, Gaspar and Melchor solemn in their white beards, and Baltasar, the black King, the buffoon who jokes with and tricks the children. Today such processions are organized by the municipal governments of many cities, but they can hardly be called spontaneous folk or religious observances.

The true autos sacramentales, the *misterios* of the Middle Ages which taught the doctrine to illiterate folk, are no longer enacted in Spain. As late as 1935 the weekly journal *Estampa* reported as of recent occurrence rude dramas given in various places in the Huerta de Murcia. Groups of men banded together to learn the lines, equip simple stages, and perform the most spectacular scenes from the traditional books. Afterwards they went through the streets of Murcia asking contributions for costs of production and for the inevitable communal meal. The most complete libretto used was that written by Gaspar Fernándes y Avila, a theologian, and printed in Murcia in 1784 (Bolarín 1935a).

This book was but one of a number of its kind, fragments of which continually turn up in small towns. In 1946 Fernández discovered a nearly complete manuscript of an *auto de los Reyes Magos* in the village of Villamol (León), a manuscript copied from older sources in 1880, apparently in part from oral tradition but obviously also based on earlier literary forms which, unlike this one, were entirely in verse. Villamol, as well as other Leonese towns, had had the tradition of giving autos of this type in earlier years, and at Fernández' urging the town agreed to do it again, basing the performance on the manuscript text. The cast, which included, in addition to the Three Kings, the Virgin, St. Joseph, Herod and his wife, Simon, Anne, and pages, ministers, wise men, and shepherds, numbered twenty-six, of whom nine were women (Fernández 1949). A recent auto also is reported from Paredes de Nava (Palencia) as if still reproduced, although the lack of description of the play, except its text, leads one to wonder whether the manuscript survives after the active tradition has died out (Teresa León 1947).[2]

Candlemas, February 2.—Forty days after the birth of Christ his parents presented him in the temple at Jerusalem, and Mary underwent the Jewish rite of purification following childbirth, thus giving origin to the Feast of the Purification, *La Candelaria.* The custom of *la cuarentena,* whereby a new mother remains in her home for forty days leading a life of little activity, is rationalized on the basis of this 40-day interval in the life of Mary. Candlemas is announced by stands of festooned candles outside church doors and in stores specializing in religious objects. Candlemas candles are not everyday tapers. They are the most elaborate expressions of the candlemaker's art, polychromed, beribboned, decorated with a bewildering variety of designs pinched out of the soft wax, works of art the housewife keeps in a conspicuous place in the house during the year.[3] Today in Spain these candles are blessed at Mass and are kept throughout the year in the belief that, if lighted when storms threaten, they will protect the home from lightning. In Asturias it is thought that this is the only day of the year when infants in limbo see light, for the brilliance of the candles lighted in honor of the Virgin reaches even to their far-off abode.

In parts of northern and central Spain children carry a special bread loaf called *torta* and a pair of live doves to Mass, the doves symbolizing the scriptural story that the Virgin, following Mosaic law requiring an offering, brought two doves when she presented herself at the temple for purification.

Horche, a small village ten kilometers south of Guadalajara, has a Candlemas celebration which, although more elaborate than most, illustrates traditional patterns. We visited the village on this day in 1950. About 9:30 the priest, accompanied by acolytes, several white-garbed girls of ten years of age or so, the youths of Catholic Action, and most of the children in town, went to the bakery, from which they emerged shortly thereafter with the torta. This turned out to be a three-layer cake with pink frosting decorated with chicken feathers dyed green, carried on a small litter by several girls. A procession quickly formed, which included another young girl carrying a pair of doves in a small basket. This procession entered the church where it was joined by an altar boy with a processional cross, the image of the Virgin of Dolores, standards, and cantors. Thus enlarged, the procession emerged through the main doors of the church, especially opened for this occasion, and made the circuit of the building to reënter through the smaller porch entrance on the right side. The cake and the doves were placed below the altar, to be picked up for a second procession during Mass which, however, went only as far as the rear of the nave before returning to the altar. After the Mass the cake was carried to the municipal building, where it was raffled off later in the afternoon. The proceeds from the chances, sold at fifteen céntimos by young girls, went to the church.[4]

San Blas, February 3.—San Blas is patron of those who suffer momentary or permanent throat ills. According to legend he lived in the fourth century in Sebaste, Armenia, where he practiced medicine, then became bishop, and finally renounced the world to live as a hermit. Renowned for his piety he was persecuted by non-Christians who rasped his body with an iron comb and then beheaded him. Consequently he is pictured with a rake or big comb. His wide fame, however, rests on saving various people from asphyxiation through choking.[5]

San Blas is commemorated by the custom of making special bread loaves known as *panecillos del santo* or *panes benditos* or *tortas de San Blas*. These little loaves—or in small villages they may be communal cakes—are blessed at Mass and each child is given a bit to eat, an act thought to protect the child from choking throughout the year. If, in spite of this protection, someone chokes, a well-wisher pats him on the back saying *San Blas, adelante o atras* ("Saint Blaise, go ahead or come back") or otherwise invokes the aid of the saint. In some places in central Spain a major fiesta is held on the day of San Blas. That of Almonacid del Marquesado (Cuenca) is described in chapter 16.

Santa Agueda, February 5.—According to legend, Santa Agueda, patron of women, was a beautiful Italian girl of the third century to whom the governor of the province made improper advances. Rebuffed and angered, he ordered her tortured by having her breasts twisted and cut off. As she lay dying in prison Saint Peter came to cure her, but new tortures followed and on February 5, 1252, she died. Santa Agueda is usually represented holding her amputated breasts on a small tray. She is the patron of women not only in general but particularly of those suffering from breast ills, and votive offerings of wax or metal in the shape of breasts are to be found hanging beside her altar in churches all over Spain.

In much of Old Castile women formerly were banded together in formal associations or *cofradías* to celebrate their fiesta on the day of Santa Agueda. In Salamanca, Zamora, Avila, and especially Segovia it was (and is still in a very few places) the custom on this day to name *alcaldesas* (female mayors) and all other town officers from among the married women of the village. On this day the men relinquished all their usual authority and allowed the women, in theory at least, to command. They were dressed in the most elaborate regional costumes available, attended Mass as a group, demanded contributions from townsmen and passersby, ate together, and danced, sometimes with a straw-filled scarecrow which was subsequently burned. In Zamora and Salamanca the festivities were enlivened with *corridas de gallos* (p. 176), the corpse of the unhappy bird being added to the larder for the forthcoming banquet.

In times past there appear to have been males more than a little indignant at the thought of women reigning for a day. The Atheneum questionnaire records the righteous indignation of one such blue-nose around the year 1900.

The stranger who arrives on the days of Santa Agueda is the victim of the impudence of these women, who will not leave him alone until he contributes a sum of money proportional to his dress, which never is less than two *reales* and may be as much as one or two *duros*. The banquets of the women are truly dionesiac orgies unworthy of women who call themselves Christians. It is almost impossible to believe that such things occur at the very gates of Salamanca. *Soy testigo*, I am a witness!

Of all the fiestas of Santa Agueda that of the village of Zamarramala, a scant five kilometers from the city of Segovia and clearly visible from the Alcázar, is the most famous. It is described in chapter 16.[6]

Carnival.—Carnival is called *Carnaval* in Castilian Spanish. The most common etymology of the word is from the Romance *car navale*, the ship-cart, or *currus navalis*, of the ancient Greeks. The term *carnestolendas*, signifying abstention from *carne*, "meat," during Lent is also widely used. The Catalonian form *carnestoltes* (or *carnistoltes*) is a variant of this. In Galicia the term is *entroido*, from the Latin *introitus*, "entrance" or "entering," in the sense of the new year or spring (the new year formerly beginning in the spring rather than in midwinter). This form is from the same root as Castilian *antruejo*, which, strictly speaking, refers to the three festive days of Carnival, Sunday through Tuesday. The term "antruejo" seems particularly characteristic of Old Castile. Covarrubias limits its use to Salamanca (1943, p. 126), although today it is more widespread.

Traditional Spanish carnival observances—today they are prohibited—follow ancient and widespread European patterns. Although the Roman Saturnalia, and to a lesser extent the Lupercalia and Liberalia, are generally credited with being the immediate origin of the carnival theme, it is also accurate to think of it as a long-continuing manifestation of ancient fertility and spring rites. Rademacher traces the path from the Greek worship of Dionysus whose image was drawn through the streets of Athens in a currus navalis, a ship with wheels, while satirical songs were sung and buffoonery reigned (1919). The ship-cart subsequently appears in Egypt, Rome, and central Europe and, as we shall see, has recent manifestations in Spain. In Germany the ship-cart carried a representation of the earth-mother goddess Hertha or, in her place, a plow; in recent times in Spain symbolic plowing has been part of the carnival observance. Other Spanish customs reflecting basic European tradition are the election of a "king," rites of inversion in which the proud are humbled, and the striking of women by men disguised as animals, to promote fertility.

In Spain, Carnival traditionally was considered to be an entire season, beginning as early as the New Year. But there were few special activities until the final weeks before Lent. In much of the country the next to last

Thursday before Carnival is called Jueves de Compadres, while the last one, immediately preceding Carnival, is called Jueves de Comadres or, as an alternate, *Jueves Gordo* or *Jueves Lardero* ("Fat Thursday"). Sometimes all three Thursdays are recognized, with *Lardero* the last, in which case Jueves de Compadres falls two and one half instead of one and a half weeks before Carnival (e.g., as described for Barcelona by Cortada y Sala and Manjarrés 1945, pp. 81-83).

Of these days "Comadres' Thursday" is the most widely observed. Many of the customs associated with it are of considerable antiquity. In seventeenth-century Madrid there was a fiesta in the Prado, and then great crowds swarmed to the banks of the Manzanares for a picnic. Lope de Vega and other playwrights of this period describe the activities of this day. Originally, in all probability, these were days on which true comadres and compadres took turns in inviting each other to eat, or gave each other small presents. But today the common pattern is that of the New Year's Eve drawings, in which at small parties youths and girls are paired off as compadres and comadres through the drawing of lots, a relationship totally distinct from that of true compadres in that, far from being a barrier to marriage, it is a common device whereby, in a society which jealously guards its adolescent girls and women, courting may be initiated and marriage follow.

Jueves Lardero, when observed, is simply a day of feasting. Young people often make the inevitable "collections" of food from friends and neighbors, sometimes begged, sometimes stolen, before adjourning to the country to prepare their picnics. Popular knowledge of the "Three Thursdays" is sometimes confused, and the days may be taken in inverse order, or one or more may be omitted entirely. And at least once, in Barco de Avila (Avila), Jueves de Comadres crops up in mid-Lent, the equivalent of the French mid-Lenten *Mi-Carême,* a custom generally lacking in Spain (Fuente Arrimadas 1925, p. 251)

The pattern of masks, street dances, practical joking, squirting of perfumed water, breaking of eggs filled with confetti, the former emptying of chamber pots on unwary passersby, and the like followed general European patterns in Spain, and are too well known to require description. Certain specialized characteristics of Carnival, however, merit attention. These include the personification of the carnival spirit, and its subsequent burial, the frequent election of a king of the Carnival, the role of the "man-mule" or "man-horse," the presence of a man dressed as a bear, the "ship-cart," and the ceremonial plowing of land.

Usually the spirit of Carnival was represented by a *monigote* or *pelele,* an enormous figure stuffed with straw, sometimes animated by a man from within. Not infrequently the figure had a wife as well, and other smaller figures, often called *cabezudos,* or "big heads," paraded. On Shrove Tuesday or Ash Wednesday the figure was burned, buried, or otherwise destroyed, sometimes following a mock trial in which it was defended by counsel before a "judge," always unsuccessfully of course.[7]

In Galicia the straw figure representing the spirit of Carnival was called *entroido*, the same term used for Carnival, or *meco*. This figure and its female counterpart were suspended from a tree on the outskirts of town where carnival festivities were to be held, sometimes as much as a month in advance. Following the passing of sentence, the figure or figures were mounted on a burro or sheep, paraded through town, and burned. In Barcelona a huge figure was called "carnestoltes" after the Carnival. It was met ceremonially by revelers on the outskirts of the city, to signify the beginning of the festivities, and after a brief reign it was "buried" on Ash Wednesday.

The destruction or "burial" of a figure appears to have been more common in northern than southern Spain, especially characterizing Catalonia, Aragón, and Navarra. In Durro (Lérida) until very recent years the carnestoltes was accused publicly of drunkenness, gluttony, and of having brought idleness to the village, for which the sentence of death was demanded. Then the defense took the floor to ask pardon, for the spirit had brought joy and happiness as well as full stomachs to everyone, but in spite of the pleas the judge ordained death. A shot was fired into the air, the figure fell dead, was carried on a litter to the plaza, burned, and only at the last minute did the animating "king" emerge from the pyre, midst the applause of the multitude, celebrating the resurrection of the king, who would again reign the coming year (Violant 1949, pp. 576-577).

The end of the Carnival was marked by the *entierro de la sardina*, the "burial of the sardine." The reason why a sardine should be buried ceremonially on the eve of its period of greatest importance is not clear. Sometimes a small representation of a fish actually was buried (Mesonero Romanos 1851, p. 180), but more often the "sardine" was not a fish at all. By the eighteenth century the "burial of the sardine" had become an important fiesta in Madrid, and great crowds adjourned to the banks of the Manzanares for picnicking, parading, and merrymaking in general. Kany says that the "sardine" originally was a dressed pig, but by the latter half of the eighteenth century it was represented by a stuffed figure or, more generally, a masked wine-skin. The revelers masked themselves to represent monks, priests, or grotesque forms, and paraded around the field chanting lugubriously and sprinkling bystanders with water from syringes or wet brooms. A hole was finally dug in the ground and in it a real sardine—but not the large figure—was buried, while the paraders feasted and drank from the wine-skin that had represented the spirit of Carnival (Kany 1932, pp. 367-368).

A hundred years later the "sardine" was sometimes a piece of pork (Basilio Sebastian Castellanos 1850) and a dozen years after that it is described as a piece of sausage (Davillier 1949, p. 750), a symbolism reminiscent of the Nuremburg butchers' Shrove Tuesday processional sausage, which at times reached a length of 650 yards (Lowie 1945, p. 80). In Rialp (Lérida) the ceremonial death through dismemberment of the carnestoltes straw figure was called "burial of the sardine." The "burial of the sardine," whatever its form, occurred at least sporadically from Extremadura east through Madrid to Valencia, and in the areas to the north. It was not characteristic of Andalusia.[8]

The ancient Greek "ship-cart," the currus navalis, has survived in very attenuated form in Spain until recent years, associated with the king or spirit of Carnival. In Albacete a cart pulled by the oldest burro in town carried a man feigning death, while other men simulating his sorrowing wife and children wept over his body. A cross from which sardines were hung preceded the cart in this entierro de la sardina procession. The cart was also important in Galicia, where the entroido, the figure representing the Carnival, was often carried in a wheeled vehicle drawn by burros or oxen. But the most spectacular sight of all was the procession in Reus (Tarragona), where a real boat manned by a real crew of sailors mounted on a wagon pulled by twelve horses passed through the streets of the town in the carnival procession (Casas Gaspar 1950a, p. 85).

Feigned animals and live birds likewise participated in some carnival observances. From Galicia to the Mediterranean, and on both sides of the Pyrenees, a form of "man-horse" appeared from time to time, the symbolism of which is not clear and was perhaps not the same in all places. In Castro Caldelas (Orense) two men disguised as a "false mule" (mula falsa) were led by a maragato, a man dressed in the customary costume of these rude people who, formerly, were muleteers who carried much of the merchandise of the region. The maragato then invited women to ride, and if the men were unable to buck her off, they ran with their rider to the tavern, where she was expected to pay for drinks for the men (Risco 1948, p. 195). In various Pyrenean villages of Lérida a "white mule" (mula blanca) ran through an act on carnival Sunday. In Sarroca de Bellera the "mule" was a man who wore a frame with a crude head on the front, a sort of hobbyhorse, the mule being further simulated by a covering which hung from the man's neck over the frame and to the ground. The mule's owner attempted to "sell" the mule, but each time a burlesque sale was consummated the mule reacted so violently, kicking and becoming unmanageable, that the sale was annulled.

Most famous of all was the "man-horse" of Lanz (Navarra), a man disguised much like the muleman of Lérida, with horse head and tail giving a slight realism to the costume. This zaldizko, accompanied by a giant and a grotesque fat-legged figure, danced with thirty or more men disguised in sheep and goat skins and, according to one account, was shot to death on Shrove Tuesday (Violant 1949, p. 570) while in another account (Iribarren 1949, pp. 191-201) the giant was killed in the more usual form of carnival ending.

Simulated bears likewise appeared in carnival rites. Although the most elaborate episodes come from the French side of the Pyrenees (Alford 1937, pp. 11-42), the earliest reference to bears at Carnival is from Barcelona in 1444 (ibid., p. 24). Lérida is again a center where, at least until the recent past, the rite has been most marked. In Sarroca de Bellera the "bear," clad in sheepskins and led by a "beggar," danced on tne night of Jueves Lardero. Similar performances, some on the days of Carnival, are reported in other villages of Lérida (Violant 1949, p. 570). Down to the present time in the city of Murcia the "bear," a man dressed in goat skins and chained to a "hunter," dances about the city, grunting and growling in protest against his captivity and running after children. And Montoto, seventy years ago, laconically reports that in Andalusia people liked to dress as bears for Carnival (1884, p. 297), a custom I have not found confirmed in other sources. Feigned bears also appeared in Asturias (Caro Baroja 1946b, p. 311), and it seems probable that at one time the custom was fairly widespread in Spain.

Cock-baiting, the several forms known collectively as *correr el gallo*, was a part of carnival festivities in north and central Spain and, of course, the sport, if such it can be called, is indulged in on other occasions as well. A cock, or occasionally a goose, is suspended by its feet from a cord stretched across a street. The players ride by on horseback rising in their stirrups to try to wring off the bird's head, an act more difficult because the cord is jerked as the horseman rises.[10] Or, lacking horses, players— often children—are blindfolded, spun, and started off towards the suspended cock, at which they lash wildly for the appointed number of turns with a wooden stick or sword.

Attenuated reflections of the ancient fertility aspects of the carnival season are manifest in the symbolic plowings which occurred, apparently primarily in Catalonia, until modern times. In Rialp (Lérida) on the afternoon of Shrove Tuesday two of the most important men of the town were yoked to a plow, guided by a real farmer, who plowed symbolic furrows in the plaza and around and between the dancers who surrounded them. This rite of inversion, the humbling of the proud, is particularly suggestive of the Saturnalian custom of masters waiting on their slaves (Violant 1949, p. 573). Plowing was similarly done in Durro (Lérida) (*ibid.*, p. 573), in Cardedeu (Barcelona) (Caro Baroja 1946a, p. 469), and in the Vallès region north of Barcelona (Alford 1937, p. 29). In the last-named region "devils" (*diablots*) clad in skin breeches and wearing cowbells on their belts danced on threshing floors, while a farmer with a team of oxen plowed a furrow around the dance space. But symbolic plowing is not limited to Carnival and Catalonia. Far to the west in the Maragatería of León in a simple agricultural rite at the beginning of the year the snow-covered fields are furrowed by an ox team driven by a youth dressed as a girl (Caro Baroja 1946b, p. 319).

Carnival died a slow death in Spain; in spite of the theoretical end with Ash Wednesday, festivities in some measure dragged on until the next Sunday, *Domingo de Piñata*, in which they again flared up for a final outburst. The gatherings were family or neighborhood parties, unmasked and relatively quiet in comparison with the early days of the week. The piñata, a clay pot or framework decorated with colored paper, was filled with candies—and live birds at more elegant parties—and suspended in the center of the room. By turns the participants were blindfolded, given a stick, spun to make dizzy, and allowed to strike at the piñata. By jerking the suspending cord it was possible to make sure the pot was unscathed until nearly everyone had had his turn. Then the lucky strike occurred, the candies and sherds fell, the dazed birds flew up, and the guests scrambled for the sweetmeats. The custom of the piñata appears to have died out in Spain, although Domingo de Piñata is still known, and in the Levante I have seen rouged and masked children fantastically dressed going about the streets in their own little party. The origin of the piñata appears to be Italian, as the form *pignatta*, Italian for "pot," would indicate.[11]

The conceptual similarity in striking the piñata and striking at a suspended cock while blindfolded is apparent; perhaps the two traits have ancient and common roots, or perhaps the piñata is a refined and debrutalized form of the cock kill.

The modern prohibition of carnival celebrations follows a long series of prohibitions against public maskings and the excesses to which the Carnival was carried. At least as early as the reign of Carlos V masks or other disguises hiding the identity of an individual were outlawed. But repeated pronouncements on the same subject bear witness to the facility with which unpopular edicts were flouted by the populace, and Carnival has had its ups and downs over the centuries. The opposition of the Church now makes it seem unlikely that, in the near future, carnival celebrations will again be observed in Spain.

Lent.—*La Cuaresma* is a traditional period of austerity and self-denial, formerly marked by closed theaters and other signs of abstention from pleasure. Although many of the popular and religious activities of this period which graced earlier centuries have died out, enough remains so that this is still one of the most impressive and interesting times of the year. Mid-Lenten festive celebrations to break the monotony of a rigorous seven weeks seem never to have been common, as they are in France and Italy, although in Murcia there was a slight relaxing of the rules when, at mid-Lent, extravagantly dressed figures of old people, called *los viejos*, were placed on terraces and balconies (Anonymous 1923, p. 501). Consequently the counting of the days until normal life and pleasures could be resumed became an important pastime.

To facilitate the count, children cut from cardboard a grotesque figure of a woman with seven feet, holding a dried cod fillet or a basket of fish in one hand. This representation of "Old Lady Lent" (*La Vieja de la Cuaresma*) was hung from the ceiling or placed on a convenient wall, and each Sunday the children gathered to tear off one of the feet. Thus one always knew at a glance how many Sundays had passed and how many remained. On Easter Sunday the figure was taken down and burned midst the general rejoicing of the day.[12]

The Friday evening *Via Crucis* processions were perhaps the most impressive of Lenten spiritual exercises. Many towns and villages have ornamental iron crosses, or more rarely small stone altars, at street corners. Each represents one of the Fourteen Stations, points at which Christ stopped on his way to Calvary. The priest led his parishioners, who carried lighted candles, from cross to cross, where all stopped and knelt and recited the prayers appropriate to each Station. In many hill towns of the Levante small chapels crown the top of hills near towns, and a cypress-lined path ascends from below. In such towns, in the province of Valencia in particular, bareheaded and barefoot men may still carry a cross from the parish church to the Calvary chapel, led by the priest and followed by the women. Via Crucis processions today are for the most part limited to Good Friday. The Franciscans, through the lay Third Order, were particular advocates of the Via Crucis processions on the Fridays of Lent, so it is not surprising that in those parts of Spain, and the New World as well, where the Franciscans have been most active, one finds the strongest adherence to the Via Crucis.[13]

Holy Week.—The activities of *La Semana Santa,* which begin with Palm Sunday (*Domingo de Ramos*) and end with Easter Sunday (*Pascua de Resurrección*), may be thought of as composed of a common core or framework of Church ritual, everywhere observed, elaborated upon according to the particular traditions and enthusiasms of each city and village. Thus to the standard observances the town of Olesa de Montserrat adds her famous passion play, Murcia her processions with the lovely sculptured works of Salzillo, Lorca her overwhelming parade of Biblical characters, Baeza her drummers, and Tudela her airborne angel, to name a few.

In towns and cities Palm Sunday is heralded by the arrival of great carloads of yellow-gold palm fronds, sent from the palm orchards of Elche, Crevillente, Orihuela, and other subtropical garden spots in Alicante. Overnight palm-selling stands spring up in front of churches and cathedrals, and each worshipper provides himself with his ramo before entering to attend Mass. Many fronds are woven into ingenious and elaborate forms.[14] Once blessed, this spray becomes an amulet to be kept at home during the year, to be burned, a little at a time, if tempests threaten and the home owner fears that a thunderbolt may strike his dwelling. Often it is lashed to a balcony, and in Madrid even the most modern apartment buildings invariably display in such fashion this token of faith in the protective power of blessed palm.[15] Palm fronds, in spite of their ubiquity, are relatively recent in those parts of Spain were they do not grow, dating primarily from the introduction of rail and highway transportation. Previously in the north—and even today in small, poor villages—the traditional ramos were of laurel and rosemary, and in the south olive branches were, and are, the most common.

Apart from the blessing of the ramos there are few traditional Palm Sunday observances. With the increasing elaboration (and commercialization) of Holy Week activities more and more cities are inaugurating their series of processions of *pasos* of sculptured scenes from the Passion, carried by masked and hooded members of religious confraternities on this

day, but in general the most important Holy Week exercises transpire between Wednesday evening and Saturday noon. On Wednesday at dusk the
first of three consecutive daily services known as *tinieblas* is held. A tall,
triangular candelabra with eleven, thirteen, or fifteen candles rests on the
altar. One by one, as the appropriate psalms and prayers are said, the
candles and other lights in the church are extinguished. Finally, only one
candle, representing the Virgin, remains. This too is then extinguished
or hidden beneath the altar, a signal in many parts of Spain for setting off
an ear-splitting hubbub in which all children present beat on pews, walls,
and pillars with fists and hammers, and swing *carracas* (wooden ratchet
noisemakers of the type used in the United States on New Year's Eve) and
other noisemakers. In some places it is said that the darkness and noise
symbolize the gloom and earthquake that followed the crucifixion. After an
interval of bedlam the lighted candle reappears, other lights go on, order
is gradually restored, and after final prayers the parishioners disperse to
their homes.

On Thursday morning the bells ring for Mass for the last time until the
toque de Gloria, which rings out during Mass on the following Saturday.
The bells, as baptized Christians, are in mourning for Christ, even as are
human beings. During these two days Mass is announced with the matraca,
a hollow wooden box, cross, or wheel to which are fastened hammers in
such fashion that when the instrument is revolved, the hammers strike it,
producing a dry rattle that can be heard at a considerable distance.

From Thursday until Saturday all altars are hidden in purple shrouds.
The Monument to the Holy Sacrament (*El Monumento*), a side altar on
which is placed a second Host, is also shrouded. The Host is consecrated
during the Thursday morning Mass, to be left until the Service of the Presanctified on the following day. On Thursday afternoon the priest or bishop
of many churches and cathedrals enacts the *lavatorio*, symbolically washing
the feet of twelve old men. Formerly the King of Spain himself invited
twelve beggars into the Royal Palace at Madrid and humbled himself by
kneeling to daub a bit of water on their bare feet. The second tiniebla
vesper service is observed at dusk on Thursday, and all that night worshippers crowd churches to pray. The presence of the Holy Spirit in the presanctified Host which rests on the Monument is the special object of their
devotion. Each worshipper genuflects before the Host, crosses himself,
advances to place a lighted candle on the Monument, steps back, kneels in
prayer or supplication, and, after a suitable interval, again crosses himself, rises, and silently departs.

In a few small villages there is a formal guard for the Monument, perhaps representing the remnant of more elaborate folk dramas of earlier
centuries. In LaGuardia (Alava), for example, pairs of armed men,
dressed as Roman soldiers and incongrously called "Jews," stand half-hour
watches throughout the night, absolutely motionless until the moment when
they are relieved by the next pair of "Jews" (Thalamas Labandíbar 1931,
p. 107). In Villamesía, near Trujillo (Cáceres) the custom is known as

guardar el cuerpo del Señor. The guards, who stand watch in fulfillment of a vow, wear long black capes and carry sabres. Similar customs are found in other villages in Cáceres, and doubtless the custom was at one time much more widespread in Spain (Ramón y Ferñandez 1950).

On Good Friday the Eucharist is not celebrated; its place is taken by the Mass of the Presanctified, the communion of the priest with the Host which has remained on the Monument overnight since its consecration the day before. The service known as the Adoration of the Cross is also a part of the offices of this day, and at dawn or dusk in many places there may be a Via Crucis procession. Then in the afternoon everyone returns to church for the Devotion of the Three Hours, which includes the sermon of the *Siete Palabras*, the reading and explanation of the seven utterances of Christ while he was nailed to the cross. This office is relatively modern, brought from Lima, Peru, where it was composed by the Jesuit Fray Alonso María in 1687.

Formerly in many churches an articulated image of Christ was raised and fastened to a cross for the Friday afternoon service, following which it was ceremoniously lowered and placed in a glass coffin or *urna*, while a sermon known as the *Descendimiento*, the Descent from the Cross, was preached. This image, an Ecce Homo known as the *Santo Entierro*, was then carried through the streets in a candlelight procession which was one of the most simple but moving of all Holy Week observances. In Barco de Avila (Avila) the image was bolted to an immense stone cross erected on the threshing floors on the outskirts of town or, in bad weather, a wooden cross in the church was utilized. The articulated Santo Entierros have been rapidly disappearing, and many of the last were destroyed during the Civil War. In Murcia we were told that a famous image made by the sculptor Nicolás de Bussi, brought to Spain by Charles II during the latter part of the seventeenth century, was used regularly until it was burned during the civil disturbances which began in 1936. Although the articulated image is very nearly a thing of the past, many, if not most, churches have reclining figures of the crucified Christ, which are carried in the procession of the Santo Entierro on Friday night.

Saturday morning Mass is marked by the blessing of new fire and five grains of incense, which are then pressed into the huge Paschal candle in the form of a cross. This *Cirio Pascual* represents Christ Risen, and the five grains of incense symbolize the five wounds of the crucified Christ. Then, at the toque de Gloria when the bells again ring out, the altar coverings fall away and all rejoice, for Christ is risen. Shortly after Mass, in many towns, a scarecrow figure representing Judas will be swung into the air on a main street, and youths and men will fire at it with guns, setting fire to the straw stuffing and bringing the image burning to the ground midst shouts of delight from all onlookers. This *quema de Judas* may also occur Saturday night or Sunday morning, especially in the north. Tudela (Navarra) is particularly famous for its Judas act. Since the beginning of the sixteenth century a *volatín*, an articulated wooden figure, has been suspended from the balcony of the town hall from Saturday until Sunday, symbolizing the suicide of Judas. By means of cords the figure is made to dance and gyrate in absurd contortions, to the great amusement of children and adults alike (Iribarren 1946, pp. 249-251).

A final procession, the *Encuentro*, which symbolizes the meeting of Christ Risen with his mother, occurs in many places on Easter morning. The black-shrouded image of the Virgin is carried along one route, while that of Christ goes by another. At a predetermined point the images meet and are tipped towards each other by their porters so that they appear to be kneeling. The black robe is drawn from the Virgin and she appears resplendent in white. Then the images are again raised, and with that of Christ in the lead a single procession returns to the church. Occasionally an Encuentro procession occurs on an earlier day in the week.[16]

The traditional Spanish Holy Week penitential rites—flagellation in their extreme forms—are largely a thing of the past. Kany describes the eighteenth-century processions in Madrid, in which barefoot and barewaisted penitents marched in the processions, scourging themselves with cat-o'-nine-tails, the knotted cords of which terminated in wax balls in which were embedded bits of glass. For some this was a devout exercise, for others a form of gallantry, to show devotion to one's lady love. If, to show his gallantry, the suitor could whip himself in such a way that his blood spurted on his beloved, it was for her the highest compliment possible (Kany 1932, p. 375).

In the common form of penitential rite an individual in response to a vow made during the year marches in the processions of Thursday or Friday, clad only in a skirt or a waist cloth. Face and head are hidden by a *capucho*, a cowl-and-mask combined, so that the marcher's identity remains unknown. Some *penitentes* carry wooden crosses on their shoulders, others whip themselves with the ancient cat-o'-nine-tails, and still others are hobbled with *grillos*, leg irons around the ankles which limit motion to tiny steps or short hops. Many are assisted by helpers called *Cirineos*, so called after Simon of Cyrene, who aided Christ.

In Alosno (Huelva) ornamental iron crosses may still be seen on the walls of a number of houses. These marked the spots where *azotador*, or self-scourging penitents, mortified themselves. Each had made a vow during the year, usually in time of family illness or distress, to do penance if his prayers were granted. On Good Friday night following the Via Crucis procession the azotador, often hobbled with leg irons, hopped his painful way to each iron cross, where he whipped his bare breast and back three times. Then he continued to the church sacristy, where his aide wiped away the blood and dressed his wounds. A good deal of fear and superstition marked these rites, and ordinary worshippers are said to have hurried home following the procession, to bar their doors securely, for the penitente would try to enter homes to find an *hermano de azote* ("brother of the lash") to help him on his rounds. This custom died out at the end of the nineteenth century.

Modified penitential rites are found to this day in scattered parts of Spain, although the action appears in most cases to be symbolic, and not to involve true flagellation.[17]

In most places the religious acts of Holy Week end with the Saturday Mass, and Lent is officially over. Family groups banquet or go on picnics, if the weather permits, and visit with friends and relatives. Easter Sunday is a day when, traditionally, good godparents present their godchildren with the *mona*, a pastry in which one or more eggs, sometimes to the number of birthdays the child has celebrated, are encrusted in the top and baked, shell and all. As to why an Arabic word (*muna*, "provisions," "supplies") has come to be used for a symbol of Christian rejoicing is anybody's guess. In passing it may be noted that the custom of coloring Easter eggs, although not entirely unknown, is generally unimportant in Spain as compared to the rest of Europe.

In nearly all Spanish cities of importance, and even in many of the smallest villages, the basic Holy Week ritual is elaborated upon—in some places "submerged" would seem to be a more accurate term—by the hours-long processions in which hooded members of religious brotherhoods carry beautifully carved and richly decorated pasos, floats depicting scenes from the Passion of Christ, through the main streets, to the accompaniment of orchestral dirges, *saeta*-singing, and the rolling of drums.

The dramatic impact of the candlelight processions of hooded and masked men carrying superbly carved figures ornamented with costly velvet and gold clothes is so appealing to Spaniard and foreigner alike that a not inconsiderable commercial element has crept into the activities. Many towns and cities publish guides to the activities of Holy Week, giving the putative schedules of the various processions, sketching the history of all the brotherhoods, and showing pictures of the more important pasos. A guide to the 1949 activities of Valladolid, for example, gives the following:

> General procession of the Sacred Passion of the Savior. This incomparable procession of the *Santo Entierro* will take place at seven-thirty in the evening of Good Friday, following the Sermon of the Seven Words, and it will be represented by 19 *pasos*, master works of the sixteenth century. All the penitential cofradías will participate, wearing their costumes of distinct colors and singular beauty.

Then follows the street-by-street itinerary of the procession, so that the visitor may take his stand wherever he wishes.

Many of the cofradías date from the Golden Age of Spain. The 1949 guide for Salamanca shows, for example, that the *Cofradía de la Santa Cruz del Redentor y de la Purísima Conceptión de María* was founded in 1503, while two others are late seventeenth-century and still another late eighteenth-century in origin. But perhaps a majority are of very recent foundation, since the end of the Civil War in 1939.

The list of cofradías is not identical in any two places, but the same figures and names are repeated countless times. Cofradías are ranked, formally or informally, in a definite social hierarchy, the oldest usually being those of greatest prestige. The pasos, which portray figures of Mary and Jesus and other personages, are likewise marked by the same names from one town to the next. Among the most common are the Santo Entierro, a reclining image usually in a glass coffin, *Jesus Nazareno*, Christ carrying the cross, *La Dolorosa*, an anguishing Mary, *La Oración del Huerto*, Christ in the garden, *La Crucifixión*, Christ crucified, *Cristo atado a la Columna*, Christ tied to the stake, *Cristo del Perdón*, and the *Ecce Homo*.

Each cofradía cares for its image in a particular church, and though it may meet several times a year to elect members and officers, to transact business, to attend the funeral of members, or for other purposes, it can be said to exist for the one week of the year. At specified times during this week the *cofrades* will meet at their church clothed in long garments and tall pointed *capirotes* which cover the face so that the wearer, looking through narrow eye slits—and to an American uncomfortably suggestive of a member of the Ku Klux Klan—is completely disguised. Each cofradía has a particular color combination, of which black, purple, and red are the most common. In addition, each has a standard of unique color and design, but all represent variations on the theme of the cross. Each paso is brilliantly illuminated, even for daytime processions, with hundreds of candles, and in front of each a number of cofrades walk, carrying still larger candles. Each cofrade who helps carry the paso is provided with a forked stick, so that, from time to time, the heavy burden can be rested. At the appointed hour the doors of the church open and the procession begins; first the standard appears, then the candle-bearers, and then the paso, in slow and measured rhythm, swaying slightly from side to side as the twenty to fifty cofrades step in unison. Progress is slow and rests are frequent. Perhaps a half-mile an hour is the maximum speed at which a paso moves, so that a march, even over a short course, will last several hours. Several pasos usually go in sequence, and a given procession, for the watchers, is a series of high points as a paso approaches and slowly glides by. Then the next is discerned several blocks away, making its slow progress, and eventually it too passes by.

The night-time spectacle of a major procession, with its brilliantly illuminated floats, splendid sculpture, shining tunics, and pointed caps, and the sad music from several bands of music playing the Miserere, is impressive beyond words to describe. Those of Sevilla are popularly reputed to be the most elaborate, but all major cities—and increasingly so in recent years—seem bent on outdoing each other in the splendor and lavishness of their processions.[18]

One of the most impressive features of the Holy Week processions is the singing of religious funeral dirges known as *saetas*. Native to Andalusia, the custom is spreading to other parts of Spain. An image, perhaps that of the Virgin known as La Dolorosa, proceeds through crowded narrow streets overhung with equally crowded windows and balconies. Suddenly a woman steps to the edge of a balcony, and in a clear, high voice begins to sing:

Quién es el hombre que no llorara	Who is the man who would not cry
Viendo a esta Madre tan quebrantada?	Upon seeing this mother so broken.
Oh qué afligida, oh que angustiada	Oh, how afflicted, oh, how anguished,
Fué la bendita Madre sagrada!	Was the blessed sacred Mother.

The procession stops and voices are silenced. The night air is still, except perhaps for the distant sound of drums or instruments, and faces are uplifted from the streets. The woman finishes her song, a form which, it is said, cannot be properly reproduced with musical notations, and appreciative cries of "Olé, Olé" greet the job well done. Perhaps the same woman will then continue with a different song, or another will step forward to take her turn. Only when silence again returns will the cofrades shoulder their heavy burden and continue their slow march. In theory, no one knows when a saeta will ring out, or where the procession must stop. In fact, the saeta-singers of ability are known in the city and appreciated for their talent, and with a little inquiry the stranger can learn the likely spots at which to hear the songs. Men, much more rarely, also sing saetas.

Music is an essential part of Holy Week processions. Wealthier cofradías often hire orchestras to follow their pasos or to parade in other processions, and *chirimía* and *clarín* flutes will be heard sounding their plaintive notes above the din. Drums, to set the tempo, are necessary in all processions, and occasionally, like cancer cells run riot, the rage of drumming will seize a town and a tradition will be established that will become a "must" for all men and youths. In Baeza (Jaén), for example, it is said that "here boys are born already drummers," and the week is known, for its continuous din, as "the week of not understanding anybody." One of the great sources of pride in many families is the possession of a fine drum, which is passed from father to son like a valued jewel. Here the drummers are divided into two cofradías of "Jews": the *Coliblancos* ("white-tailed ones"), also called *Los de arriba* ("the upper ones"), and the *Colinegros* ("black-tailed ones"), also called *Los de abajo* ("the lower ones"). Each group tries to outdo the other, a pastime which in the past led to cracked skulls and other forms of bloodshed (Rosa 1935).

In other towns, too, membership in *La Judea*, the Jews' cofradía, is eagerly sought after, and a writer of the past century describes, tongue in cheek, how the aspirant to this cofradía must possess *buena sangre*, i.e., be descended from Old Christians unmixed with other races, neither Moors nor recent converts to the Holy Catholic Faith, a precaution gravely stated as necessary to prevent the role from corrupting the habits and beliefs of the participants (Córte 1842).

Jews otherwise participate, in name or act, in Holy Week activities: in places as distant as Asturias and Barcelona the uproar following the tinieblas, the beating on walls and benches, the sounding of carracas and other noisemakers, is known as "killing Jews."

Formerly a number of towns and villages enacted the ritual of Holy Week in the form of a Passion Play. In Villanueva del Río Segura (Murcia) we were told that until about 1912-1920 *La Pasión* was regularly reënacted. The actors studied and practiced their parts for three months or more, and stages were erected in various parts of the village for the several scenes, which included the Last Supper, the Judgment, Christ in Jail, and the Crucifixion. The actor taking the part of Christ was tied to a cross, nails were driven between his fingers and toes, chicken blood was smeared on his head, hands, and feet, and an animal bladder of blood was concealed under his loincloth, so that when the Roman centurion's lance pierced him it spouted in realistic fashion. Barabbas went around with chains draped from his arms and legs, and other characters, who are now beginning to be forgotten, participated. The modern Villanuevans think that theirs is the only village in the region in which this was the custom.

Madrid newspapers in 1950 reported a traditional Passion Play in the village of Cájiz, thirty kilometers from Málaga. The lines were recited in verse in settings that included the Last Supper, the Tribune of Caiphas, and the houses of Pilate and Herod. The Last Supper was skillfully reenacted, Christ was judged, Veronica covered his face with a cloth which, when removed, revealed three pictures of Christ stuck to it, Judas committed suicide, and the crowd howled its approval. So deeply are the actors identified with their roles, say reports, that in this land of nicknames all actors are known by the part they play in the drama rather than by their true names (Casares 1950).

Most famous of modern Passion plays in Spain is that of Olesa de Montserrat (Barcelona). Actually this drama is of no great antiquity, having been written by a monk of Montserrat, Antón de Sant Jeroni, and having been first produced in Manresa in the middle of the eighteenth century. In Olesa it dates from the beginning of the nineteenth century.[19]

But, if the true Passion Play scarcely exists in Spain today, dramatic and theatrical aspects of Holy Week are present in many forms.

The urge to dress up, to masquerade, to act is satisfied not only in the processions of pasos, but also in isolated little dramas, and in the parading of Roman soldiers, Jews, the apostles, and in Biblical and allegorical figures. In Baena (Córdoba) two "Jews" offer money to Judas; the sum is too small, and more and more is offered until he accepts. In another little act the Evangelists hear trumpets announcing the divine inspiration and, although heckled by "Jews," succeed in writing down the true word. The *Prendimiento*, the arrest of Jesus, is enacted by another group and—apparently as an added dividend—Adam appears eating an apple in the Garden of Eden (Rosa 1935). Murcia and Lorca are other cities particularly noted for the elaborateness and numbers of parading figures (Bolarín 1935b). But questioning led us to believe that Puente Genil (Córdoba) was the town with the most exciting Easter Week dramas and tableaus, a conclusion amply borne out by a three-day visit in the spring of 1950. Since these festivities have been described and illustrated from our joint notes by Caro Baroja (1957b), they are not discussed here.

REFERENCES

Excellent data on fiestas and feast days in the yearly cycle are found in such sources as Alford (1937), Almerich (1944), Anonymous (1923), the various publications of Cabal, Caballé y Clos (n.d.), Caro Baroja (1946b), Cortada y Sala and Manjarrés (1945), Deleito y Piñuela (1944), Flores (1877), Kany (1932), Répide (1914), Serra Boldú (1946) and Violant y Simorra (1949).

Specific data on the events described in this chapter include:

Old and New Years: Almerich (1944, pp. 7-9); Cabal (1925a, pp. 105-107), Basilio Sebastian Castellanos (1845a, b, c), Flores (1877, pp. 1-11, 275-277), Montoto (1884, pp. 283-286), Morán (1950), Olavarría y Huarte (1884, pp. 11-16), Pla Cargol (1947, pp. 284-285), Répide (1914, pp. 5-8), Violant y Simorra (1949, pp. 565-567).

Epiphany: Almerich (1944, pp. 9-11), Bolarín (1935a), Cabal (1925a, pp. 110-113), Caballé y Clos (n.d., pp. 358-365), Cortada y Sala and Manjarrés (1945, pp. 31-37), Fernández (1949), Flores (1877, pp. 13-14), Fuente Arrimadas (1925, p. 250), Iribarren (1946, pp. 115-120), Kany (1929, pp. 11-14), Martin Granizo (1929, pp. 53-54), Montoto (1884, pp. 286-288), Olavarría y Huarte (1884, pp. 90-95), Pla Cargol (1948, pp. 35-36), Répide (1914, pp. 8-10), Teresa León (1947), Violant y Simorra (1949, pp. 567-568).

Candlemas: Almerich (1944, p. 21), Cortada y Sala and Manjarrés (1945, pp. 54-56), Flores (1877, p. 19), Fuente Arrimadas (1925, p. 250), Giner Arivau (1886, p. 238), Gozalo Blanco (1921), Iribarren (1946, pp. 120-121), Ramón y Fernández (1948).

San Blas: Castillo de Lucas (1943, pp. 19-24), Flores (1877, pp. 19-20), Iribarren (1946, pp. 81-82), Kany (1929, p. 24), Martínez Corbalan (1930), Ramón y Fernández (1948).

Santa Agueda: Almerich (1944, pp. 21-22), Avrial (1839), Casas Gaspar (1950b), pp. 188-192), Castillo de Lucas (1943, pp. 25-30), Cedilla (1931), Hoyos Sancho (1951), Iravedra and Rubio (1949, p. 108), Iribarren (1946, pp. 60-61), Vergara y Martín (1909, pp. 33-37).

Carnival: Alford (1937), Almerich (1944, pp. 22-27), Bouza Brey (1949), Caballé y Clos (n.d., pp. 215-225), Caro Baroja (1946b), Casas Gaspar (1950a; 1950b, pp. 208-218), Basilio Sebastian Castellanos (1850), Cortada y Sala and Manjarrés (1945, pp. 81-87), Davillier (1949, p. 750), Deleito y Piñuela (1944, pp. 23-29), Flores (1877, pp. 191-209), Fraguas Fraguas (1946), Fuente Arrimadas (1925, p. 251), Iribarren (1949, pp. 191-202), Kany (1929, p. 26; 1932, pp. 367-368), Mesonero Romanos (1851, pp. 177-181), Montoto (1884, pp. 295-304), Pfandel (1942, pp. 241-242), Rademacher (1919), Ramón y Fernández (1945b), Répide (1914, pp. 29-42), Risco (1948), Tal (1899, pp. 89-91), Violant y Simorra (1949, pp. 569-577).

Lent and Holy Week: Almerich (1944, pp. 33-38), Amades (1953, pp. 424-436), Anonymous (1923), Bolarín (1935b), Caballé y Clos (n.d., pp. 32-41), Caro Baroja (1957b), Casares (1950), Basilio Sebastian Castellanos (1850), El Marqués de Castellanos (1953, pp. 332-345), Cortada y Sala and Manjarrés (1945, pp. 87-89, 114-140), Córte (1842), Coves (1929), Díaz Roncero (1930), Flores (1877, pp. 36-59), Fuente (1841), García Mercadal (1928), García Sanz (1948), Gillet (1933), Iravedra and Rubio (1949, pp. 95-100, 107-108), Iribarren (1946, pp. 131-139, 221-263), Llorca (1930), Manrique (1952, pp. 516-520), Marcos de Sande (1945, p. 459), Martínez (1884, pp. 10-11), Martínez Corbalan (1931), Pla Cargol (1947, pp. 279-282; 1948, pp. 35-38, 89-118), Puche (1928), Ramón y Fernández (1950, pp. 96-103), Rosa (1935), Sánchez de Alba (1845), V. Sánchez-Ocaña (1933), Sarthou Carreres (1930), Serra Boldú (1946), Thalamas Labandíbar (1931).

NOTES

[1] These Spanish New Year's customs appear to be poorly developed in Hispanic America.

[2] *Reyes* is celebrated in Spanish America much as in Spain. Children traditionally put their shoes on balconies to receive gifts from the Magi, and in uncounted towns the Three Kings dress up and parade through the streets in a simple ceremony (e.g., Tzintzuntzan, Mexico, Foster 1948a, p. 204). Toor (1947, p. 193) describes a Mexican equivalent of the haba in a *rosca*. Among city people, porcelain kewpie dolls representing the Christ child are baked in a rosca, which is eaten at a party. Whoever finds one of the dolls must in turn give a party.

[3] Equally elaborate candles characterize Candlemas in Spanish America. The custom may be Moorish; I have seen similar candles in the great bazar of Damascus.

[4] Candlemas in America is religiously important, but it generally lacks the color found in Spain.

[5] San Blas is appealed to for throat ailments in Spanish America, but apparently there are few fiestas in his honor. Starr describes cords blessed in Mexico during Mass, which are afterwards worn as amulets to ward off throat-troubles (1899, p. 131).

[6] Santa Agueda appears to have little importance in America. This is surprising, in view of her importance in the list of Church saints and in view of the fact that many immigrants came from the area in which her cult is important.

[7] Personification of the spirit of Carnival appears to have been much less important in Spanish America than in Spain. In several towns of Jalisco (Mexico) a *Rey del Buen Humor* ("King of Good Humor") was elected; the data indicate that this occurred before the War of Independence in the early nineteenth century (Vázquez Santana and Dávila Garibi 1931, pp. 90-93). Toor describes *No Carnavalón*, a grotesquely stuffed figure that rides a llama in the festivities of Puno (Peru) (1949, p. 86). Cortazar elaborates on the *pujllay* of northwestern Argentina, a life-size figure that represents Carnival (1949, pp. 209-216).

[8] The burial of the sardine, as such, seems to be lacking in America, but the concept of the burial of the spirit of Carnival is found on a limited scale. Cortazar describes the ceremonial burial of the pujllay in northwestern Argentina (1949, pp. 209-216), and Olivares Figueroa tells of a Venezuelean custom in which "the subject which symbolizes the Carnival" is buried with much rejoicing (1949, p. 101). In Mérida (Yucatán) *Juan Carnaval*, a symbolic figure that has ruled for four days, is carried in a coffin and buried on Ash Wednesday, after a notary reads his will bequeathing his possessions to the mourning widow and other relatives (Vázquez Santana and Dávila Garibi 1931, p. 68). More commonly *El Mal Humor* ("Bad Humor"), represented by a figure carried through the streets in a coffin, is buried, e.g., in Guadalajara and Mazatlán (*ibid.*, pp. 78 and 98). Toor also briefly mentions a ceremony at the Peñón, on the outskirts of Mexico City, where "Sadness and Bad Humor" are buried at the end of a carnival play (1947, p. 196).

[9] Feigned animals appear to be less common in Spanish America than in Spain, but they do occur. Olivares Figueroa speaks both of a "horse" and a "bear" in Venezuela (1949, pp. 85-86, 99). The *burriquita* (literally "little burro," i.e., the horse) is a man in woman's dress wearing a burro's head of cloth, leather, and cardboard, who dances through the streets singing. The feigned bear, in the state of Trujillo, is chained to a keeper, and goes through the streets asking people to dance with it. An account of the 1958 Carnival in the village of San Juan de Aragón, on the eastern outskirts of Mexico City, also describes a dancing bear, a man in simulated bear skin, led by a "viuda de pandero," a man in woman's clothing, with whom the bear danced (Poniatowska 1958). The leader in the Mixe Indian dance called "Los Caballitos" is dressed in a hobbyhorse head and saddle frame suggestive of that of the man-horse of Lanz (author's field notes, Oaxaca, July, 1958).

[10] This is also an important part of some Spanish American carnivals, and is common on many other festive occasions as well.

[11] Domingo de Piñata does not appear in ethnographic accounts of Spanish America, although it is mentioned as a dance, *El baile de piñata*, which closed the Carnival in Mérida (Yucatán) (Vázquez Santana and Dávila Garibi, 1931, p. 68). In the form of the Christmas *posadas* and at birthday parties the piñata today enjoys a more vigorous life in Mexico than in Spain.

[12] I know of no instances of La Vieja in Spanish America.

[13] E.g., in Tzintzuntzan (Mexico) (Foster 1948a, pp. 209-210).

[14] Palm fronds are woven in similar fashion in Spanish America.

[15] Blessed palm is also believed in Hispanic America to protect against tempests.

[16] The basic pattern of the Spanish Holy Week has been duplicated in Hispanic America. The matraca calls people to worship from Thursday to Saturday, all altars are hidden in purple shrouds, the priest enacts the lavatorio with twelve old men, and all Thursday night people crowd churches. The articulated Santo Entierro is found in much of Hispanic America, and it, or another Ecce Homo, rests in its glass coffin. The burning of Judas today is more widespread in Hispanic America, and particularly in Mexico, than in Spain. The Encuentro procession may take place on any one of several days, e.g., Tzintzuntzan, the Friday before Ash Wednesday (Foster 1948a, p. 209), and among the Yaqui Indians of Hermosilla (Sonora, Mexico), on Good Friday (Barker 1957b, p. 261).

[17] Penitential rites held great attractions for Indians and mestizos in the New World. As is well known, they occur in their most extreme form in the American Southwest (e.g., Barker 1957a) but they are also found today in parts of Mexico, as in Tzintzuntzan where penitentes clad only in loincloths, faces hidden by capuchos, scourge themselves (at least symbolically) with cat-o'-nine-tails, in front of crosses scattered around town, and wear grillos or carry wooden crosses (Foster 1948a, p. 213). Toor (1947, p. 218) says she has seen penitentes in Mexico, apart from Tzintzuntzan, only in the state of Guerrero.

[18] The elaborate processions of pasos are not common in Spanish America. Popayán (Colombia) is perhaps the only Hispanic American city where a true Spanish-type Holy Week series of processions of pasos is found. Holy Week has been celebrated in this fashion in Popayán at least since 1558 (Whiteford 1954).

[19] In 1954 Dr. George Barker witnessed a Passion Play, *La Passió*, in the village of Esparraguera at the foot of Montserrat. The tradition here is said to be about three centuries old (communicated).

Passion plays are still common in Hispanic America and especially in Mexico where, again, that of Tzintzuntzan is one of the most famous (Foster, 1948a, pp. 212-213; Toor 1947, pp. 212-217).

CHAPTER XV

FEAST DAYS AND FIESTAS: MAY TO CHRISTMAS

LA MAYA.—Traces still remain in Spain of a variety of popular observances associated with the month of May, and particularly with the eve of May 1. These activities center around the old European custom of erecting a Maypole, crowning a queen, dancing, and serenading the village girls. The term *la maya*, the feminine form of *Mayo*, the month of May, is applied both to the queen and to any village girls who take part in the festivities. *Cantar la maya* is the expression used when girls are serenaded during May. The term *mayo* is applied to the Maypole, and to the occasional King of May.

Before the night of April 30, village youths cut a tall tree, strip it of branches except for a cluster at the top, decorate it with flowers and ribbons, and at midnight erect it in the village plaza, where it remains throughout the month. The same night a youth places a *ramo*, or *enramada*, a tree branch adorned with flowers and fruits, at the window of his sweetheart and then the young men, in groups, make the rounds, serenading the girls.

The election of the May Queen is often, though not invariably, associated with the Maypole. Traditionally, the loveliest maiden of the village is chosen, clothed in white, crowned with flowers and leaves, and enthroned near the Maypole. While the young people dance and sing around pole and girl, other passersby contribute small sums to the queen, with which the youths purchase the necessities for the day's picnic. In Galicia a king rather than a queen is elected: a youth is clothed in leaves and flowers and, in the company of others, roams the streets begging chestnuts and other delicacies.

The Maypole, though particularly characteristic of the eve of May 1, appears on other occasions as well, such as the San Juan festivities of San Pedro Manrique (Foster 1955) and other villages. Sometimes it becomes a cucaña, the greased pole of Spanish fairs and fiestas. In parts of such provinces as Gerona, Logroño, and Santander a live chicken is fastened to the top of the Maypole, a prize for the most agile youth. The Maypole, as a part of an ancient tree cult, characterizes Spain from Galicia to Catalonia and south through Old Castile. It is not common in the south.

The origin of May festivities in Spain is lost in antiquity, but obviously they come down, in part at least, from pre-Christian times. Several hundred years ago they were popular not only in the country but in the city as well, and such playwrights and dramatists as Lope de Vega and Quiñones de Benavente utilized the theme in their plays. Because of real or imagined

excesses Church and State tried to repress May Day festivities as early as
the sixteenth century, and successive bans appear practically down to the
present time. But, as with other banned Spanish popular customs, the
natural vitality of custom was so great that the only forces that could
discourage tradition are those we know as "modern times." [1]

The Invention of the Cross, May 3.—This date is revered as the anniversary of the "invention" of the Cross (*La invención de la Santa Cruz*),
though why a rediscovery is called an invention is not clear. The story
of the recovery of the Cross is also one of the earliest accounts of an
archaeological expedition. According to history and legend, the Empress Elena, mother of Constantine, made a pilgrimage to Jerusalem,
probably in 326, to search for the cross on which Christ was crucified.
Excavations on the hill of Golgotha turned up three crosses, two of which
presumably were those of the thieves, the third that of Christ. But which
was which? Elena, obviously no mean archaeologist and a pious woman as
well, put them to a test. A mortally ill woman was touched with the three
crosses in succession. The first two made no impression on her, but with
the touch of the third she arose, miraculously cured, so that all knew the
True Cross had indeed been found.

Today religious observances on May 3 are usually restricted to a special
Mass and perhaps a brief street procession. The pleasure in the day lies
in popular rather than church activities. Girls in each neighborhood
decorate crosses on street corners or in homes, tying flowers and ribbons
to them, and lighting candles at their base. When there are several
crosses in a village, the evening may be spent in going from one to another,
to compare the elaborateness of decoration, to comment on the jewels which
are sometimes hung from the arms, and to visit with friends.[2] In Andalusia and Extremadura the custom of decorating an entire room and
dancing in front of the cross, as described for Alosno (p. 127), is still
occasionally found.

The dramatic representations of the discovery of the Cross by the
Empress Elena, enacted in several towns in Badajoz Province, are the
most striking of all popular activities of this day. Gallardo de Alvárez
(1949) has described that of Fuente del Maestre in detail. An extensive
cast portrays in pantomime the activities of Elena, while a chorus of young
girls chants the story.[3]

In Spain the Cross is revered by the population at large; it is not the
patron of any special group. This is in contrast to the Mexican pattern,
where the Cross is patron of masons and bricklayers and where this group
celebrates May 3 by decorating buildings under construction with flowers
and colored paper, by shooting fireworks, and by eating and drinking at
the expense of the owner or contractor.

San Isidro, May 15.—San Isidro, patron saint of farmers and of the
city of Madrid, was a humble field hand, who plowed near the city when
it was simply one among many Spanish villages. Born about 1080, he
became the object of devotion of the Madrileños and of farmers long

before his canonization in 1622. His fame rests on several miracles. One scorching day his master requested a drink from his water bottle while he was plowing beside the Manzanares River. But Isidro was unable to oblige, for he had succorred passing beggars with the last drops. Terrified, he fell to his knees in supplication and implored the Lord to help him, and upon arising he cried out "When God wishes, there will be water here." As he arose he struck a near-by rock with his ox goad, and from it there gushed a stream of cool, clear water which, legend tells, has continued unabated except for a dry period in 1598. Another time, field hands who were jealous of his piety accused Isidro of neglecting his oxen to pray. His master, verifying the charge, was astonished to see that while Isidro knelt in prayer an angel appeared and guided his animals.

Isidro's fame and eventual canonization were assured in 1528 when the Empress Isabela, wife of Carlos I and mother of the future emperor, sent for the miraculous waters of Isidro's fountain to cure the little Infante Felipe of a fever. He quickly recovered, and the grateful mother ordered built the shrine that stands today. Pope Gregory XV canonized Isidro on the same occasion as Saint Ignatius Loyola.

At first the fountain of San Isidro was a shrine to which pilgrims, known as *isidros,* went in search of health. But as the years passed families, lured by fine spring days, sought the fields beside the Manzanares, where Isidro once plowed, for picnics and relaxation. Gradually the atmosphere became that of a verbena, a carnival, with music and dancing and only slight thought of piety and worship. After the Civil War the outing was transferred to the more distant *Dehesa de la Arganzuela,* but the pattern remains as before. The saint's mummified body is interred in a silver coffin in the Church of San Isidro, the provisional cathedral for the diocese of Madrid-Alcalá.

San Isidro's cult in other parts of Spain grew with the importance of Madrid as the new capital of the nation. The day is observed with a special Mass, often paid for by local field hands, and sometimes there is a procession with the saint's image, and singing and dancing in the streets. But the day is less important outside Madrid than in most of Latin America.

Corpus Christi.—According to the old saying:

Tres Jueves hay en el año	Three Thursdays there are in the year,
Que relumbran más que el sol,	That shine more brightly than the sun,
Jueves Santo, Corpus-Christi,	Holy Thursday, Corpus Christi,
Y el día de la Ascensión.	And Ascension Day.

Of the three Thursdays which "shine more brightly than the sun" El Corpus was, without doubt, anticipated with most excitement by young and old alike. This festival in honor of the Real Presence of Christ in the Eucharist was, and is, a solemn day, but it is also one of happiness and joy, as contrasted to the sorrowful mood of Holy Week. Religious fervor was gratified by the sight of the Host exposed in procession in the magnificent *custodia* (monstrance), Biblical history was reëmphasized by the costumed parading characters, the Christian moral was taught in the autos sacramentales, and funny bones were tickled by the dancing "big heads," the careening giants, and the fire-belching *tarasca* dragon, which wove through the streets to the tune of pipe and drum. Free reign to popular imagination in the Corpus processions is now largely a thing of the past, but tradition and history have recorded the life history of the Spanish customs.

Corpus Christi was the last of the major Church observances to appear. Originally the mystery of the Eucharist was honored on Holy Thursday, but with the elaboration of Holy Week activities the role of the Eucharist slipped more and more into the background. Pious legends, however, maintained interest in the dogma of the transformation of the consecrated wafer into Christ's body, and at least as early as the eleventh century the mystery was honored in scattered places with processions.

One of the most famous of the miracle legends is commemorated today in Spain with pomp and splendor in the town of Daroca (Zaragosa). Although the legend follows the general Medieval pattern it has its own characteristic Spanish twists. The great king Jaime I of Aragón undertook the reconquest of Valencia in 1238 and, successful, he left his troops under the command of Don Berenguer de Entenza while he set off about other business. Berenguer, desiring to occupy his troops as well as to add luster to his own name, decided to lay siege to the fortified castle of Chío, amply garrisoned by Moors. With regiments from Calatayud, Teruel, and Daroca, Berenguer camped on a hilltop near the castle where, before attacking, he ordered Mass said in front of a portable field altar, and communion taken by himself and his lieutenants. But scarcely had the Hosts been consecrated when the Moors attacked, and the Christians were forced to dash off to battle.

The chaplain quietly terminated Mass and then, being unable to administer the sacrament to the Christian leaders, folded the six consecrated wafers in the corporals and hid them in near-by rocks. The Christians vanquished the Moors and returned to take communion. But, to the astonishment of all, when the corporals were unfolded it was found that they were bathed in blood, and the wafers had become as if a part of the cloth itself.[4] After prostrating themselves on the ground before this miracle, the soldiers and their leaders fell to quarreling about who should have the precious relics. Seeing that agreement was impossible, Berenguer sought the intervention of Divine Will. The corporals were placed in a small silver ark, which was lashed to the back of a mule, and the animal was turned loose to wander at will. It immediately set out on the road to Aragón and, followed by chaplain and soldiers, reached the gates of Daroca two weeks later. Upon approaching the town by the Lower Gate, the mule fell dead in front of the Hospital of San Marcos. By this sign all knew that Divine Will ruled that the corporals belonged to Daroca. According to popular Spanish belief this miracle, properly brought to the attention of the Pope, was instrumental in the setting aside of a special day on which to honor the mystery of the Eucharist.

Actually Corpus Christi was set aside as a universal feast day in the Church by Pope Urban IV, but this decision was not finally implemented until a 1311 decree of Pope Clemente V. Subsequently the Feast was quickly adopted in most parts of Christendom, and the characteristic forms of the day took shape.

In Spain Barcelona was the first city to celebrate the new Feast, in 1319 or 1320, and in general the entire Levante appears to have placed great emphasis on this day at an earlier period than the Castiles. But during the next two centuries the eucharistic festival came to be the supreme symbol of Spanish Catholicism in all the country, first as a crusade against the Moors and afterwards, following the Council of Trent (1545-1563), as a public manifestation of resistance to spreading Protestantism. During these centuries the forms of the processions were worked out, the participation of municipal authorities, trade-guildsmen, religious confraternities, and clergy was established, the one-act plays known as *entremeses* and *autos sacramentales* developed their roles, and the grotesque *peleles*—dragons, giants, big-headed dwarfs and the like— made their appearance.

The day's events, by all accounts, represented the blending of sacred and profane elements which characterizes so many Spanish feast days. The sermons, the autos sacramentales, the public display of the Host, the parading of Biblical characters reaffirmed the truth of Catholic doctrine and stimulated the natural religious fervor of the masses. At the same time the popular aspects of the day, and particularly the preparation and activating of the mythological figures and characters, afforded a major social and recreational outlet for a people who had few other formal entertainments. Following Mass in the church or cathedral the great procession, sometimes hours long, wound its way along a predetermined route lined with thousands of spectators, who crowded the tapestry- and flower-hung balconies or pressed against the walls of buildings along the narrow streets. The central object in the procession was, of course, the consecrated wafer believed by Catholics to be the true body of Christ, which was exhibited at first in a small *custodia de mano* monstrance and later in an elaborate Gothic shrine of gold and silver, the custodia proper, which in the fifteenth and sixteenth centuries represented one of the highest forms of the goldsmith's art.

The great custodia was accompanied by churchmen of all ranks, lavishly dressed in rich vestments, by members of religious and lay orders, seminary students, the artisans of guilds carrying banners or symbols of their occupations, and by royalty, visiting ambassadors, and other persons of the highest stations in life. From early times various lay and religious groups prepared floats with sculptured or live figures depicting scenes from the Bible, and costumed and masked figures, real and mythological, legendary and allegorical, mingled with huge eagles and dragons and giants and dwarfs. After the procession the autos were enacted, sometimes in front of the cathedral, but, in their heyday, in the great city plazas before the king and his court.

The development and decline of the Corpus procession is documented in the archives of Spanish cities. Probably the earliest to reach full-blown dimensions was that of Barcelona. A 1424 account describes trumpeters who, mounted on horseback, led the long lines, followed by the banner of Santa Eulalia, patron of the city, by ecclesiastics with the standards and processional crosses of all of the churches and convents of the city, by guildsmen, entremeses (religious tableaux), angels, and a great papier-maché eagle. All these preceded the custodia and the bishop, upon whose heels came angels struggling with devils and, finally, two "wild men," who threatened the crowd with distaffs (Almerich 1940, p. 46; Johnson 1941, p. 77).

Thirty-five years later the Barcelona procession had swollen to incredible size. The entremeses of 1461, to mention only a few, included "The Creation of the World," with twelve angels; "Hell," with Lucifer, four devils, San Miguel with a dragon, and twenty-four more devils under the command of a mayoral, or overseer, who struggled with twenty angels; "The Garden of Eden," with Adam and the angel, another Adam with Eve, Cain, and Abel; "Noah's Ark," "with all the necessary apparatus"; "Abraham and Isaac"; "Jacob and the Angel"; "The Daughters of Lot, and Lot and his wife"; "David and Goliath," "The Twelve Tribes of Israel"; all of these, and more, were the work of the trade guilds, which early made Corpus Christi their special day. Cathedral confraternities brought forth Moses and Aaron, all the prophets, John the Baptist, Susan and the angel, the Annunciation, the Nativity, the three Kings, Herod and his doctors, and a great number of saints. Other confraternities portrayed the figures of the Passion, the apostles, more angels and more saints, with a lavishness impossible to describe. Realism was great; in fact, the portrayal of Adam and Eve was so remarkable that subsequently, "for reasons of decency," it was found desirable to suppress this entremés (Almerich 1944, pp. 46-48).

Other particularly noteworthy processions were those of Gerona, Valencia, Sevilla, Toledo, and, in later years, Madrid. An account of the participants in the procession of 1623 in Madrid reads like a *Who's Who* of Spain's Golden Age: two cardinals, the Papal Nuncio, the Bishop of Pamplona, the Inquisitor General, the Patriarch of the Indies, the Ambassadors of Poland, France, Venice, England, and Germany, the Conde-duque of Olivares, the Spanish Grandees, and many more (Mesonero Romanos 1851, pp. 83-84). On the eve of Corpus Christi the *tarasca*, the *mojigón*, and the *tarasquillas* paraded as a group, bowing, dancing, and gesticulating to the sound of pipe and drum, marking the course to be followed the next day by the main procession. The tarasca was a dragon-like creature which rolled on wheels, manipulated by men who walked inside. It had a long neck which, by means of cords, could be made to dart in any direction, to the squeals of children who had come for the purpose of being frightened. The tarasquillas were a pair of wooden figures dressed in the latest mode which rode on the back of the tarasca, while the mojigón was a grotesque and ugly giant, stuffed with inflated bladders, who staggered recklessly from side to side.

A woman's figure, popularly reputed to be that of Anne Boleyn, rode on the back of Toledo's fearsome tarasca. The four pairs of giants that paraded during the eighteenth-century heyday of Toledo's processions represented the four corners of the earth to which Spain had carried the Catholic doctrine: Europe, America, Africa, and Asia. Another figure, with sword in hand, was no less than Spain's great eleventh-century champion against the Moors, *El Cid Campeador*.

With the passage of time the entremeses declined in importance, and because of the "excesses" into which many Spanish popular festivities seemed always to degenerate, they were prohibited by Carlos III in 1780. But the allegorical figures, the *gigantes, cabezudos, enanos, águilas*, and tarascas, continued to play a role much longer, sometimes in the procession, but more often, like the Madrid mojigón and its companions, by tracing the route on the eve of the festival. In Gerona, Barcelona, Valencia, and perhaps other cities of the Levante, eagles, giants, and "big heads" still appear each year, though in other parts of the country the custom seems decadent.

The origin of these creatures is not entirely clear, though they are, of course, survivals of the general Medieval urge towards grotesque buffoonery on the most sacred occasions. The tarasca, in name at least, comes from Tarascon, in Provence, where, as early as 1465, a similar monster, the *tarasque*, participated in the processions of Pentecost and St. Martha (July 29). The tarasque, according to French legend, was a great dragon who devastated the countryside until rendered harmless by St. Martha. In gratitude the people adopted Christianity and made her the patron of the city (Dumont 1951, p. 49). The *dragón* and a giant are mentioned in the 1513 Corpus procession in Gerona, and a 1557 report again speaks of a single giant, suggesting that at this time the pairs had not yet evolved (Pla Cargol 1948, p. 85). Strangely, in spite of linguistic and cultural similarity, and of earlier political unity with Provence, the term "tarasca" seems not to be used in Catalonia. This suggests a relatively late introduction of the word direct from Provence to Castile.

It is possible that the gigantes arose from the entremés of David and Goliath. The latter was portrayed in Barcelona as early as 1391 as a giant, a cover over a frame, chained to a David of normal size. Not until 1568 is there mention of a *giganta*, a female companion (Almerich 1944, p. 50), and presumably the symbolism of the four continents was an outgrowth of this pair, as Spanish conquests covered the earth. Catalonian giants of recent years are often reduced to a single pair, elaborately dressed as Gothic kings and queens. Big heads too, still dance, although they are mere clowns or *payasos*, designed only to evoke laughs. The eagle, unlike the other figures, seems to be peculiar to Catalonia and its daughter kingdom of Valencia. Its antiquity is probably as great as that of David and the giant. The "big heads," on the other hand, appear to be much more recent, perhaps of the eighteenth century. They do not appear in Gerona until even later, in 1868 (Pla Cargol 1948, p. 87).

For three centuries or more, dramatic representations were an integral part of the Corpus festivities. In contrast to the simple, usually jocular skit of the entremés, the auto sacramental was a serious one-act play dealing with a religious theme, enacted during the days between Corpus Christi and the octave. The primitive autos were the work of the clergy, and took place inside churches and cathedrals. In the sixteenth century the clergy were prohibited from participating, and the representations were taken over by lay groups, particularly trade guilds and confraternities, and were henceforth given out of doors, usually in front of the cathedral where the custodia was displayed, in the afternoon following the procession.

The early autos were associated with Corpus only by being presented on this day. Most of the sixteenth-century representations are anonymous. The art developed under Lope de Vega and Tirso de Molino and reached its perfected form in the autos of Calderón de la Barca, in which the mystery of the Eucharist is dwelt upon in theological allegories, purged of the earlier popular and historic aspects. In the seventeenth century these autos were sumptuously staged in the Plaza Mayor of Madrid in the presence of the king and his court, as well as such commoners as could crowd into the restricted space. Apparently the art could go no further than this. Calderón's followers limited themselves to imitation, and by the beginning of the eighteenth century new autos were no longer being composed. The representations dragged on with decreasing vigor, and the final prohibition by Carlos III in 1763 was scarcely necessary, for the vitality had vanished a century earlier.

Religious dances, a part of many Spanish festivals and romerías, are also associated with the observances of Corpus Christi. In Valleruela de Pedraza (Segovia) sword dancers click castanets as they weave their intricate steps in front of an image of the Virgin. The eight youths who dance are dressed in white skirts trimmed in red worn over white shirts, pants, stockings, and sneakers. Plumed mitres cover their heads and colored ribbons and handkerchiefs fly from their shoulders and sleeves (Martínez Alcalde 1930, pp. 71-73). Sword dancers also appear to have been common in southern Spain: a Sevilla decree in 1532 prohibited cofradía and guild sword dancers from preceding the custodia, relegating them to the tail end of the procession and to performing only in authorized places (Rosa y López 1904, p. 189).

The most spectacular Corpus dancers are the *seises* (choir boys) of the Sevilla cathedral. These *niños cantorcicos*, as they were first called, are mentioned in 1508 in such manner as to imply that they had sung and danced for many years before. Dressed as angels with wings and crowned with garlands of flowers, they danced before the primitive wooden custodia of the cathedral, not only on the occasion of Corpus Christi but also on such other feast days as Christmas and during Holy Week. The name "seises" probably stems from the fact that originally there were six singers, although the number has oscillated considerably over the centuries. In 1565 it was fixed at ten, the number that dance today (Rosa y López 1904, p. 244).

The seises of Sevilla formerly received a thorough musical and literary education in the San Miguel School. Subsequently this was reduced to a primary education, with emphasis on music and Latin. Since the musical life of the seises ended with their changing voices, like choir boys in other parts of Europe they were sometimes castrated. This practice is first mentioned in 1620, and as late as 1829 one of the seises was so mutilated (Rosa y López 1904, p. 137).

Today the seises, as they dance and sing before the high altar in the cathedral in Sevilla on Corpus Christi and on the anniversary of the Immaculate Conception (December 8), provide one of the most moving of all Spanish religious spectacles. The seises of Toledo, of whom there are seven, have not fared as well. Formerly they appeared on Christmas, at Corpus, on the occasion of the celebration of the Virgin of August, at receptions for royalty, and on other special days of national rejoicing. But since 1866 they have not danced and are, as a result, little known compared to their brothers of Sevilla.

Although the modern Corpus Christi processions of Catalonia and the Levante today are more interesting than those of the rest of Spain, we found it most convenient in 1950 to visit Toledo. Here the procession is purely religious, and, though splendid and striking, there is nothing popular about it.

Intrigued by the rumor that two "small" giants—not the traditional figures—had paraded the preceding evening, we visited the cathedral, and in an obscure and out-of-the-way corner discovered what appear to be the remains of the wonderful figures brought from Barcelona in 1755 in the heyday of tarascas, "big heads," and giants. The tarasca was a turtlelike creature about three meters long, its single head mounted on an accordion frame so that it could be made to dart out from its shell. This realistic touch was further heightened by an ingenious lower jaw that could be made to snap shut when activated by a string concealed in the neck. A small angel, a reduced tarasquilla by no stretch of the imagination an Anne Boleyn, rode on the tarasca's back.

The eight dust-covered giants were in a less well preserved state, but it was still possible to associate them with the descriptions of earlier centuries. The construction of all was the same: hands and faces of carved and painted wood mounted on a framework four meters tall covered with cloth. Men as well as women wore skirts. Two giants represented America. Señor América sported a long jacket and a raccoon cap and carried a medallion of the Virgin of Guadalupe. La Señora de América held a cornucopia, wore great earrings, and carried a medallion of the Virgin of Guadalupe hanging on a cord around her neck.

The African pair were easily identified by their black skins. The man held a huge sword and the woman a dove, perhaps symbolizing the presence of the Holy Spirit in darkest Africa as well as in the centers of civilization. The female caretaker who had so obligingly admitted us to this storeroom said that two other figures were "Turks," although the man, at least, with his shaved head, mandarin mustache, and wide-bladed cutlass, looked more Chinese than Turkish. Europe was represented by a red-jacketed "Spain" armed with a sword, and by a jaunty "Cid Campeador" with a great scimitar, plumed hat, and a medallion of the Virgin of the Sagrario hanging around its neck.[5]

San Juan, June 24.—In its advance over Europe primitive Christianity, through a process of syncretism, quickly captured and tamed most of the pagan rites and beliefs which might threaten it. The winter solstice was dominated by the birth of Christ, spring fertility rites became identified with the death and resurrection of the Savior, and vengeful spirits of the dead were cajoled in the observances of All Saints' and All Souls' days. One day alone could not be subdued. Although the summer solstice with its purification by fire and water was early dedicated to St. John the Baptist, who cleansed with water, it has remained an uneasy captive throughout Europe over nearly two thousand years, and the pre-Christian customs are still clearly evident.

In Spain no other occasion equals the eve and morning of San Juan for variety and interest of folk activities. Insofar as there is geographical difference, it is the familiar division between north and south Spain, between those areas in which Celtic and Gothic strains have remained near the ethnic surface and those regions repopulated from the north after the expulsion of the Moors. And, following the rule of greater variety in the less disturbed areas, it is in the north that more distinct customs are apparent. Nevertheless, in spite of differences there is a Pan-Spanish pattern that recognizes both fire and water as purificatory agents, that associates magic and curing with this occasion, that allows amatory rites and activities of various types, and lets people persuade themselves that this morning they see the sun rise "dancing."

Fires—the Midsummer's Night fires of antiquity—blaze from the hilltops soon after dark on the evening of June 23, and spring forth at street intersections and in public plazas in the cities. When the flames have died down, the children who have danced around the fires jump over them, believing they will thus protect themselves from illness and misfortune throughout the year. In the valleys of the Central and Eastern Pyrenees, men and youths gather in the mountains above their villages, carrying pine-pitch torches called *falles*. After dark the torches are lighted and the participants race down the mountain side, to deposit torches in great fires in public plazas or before churches.

Especially in the north, Maypole festivities, usually combined with the custom of placing wreaths or sprays on the windows of girls, are common. But even in the south, as in Alosno (Huelva), youths and maidens go in groups to the hills on the eve of San Juan and cut pine trees, which they erect in the middle of streets. After dark the young people of each neighborhood sing and dance around their "Maypole," an activity known as *bailando el pino*, "dancing the pine." Next morning *los cascabeleros*, seventeen men from the Hermandad of San Juan wearing *cascabeles* (sleighbells) around their ankles, dance in front of the image of the saint as it passes through the streets in procession, and upon returning to the church they again dance in front of the altar.

Curing practices and preparations are especially efficacious on San Juan. The magical purificatory power of water is exploited in many ways, particularly by the act of bathing in fountains or streams at midnight or dawn. At least in the north such an immersion is known, after the saint's name, as a *sanjuanada*. In the ports of Galicia it is believed that he who bathes at midnight and is splashed by nine waves will recover from whatever ails him or will be preserved from illness throughout the year. The dew of the dawn of San Juan is unlike that of any other morning of the year. Those who suffer from skin diseases, and especially those mangelike afflictions known as *sarna*, may disrobe and roll in the cool, damp grass, sure that their suffering will be alleviated. The *flor del agua*, the "flower of water," is equally efficacious, if somewhat more elusive. Some believe the flor to be a real, if magical, flower, while others say it is the topmost microscopically thin layer of water over which falls the blessing of St. John. In either case the maiden who can discover or obtain the flor del agua achieves complete felicity.

Medicinal herbs gathered the eve of St. John are especially potent as compared to those plucked at other times of the year. Verbena and sweet basil are thought of as the flowers of St. John, but all other common herbs are more effective if picked this night and, for the very best results, left *al sereno*, exposed to the night's dew until morning.[6]

Assumption Day, August 15.—On *el día de la Asunción* a catafalque is erected in churches and on it an image of the Virgin reposes until the octave a week later. There is a special Mass and occasionally a street procession. A few minor superstitions are associated with this day in various parts of the country. In Puebla de Guzmán (Huelva) people sometimes break a small olive branch from a tree and gather several heads of wheat, which they nail to the walls of their homes, saying that, if this is done, *ni le faltará ni paz ni pan por todo el año*, neither peace nor bread will be absent during the year.

The most noteworthy event of Assumption Day in Spain, however, is the famous mystery play produced in Elche (Alicante), a drama so spectacular that in 1931 it was declared a "national monument" (Serra Boldú 1946, p. 587). The origin legend of the appearance of the miraculous image of the Virgin now in the church of Santa María de la Asunción follows a familiar Spanish theme. In 1370 a chest marked "For Elche" floated ashore at the near-by fishing village of Santa Pola. Since the jurisdiction of the coast at this point was divided between Elche, Orihuela, and Alicante, authorities of all three cities were advised. To make sure the "For Elche" address was not spurious they ordered the chest placed upon the back of a blindfolded horse, so that the Divine Will would make itself known. The horse had no doubts; it walked directly to Elche and stopped in front of the Hermitage of San Sebastián. After great difficulty workmen succeeded in opening the chest, which had no visible exterior aperture, and inside they found the image and a parchment with instructions for an annual fiesta to be held in honor of the Virgin.[7]

The first act of the modern drama takes place the afternoon of August 14 in the church where a cloth "sky" has been stretched under an opening in the dome, beneath which stands a stage. As the scene opens, a sorrowing Virgin, accompanied by two "mute" Marys and a chorus of angels, all played by youths, kneels and chants her desire to die and join her Son. The "sky" opens and a great blue ball representing a pomegranate is lowered to the stage, where it falls open, revealing an angel who bows to the Virgin and tells her that in three days her wish will be granted. Mary asks that the apostles be permitted to join her. All except Thomas arrive, the Virgin greets them, says goodbye, and expires. The apostles care for her body, substituting the original image which rests on the catafalque for the youth who plays the living part. Celestial music sounds, the sky opens again, and the Ara Coeli, the altar of the sky, is lowered. On it rests an angel, who superintends four cherubims playing harps and guitars. They take Mary's soul, represented by a small effigy of the Virgin, back to heaven.

The second scene takes place the next afternoon after morning Mass and an impressive procession in which the apostles—Thomas still missing —carry the image of the Virgin on its bier. On the stage the image of the Virgin is surrounded by praying apostles and angels. The apostles raise the body and carry it to a tomb, an opening in the floor of the stage. But suddenly a noisy and ill-mannered group of ten "Jews" enters. They dispute the real death of the Virgin with the apostles, fight with them, and then accept conversion to Christianity. At this moment the heavens again open, the Ara Coeli descends with the angel and the soul of Mary, and the chorus chants an invitation to Mary to ascend to her eternal home. The sequence is briefly interrupted as a breathless Thomas appears, apologizing profusely for his tardiness, explaining that urgent business in the Indies has delayed him. After this comic relief the image of the Virgin is placed on the Ara Coeli which rises to midair, where it pauses. Simultaneously another group of live figures representing the Holy Trinity is lowered until the priest who plays the part of the Eternal Father can place a silver crown on the Virgin's head. Thus crowned as Mother of God, Mary, with the Holy Trinity, disappears in the sky, the municipal band plays the Royal March, the organ bursts out in thunderous sounds, bells are rung, and the audience gives vent to its last outburst of enthusiasm until the same time next year.[8]

All Saints' and All Souls' Days, November 1-2.—November 1, the day of *Todos los Santos* and November 2, *día de difuntos* or *día de las benditas ánimas*, are observed in much the same way in all parts of the country. Both days have special offices for the morning Masses and on one of the two days, depending on local custom, everyone visits the cemetery to pay homage to the dead. In the larger cities the visits have been rather festive and social events for several generations, but in smaller villages the visits are still impressively marked by solemnity and signs of piety. Shawled women carry covered baskets from which they draw flowers and oil lamps or candles to light the graves. The chrysanthemum is the flower most in evidence, not because of sacred significance but because at this time of year it is most plentiful. In some places, especially Catalonia, the small yellow "everlasting" *siempreviva* is much used, suggestive of the similar yellow *simplasuche* of the Mexican Aztecs, which is still the traditional flower of the dead in Mexico.

In much of northern Spain (Basque provinces, northern Old Castile, and Aragón) offerings of wheat or bread and wine were taken to Mass to be blessed, or were placed directly on graves. The custom appears not to have been common in the south, and even now it has almost disappeared in the north.[9] Belief that the souls of the dead return to earth to partake of this food scarcely exists any more, although formerly in Asturias this thought was so firmly engrained that, in Proaza for example, few people went to bed the eve of *ánimas*. Most people left their beds free so that the souls of departed relatives could rest if they wished during their night on earth (Giner Arivau 1886, p. 246).

The traditional activity of the eve of All Souls' Day is the night-long tolling of the church bells by boys, and sometimes adults as well, who warm themselves around a bonfire, roast chestnuts, and drink wine.[10] In many small villages of northern and central Spain youths go from house to house asking alms for the dead, sometimes praying for the souls of the dead of each house as the request is made. The alms, either in kind or in cash, are turned over to the priest, who is expected, in return, to supply the night's refreshments.

Our quest for typical All Saints' and All Souls' Day observances led us to Hoyos del Espino (Avila), a bleak village of six hundred inhabitants near the Parador de Gredos, high in the sierra of the same name. Here the parish church of Nuestra Señora del Espino is situated some distance above and to the west of the village, which it dominates from an open hillside. A miracle legend of stock form explains the unusual location for a village church. Centuries ago an image of the Virgin appeared to a shepherd girl at an *espino*, a hawthorne tree that stood at this spot. The villagers, delighted to have a "miraculous" virgin, carried the image to a hermitage near the center of the settlement. But next morning the image had disappeared, and only after diligent search was it re-discovered at the spot where it first appeared. Twice again the image was carried to the hermitage, and twice again it returned to the espino. Only then did the villagers understand that they were to build a new shrine, the church where today the *Virgen del Encino* stands enshrined, surrounded by paintings, *milagros*, that tell of some of the wonders she has worked.[11]

One picture represents her appearance to the shepherd girl. A second portrays a young girl suspended in midair between high cliffs over a cruel river; the unfortunate child slipped and fell but, when she called on the Virgin to save her, her descent was abruptly checked and she floated to safety. Another picture shows a paralytic leaving her crutches behind; this young woman had begged the Virgin to aid her and, overcome with emotion upon ending her prayers, she stood up without thinking and walked unaided out of the building. A final picture tells of still another miracle. A terrible fire broke out in the neighboring village of Barajas which threatened to destroy all the buildings. In desperation some of the inhabitants raced to Hoyos to carry the Virgin to save their homes. But midway between the villages the image became so heavy that it could not be moved. Sadly the men turned their backs on their burning village to return the Virgin who had blasted their faith, but as they did so the flames miraculously died down and the fire went out. But the Virgin is most loved, locally at least, because within the memory of living man no son of Hoyos has died in battle.

Here, on a cold and blustery November 1 we found ourselves attending Mass. As in many other churches in Spain the youths stood in the balcony while the men stood beneath. The women knelt over the ancient family floor tombs in the center of the building and the town officials sat on the two benches flanking the altar that were reserved for such dignitaries. After Mass the men hurriedly left but the women tarried to place flowers, candles, and oil-burning *luminarios* on the gravestones, which were first covered with white cloths. Then the priest, accompanied by two acolytes, went from grave to grave to bless them, after which the women departed for home and a late meal. Later in the afternoon a Rosary was said in a new hermitage in the village and then a procession formed to walk to the near-by, new, open-air cemetery, where the grave decorations and blessings of the morning were repeated.

Meanwhile the parish bells began to toll. Pairs of young girls climbed the low stairs to the belfry—a construction separate from and to one side of the church—and several times struck each of the two bells. This was done by dashing the clapper of the stationary bells from side to side with a rope attached for this purpose. Then the girls descended the stairs and entered the church to pray at several Stations of the Cross, their places at the bells taken by other waiting pairs. By dusk it was the turn of the youths and, still later and until past midnight, married couples made the pilgrimage up the slopes to toll the bells for their dead.

Although youthful bell-ringers no longer light a fire and gather to roast chestnuts and drink wine, fires in honor of the souls appeared on surrounding hills, set by shepherds in their solitary watches. And in Barajas, on our way back to the Parador, we found a group of children who, though not bell-ringers, were enjoying themselves roasting chestnuts and jumping over their bonfire. Next day the catafalque was erected, a large black cloth-covered bier on one end of which rested a bleached human skull. This *tumba,* we were told, would remain during the octave, to be removed a week hence.[12]

Christmas.—The Christmas season begins in Spain on the day of the Immaculate Conception, December 8. From this time on groups of carolers are heard singing Christmas carols *(villancicos),* the clay and pasteboard figures and settings of Nativity scenes appear in marketplaces, and special foods like the honey-and-almond *turrón* and marzipan are offered for sale. Carols are accompanied by strange and wonderful instruments: the *zambomba* friction drum, the druggist's brass mortar and pestle, iron triangles, tambourines, hand bells and the *carraca,*[13] a corrugated tin tube over which a wire brush or stick is scraped. In Andalusia such carolers are called *campanilleros* because of the bells they carry. At each home where they stop to sing they hope to be invited in to receive the Christmas *aguinaldo,*[14] a food delicacy or perhaps a small coin.

No city home is complete without its miniature Nativity scene, and families vie to outdo each other in the elaborateness of their settings. The Spanish custom of such scenes, known variously as *pesebres* (mangers), *belenes* (Bethlehems), and *nacimientos* (from *nacer,* "to be born") is Italian in origin. The first recorded Nativity scenes with clay figurines (as contrasted to painted or carved representations) are from Naples, in 1478, although the custom there appears to have begun sometime earlier (Pérez-Cuadrada 1948, p. 20; Ferrandis 1951, p. 27). These early Nativity representations were placed in churches, and were not characteristic of homes. In the sixteenth century small sculptured scenes of the birth of Christ began to appear in Spain, and in the seventeenth century such artists as Eugenio Torices, Luisa Roldán, and José Risueño created miniature and life-size representations of the Nativity, some modeled in wax and some carved in wood.

But the popularization of Nativity scenes in Spain is a phenomenon of the latter part of the eighteenth century. When Charles III left the throne of Naples to become Emperor of Spain in 1759 he brought with him, among other artistic influences, a keen interest in belenes. The Valencian artists José Esteve Bonet and José Ginés were commissioned by him to produce a collection of Nativity figurines in the Neapolitan style as a present to his son, the Prince of Asturias. The custom quickly caught on among the nobility who, in imitation of their monarch, commissioned other Levantine artists for similar works. Of these the most famous were the Murcian Francisco Salzillo (1707-1783) and the Barcelonese Ramón Amadeu (1745-1821). Salzillo's full-sized images of Christ and the Virgin, which may be seen in a number of churches and convents in Murcia, are among Spain's finest artistic treasures, but to the anthropologist his exquisite painted pottery Nativity figurines in the Museo de Murcia are even more interesting. For, like the Neapolitan nacimientos, these figures portray not only the Biblical characters of the Nativity, but artisans and craftsmen of the artist's period and environment, complete in every detail of costume, tools, and activities. Amadeu, like Salzillo, created full-sized religious images of great merit, but his fame rests on his painted pottery figurines, which show much the same range of imagination and artistry as those of his Murcian counterpart.

But belenes today, in the sense of individual home Nativity scenes, belong in the realm of folk art, even though many of the figurines are factory-produced. The members of each family visit markets early in December to make their selection of humans, animals, trees, houses, and other props, so that when finally erected at home, no two Nativity scenes are identical. The growth of the custom of belenes as a folk activity follows the same principle previously mentioned in the discussion of clothing (p. 96), the outward and downward flow of forms and ideas from the upper classes and the nobility, so that culture which, in one century, is of the elite may in the next be taken over by the masses through the process of imitation and copy. In this popularization of the custom of belenes the Franciscan Order, which from the time of St. Francis has shown a special interest in the Nativity, has played an important part.

Today Nativity figures are made in many cities, but Olot (Gerunda) has inherited the mantel of Barcelona, probably as the result of the years Amadeu spent there at the beginning of the nineteenth century, while in Murcia the industry is carried on in four flourishing workshops. We visited Mirete Rubio's shop, where we found the figures were cast in molds before firing and painting. The finest type, of which there were ninety-five different models, are copied after the Salzillo figurines, and like these are of considerable ethnographic interest because they portray eighteenth-century Murcians in peasant garb engaged in a variety of traditional occupations.[15]

Christmas Eve (nochebuena) and Christmas Day are family occasions when relatives eat together and attend church in a group. Less frequently than formerly the season and day of the Nativity, La Navidad, are symbolized, usually by a great yule log but occasionally by a straw-filled figure. This Christmas log, el nochebueno, is also called by local terms: tuero in western Andalusia, cabezero in eastern Andalusia and Murcia, and tío ("uncle") in Catalonia. In Basque, Christmas is called olentzero or a variant term, and the log becomes olentzeroenbor. Here the season's spirit is represented by olentzero, the "red-eyed" one, a straw-stuffed figure who, with scythe in hand, sits in the chimney corner to watch over the yule log or parades through the streets in the company of carolers.

Pla Cargol describes the lively fiesta del tío in Gerona (1948, pp. 32-33). A great log covered with a cloth is placed near the fireplace. On Christmas Eve the children pray briefly in an adjoining room that "uncle" will favor them. Then with loud laughter they enter "uncle's" room, beat him unmercifully with stout sticks, and shout "Uncle, uncle, defecate a turrón, and if you don't, blows from our sticks!" When "uncle" has been well beaten, his cloth is removed, revealing packages of turrón and other candies beside the log. Only then is "uncle" put on the fire to burn.[16]

The *Misa del gallo*, the midnight Christmas Eve Mass, was formerly the scene for folk dramas known as *autos de nacimiento* in which the birth and adoration of Christ were portrayed. These representations enjoyed their greatest popularity from the fifteenth to the seventeenth centuries, but in greatly reduced form they continued down into the present century as *Los pastorcillos de Belén*. Fernández-Núñez (1914, pp. 392-399) describes how in La Bañeza (León) shepherds arrived for the midnight Mass in company with the townspeople. A fire was lighted on the stone floor of the chancel and the shepherds lay down, feigning sleep. The youngest shepherd apprentice, the *zagalillo*, appeared, dressed as an angel, to announce to the slumbering herders the birth of the Lord in a far-off land. But the shepherds slept soundly and only their chief, the mayoral, perceived, as if in a dream, the visit of the angel. He prostrated himself before the angel, awakened his companions, and expressed his belief that they had been elected to bring to mankind the news of the fulfillment of the ancient prophecy of the Saviour. The sleepy shepherds voiced disbelief, but then in their sleepy stupor they heard the Divine Voice and, enthused by their mayoral, they broke into shouts of rejoicing, which died away only as they left the fire to follow the star of Bethlehem.[17]

Formerly the Misa del gallo was lively for other reasons as well. In small towns tambourines, drums, flutes, and castanets added rhythm to the choral efforts of the singers, and in towns and cities the organist was allowed to play fandangos, Galician folk dances, and other popular tunes in addition to ritual music. But the excesses of the custom were such that eventually this exuberance was prohibited, and today the Cock's Mass is marked by the same decorum as all other Masses.

Inocentes.—Christmas Day is followed by *Los santos inocentes*, December 28, the anniversary of the day of Herod's massacre of infants in the futile hope of killing the Christ child. In spite of the grisly nature of the origin of the day, for centuries it has been a kind of All Fool's Day marked by burlesques and jokes. The election of a Boy Bishop from among the cathedral cantors and the burlesques which he and his fellow cantors disguised as canons carried out are no more, but there is still a good deal of informal horseplay. Children cut out paper dolls and pin them to the skirts of unsuspecting women, or try to send friends—children and adults alike—on false missions.

Jokes of former years were less innocent. Pranksters heated coins or horseshoes to nearly red heat and then dropped them in the streets in the hope that some passerby would think he had found good luck and thus burn his fingers. Artisans were expected to deceive their new apprentices, sending them for the equivalent of "left-handed monkey wrenches," and the public at large was not spared molestation, for spaghetti-makers put strings in their product, pastry-makers esparto grass in their cakes, and candlemakers false wicks in their tapers.[18]

COMPARISONS AND COMMENTS

Several general geographical distributions emerge from the analysis of the major fiestas of the ceremonial year in Spain. The following traits particularly characterize north or north-central Spain, as contrasted to the south: Epiphany's broad-bean-in-bread and its trick-or-treat, the Candlemas torta, Santa Agueda and its alcaldesas, the burial of the king as a part of Carnival celebrations, and la maya. The Carnival "sardine" is buried in Extremadura and, as pointed out, reached great importance in Madrid, but this custom seems to have been of very slight consequence in Andalusia. The piñata may have been more important in east Spain, because of introduction from Italy, but it is difficult to tell at this date.

It is clear that those feast days the Church considered central to dogma are well established in America, while those in which it had less interest are either absent or celebrated only to a limited degree. There is both positive and negative evidence to indicate this. The much greater importance of San Isidro in America than in Spain, for example, probably stems from the fact that the fiesta in his honor, as patron of Madrid, became a part of formally transmitted religious culture, and so was incorporated in the annual cycle of feast days in America from the earliest days. By way of contrast, the day of Santa Agueda, celebrated so colorfully only a few miles away in Segovia, was of no great interest to the Church, and it dropped by the wayside. The same is true of San Blas fiestas. Positive sixteenth-century opposition to la maya may explain why customs of this day are rare in Spanish America.

REFERENCES

La maya: Alford (1937, p. 40), Anonymous (1923, pp. 473, 477, 480, 497, 501), Bautista Merino (1949, p. 47), Caro Baroja (1946b, pp. 469, 483), Casas Gaspar (1947, pp. 246-247), Coloma y Santana (1930), Fuente Arrimadas (1925, p. 253), Giménez de Aguilar (1928), González Palencia and Mele (1944), Violant y Simorra (1949, pp. 585-587).

Invention of the Cross: Deleito y Piñuela (1944, pp. 29-31), Flores (1877, pp. 70-72), Gallardo de Alvárez (1949), Gonzáles Palencia and Mele (1944, pp. 71-72), Hernández de Soto (1883-1884), Hoyos Sancho (1953b), Marcos de Sande (1945, pp. 450-451), Martínez (1883-1884; 1884, pp. 10-13), Mesonero Romanos (1851, pp. 17-19), Répide (1914, pp. 102-104), Serra Boldú (1946, pp. 547-554).

San Isidro: Anonymous (1926a), Castillo de Lucas (1943, pp. 41-47), Cortada y Sala and Manjarrés (1945, pp. 164-166), Deleito y Piñuela (1944, p. 44), Flores (1877, p. 75), Kany (1929, p. 63; 1932, pp. 366-367), Mesonero Romanos (1851, pp. 17-19), Olmo (1928), Pla Cargol (1947, pp. 285, 366), Répide (1914, pp. 107-113).

Corpus Christi: Alford (1937, p. 40), Almerich (1944, pp. 45-52), Anonymous (n.d.; 1844; 1923, pp. 489, 494; 1926b), Capmany (1944, pp. 364-377), Chía (1895), Colón y Colón (1840), Corbató (1932), Cortada y Sala and Manjarrés (1945, pp. 177-196), Dumont (1951), Durán y Sanpere (1943), Flecniakoska (1954), Flores (1877, pp. 87-92), Garrido Atienza (1889), Gascón de Gotor (1916), Iribarren (1946, pp. 145-148), Johnson (1941), Kany (1929, pp. 81-85; 1932, pp. 368-373), Magán (1841),

Martínez Alcalde (1930), Mesonero Romanos (1851, pp. 83-86), Otañón (1928; 1934), Pfandl (1942, pp. 156-161, 224-226), Pla Cargol (1947, pp. 291-296; 1948, pp. 76-88), Puigarrí y Llobet (1857), Répide (1914, pp. 115-127), Rodríguez Elías (1934), Rosa y López (1904), Serra Boldú (1946, pp. 554-571), Thalamas Labandíbar (1931, pp. 54-55), Varey and Shergold (1953).

San Juan: Almerich (1944, pp. 53-55), Anonymous (1928), Cabal (1925a, pp. 193-222), Caro Baroja (1948; 1950b), Chico y Rello (1947), Cortada y Sala and Manjarrés (1945, pp. 213-219), Deleito y Piñuela (1944, pp. 53-67), Foster (1955), Giner Arivau (1886, pp. 243-244), Hoyos Sáinz and Hoyos Sancho (1947, pp. 102-104), Iribarren (1949, pp. 135-157), Jiménez Sánchez (1954), Kany (1932, pp. 100-101), Llano Rosa (1919, pp. 182-183), Pérez Vidal (1945), Pla Cargol (1947, pp. 242, 290; 1948, p. 118), Ramón y Fernández (1950, p. 83), Rodríguez López (1948, pp. 151-156), Taboada (1952), Tal (1899, pp. 6-8), Violant y Simorra (1949, pp. 588-597).

The drama of Elche: Davillier (1949, pp. 1087-1089), Herrera (1896), Ibarra y Ruiz (1895, pp. 250-268), Llopis (1928a), Serra Boldú (1946, pp. 582-587).

All Saints' and All Souls' days: Alford (1937, p. 58), Almerich (1944, pp. 71-75), Anderson (1939, pp. 305-307), Anonymous (1923, p. 490), Caballé y Clos (n.d., pp. 237-241), Castellanos (1953, pp. 348-349), Cortada y Sala and Manjarrés (1945, pp. 285-292), Ford (1846, pp. 250-251), Fuente Arrimadas (1925, p. 256), Giner Arivau (1886, pp. 246-247), Kany (1929, pp. 120-121), Manrique (1952, pp. 521-522), Marcos de Sande (1945, p. 460), Répide (1914, pp. 184-193).

Christmas: Alford (1937, pp. 13-14, 97, 137), Almerich (1944, pp. 82-89), Caballé y Clos (n.d., pp. 333-364), Caro Baroja (1946b), Cortada y Sala and Manjarrés (1945, pp. 313-318), Córte (1844), Fernández-Núñez (1914, pp. 392-399), Ferrandis (1951), Flecniakoska (1954), Flores (1877, pp. 177-180), Fraguas Fraguas (1947), Gallardo de Alvárez (1944), Garrut (1950), Kany (1932, pp. 134-140), María de Azkue (1935, pp. 323-370), Pérez-Cuadrado (1948), Pla Cargol (1947, pp. 358-359; 1948, pp. 32-35), Répide (1914, pp. 195-201), Serra Boldú (1946, pp. 508-514), Tal (1899, pp. 29-48), Violant y Simorra (1949, pp. 558-564; 1953, pp. 115-124).

Inocentes: Almerich (1944, pp. 89-91), Cortada y Sala and Manjarrés (1945, pp. 319-322), Pla Cargol (1948, p. 34), Répide (1914, pp. 201-202).

NOTES

[1] Elaborate May Day festivities do not generally characterize Spanish America, but the Maypole itself, in the form of the *baile de cintas*, occurs as a part of fiestas in several countries, notably as the *sebucán* in Venezuela (e.g., Liscano 1950, p. 209; Olivares Figueroa 1949, pp. 84-85), in Argentina (Coluccio 1950, p. 121), and in Mexico, where the dance was performed in Tlaxcalla at least as early as 1538 (Mendoza 1957, p. 13). The cucaña is, of course, a traditional part of fiestas in Hispanic America. The attitude of the Church is probably the major reason why May Day festivities in America are essentially lacking.

[2] This is a common Spanish American pattern (cf. Tzintzuntzan, Foster 1948a, p. 215).

[3] I have not encountered this presentation in Spanish America.

[4] The miracle at Tepeyac, when the image of the Virgin of Guadalupe was impressed in the *tilma* cloth of the devout Indian, Juan Diego, suggests this theme.

[5] Modern Corpus Christi observances in Spanish America appear to have lost the pomp and variety of former years. In colonial times processions apparently were much like those of Spain, with religious orders and trade guilds taking part. The Tzintzuntzan representation of muleteers, crate carriers, and farmers with oxen appears to be a folk-level reflection of former times (Foster 1948a, pp. 216-217). In Ayacucho (Peru) altars are erected and decorated in the plaza by artisans—bakers, tailors, blacksmiths, leather tanners, shoemakers, carpenters, hat-makers and others (Bustamente 1943, p. 85). This is also done in Cuzco (Toor 1949, p. 173). *Gigantones* appear in various

Spanish American festivals; I have seen them on December 8 in Pátzcuaro, Mexico, and I have seen the figures, reputedly used for Corpus Christi, in Ciudad Vieja (Antigua, Guatemala). The tarasca was introduced to America but, to judge by surviving traces, it must not have been important. Starr writes: "Everywhere . . . the day [Corpus Christi] is looked forward to by children, who promptly beg for their tarasca on getting up in the morning. These are sold on the streets. They are figures of a curious winged creature, somewhat like a dragon. They are usually set úpon little wagons, sometimes in such fashion that when dragged the tarasca moves, rising or falling" (1899, p. 82). Both the tarasca and the dragón formerly marched in Corpus processions in Venezuela (Olivares Figueroa 1946, pp. 136-137). In Colombia the tarasca is a wild, mythological creature, a bogeyman, who lives in caves and is evoked to frighten children (Escobar Uribe 1950, pp. 95-97). The Corpus tarasca must have given rise to him. Seises formerly danced in the cathedral in Cuzco; I do not know whether they were found in other American cities or not, but they are suggested by the *Santiaguitos* of Chila, Sierra de Puebla (Mexico), ten young boys who dance in front of the church altar during a February fiesta (Kurath 1949, p. 87).

[6] American San Juan observances are similar to those of Spain, but again perhaps somewhat less intense. Fires commonly are lighted, particularly in the highlands of Peru and Bolivia (e.g., Toor 1949, p. 134; pp. 217-218; Rigoberto Paredes 1920, p. 205). Bathing is widespread, from Mexico on south. Divination techniques similar to those of Spain are common, particularly among non-Indian groups. In Venezuela, as in northern Spain, the belief exists that *el sol sale bailando* on the morning of San Juan (Olivares Figueroa 1949, p. 140).

[7] The theme of the chest floating ashore bringing a miraculous image is found in Hispanic America. The image of *Nuestro Señor de los Temblores* in Cuzco was found floating off the shores of Callao. It was so heavy that it could be moved only when Cuzco was mentioned, thereby showing that it was intended for that city, rather than near-by Lima (Toor 1949, p. 120).

[8] The Feast of the Assumption is important in Spanish America, but I know of no fiesta that approaches that of Elche in elaborateness.

[9] Similar visits to graves particularly characterize Mexico.

[10] Bell-tolling and cooking food over an open fire is still done in Mexico (cf., Tzintzuntzan, Foster 1948a, p. 220).

[11] This is one of the most common types of legends of the origin of miraculous images in America. Morote Best classifies it as "type 12," and gives a number of Peruvian examples (1953, pp. 91-95).

[12] The catafalque is common in Mexico on this occasion and, I assume, in other Spanish American countries as well.

[13] Could the carraca be an Afro-American introduction? It suggests the Venezuelan *charrasca* (made of wood) used in aguinaldo Christmas songs (Liscano 1950, p. 100), and of similar instruments, often notched gourds, found throughout the West Indies.

[14] Groups of carolers singing Christmas hymns (aguinaldos) are common in America.

[15] Nativity scenes are universal in Spanish America. In Mexico they usually are called "nacimientos." In South America the more common Spanish term "pesebre" seems to predominate.

[16] These sound like pagan beliefs that the Church would be anxious to keep from reaching America; apparently it was successful.

[17] *Pastorela* Nativity plays have been common in Mexico.

[18] Similar horseplay characterizes *Inocentes* in Spanish America.

CHAPTER XVI

ROMERIAS AND FIESTAS

IN SPANISH AMERICA

IN addition to the religious observances incident to the annual cycle of church feast days, each community normally celebrates its own special fiesta. Usually this is in honor of its patron saint, although sometimes some other day is selected. These exceptions occur particularly when a community is the possessor of a "miraculous" image of Christ or the Virgin. Fiestas are the occasion for visits from people from other villages, and sometimes such visits are formalized as pilgrimages, or *perigrinaciones,* in which groups, carrying religious standards or banners, travel together. The pattern of Hispanic American fiestas is drawn almost completely from Spain, although local elaborations obviously have crept in during the course of centuries.

IN SPAIN

In this chapter three Spanish fiestas are described, based on my field notes; they appear to be quite typical of villages and small towns, and to represent traditions that probably have changed little since the time of the Conquest. The account of Moors and Christians is drawn from published sources.

The fiesta of San Blas in Almonacid del Marquesado (Cuenca).—Almonacid is a village of eleven hundred people 115 kilometers southeast of Madrid, 15 kilometers off the Valencia highway. It looks like hundreds of other drab communities in the wheatlands of central Spain: desolate, dirty, barren of trees. The physical unattractiveness of the village on the day we visited it was added to by the grey February skies, biting wind, and occasional spit of snow which stung our faces upon our arrival. But the warmth of our unheralded reception and the frenzies of the devil dancers we had come to see made up for the discomforts attendant upon long hours of sitting in a cold church and standing in wind-whipped streets.

Almonacid's fiesta dates from a shepherd's miraculous discovery of an image of San Blas near the boundary of neighboring Puebla de Almenara. People from "La Puebla" came with oxen to escort the image to their church, but in spite of these mighty teams they were unable to move it. Then the inhabitants of tiny Almonacid came with their *burricos,* their little burros, and without effort carried the image to their church. Ever since, the people of La Puebla have had a special devotion for San Blas and have come in large numbers to the fiesta. But they feel that in some way, through chicanery or deceit that they cannot quite fathom, they were done out of their rightful due. The original "miraculous" image was destroyed during the Civil War, and the one now carried is a modern copy.[1]

The fiesta is in charge of two groups of men. The *Hermandad de San Blas* is composed of all youths and men who wish to be members, and all are called, in unusual fashion, mayordomos. In 1950 there were fifty-nine participants who paid for the Mass, for candles, and for the considerable quantities of liquor consumed. The devils *(los diablos)* are usually men and boys who have made a vow, at a time of serious family illness or trial, to dress as devils and dance in the fiesta. The vow may be for as little as a single year, or for an entire lifetime. Other "devils" dance out of pride for family tradition, as a right and obligation handed down from father to son. Children can begin at almost any age, and half the thirty-five devils we saw appeared to be minors. The devil who has danced longest automatically becomes the "principal" who directs the others. In 1950 the principal was finishing his sixtieth year, having first danced at the age of nineteen.

The fiesta begins on February 1, when the devils visit the mayor and ask his permission to dance that night in front of the church. Next day, Candlemas, when doves and cakes are carried to Mass, the devils dance in the church itself and then spend the rest of the day asking alms at each house. All that night they dance through the cold streets, making, for reasons that will be forthcoming, such an infernal din that sleep is almost impossible for the citizens. The dancing continues through February 3, the main day of the fiesta, and all that night and the next day until the evening of February 4, when the devils assemble for the annual banquet, paid for by the alms collected on earlier days.

We arrived in Almonacid on the morning of February 3. The plaza, church, and town hall were nearly empty of people, except for the proprietors of two pathetic, wind-buffeted stands selling candy and trinkets. Then in the distance we heard a violent ringing of bells, and presently the devils danced into view. A third or more wore pants and shirts of cheap but brightly colored cotton prints, the others old or castoff clothes. Several were clad in aviators' old overalls. All were masked, most with home-improvised face coverings—one dancer was disguised with the frame of an old gas mask, a grisly reminder of the Civil War—and all wore bishop's mitre hats of red paper with a gold cross on the front. But the most astonishing part of their garb was the *cencerros*, cowbells hung on backs and buttocks. The largest were enormous brass bells 40 cm. long, worn in sets of three and carried on stout shoulder harnesses. Smaller bells in larger numbers were worn by others, but no dancer was without his noisemaking apparatus.[2] Most devils carried a staff with a crudely carved head, some with horsehair for scalps, and one carried a skillfully carved figure of a devil with horns and long tail (pl. 7, right).

The devils' "dance" was simple but effective, a type of hula step which threw out the hips, causing the bells to rise and fall and thus to ring. Sometimes the pace was fast, other times less rapid, as the dancers worked up and down a street, back and forth, so that progress in any direction was slow. A bit before noon church bells announced Mass, and the devils went to the town hall *para sacar la justicia,* to escort town functionaries to the church. People were packed inside the church building leaving little more than a narrow aisle free, down which the devils danced as outside, their bells reverberating from the stone walls of the building. Then the members of the hermandad shouldered San Blas' image and followed the dancers out of the church on a half-hour procession around the streets of the village and back to the church. The church was quickly vacated, and the streets were lined with spectators to watch the progress of the parade. In great leaps the devils ran one hundred meters or more in front of the image, stopped abruptly, ran toward the image, leaped into the air before it, and crouched to the ground, to repeat the runs until it seemed they must drop from exhaustion. Once again in the church, the devils danced while San Blas was set in his usual resting place. Then, after backing out of the church, somewhat as if protesting at having to leave, they adjourned to the house of one of the group to fortify themselves with strong drink.

The devils gone, Mass now began. It was marked by a very long sermon, which described the exemplary life of good San Blas, an account followed by few listeners. It was, in fact, the most casual Mass I have ever witnessed: people came and went at will, talked audibly with their neighbors, forgot to cross themselves. Many grown girls wore no head covering, and others stood or sat on the side altars in order to obtain a better view. It was obvious that the priest's competition was more than he could cope with, but when he finished his long peroration he was obligingly given a loud huzzah. At this point the devils again entered, their dancing more frenzied and unsteady than before. Down the aisle they charged, sometimes shaking their fists and gesticulating in apparent anger before San Blas, sometimes holding their hands upraised as if in supplication. Each in turn rushed headlong from the door down the long aisle, leaped into the air before the image, and then veered to one side to make room for the next. The racket was now extreme, and all spectators watched in rapt attention. Finally, after fifteen or twenty minutes the dancers were exhausted; they left the church, while the townspeople followed them out to return to their homes. The mayor and his councilmen, the priest, members of the hermandad, dancers, and visiting ethnologists hurried to the town hall for liquid refreshments and tiny cakes.

Once inside the building, the priest turned to me. *"Costumbres del pueblo,"* he said, half by way of apology for the strange goings on and half in pride. He was a native of Almonacid, and had been its priest for more than twenty years. His superiors did not approve of the fiesta, he said, but he felt that it did no harm and meant much to the villagers. "What do the staffs with devils' heads mean?" He did not know, except that they are very old. "And the cattle bells?" That is easy. At the time of the discovery of the image of San Blas all the men were shepherds, and the ringing of their bells was the only way they knew to show respect to the saint. This is subsequent rationalization, since cencerros appear in a multitude of Spanish fiestas (and Mediterranean ones, at least as far east as Greece), but it was a good attempt at explanation.

And the origin of the fiesta itself? The priest said it represents the temptation of San Blas during his tortures, when he was being abjured to renounce Christianity. But we liked another origin explanation better: after giving birth to Christ, said one of the devils, the Virgin wished to attend Mass but was ashamed to do so. The devils obligingly appeared, to attract attention so that she could attend unobserved. Actually no one knows the origin of the devils; the dance is obviously an ancient rite, with more than a little paganism remaining. Though we did not see it, we were told that on Candlemas the devils throw jibes and insults at the image of the Virgin, a story which does not seem in keeping with the folk legend that they are doing her a favor in distracting attention while she attends Mass.[3]

The fiesta of Santa Agueda in Zamarramala (Segovia).—On the day of Santa Agueda, it will be remembered, female mayors (alcaldesas) are appointed in villages in Old Castile and León. The famous fiesta in Zamarramala is particularly interesting from an ethnographic standpoint because of an 1839 account which makes possible a comparison of today's and yesterday's customs. At that time the alcalde and his councilmen surrendered their *bastones,* their staffs of office, to their wives, who thereby automatically became alcaldesas to reign for the day. During Mass they sat on the bench reserved for male town authorities and afterwards they stationed themselves on each side of the church door, silver tray in hand, to extract contributions from the men as they emerged. Then they went to their respective homes to eat, where the normal routine was completely inverted. Husbands attempted to spin with the distaff, fed the babies, and otherwise humbled themselves before their wives. At the sound of flute and drum the women bade adieu to their husbands and gathered at the threshing floors where, with great solemnity, they danced around the musicians, fortifying themselves against the cold with copious drafts of white wine and attacking with hatpins any rash male who might have the temerity to try to join the dancers' ring. At nightfall the dance ceased, wives again ate at home, and authority passed back to the relieved men. On the next day, called *la santa Aguedilla,* the dance was repeated, this time with the participation of unmarried girls and men and boys. Even at this early date a high proportion of the onlookers were outsiders, drawn by the curious custom of the alcaldesas (Avrial 1839).

We observed the festivities in 1950, and found them still amusing in spite of changes in the more than one hundred years that had elapsed. February 5 is apt to be cold, gray, and disagreeable in the high plains of Old Castile. This day was no exception, and the cold winds and occasional flurries of snow somewhat dampened the enthusiasm of participants and spectators. Festivities began when the flute and drum players marched through the streets playing *pasodobles* to call at the home of the alcaldesas and the priest to conduct them to the church. This year there were only two alcaldesas, who wore costumes now the property of the municipal council; these are all that have survived the rigors of time and Civil War. But the two alcaldesas were certainly as spectacular as their great-grandmothers. They were dressed in the traditional red and black velvet and wool skirts, jackets and aprons, with mitrelike head coverings over white lace shawls. Coral necklaces hung arounds their necks, and in their hands they carried the silver tray and *bastón* of authority, a dainty stick which an orchestra conductor might wield with ease (pl. 6, right).

Inside the church the procession formed: schoolchildren with the standard of San Antonio, youths with a white banner, three acolytes with the processional *cruz alzada*, men, musicians, the little image of Santa Agueda holding her pathetic little amputated silver breasts on a tray, the priest, the two alcaldesas, and last, the women of the village. This procession circled the church to the sound of the Royal March and cries of "Viva Santa Agueda!" Upon reëntering the building, the alcaldesas took the council seats on each side of the altar, while the other women knelt in the front third of the church over the ancient family tombs, and the men sat on benches to the rear. A violinist and cellist brought from Segovia for the day, a harmonium and its player, and two nuns and several young girl singers placed in the midst of the women provided music beyond that of the usual Mass. After the consecration of the Host the priest blessed a large basket of bread, to be eaten at the Women's banquet. Then the most recent woman to marry kissed all the other women, a kiss known as the *pestéculo*, the priest announced the names of the alcaldesas and alternates for the coming year, and Mass was over.

After leaving the church, the women danced in the tiny plaza which faces it. A few traditional Castilian *jotas* were played by a clarinet and drum, but the music quickly degenerated into jazz, particularly the *Raspa*, which in 1950 was enjoying tremendous popularity in Spain, and ballroom dancing replaced the old *baile de rueda*, the circle dances. But men did not participate. The biting wind and gray skies were not conducive to outdoor gaiety, and after a period only long enough to comply with custom the women hurried to their banquet at the town hall, a banquet of bread, ham, sausage, and wine at which the priest was the only male guest. The men, however, did not suffer; they assembled for their own banquet in another building, where they feasted to the tunes of the musicians. After eating, the alcaldesas stationed themselves in the unpaved road from Segovia, the only road to enter the village, and stopped all cars and foot-travelers to demand a contribution for the costs of Mass, the banquet, and incidental expenses. With this the festivities ended; the Aguedilla of yesteryear is no longer known.[4]

Fiesta of the Virgen de la Peña.—The late April romería of the Virgin of "The Rock" in Puebla de Guzmán (Huelva) is typical of hundreds of out-of-the-way village and small town fiestas in which homage is paid to the patron of the community. Because of the relative isolation of the town and its poor facilities for lodging crowds and because the image is overshadowed by its famous neighbor, the *Virgen del Rocío* in Almonte, the fiesta is visited by few Spanish tourists and by even fewer foreigners. Unspoiled and uncontaminated, it preserves much of the natural and spontaneous atmosphere of past years, a traditional Andalusian romería, in which touches of commercialism are just beginning to appear.

La Puebla de Guzmán is a town of considerable importance in the heart of the Cerro de Andévalo hill region, 70 kilometers from the provincial capital and 25 from the Portuguese border. Fortunately for the townspeople the surrounding land is of only modest fertility, spotted with crags and rock outcroppings, satisfactory for grazing but of limited value for agriculture. Probably as a result of this the land was never taken up in the big estates that mark much of Andalusia, so that a rather high proportion of the 1,200 family heads own their lands, and the standard of living is relatively higher than in many other towns of 6,000 in the south. La Puebla looks much like other Andalusian communities: more or less straight streets spilling over hillsides, lined with whitewashed red-tiled houses, two stories high near the center of town and one story high on the outskirts. Until recent years whitesailed windmills dotted the surrounding hills, and on the edge of town there still stands a tower, the remains of the last in which grain was ground. Although La Puebla for some years has been connected by road with the city of Huelva, public transportation in 1950 was still limited to a single decrepit bus which went down in the morning and returned in the afternoon, and consequently urban influences remained weak. Pueblereños still speak fondly of the days, not far distant in the past, when their women wore the *mantellina,* a heavy head garment which fell to the waist, leaving visible only the eyes and nose. But the tradition that means most to them is the adoration of their Virgin of the Rock.

According to tradition, one Alonso Gómez, a humble shepherd and pious devotee of the Virgin in the manifestation of the Immaculate Conception, was paying such homage to her as was possible while tending his flocks on the morning of December 8, 1460. As day dawned, an aurora of supernatural brilliance blinded him, and from the center of the brilliance came the words, "May you be more pure than the dawn." Overcoming his stupefaction, he approached the light and discovered, not one but two images of the Virgin. As he knelt in awe they said, "We are from Ayamonte. When Spain was lost to the Moors, we were hidden here by devotees. Carry one of us to the Cerro del Aguila, and leave the other here for the protection of this land."

Following these instructions, the shepherd left one image, which became known as the *Virgen de Piedras Albas* and is still worshipped today in a hermitage built on the spot. He carried the other to the summit of the "Hill of the Eagle," a lofty eminence near La Puebla de Guzmán, which dominates the countryside for a great distance in all directions. Here pious people built a hermitage to house the image, which became known as *de la Peña* because of the rock cliff which rises behind the buildings.

The chronicles are silent until the midseventeenth century when, in the face of a raging plague—"apparently spread from Portugal," the account adds—the townspeople vowed to celebrate annually a fiesta in honor of their Virgin, and almost immediately the plague died out. Since that time, according to tradition, the citizens have gone out together to climb the hill to the sanctuary five kilometers away, to give thanks to their protectress and to renew their solemn vows. In 1918 the fiesta was placed on a more formal footing by the establishment of the brotherhood of the Santísima Virgen de la Peña, whose statutes were approved by the Cardinal of Sevilla. Whereas formerly the expenses of the fiesta were borne by a few pious families, now, through the institution of the mayordomo, increasingly elaborate arrangements are made.

The Romería of the Virgen de la Peña takes place on the last Sunday of April, with festivities beginning the preceding Saturday and continuing through Tuesday. Early in December of 1949, in the company of Julio Caro Baroja and Arcadio Larrea, noted Spanish musicologist, I had visited La Puebla. We were delighted with the warmth of our reception, the obvious enthusiasm the people felt for their Virgin, and the picturesqueness of the sanctuary itself, high on a lonely hill, isolated from all human habitation. In company with Don Celestino Luque, town physician and most enthusiastic devotee of the Virgin, we had climbed to the crest of the Hill of the Eagle where, in a most unusual gesture of hospitality, a small replica of the annual fiesta had been arranged. Mass was said, and then the sword dancers, led by the *tamborilero* with his flute and drum, circled the hermitage, just as is done for the real fiesta.

The shrine is a low, whitewashed chapel which nestles against the eroded cliffs (pl. 8). To the left are several small buildings: a kitchen and storehouse in which to prepare the immense quantities of food consumed during the fiesta, a dining-room for brotherhood members and their guests, and rooms in which the mayordomos and their families remain during the days of the fiesta. Except for a *santero*, a guardian who stays in a small house nearby, no one lives within sight. The wind blows softly over the hill, the grass rustles, and an occasional cuckoo is heard. From down the hillside, comes the sound of sheep bells, but the principal sensation of the visitor is that of wild beauty, peace, and isolation.

The discovery here some years ago of a Roman lapidary tablet, now kept in the chapel, suggests that this remote hilltop was, in pre-Christian times, the site of religious observances. Early Christians built churches on the sites of pagan worship, thus capitalizing on the religious associations of the people who were to become good Christians. Often, to add force to the new religion, a miraculous image appeared on the site, or as at Tepeyác in Mexico, the Virgin herself appeared to some humble soul. It is not improbable, therefore, that the placing of the miraculous image of the Virgen de la Peña on this hilltop was a part of the Christian campaign to reëstablish the faith in Andalusia after long years of Moorish domination.

The interior of the shrine, badly damaged during the Civil War, is without notable architectural features, a modest contrast to the ornateness of the nearly life-sized image, which has recently been restored. The Virgin is clothed in rich gold and silver brocades and wears on her head an enormous, glittering, and ill-fitting diadem. She holds a sceptre in her right hand, while in her left arm a chubby Christ child nestles. The expression on her face is calm and composed, neither joyful nor sorrowful, a stylized realism duplicated in many other Spanish images (pl. 7, left). Although this image has little real artistic merit, it is well made, and one can understand the affection and enthusiasm it evokes in the hearts of its followers.

When Don Celestino and his friends urged us to return in April for the fiesta, it was not difficult to decide to do so. Consequently, the three of us arrived the afternoon of April 28, 1950, "Tripe Friday," so nicknamed because the animals that will feed the multitudes are this day slaughtered at the sanctuary.[5] La Puebla had already decorated for its fiesta. Wooden railings lined the sidewalks of the main street to prevent horsemen from surging over curbstones, and from tall poles in front of houses colored flags fluttered. Each bar and tavern likewise had stout barricades at its door, a wise precaution to prevent exuberant horsemen from trying to enter the building on horseback.

Unlike comparable Latin American fiestas, very few commercial people had come from outside to set up food and entertainment stands. Three *churreros* stood beside their cauldrons of oil, squeezing spirals of bread dough onto the boiling surface from bakers' syringes, and at half-a-dozen other stands one could buy cookies, candy, and *turrones*. But there were no casseroles of turkey or chicken, rice and beans, tripe in broth, or the dozens of other staples from which one makes a meal on the other side of the Atlantic. Nor in other ways, it soon became apparent, did La Puebla need the artifices of the modern world to make its fiesta a success—no lotteries, no bingo games, no juke boxes, not one loudspeaker. A single furtive man with a folding table and wheel had little trouble in avoiding the glances of the police. His game could hardly be called gambling, for the lucky player won nothing but a pocket comb! La Puebla's one condescension to modern times, and a source of immense satisfaction to her sons, was an enormous electric arch across the street from which blazed, night and day, the words *Viva la Virgen de la Peña*.

On Friday evening after vespers in the parish church there was a short rocket-illuminated procession to the town house of the hermandad, where the white silk banner of the brotherhood, with a blue-and-gold embroidered representation of the Virgin, was placed. As we walked, Don Celestino told us of the mayordomos. This year three men had banded together to share the cost, estimated at 50,000 pesetas, a staggering sum for most rural Spaniards. But Don Celestino was also worried. There was no indication that anyone would "seize the *pendones*," the yellow silk, brocade banners symbolic of mayordomoship, in the final service, signifying intention to be mayordomo the following year. The increasing cost of each fiesta was frightening away potential mayordomos. It was becoming a rich man's activity so that almost no one, in years of drought, could bear the cost. Should no one volunteer, the brotherhood itself would have to put on the fiesta, as had been done in 1947, but this was a violation of tradition and a reflection on the love and veneration in which the Virgin was held.

The same night Don Celestino presented us with our copies of the *Revista de N.tra S.ra de la Peña*, an elaborate 50-page program printed on glossy paper, with a polychrome cover reproducing a painting by a native son, the well-known Spanish artist Don Sebastián García, showing a mayordomo and his wife dressed in the rich garments of former years. The program—a "must" for all Spanish romerías with pretensions—contained the story of the origin of the fiesta, and data on La Puebla and the hermandad. Dedicated to Pope Pius XII, it also contained an "offering" to Sra. Eva Duarte de Perón, who the preceding year had visited Spain, a paragraph of congratulations from the Argentine Ambassador to Spain, words on the intensity of the Marian devotion from the Minister of Justice, and various eulogies and praises to the Virgen de la Peña from other eminent persons and aspiring local writers and poets.

About three o'clock Saturday afternoon the *caballería* formed. This was a procession of more than a hundred horsemen and horsewomen, including two mayordomos with their pendones, the hermano mayor of the brotherhood, other hermanos, and anyone else who wished to ride and had a horse. Mayordomas (the wives of the mayordomos) were dressed in the elaborate traditional costume of La Puebla: full, scarlet, velvet skirt trimmed at the hem with gold braid, gold-embroidered blouse, long-sleeved, tight-fitting, black velvet bodice, and red-and-gold embroidered slippers. On her head each mayordoma wore a white lace shawl which fell to the waist, and over this was perched a plumed black felt hat with tall, square crown and narrow brim, of very nearly the lines of an opera hat. Heavy gold and silver necklaces with crosses, scapularies, and medallions crowded one another around the neck. The mayordomos wore ordinary business suits. The short black velvet pants with red tassel at the knee, gold-brocaded waistcoat, red sash, tight dark jacket, and jaunty *sombrero calañés* with its low crown, curled brim, and red tassel which mayordomos formerly wore have fallen victim to modern times.

Other women were dressed in gay *sevillana* costumes, long, full, cotton print dresses with white polka dots on a blue or scarlet background, and one beautiful girl, a visitor from Huelva, appeared in the stunning *traje de amazonas* (Amazon's dress) with long, black wool skirt, black jacket, white pleated shirt with starched collar, black flat-crowned, wide-brimmed cowboy hat, and a red hibiscus in her hair. All women, except the mayordomas, rode side-saddle, as is still customary in Spain. The mayordomas were mounted in *jamugas*, legless wooden chairs with arms and backs lashed securely to the backs of mounts, facing to the right rather than the left of the horse. All horses were groomed to the last hair: tails bound with ribbons to form billy-clubs, manes braided with more ribbons, tassels fastened to ears, colored blankets thrown over saddle pommels, and multicolored tasseled bands draped across chests. Among the younger set it was fashionable for girls to ride side-saddle behind horsemen, their arms decorously circling the waists of their escorts. A riding horse is a luxury, kept for the most part to be ridden during the romería, a mark both of social distinction and of piety and devotion to the Virgin.

The procession got under way to the accompaniment of a great stamping of hoofs and clouds of dust, to follow the ritually prescribed route to the summit of the hill. The hour's ride was an exciting experience. Spring meadows had broken out with the first flush of aromatic plants—gum cistus, rosemary, thyme, and furze—and the soft air stimulated horses and riders alike. From time to time the group broke into song, coplas de caballo and fandanguillos:

La madre de mi caballo,	The mother of my horse,
Era una yegua lozana,	Was a spirited mare,
Que me costó cien doblones	Which cost me 100 doubloons,
En la feria de Triana.	At Triana's fair.
Es la Virgen de la Peña,	It's the Virgen de la Peña,
La que más altares tiene,	Who has the most altars,
No hay un hijo de La Puebla,	There's no son of La Puebla,
Que en su pecho no la lleve.	Who does not guard her in his breast.

As the group neared the hermitage it was met by nine lanzador sword-dancers, the drummer with his flute and tambor drum (pl. 9, right)[6] the third mayordomo, and the priest. To the tunes of the tamborilero the dancers gracefully wove in and out, doubling back and passing under their glistening swords, in steps not unlike those of the sword dancers of the Basques and other parts of the Pyrenees. Their costumes likewise were similar to those of the north of Spain: black alpargata slippers, white stockings, black knee-length pants with four silver buttons, wide red sash at the waist, near-white shirts with the slightest hint of salmon color, and white kerchiefs except for the cabeza and er rabión, the leader and the tail, who wore red.[7]

After the dancers had led the procession counterclockwise around the sanctuary, horses were tied and everyone crowded inside for vespers, after which the dancers performed inside the chapel and, still dancing, led the mayordomos and their wives to the rooms in the adjacent structures which traditionally were to be their temporary homes during the next three days. Then the members of the procession went next door to the casa fonda for a dinner of steaming cauldrons of caldereta (stewed goat and mutton), clear broth with bread slices topped with mint leaves, fresh bread, and white wine. We took this occasion to inspect the stores for the days ahead, and discovered the carcasses of 4 beeves and 25 smaller cattle for a total of more than a ton and a half of meat, and 600 great loaves of bread, a ton in all.

Customarily the mayordomos remain at the hermitage but in 1950, as an innovation, a young lawyer was scheduled to deliver a *pregón*, a dramatic and sentimental eulogy to the Virgin, in the local theater, after which the lanzadores were again to dance. This necessitated the return of nearly everyone to town.

Sunday morning was the occasion of another innovation, the arrival of affiliated hermandades from Huelva and Ayamonte, from whence, according to legend, the image had come. The recent creation of affiliated brotherhoods was considered proof, as indeed it was, that the beloved Virgen de la Peña was growing in fame and importance. Mayordomos, brotherhood members, and most townspeople awaited the coming of the two busloads of distinguished visitors at the edge of town. Presently clouds of dust on the horizon announced the impending arrival, and the crowds pressed to the road as the wheezing and steaming old vehicles rolled to a halt. Several dozen men and women stepped from each bus, led by the hermano mayor of each group, who carried a banner similar to that of the hermandad of La Puebla. Two affiliated hermandades were not many, compared to the forty or more auxiliaries of the hermandad of the Virgen del Rocío, some from as far as Sevilla, but everyone felt that two would be four next year, and four eight the following year, and that by 1960, when official coronation of the Virgin was hoped for, who knew but what La Puebla would have as many affiliates as El Rocío. Certainly, no affiliated hermandad of El Rocío ever received a more animated reception, to the sound of huzzahs, exploding rockets, and cries for the Virgin.

The town and its guests then moved to the sanctuary, one group again riding but most people going by bus and truck to the foot of the hill, which they ascended on foot. The crowd was enormous, 6,000 we estimated, and clusters of *romeros* scattered over the hillside, seeking the shade of the few oaks which grew in this waterless area, while others gathered in the chapel to await Mass. But more startling than the size of the crowd was the presence of great numbers of ragged, dirty, maimed, crippled beggars, the dregs of humanity for miles around. They had come, limping and crawling, for the few pesetas they would receive from more fortunate persons—who, they hoped, would be reminded of their Christian obligation of almsgiving —and for the two *comidas de pobres*, the "beggars' banquets" served by the mayordomos to the poor.

The sword-dancers escorted mayordomos and priest from their rooms to the altar, and after Mass the image of the Virgin in her flower-banked tabernacle was carried around the building in counterclockwise direction in ceremonial procession, preceded by drummer, dancers, mayordomos, and priest, and followed by all who wished to pay homage to her. Then the mayordomos turned to what they felt was the most unusual and most praiseworthy of all aspects of the romería, the "beggars' banquet." A roll of white muslin a hundred meters long was stretched over the meadow below the hermitage and the beggars, six hundred or more, with a weird assortment of battered plates, cups, tin cans, and other containers crowded to the sides, jostling like animals to be as near the head of the line as possible. A visiting priest said grace and then the food was brought on: goat stew and chick peas ladled from great copper cauldrons, chunks of bread from gunny sacks, and white wine from buckets. Fulfilling their ritual obligations, the mayordomos distributed the food to every person in the long and impatient lines. Disputes arose, some beggars hiding their bread and then swearing they had been passed by, while others gulped their wine and insisted, while holding out still moist containers, that they had received none. Some years the mayordomos take the vow to seat themselves between the dirtiest and poorest of the beggars to eat, a further humbling of themselves which, however, did not take place this year.

Back in La Puebla the gaiety reached its peak in the evening. After sundown the streets were packed with strollers who ascended and descended the steep streets, while horsemen whipped their steeds among them in wild charges. Girls fortunate enough to have swains with horses mounted side-saddle behind them to accompany the men as they made the rounds from bar to bar. Horses were reined up in front of the doors, while waiters, safe behind the stout wooden barriers, passed glasses of wine and brandy to the mounted men—but only rarely to the girls—in an arrangement that might be called an "equestrian ride-in." Then horsemen and girls dashed off to the next bar, songs in honor of the Virgin on their lips, and more drinks and still more drinks until it seemed impossible that they could stay astride their mounts. In fact, however, as at other Spanish fiestas, there was very little real drunkenness.

Meanwhile a guitar and an accordion played in a large room rented by the hermandad, and couples danced sevillanas and fandanguillos. Cardinal Segura of Sevilla had prohibited ballroom dancing in all Andalusia, so the brotherhood was obliged to forego a real orchestra. In a small bar and restaurant, however, a small orchestra played and several hardy couples who dared defy the bann risked a few furtive foxtrots. By midnight the crowds had thinned and most people had gone home to bed. But, to our astonishment, when we emerged onto the streets next morning, we found a few persistent riders who, somewhat unsteadily to be sure, still sang and drank after more than twelve hours in the saddle.

Monday's festivities were a duplication of Sunday's, except that crowds were smaller. On Tuesday Mass was said in the parish church, but the main function, the "sermon of supplication" at which new mayordomos were expected to be named, took place at the sanctuary in the late afternoon. A man usually undertakes a mayordomía in response to a vow made to the Virgin. The officiating priest was a young Aragonese; a second priest stood in front of the image, and two others flanked the altar. The outgoing mayordomos and their wives sat near the image, pendones in hand. The sermon was a eulogy of the Virgin, coupled with an emotional lesson about the importance of the cult and of the fiesta. After some minutes the mayordomos gave their pendones to the priest who stood in front of the image. This was the signal for the new would-be mayordomos to rush up and tear the yellow banners from the priest's hands, disputing with each other the right to serve. This year no such thing happened. In a year of drought and poor crops potential mayordomos thought of the 50,000 pesetas and resolved to await a more auspicious year.

The predicating priest became more and more nervous as the minutes dragged on. All classes of earthly and spiritual benefits were promised to the pious souls who would take over, but still no flicker of interest appeared. Supplication gave way to taunts and sarcasm; was there no one in La Puebla that loved the Virgin enough to be a mayordomo? The veins swelled in the neck of the perspiring priest, and his face was flushed. It was a personal failure for him, for his oratory failed to inspire the masses. The priest with the pendones, likewise fearful, broke out with loud shouts of "Cowards, cowards, you are all cowards." But shame swayed the crowd no more than taunts, sarcasm, and beseeching. Finally the heads of the hermandad held a hurried, whispered conference, and the hermano mayor stepped forward, interrupting the exhortations, to announce that in 1951, as in an earlier year, the hermandad itself would undertake the romería. It was a sad and somewhat sour note on which to end the fiesta, and the crowd knew it. Ashamed that no one was willing or able to volunteer, it descended quietly to the town, with none of the gaiety and enthusiasm of earlier in the day. The fiesta was over, and not until the next year would the days be so exciting.[8]

Fiestas of Moors and Christians.—The Spanish love of folk drama and dancing, of symbolic battle and victory of Spanish armed might, of the triumph of culture and religion over pagan and infidel forces is nowhere more perfectly represented than by the *combates de Moros y Cristianos,* the combats between Moors and Christians. In these dramas, whose recognizable form reaches back in time for more than eight centuries, the participants and onlookers relive real and imaginary events in the reconquest of Spain from the Moors. Transplanted to America, versions of Moors and Christians became popular with all classes, and were a significant element in propagating the faith among Indians (Ricard 1933, pp. 224-225). In broad outline the representation of Moors and Christians is a drama which takes place in the streets and plazas of a city or town. The actors, who sing or chant their lines and sometimes execute crude dance steps, take the part of "Christians" and "Moors." The Moors challenge the Christian stronghold, overpower it, and again have it wrested away from them by the Christians, although not without a hard struggle in which the outcome for long seems in doubt. Usually, the Moors are converted to Christianity in the final scene.

Although Spanish history is the apparent source of the *Moriscas*—the generic name by which the performances are known to students of the dance—it seems probable that they actually represent religious acculturation, in that more ancient pagan dances associated with spring fertility

rites and other events received a new lease on life when they were transformed into festivals to celebrate Christian victory over the infields (Alford
1937, p. 227; Larrea 1952, p. 12). If this hypothesis is true, the spread of
Morisca dances over most of Europe (except Scandinavia) is much more
understandable. Pan-European, pre-Christian, stick-and-sword dances,
now dignified as religious and historical representations, became *Morisken-
tanz* in Germany, Morris dances in England, and *moreška* in Dalmatia.

In Spain there appear to be five principal geographical nuclei in which
representations of Moors and Christians are given or have been given until
recent times: Aragón-Catalonia villages in Zaragosa, Huesca, Lérida, and
Tarragona; Orense; Alicante (including several adjacent villages in Albacete and Valencia) ; the Balearic Islands (Palma, Soller, Pollensa) ; and
Andalusia (Benamahoma in Cádiz, Benadalid in Málaga, Carboneras in
Almería, and several villages in the Alpujarra). The drama also has been
reported recently in the province of Toledo (Brugarola 1955).

The Old Kingdom of Aragón seems beyond reasonable doubt to have
been the land that gave birth to representations of Moors and Christians
(Alford 1937, p. 204). The earliest performance known to me took place
in the cathedral of Lérida in 1150, upon the occasion of the marriage of
Queen Petronilla of Aragón to the Catalan count, Ramón de Berenguer IV,
when a company of Moors and Christians feigned combat (*ibid.*, p. 221).
As the Christians pushed the frontier steadily southward toward Valencia
and Murcia, mock combats appeared in more and more towns until the
coast was reached, and from this drive dates the modern nucleus in Alicante. The Balearic performances, of course, follow upon the thirteenth-
century reconquest of these islands. The Andalusian performances are
later in time (this was the last region given up by the Moors), but little
is known about the introduction of the custom into this area. Likewise
little is known about the time of origin of the Orense performances, although it is possible they are linked historically with similar dramas which
at one time were very popular in Portugal. At present, then, it is pre-
mature to say whether the five nuclei outlined represent in fact historical
reality, or whether they are simply surviving "islands" which will be joined
together when more research has been done.

Although there is considerable variation in Spanish Moros y Cristianos,
the principle division seems to be that which separates the Aragonese-
Catalonian dramas from those of the rest of the country. In the former
area the actual representation of Moors and Christians is usually only
one episode in a series of dances and dramas with such names as *Furias de
Luzbel, Soldadesca, Guirnaldas,* and *Coloquios,* which are known collectively as the *dance aragonés* (Larrea 1952, pp. 11-22). These representations are given on the occasion of the fiesta of the patron of the town or
village or on some other important feast day, are intimately associated
with the image of a saint or the Virgin, and are marked by sword dances
of a type found in many parts of Spain. Often the first part of the series
consists of one or more *rabadanes* (shepherds) who, disobeying the orders

of their mayoral (head shepherd) have come to town to enjoy the fiesta, which is to include the representations of Moors and Christians. Following long arguments, in which the Devil often incites the participants, the rabadanes and mayoral comment, in verse, on the nature of the past agricultural year and poke fun at the indiscretions or characters of local citizens.

The following act is that of Moors and Christians proper: the Moors—often they are called Turks—attack to carry off the miraculous image of the Christians or to protest failure of the subject Christians to pay the annual tribute of *cien doncellas,* "one hundred maidens." Helped by the Devil, the infidels nearly succeed in their aim, but the Guardian Angel appears in the nick of time to save the Christians. The principal Moors are killed, and often those who remain ask Christian baptism.

The relationship of the Aragonese form of Moors and Christians to the Moriscas of other European countries, and to the Spanish sword dances of the Basques and other parts of the country, is apparent in the importance of the dance steps themselves—precisely executed movements which correspond to those of dances in which Moors and Christians are lacking.

In the rest of the country the drama itself (though not the spoken lines) is much more highly developed, but the "dancing"—if the motions can be so dignified—is perfunctory and incidental to the other aspects of the representation. In the Alicante towns of Alcoy, Villena, Jijona, Biar, Castalla, Sax—to name a few—the *combate* of Moors and Christians is presented as the *pièce de resistance* on the occasion of the principal fiesta of the community. Cofradías which exist for the purpose contribute a number of *comparsas* of actors, identified either with the Christians or the Moors, while half-a-dozen or more named actors, representing the Moorish and Christian leaders, speak long lines in verse. Usually on the first day there is a ceremonial entrance of the various troupes into town; on the second, the Christians, defending a cardboard-and-wood castle in the main plaza, are attacked and beaten by the Moors; and on the third day, in a counterattack, the Christians rout the Moors and retake the castle.

Probably the most famous of all contemporary representations is that of Alcoy (Alicante), although that of Villena (Alicante) is not far behind. History tells that in 1276 the Moorish caudillo Alazrach gave orders to attack Alcoy and neighboring towns, which had been liberated from the Moors scarcely a generation earlier. Led by their *mosén* (priest), Ramón Torregrosa, the men of Alcoy, hopelessly outnumbered, prayed to the saint of the day of the attack, Saint George (April 23), and then joined battle with the enemy. When the battle was fiercest and the danger greatest, to their great joy the Christians saw a white cloud in the sky, over which hovered a white horse bearing a warrior marked by a red cross on his breast. The sky-borne warrior let fly a rain of arrows that killed many Moors, including the odious Alazrach himself, and the Christians, taking heart at the sight of Saint George fighting with them, redoubled their efforts and soon won the day. Saint George was henceforth to be patron of the town, a church was erected in his honor, and some years later the drama of Moors and Christians was initiated, to recall to mind the stirring events of that April 23 (García Figueras 1940a, pp. 8-9).

As described for 1935, the fiesta was marked by nine comparsas of Christians, including "smugglers," negro slaves, *Cides* (from *El Cid Campeador*), Mozárabes, Visigoths, Aragonese, and farmers, and thirteen comparsas of Moors, including Mudéjares, Berbers, Moroccans, and Jews. The costumes of each group were elaborate, but those of the Moors were more splendid, and to be a Moor was considered more desirable than to be a Christian. Negroes wore rings in their ears and noses, smugglers were disguised as Andalusian bandits, Cides wore medieval tunics, while the Moorish comparsas featured feathered turbans and brilliant long robes. Comparsas change somewhat from year to year, one group failing to appear, its place taken by a new one, so that over the years there is considerable latitude for imagination.

On the morning of April 22 the Christian comparsas entered the city, dancing shoulder to shoulder in a sort of primitive dance, each to the rhythms of its own musical band. The Christian governor met the Christian captain and subaltern (*alférez*), and gave them the keys to the castle, a wooden structure six meters or so high in the plaza, with the admonition that they defend it well. Then in the afternoon the comparsas of Moors, led by the Moorish captain, entered in similar fashion. Next morning the Christians were in possession of the castle, their banner flying gaily from the highest tower, when a Moorish emissary appeared, asking them, in vain, to surrender to the great Alazrach. The Christian captain showed great rage, tore up the letter, and threw the pieces in the face of the emissary, who fled at great speed. Now the Moorish ambassador appeared, more imperious than the messenger, first vouching friendship, always in verse, and then threatening destruction to the Christians. But the Christian captain and ambassador taunted the Moor, who in turn flung insults at the Christians. Then the battle broke loose; the opposing armies fired at each other at point-blank range, and rockets and firecrackers added to the din of the blank cartridges. Little by little the Moors flung back the Christians, finally overrunning the castle and forcing the latter to flee. The Moorish governor sank his sword in the chest of his Christian counterpart in dramatic hand-to-hand combat, while the Moorish captain and subaltern finished off their opposite numbers in similar style. The crescent flag flew from the tower, and it appeared that the Christians were finished.

But in the afternoon the roles were reversed. This time the Christian emissary asked, in vain, the surrender of the Moors, the battle began anew, the air filled with smoke and shouts, and to the cries of Christian avengers the Moors fled the castle. The crowd shouted its satisfaction and, as darkness approached, gathered to watch the *luces de bengala*, fireworks in which the figure of Saint George on horseback appeared over the tower of the castle (Sánchez-Ocaña 1935).

Far to the northwest, in Sainza (Orense) a similar drama is reënacted in the fall. The Moors occupy a ruined castle, in which Christian prisoners are held chained. In a fashion similar to that of Alcoy and Villena the Christian general demands the rendition of the castle: "In the name of the All Powerful, and in honor of my beloved Patria, I come to demand that you deliver up the castle which you so unjustly hold, and release the Christian captives, my beloved subjects, whom you hold in your power." "In the name of Mohamet, my true God and Prophet," replies the Moorish general, "I will never surrender it unless you win it with the sword." Insults are hurled back and forth, and presently the battle breaks out, enlivened by the presence of "artillery," tin cannons from which explosive charges are fired, producing a din comparable to a real battle. Finally the castle is stormed, the Moors are taken prisoner, put in their own chains, and offered as slaves to the *Virgen de la Merced*, in honor of whom the fiesta is held (Ramón y Fernández 1945c).

COMPARISONS AND COMMENTS

The three fiestas described from my field notes have no direct American counterparts. But, even though they are in many ways quite distinct from American forms, it is clear that many of the elements that characterize them have crossed the Atlantic. This is true, for example, of the "heavy image" motif in miracle legends, of devil dancers who participate in response to a vow, of the use of flute and arum for much fiesta music, of feasting, of horseback riding, and the like. And of course, in America, as in Spain, religious brotherhoods assume responsibility for the expenses and arrangements of fiestas.

The drama of Moors and Christians was introduced early into America, and has continued as a popular presentation down to the present time. The American forms, however, have experienced the reduction that characterizes so much conquest culture. Dramatic aspects are few, and more often than not the "drama" is limited to dancing. Possibly, in the early days of the Conquest, Moors and Christians more nearly resembled Spanish forms. Toor (1947, pp. 347-349) says that in Mexico Spaniards formerly participated in the activity on the occasion of bullfights and other fiestas and that later the dramas were performed on a grand scale only at religious fiestas. Since about 1910, she says, the dance has declined in elaborateness.

REFERENCES

(I have not personally examined asterisked items; they are included for the sake of completeness).

Santa Agueda: Avrial (1839), Cedilla (1931).

Moors and Christians: Alford (1937), Arco y Garay (1943, pp. 110-345), Brugarola (1955), Cala López and Flores González (1918),* Capmany (1944, pp. 389-394), Castillo y Arista (1919), Díaz de Villegas (1936),* Fernández Martínez (1931, pp. 288-293),* Flores González (1936),* García Figueras (1933,* 1939, 1940a, 1940b), Giese (1937, pp. 216-220), Larrea Palacín (1952), Llopis (1928b), Pérez Vidal (1951), Ramón y Fernández (1945c), Ricard (1933, 1938, 1940, 1945, 1946, 1952, 1953), Sánchez-Ocaña (1935), S. (1839), Taboada (1955), Touceda Fontenla (1952).*

NOTES

[1] The "heavy image" theme is widespread in Spanish America. The *Santo Entierro* of Tzintzuntzan arrived in this fashion (Foster 1948a, pp. 192-193), and similar accounts are found in other parts of Mexico. This is Morote Best's "type 11" in his classification of Peruvian legends (1953, pp. 89-91).

[2] I know of only one place in America where cowbells are hung from the waists of dancers: the bells used by the "devils" of San Francisco de Yare in Venezuela (Diaz Ungria 1952, p. 98).

[3] "Devil" dancers are common in Spanish America. Those of Corpus Christi of San Francisco de Yare, however, are the ones that particularly resemble, but are not identical with, those of Almonacid. The "devils" dance in response to a vow, but they are never permitted to enter the church.

[4] As previously pointed out, Santa Agueda, as a fiesta day, seems to be completely unknown in Spanish America.

[5] Caro Baroja, drawing upon our joint field notes, has also published an account of this fiesta (1957a).

[6] The tamborilero is the traditional fiesta musician in Spain, now unfortunately often replaced by a wind-and-string orchestra. The three-holed flute, called gaita (not to be confused with the Galician bagpipe, also called gaita) in Huelva and many other parts of Spain, and called *chirimía* in other provinces, is held and played with the fingers of the left hand. The Huelva drum, or *tambor*, is of large size. The one used at the fiesta described was approximately 70 cm. long and 45 cm. in diameter. This drum is suspended from the left elbow by a heavy leather strap, and is played by a single drumstick held in the right hand. The head of the drum is of goatskin, said to give a better tone than other covers, and a cord is stretched taut across this head so that it vibrates when the drum is struck, amplifying the sound (pl. 9, right). This head-string is also found in other parts of Spain, for instance, in the province of León, but I do not know whether it is universal or not. In some provinces the drums are smaller, apparently reaching their smallest size in Mallorca, where they dangle gracefully from the left wrist. None appears to be as small as the tiny drums used in Mexican fiestas (as in the *volador* pole "dance"), which are suspended from the little finger of the left hand. (The photograph [pl. 9, right] shows the drummer of the fiesta of San Benito in Cerro de Andévalo. The instruments are identical to those of La Puebla.)

A tamborilero is usually a full-time specialist. The one at the romería of the Virgen de la Peña came from near-by Villanueva de los Castillejos, and was paid 200 pesetas for five days, in addition to which he received a good deal in the form of tips.

[7] The lanzadores form a hereditary company, and those who danced in 1950 were all relatives. The oldest was 73, a veteran of 50 years of dancing, the youngest was still in his 20's. Socially they belonged to the lower middle class, and were laborers rather than farmers or professional men like the mayordomos. Although they received 35 pesetas for their fiesta performance—a fact which placed them in a very different category from mayordomos—their real reason for dancing was pride and pleasure in being known as skilled craftsmen.

[8] The account of this fiesta is given to serve as a type, in contrast to the fiestas of patron saints of towns in Spanish America described in detail in a series of ethnographies. The origin given here of the miraculous image is a common motif in Spain (except for the "double discovery" feature), and also in Spanish America. Morote Best does not classify it as a separate type (as I believe he should), but gives an almost perfect type-example parallel, that of the Virgen del Socorro, from the province of Trujillo (1953, p. 83). In general the Spanish romería is quite different in "feel" from the common fiestas of Spanish America.

CHAPTER XVII

THE CONCEPT OF CULTURAL CRYSTALLIZATION

IN conclusion, I now wish to consider very briefly what happens to a conquest culture—that of Spain, of course—in a new world. Conquest culture, as pointed out in chapter 2, represents but a small part of the totality of traits and complexes that comprise the donor culture. Then, through a second screening process in the geographical region of the recipient peoples, conquest culture is still further reduced, in the process of playing its role as a builder of colonial culture. Two distinct but related analytical approaches help us to understand this reduction process. The first deals with the social and psychological mechanisms whereby recipient peoples, in those situations in which they are allowed choice, exercise discretion in accepting and rejecting elements presented to them. The second deals with the time dimension, with the sequence in presentation of conquest culture. It suggests a concept, which may be called "cultural crystallization," illustrating how essentially nonsocial and nonpsychological factors may be very significant in determining what the final stabilized forms of an acculturated society will be. These approaches, and the conclusions they lead to, are discussed in turn.

The operation of social and psychological mechanisms both produces and is governed by the structure of the contact situation. In relation to areas of high culture, and especially to Mexico, it is well to bear in mind that, although we tend to think only in terms of Indians acculturating to Spanish ways, there were, in fact, two recipient groups in process of change: Indian and Spanish. Every Spaniard in America represented some phase of the donor culture, and thereby helped carry conquest culture. At the same time each Spaniard was exposed not only to Indians, but also to other Spaniards, who often faced him with laws and regulations, and with less formal cultural items, many of which were very strange to him. That is, the Spaniard as well as the Indian was exposed to conquest culture. Both were faced with a similar problem of selection and adjustment. The Spaniard did not have to adjust to metal tools, domestic animals, the plow, and Christianity, but he did have to come to terms with a new sociopolitical and environmental situation and to other Spaniards and their customs as well as to the Indians.

The manner in which both Indian and Spaniard and their mestizo offspring were exposed to conquest culture was structured by the social setting, and particularly by the division of society into urban and rural components. This division, as it existed in pre-Conquest times, can be thought of in terms of the familiar folk-urban continuum with, to use Aguirre Beltrán's terminology, a "ceremonial center" pole representing the elite tradition and a "community culture" representing the peasant tradition (1957, pp. 26-33).

In the very first years of the Conquest, acculturation must have been marked by much direct transmission from Spaniards to Indians all along this continuum, and from Spaniards to Spaniards. But as Spanish cities were founded and native cities were rebuilt, the picture changed. The native urban-elite authority structure was replaced by the Spanish equivalent so that, instead of a continuum both poles of which represented variants of a single culture, there now existed a continuum for which the authority pole was Spanish. After this modified continuum was established, and after the initial culturally mixed mestizo populations came into being, the acculturation process took the familiar pattern of flow of influence downward and outward, from the urban-elite pole to lower classes and peasants. Spanish, hispanicized, and partly hispanicized peoples all along this continuum therefore continued to be exposed to new Spanish influences as they were passed along from cities, and these peoples in turn became a point of diffusion of the items they accepted, to other populations less influenced by Spain.

The sociopsychological mechanisms whereby the peoples along this continuum screened conquest culture, accepting what they perceived to be desirable and within their reach and rejecting what they perceived to be undesirable and within their ability to refuse, can be best observed in relation to Indian culture reacting to conquest culture, since this offers the maximum contrast. Without attempting a thorough study of these mechanisms, the following observations may be made:

1. In the field of material culture and techniques, Spanish forms were welcomed when they were recognized by the Indians as useful, and when there were no indigenous counterparts or when indigenous counterparts were rudimentary. New crops, agricultural implements, and domestic animals were recognized by most Indian groups as useful. And since indigenous patterns of care of the few domestic animals known did not furnish a broad enough base on which radically to modify Spanish practices of animal husbandry, these are overwhelmingly predominant in America. Where agriculture with some other tool than the digging stick was feasible, the utility of Spanish methods, especially the plow and ox, was usually apparent; hence in much of America, Spanish agricultural techniques used in preparing the ground, sowing, and harvesting (e.g., broadcast sowing of grain and the division of fields into melgas) predominate. With respect to heavy transportation the Spanish solid-wheeled oxcart, the *carro chirrión,* had no native competitor in America, and it was soon widely adopted. Indigenous metalworking techniques were so limited that they offered no serious competition to European methods.

Conversely, where there were satisfactory native counterparts, Spanish influence was much less marked. This is particularly apparent with respect to food, and in the practices and beliefs associated with the life cycle. Although religious, political, and social institutions were well developed in America, and therefore might be expected to have changed less rapidly than they did, the special manner in which they were singled out for formal attention by the conquerors caused the native institutions to disintegrate at a rapid rate.

2. Again, in the field of material culture and techniques, Spanish forms set the pattern when they were recognized by the Indians as obviously superior to, or representing a significant extension of, their indigenous forms. The Moorish roof tile, the primitive Iberian potter's kiln, and the Spanish carpenter's simple tools were all widely (but by no means universally) adopted. The ubiquity of Spanish-type fishing devices certainly again reflects the fact that they were recognized by Indians as preferable to their own types. At least some Spanish costume was better than existing Indian types: outside the area of the llama, wool cloth made possible by the introduction of sheep was an enormous boon to both sexes. The fulled bayeta skirt must have brought previously unknown comfort to Indian women, and woolen blankets, blouses, and jackets must have been appreciated by all wearers in cold areas. The Spanish flat-bed loom, although by no means replacing the native back-strap loom, quickly found its place, further contributing to more adequate clothing and a more comfortable bed. (It must be remembered that the patterns of Indian clothing in parts of Colonial America were also set by decree.) And the Old World crops of wheat, rye, barley, sugarcane, and many vegetables and fruits, as well as Spanish animals—sheep, cattle, horses, the chicken, burro, and pig— represent significant extensions of indigenous content.

3. In the field of folk culture, in a somewhat limited sense of the term, the processes at work in the acceptance or rejection of Spanish elements by Indian cultures are less clear than in the two foregoing categories. We are dealing here with areas of culture not of primary concern to State and Church and with areas of culture in which obvious superiority either does not exist or cannot be easily recognized. This is an area in which chance, and perhaps the personality of unusual individuals, both Spanish and Indian, seems to have played a very important role. With respect to such things as dietary patterns, superstitions, folk medicine, folklore, and music, Spanish traits found themselves in competition with indigenous traits, and often with no clear advantage. Here individual motivation is an important factor, but at this distance in time it is difficult to work out these motivations. We can assume that the motivations that are important in contemporary culture change—prestige and curiosity, to name two—were equally important in sixteenth-century America, but it is difficult to link these general motivations to the introduction of specific traits. To the extent that it can be done, it must be done with historical techniques.

Now let us turn to the second of the two approaches—that involving a time dimension—which help in understanding what happens to conquest culture in the recipient area. This approach concerns the question of the geographical origin in Spain of Hispanic American traits and complexes. The problem is whether we can find Spanish foci or distribution areas for prototypes of such things as agricultural tools, transportation devices, fishing techniques, clothing forms, beliefs and practices associated with the life cycle, and popular religious observances. If we find such distribution areas, what implications do they hold for understanding the sequence of presentation of conquest culture to America? And what do they have to do with the concept of "cultural crystallization?"

Although peninsular distribution areas for Hispanic American proto-types have not been worked out in detail, certain broad patterns, which will shortly be pointed out, do exist. That is, Spanish culture in America does not represent an equal and balanced selection from all parts of the country; some areas of Spain are much more heavily represented than others. Why is this? A common explanation is based on the theory of what may be called "proportional representation." Since we know that cultures meet through their carriers, each individual—each emigrant of a donor cul-ture—is a potential device for transmitting something of his local culture to the new region. Therefore, it might be expected that each geographical area of such a country as Spain would be represented culturally in America in proportion to its share of the total numbers of emigrants who left the peninsula. The apparent predominance of Andalusian and Extremaduran traits in America is therefore often "explained" by saying that "a majority of conquistadors and settlers came from these areas."

If we utilize the data presented in this monograph to determine whether in fact the cultures of Andalusia and Extremadura are most heavily represented in America, we come to the conclusion that this popular belief is essentially correct. Minor modifications are needed: eastern Andalusia appears less important, and much of New Castile and the southerly parts of Old Castile and León must be included in the area of greatest influence. Here are samples of the data that lead one to this conclusion:

Agriculture.—In America the Andalusian and Extremaduran plow is found to the apparent exclusion of all other peninsular forms. The highly useful Castilian threshing sledge (tribulum) is unknown, while the absence of the modern Andalusian threshing cart (the ancient plostellum) can be explained on the basis of its nineteenth-century reintroduction into southern Spain, so that it was not available in earlier centuries for export to America. For drawing plows and carts the north-Spanish neck yoke is uncommon or absent in America, its place taken by the central-southern Spanish horn yoke.

Fishing.—American net types and terminology, especially the various parts of the jábega-chinchorro seine, suggest the Andalusian coast rather than Galicia or Catalonia. I have no explanation, however, for the puzzling fact that the term "chinchorro" appears to be used in all Spanish America to the complete exclusion of the more common Spanish term "jábega," and the near exclusion of the term "boliche." Perhaps American net forms are drawn from a very limited area of Andalusia where the term "chinchorro" predominated. In view of the great variation in terminology applied to similar nets along Spanish coasts, this is certainly a possibility.

Arts and crafts.—Spanish American folk pottery techniques of peninsular origin appear to draw most heavily on Spanish forms found from Granada west, and then north to León, while American manufacture of finer ware, such as Talavera, is due to Sevillian and Toledan influence. With respect to the textile arts, the south-Spanish horizontal spinning wheel rather than the north-Spanish upright model is found in America. Spanish American folk costume suggests south Spain rather than north Spain; for example, the garments of peasant women from Old Castile north are surprisingly different from those of women in rural America. Some specific items, like the *tapada* of colonial Peru, quite obviously come from Andalusia. Salamancan jewelry, especially such things as articulated silver fish, appears to be ancestral to many Peruvian and Mexican forms.

Social patterns.—To the extent that a peninsular type of compadrazgo is ancestral to Hispanic American variants, it is Andalusian. Negatively, the absence in America of the widespread Old Castilian-Leonese institution of bachelors' societies (p. 126), and of most of the popular wedding customs and forms of horseplay of north-central and northwest Spain, is significant.

Funerary practices.—On the basis of available data the customs of Extremadura, Huelva, and parts of New Castile are particularly suggestive of America, although the baile del angelito points to the southeast. At the time of the Conquest, however, this custom may well have been much more widespread. Negatively, the north-Spanish funeral orgy appears not to have characterized America, nor have paid mourners been noted in the New World. Likewise, north-Spanish inheritance patterns seem to have had little influence in America, whereas south-Spanish forms have been important.

Popular religious practices.—A number of widespread central and northern Spanish activities are little known or lacking entirely in America. Among these are the pig of St. Anthony, the Candlemas torte, the festivities of Santa Agueda and the married women's cofradía, and la maya. The "burial of the sardine," general in central and northern Spain in earlier years, was absent in Andalusia, and very rare in America.

Speech.—Although linguistic acculturation is an enormously complicated subject, which cannot be touched upon here, in a general way it seems that southern and western Spanish variants of Castilian were more important in America than central and northern forms.

This list deals primarily with cultural elements brought to America through informal channels. It is clear that the formally transmitted categories of culture, in which Church and State policy were predominant, are Castilian rather than Andalusian-Extremaduran. This is to be expected, for the obvious reason that Castile was the kingdom of the ruling house and of the administrators and churchmen most concerned with government.

If we therefore ignore these formally transmitted categories of culture, it looks as if we have a good case for the hypothesis of "proportional representation" as it is popularly expressed: a preponderance of southern and western influences, because of a preponderance of emigrants from these areas. But we know now, from data presented in chapter 3, that the old belief in the importance of settlers from Andalusia and Extremadura is not borne out by demographic data. Sufficiently large numbers of emigrants came from nearly all parts of the country, so that we might logically expect less Andalusian-Extremaduran influence and more from Old Castile, Asturias, Navarre, Aragón, León, and Galicia. What explanation can be advanced to explain the seeming anomaly of a disproportionately large total of cultural influences stemming from Andalusia-Extremadura as compared with the numbers of emigrants from these regions?

The answer appears to lie in the *sequence* of formation and presentation of conquest culture. It is probable that at any given time undirected conquest culture (i.e., that not controlled by Church and State) was made up of elements which reflected at least a rough correlation between subcultural areas and numbers of emigrants from these areas. This means that conquest culture was not formed overnight, to remain essentially static over a long period of time. Rather, it was fluid, changing over the years as the composition of its carriers changed. At any specific time it was given shape by the culture type of the most numerous groups of emigrants, at least as far as informally transmitted elements are concerned.

In its earliest manifestation, then, it must have represented the local culture of the first waves of conquistadors and settlers. And these people, we know, did come in significant numbers from Andalusia and Extremadura. While it is true that, if we consider the entire sixteenth century or even the first fifty years of widespread emigration, nearly all parts of Spain were represented in significant quantity, it is also true that during the first two or three decades the provinces of western Andalusia, Extremadura, New Castile, southern León, and southern Old Castile were particularly well represented. This is by no means a homogeneous culture area, but there are basic similarities which stem from the fact that its northern part had recolonized its southern part several centuries earlier.

Therefore, during the very first years of conquest and settlement in America, in its unplanned aspects conquest culture represented southwest and west-central Spain rather than the north. This initial phase was relatively short, although I hesitate to set a time span. It was a highly fluid, formative period in America in which the basic answers to new conditions of life had to be found, and a rapid adaptation to changed conditions on the part of both Indians and Spaniards was imperative. This was the period of the blocking out of colonial cultures. Quick decisions, individual and collective, conscious and unconscious, had to be made on innumerable points. And the information on which settlers had to draw, in making these decisions, was the knowledge that characterized their particular variants of Spanish culture.

The basic outlines of the new colonial cultures took shape at a rapid rate. Once they became comparatively well integrated and offered preliminary answers to the most pressing problems of settlers, their forms became more rigid: they may be said to have crystallized. After crystallization, and during a period of reasonably satisfactory adjustments to social and natural environments, the new Spanish American colonial cultures appear to have become more resistant to continuing Spanish influence. These stabilizing cultures were then less receptive to change and less prone to accept new elements from the parent culture which had been left behind or rejected in the initial movement.

When, then, increasing numbers of emigrants from more northerly areas reached the New World, they encountered a going concern to which they had to adapt themselves. The culture they brought with them, which would have been perfectly adequate in working out solutions to new problems in America, was now less important, simply because it came later in the time sequence.

The duration of the initial period of fluid cultural conditions and hospitality to Spanish forms is difficult to determine. It varied from place to place, depending on the date of effective conquest. On the mainland this initial period began and ended first in central Mexico, whereas in South America it came some years later. Writing about Yucatan, Scholes says that the basic pattern of Hispano-Indian society

was clearly marked out by the end of the sixteenth century or about sixty years after the Conquest. By that time a new ruling caste of foreign origin, extremely jealous of its privileges, had obtained firm control over the destinies of the Maya race; . . . and a considerable amount of fusion of culture, especially in the realm of religion, had taken place. *During the remainder of the colonial period these basic problems of provincial society remained essentially the same* (1937, p. 531, my italics).

There is evidence for the validity of the concept of cultural crystallization from other sources. Herskovits, faced with the problem of reconciling the fact that slaves were drawn from a wide African area but that major Negro influences in America apparently represent a relatively restricted area on the west coast, has come to similar conclusions. He believes the answer to his problem lies in the fact that "the slaves who came late to the New World had to accommodate themselves to patterns of Negro behavior established earlier on the basis of the customs of the tribes" that preceded them (1941, p. 52), just as Spaniards who came to America after the earliest phases of conquest had to adjust to prevailing circumstances.

Pursuing this line of reasoning further, he suggests that in colonial United States the early Senegalese arrivals

were overshadowed by the traditions of the more numerous Guinea coast Negroes; while as for late-comers such as the Congo Negroes, the slaves they found were numerous enough, and well enough established, to have translated their modes of behavior . . . into community patterns (*ibid.*, p. 52).

I believe that similar processes explain the apparent predominance of southern and western Spanish forms in America. In the very early years of the conquest of America, Andalusian and Extremaduran emigrants were numerically superior to those from all other areas, even though well before the end of the sixteenth century this pattern had shifted drastically. Moreover, to the extent that items of material culture were carried to America—plows and nets, for example—they would certainly be objects locally manufactured near the seaports which traded with the Indies. Poor internal transportation in Spain would preclude the hauling of Castilian plows and Navarense yokes to Sevilla, when perfectly adequate local models were available.

The early decades in America were decades of decision, a time when new adjustments and colonial cultures were roughed out and the basic outlines set. To the extent that Church and State did not take charge, the customs and ways of the earliest immigrants had the best chance of surviving, of finding niches in the new societies. Equally satisfactory competing forms, which came with more northerly immigrants only a few years later, would find the functions they fulfilled already taken care of, and their carriers, like the later African slaves in the United States, had to adjust to the forms already set. After the first several decades a comparative hardening of colonial cultures occurred which, for a significant period of time, made these cultures less receptive to new items and less tolerant in their appraisal of later Spanish cultural influence.

If the concept of cultural crystallization is valid, it is clear that the common anthropological emphasis on social and psychological phenomena to explain acceptance or rejection of new elements by a subordinate people can never fully explain what takes place in an acculturation situation. The time sequence of formation and presentation of conquest culture plays an equally important role in determining the final selection of imported traits by native and colonial cultures. The sociopsychological reasons for acceptance and rejection can never be fully understood until they are placed in the perspective of time sequence and until it is recognized that new hybrid and drastically altered native cultures must make rapid decisions and then abide by most of these decisions, if they are to endure.

BIBLIOGRAPHY

(For RDTP read *Revista de Dialectología y Tradiciones Populares*)

ABU ZACARIA (Iahia Aben Mohamed Ben Ahmed Ebn el Awam)
1802. *Libro de agricultura.* 2 vols. Madrid.

AGUADO BLEYE, PEDRO
1947. *Manual de historia de España.* Vol. 1, " Prehistoria, edades antigua, y media."
Madrid.

AGUILERA, EMILIANO M.
1948. *Los trajes populares de España visto por los pintores españoles.* Barcelona.

AGUILERA Y ARJONA, ALBERTO
1916. *Galicia: derecho consuetudinario.* Madrid.

AGUIRRE BELTRÁN, GONZALO
1957. *El proceso de aculturación.* México, D.F.

AGUSTÍN SÁNCHEZ, RODRIGO
1932. *Folklore serradillano.* Serradilla (Cáceres).

AITKEN, ROBERT
1945. "Routes of Transhumance on the Spanish Mesta," *The Geographical Journal,*
106:59-69.

AITKEN, ROBERT, AND BARBARA AITKEN
1935. "El arado castellano, estudio preliminar," *Anales del Museo del Pueblo
Español,* 1:109-138. Madrid.

ALFORD, VIOLET
1937. *Pyrenean Festival. Calendar Customs, Music & Magic, Drama & Dance.*
London.

ALMELA Y VIVES, FRANCISCO
1946. *El traje valenciana.* Valencia.

ALMERICH, LUIS
1944. *Tradiciones, fiestas y costumbres populares de Barcelona.* Barcelona.

ALONSO DE HERRERA, GABRIEL
1790. *Agricultura general.* Madrid.

ALTAMIRA Y CREVEA, RAFAEL
1905. *Derecho consuetudinario y economía popular de la Provincia de Alicante.*
Memoir, Real Academia de Ciencias Morales y Políticas. Madrid.
1949. *A History of Spain from the Beginnings to the Present Day.* (Translated by
Muna Lee.) New York, Toronto, London.

ALVAR, MANUEL
1955. "Las encuestas del 'atlas lingüístico de Andalucía'," RDTP, 11:231-274.

AMADES, JUAN
1939. *Indumentaria tradicional.* Barcelona.
1953. "Calendario de analfabetos," RDTP, 9:416-466.
1955. "Imágines marianas de los Pirineos orientales," RDTP, 11:80-118, 275-306.

AMBROSETTI, JUAN B.
1917. *Supersticiones y leyendas, región misionera—Valles Calchaquies—Las Pam-
pas.* Buenos Aires.

ANDERSON, RUTH MATILDA
1939. *Gallegan Provinces of Spain: Pontevedra and La Coruña.* The Hispanic
Society of America. New York.
1951. *Spanish Costume: Extremadura.* The Hispanic Society of America. New
York.

ANONYMOUS
1844. "Los corporales de Daroca," *Semanario Pintoresco Español*, 9:182-183. Madrid.
n. d. "Corpus Christi," in *Enciclopedia Universal Ilustrada Europeo-Americano* (Espasa-Calpe), 15:842-844. Barcelona.
1923. "Folklorística y etología," Fourth section of Chapter 2 of "España política" in *Enciclopedia Universal Ilustrada Europeo-Americano* (Espasa-Calpe), 21:450-507. Barcelona.
1926a. "Isidro," in *Enciclopedia Universal Ilustrada Europeo-Americano* (Espasa-Calpe), 28(2):2065-2066. Barcelona.
1926b. "Sacramental," in *Enciclopedia Universal Ilustrada Europeo-Americano* (Espasa-Calpe), 52:1138-1143. Bilbao-Madrid-Barcelona.
1928. "Las fiestas de San Juan en Castilla," *Estampa*, No. 25, June 19. Madrid.

ARANZADI, TELESFORO DE
1897. "Der ächzende Wagen und Anderes aus Spanien," *Archiv für Anthropologie*, 24:217-225.
1943. "Aperos de labranza y sus aledaños textiles y pastoriles." In *Folklore y costumbres de España* (F. Carrera y Candi, Director), 1:289-376. Barcelona.

ARANZADI, TELESFORO DE, AND LUIS DE HOYOS SÁINZ
1917. *Etnografía, sus bases, sus métodos y aplicaciones a España*. Madrid.

ARCO Y GARAY, RICARDO DEL
1924. *El traje popular altoaragonés*. Huesca.
1930. *Costumbres y trajes en los Pirineos*. Zaragoza.
1943. *Notas de folk-lore altoaragonés*. Consejo Superior de Investigaciones Científicas, Instituto Antonio de Nebrija, Biblioteca de Tradiciones Populares, No. 1. Madrid.

ARENAS, PEDRO
1934. "Los trabajadores del barro," *Estampa*, No. 334, June 2. Madrid.

ARIAS GIRÓN, J.
1839. "Las bodas de los charros," *Semanario Pintoresco Español*, 1:211-212. Madrid.

ARTIÑANO, GERVASIO DE
1946. "Gente de mar." In *Folklore y costumbres de España* (F. Carreras y Candi, Director), 3:7-136. Barcelona.

ASH, HARRISON BOYD (translator)
1941. *Lucius Junius Moderatus Columella on Agriculture*. 3 vols. London.

AVRIAL, J. M.
1839. "El día de Santa Agueda en Zamarramala," *Semanario Pintoresco Español*, 4:257-259. Madrid.

BALMASEDA, FRANCISCO JAVIER
1885. *Tesoro del agricultor cubano*. Vol. 1. Habana.

BARANDIARÁN, JOSÉ MIGUEL DE
1935. "Vida pastoril vasca; albergues veraniegos. Transhumancia intrapirenaica," *Anales del Museo del Pueblo Español*, 1:88-97. Madrid.
1949. "Materiales para un estudio etnográfico del pueblo vasco: en Liginaga," *Eusko-Jakintza* (Revue d'Etudes Basques), 3:433-449.

BARKER, GEORGE C.
1957a. "Some Aspects of Penitential Processions in Spain and the American Southwest," *Journal of American Folklore*, 70:137-142.
1957b. "The Yaqui Easter Ceremony at Hermosillo," *Western Folklore*, 16:256-262.

BAUTISTA MERINO, JOSÉ J.
1949. *El folklore en el valle de Ojacastro*. Instituto de Estudios Riojanos. Logroño.

BEALS, RALPH L.
1946. *Cherán: a Sierra Tarascan Village*. Smithsonian Institution, Institute of Social Anthropology Publ. No. 2. Washington, D. C.

BEDATE Y BEDATE, PETRA
1928. "Zamora, trajes y costumbres." Unpublished manuscript, Museo del Pueblo
Español, Madrid.

BENAVIDES, JOSÉ D.
1932. "Los pintorescos y trágicos amores de los campesinos ibicencos," *Estampa*,
No. 256, December 3. Madrid.

BENITO MELERO, B.
1947. *Nomenclator estadístico de España*. Madrid.

BERGMANN, WERNER
1934. *Studien zur volkstümlichen Kultur im Grenzgebiet von Hocharagón und
Navarra*. Hamburger Studien zu Volkstum und Kultur der Romanen,
Vol. 16. Hamburg.

BIERHENKE, WILHELM
1929. "Das Dreschen in der Sierra de Gata," *Volkstum und Kultur der Romanen*,
2:20-82. Hamburg.
1932. *Ländliche Gewerbe der Sierra de Gata. Sach- und wortkundliche Unter-
suchungen*. Hamburger Studien zu Volkstum und Kultur der Romanen,
Vol. 10. Hamburg.

BIESANZ, JOHN AND MAVIS BIESANZ
1944. *Costa Rican Life*. New York.

BISHKO, CHARLES J.
1956. "The Iberian Background of Latin American History: Recent Progress and
Continuing Problems," *Hispanic American Historical Review* 36:50-80.

BOAS, FRANZ
1912. "Notes on Mexican Folk-lore," *Journal of American Folklore* 25:204-260.

BOLARÍN, ANDRES DE
1935a. "Los Reyes en la Huerta de Murcia," *Estampa*, No. 364, January 5. Madrid.
1935b. "Viernes Santo en Lorca," *Estampa*, No. 387, April 13. Madrid.

BOUZA BREY, FERMÍN
1949. "Teatro de carnaval en Galicia," RDTP, 5:406-414.

BOUZA BREY, FERMÍN, AND JORGE LORENZO
1947. "La casa, el trabajo y la cántiga en Pías (Mondariz, Pontevedra)," RDTP,
3:3-30. Madrid.

BRENAN, GERALD
1957. *South from Granada*. New York.

BRINKMANN, WALTER
1938. *Bienenstock und Bienenstand in den romanischen Ländern*. Hamburger
Studien zu Volkstum und Kultur der Romanen, Vol. 30. Hamburg.

BRUGAROLA, MARTÍN
1955. "Moros y cristianos ante el castillo de Maqueda," RDTP, 11:530-536.

BUSTAMANTE, MANUEL E.
1943. *Apuntes para el folklore peruano*. Ayacucho.

CABAL, C.
[1924]. *Los cuentos tradicionales asturianos*. Madrid.
1925a. *Las costumbres asturianas, su significación y sus orígenes: el individuo*.
Madrid.
1925b. *La mitología asturiana: los dioses de la muerte*. Madrid.
1925c. *La mitología asturiana: los dioses de la vida*. Madrid.
1928. *La mitología asturiana: el sacerdocio del diablo*. Madrid.

CABALLÉ Y CLOS, TOMÁS
n. d. *Costumbres y usos de Barcelona*. Barcelona.

CALA LÓPEZ, RAMÓN, AND MIGUEL FLORES GONZÁLEZ
1918. *La fiesta de 'moros y cristianos' en la villa de Carboneras*. Cuevas.

CAPMANY, AURELIO
1944. "El baile y la danza." In *Folklore y costumbres de España* (F. Carreras y Candi, Director), 2:168-418. Barcelona.

CARANDELL, JUAN
1924. "Datos para la geografía física y humana del litoral atlántico de la provincia de Cádiz. Estudios de una población típica: Rota," *Boletín de la Real Sociedad Geográfica, Revista de Geografía Colonial y Mercantil*, 21:301-334. Madrid.

1934. "El habitat en la Sierra Nevada," *Boletín de la Sociedad Geográfica Nacional*, 74:644-698. Madrid. (Now *Boletín de la Real Sociedad Geográfica*.)

CARDONA, MIGUEL
1954. "Creéncias y supersticiones diversas," *Boletín del Instituto de Folklore*, 1:76-82. Caracas.

CARO BAROJA, JULIO
1943. *Los pueblos del norte de la península ibérica*. Consejo Superior de Investigaciones Científicas, Instituto Bernardino de Sahagún. Madrid.

1944a. "El toro de San Marcos," RDTP, 1:88-121.

1944b. *La vida rural en Vera de Bidasoa (Navarra)*. Consejo Superior de Investigaciones Científicas, Instituto Antonio de Nebrija. Madrid.

1946a. *Los pueblos de España. Ensayo de etnología*. Barcelona.

1946b. "Olentzaro. La fiesta del solsticio de invierno en Guipúzcoa oriental y en algunas localidades de la montaña de Navarra," RDTP, 2:42-68.

1948. "Mascaradas y 'alardes' de San Juan," RDTP, 4:499-517.

1949a. "Los arados españoles (sus tipos y reparticiones)," RDTP, 5:36-96.

1949b. *Los vascos*. San Sebastian.

1950a. "Teoría de las ciudades viejas," *Clavileño*, 1(1):65-70. Madrid.

1950b. "Una fiesta de San Juan en Castilla," *Clavileño*, 1(5):57-64. Madrid.

1951. "Dos notas descriptivas: la agricultura en Vera de Bidasoa y caza de palomas en Echalar," *Eusko-Jakintza* (Revue d'Etudes Basques), 5:107-119.

1952a. "Disertación sobre los molinos de viento," RDTP, 8:212-366.

1952b. "Las 'nuevas poblaciones' de Sierra Morena y Andalucía," *Clavileño*, 3(18): 52-64. Madrid.

1954. "Norias, azudas, aceñas," RDTP, 10:29-160.

1955. "Sobre la historia de la noria de tiro," RDTP, 11:15-79.

1956. "En la campiña de Córdoba," RDTP, 12:270-299.

1957a. "Dos romerías de la provincia de Huelva," RDTP, 13:411-450.

1957b. "Semana Santa de Puente Genil (1950)," RDTP, 13:24-49.

CARRAL, IGNACIO
1929. "Como se casa la gente en Castilla," *Estampa*, No. 97, November 19. Madrid.

1935. "Boda en Castilla," *Estampa*, No. 381, May 4. Madrid.

CARRERAS Y CANDI, F. (Director)
1943, 1944, 1946. *Folklore y costumbres de España*. 3 vols. Barcelona.

CASARES, FRANCISCO
1950. "La Pasión de Cájiz," *Ya*, No. 3435 (Apr. 12). Madrid.

CASAS GASPAR, ENRIQUE
1947. *Costumbres españolas de nacimiento, noviazgo, casamiento y muerte*. Madrid.

1950a. "El carnaval en España," In *Homenaje a Don Luis de Hoyos Sáinz*, 2:80-87. Madrid.

1950b. *Ritos agrarios. Folklore campesino español*. Madrid.

CASAS TORRES, JOSÉ MANUEL
1943. "La barraca de la Huerta de Valencia," *Estudios Geográficos*, 4:113-178.

1944. *La vivienda y los nucleos de población rurales de la Huerta de Valencia*. Consejo Superior de Investigaciones Científicas, Instituto Juan Sebastián Elcano. Madrid.

CASAS TORRES, JOSÉ MANUEL, AND JOSÉ V. ARAUS AZLOR
1945. "Un mapa de los mercados de la provincia de Teruel," *Estudios Geográficos,* 6(20-21):525-555.
CASAS TORRES, JOSÉ MANUEL, AND ALFREDO FLORISTÁN SAMANES
1945. "Un mapa de los mercados de la provincia de Huesca," *Estudios Geográficos,* 6(20-21):461-487.
CASAS TORRES, JOSÉ MANUEL, AND ANGEL ABASCAL GARAYOA
1948. *Mercados geográficos y ferias de Navarra.* Consejo Superior de Investigaciones Científicas, Diputación Foral de Navarra. Zaragoza.
CASAS TORRES, JOSÉ MANUEL, AND JOAQUÍN PARDO CAJAL
1945. "Un mapa de los mercados de la provincia de Zaragoza," *Estudios Geográficos,* 6(20-21):489-523.
CASTELLANOS, BASILIO SEBASTIÁN
1845a. "De los aguinaldos o regalos de Año Nuevo," *Semanario Pintoresco Español,* 10:3-4. Madrid.
1845b. "Del origen de los llamados años, y estrechos de año nuevo y día de Reyes," *Semanario Pintoresco Español,* 10:18-20. Madrid.
1845c. "Jurado de los estrechos de amor de Castilla y de Aragón," *Semanario Pintoresco Español,* 10:27-29. Madrid.
1850. "La Pascua de Resurrección," *La Semana, Periódico Pintoresco Universal,* 1:365-366. Madrid.
CASTELLANOS, EL MARQUÉS DE
1953. "Tradiciones religiosas de Pascualcobo (Avila)," RDTP, 9:329-349.
CASTILLO DE LUCAS, A.
1943. *Folklore médico-religioso. Hagiografías paramédicas.* Madrid.
CASTILLO Y ARISTA, ISABEL DEL
1919. "Estudio del traje típico de Jaén." Unpublished manuscript, Museo del Pueblo Español, Madrid.
CASTRO, AMÉRICO
1954. *The Structure of Spanish History.* Princeton, New Jersey.
CEDILLA, EL CONDE DE
1931. "Las fiestas de Santa Agueda en Hoyuelos," *Boletín de la Sociedad Española de Excursiones,* 39:169-182. Madrid.
CERVANTES, ENRIQUE A.
1939. *Loza blanca y azulejo de Puebla.* 2 vols. México, D.F.
CHÍA, JULIÁN DE
1895. *La festividad del Corpus en Gerona.* Gerona.
CHICO Y RELLO, PEDRO
1947. "El portento de caminar sobre el fuego," RDTP, 3:78-85.
CHRISTIANSEN, FRIEDRICH
1928[?]. *Spain in Pictures.* New York.
COELLO, FRANCISCO
1848-1870. *Atlas de España y sus posesiones de ultramar.* Madrid. (Series of provincial maps published during this approximate period. Maps also contain plans of principal cities of each province.)
COLOMA Y SANTANA, JOVITA
1930. "Folklore de la provincia de Palencia." Unpublished manuscript, Museo del Pueblo Español, Madrid.
COLÓN Y COLÓN, J.
1840. "La procesión del Corpus en Sevilla," *Semanario Pintoresco Español,* 2:187-188.
COLUCCIO, FÉLIX
1950. *Diccionario folklórico argentino.* 2nd. ed. Buenos Aires.
COLUCCIO, F., AND G. SCHIAFFINO
1948. *Folklore y nativismo.* Buenos Aires.

COLUMELLA. (See Harrison Boyd Ash.)

CORBATÓ, HERMENEGILDO

1932. *Los misterios del Corpus de Valencia.* University of California Publications in Modern Philology, 16(1) :1-72. Berkeley.

CORDERO, AUGUSTÍN

1780. "Sobre el trillo de Lucas Veléz," *Sociedad Económica (Matritense),* Memoir 1, pp. 48-51. Madrid.

[CORTADA Y SALA, JUAN, AND JOSÉ DE MANJARRÉS Y DE BOFARULL]

1945. *El libro verde de Barcelona.* Barcelona.

CORTAZAR, AUGUSTO RAÚL

1949. *El carnaval en el folklore calchaquí.* Buenos Aires.

CÓRTE, JUAN ANTONIO DE LA

1842. "Costumbres andaluzas. Los judíos de la Semana Santa," *Semanario Pintoresco Español,* 7:92-94. Madrid.

1844. "Navidad y Reyes," *Semanario Pintoresco Español,* 9:6-8. Madrid.

CORTÉS Y VÁZQUEZ, LUIS L.

1952a. "Ganadería y pastoreo en Berrocal de Huebra (Salamanca)," RDTP, 8:425-465, 563-595.

1952b. "Medicina popular riberana y dos conjuros de San Martín de Castañeda," RDTP, 8:526-537.

1953. *La alfarería popular salmantina.* Centro de Estudios Salmantinos, Universidad de Salamanca. Salamanca.

1954a. "La alfarería en Pereruela (Zamora)," *Zephyrus,* 5:141-163. Centro de Estudios Salmantinos, Universidad de Salamanca. Salamanca.

1954b. "Questionnaire sur la poterie populaire de la province de Salamanque (Espagne)," *Orbis,* 3:250-257.

1958. "Alfarería femenina en Moveros (Zamora)," *Zephyrus,* 9:95-107.

COSTA, JOAQUÍN

1915. *Colectivismo agrario en España.* Partes I y II, Doctrinas y Hechos. Obras Completas, Vol. 5, Madrid.

COSTA Y MARTÍNEZ, TOMÁS

1918. *Apuntes para la historia jurídica del cultivo de la ganadería en España.* Memoir, Real Academia de Ciencias Morales y Políticas. Madrid.

COVARRUBIAS OROZCO, SEBASTIÁN DE

1943. *Tesoro de la lengua castellano según la impresión de 1611, con las adiciones de Benito Remigio Noydens publicadas en la de 1674.* Barcelona.

COVES, FRANCISCO

1929. "Las cofradías de Sevilla," *Estampa,* No. 61, March 5. Madrid.

1935. "Recetario sevillano para sacar novio," *Estampa,* No. 381, May 5. Madrid.

CURIEL MERCHÁN, MARCIANO

1945. "Juegos infantiles de Extremadura," RDTP, 1:162-187.

DANTÍN CERECEDA, JUAN

1935. "El carro leonés del Concejo de Gordón," *Anales del Museo del Pueblo Español,* 1:139-148. Madrid.

1942. *Regiones naturales de España.* Consejo Superior de Investigaciones Científicas, Instituto Juan Sebastián Elcano. Madrid.

DAVILLIER, CHARLES

1949. *Viaje por España.* Madrid.

DELEITO Y PIÑUELA, JOSÉ

1944. *También se diverte el pueblo. (Recuerdos de hace tres siglos.)* Madrid.

DÍAZ MORALES, J. J.

1928. "Una boda en Lagartera," *Estampa,* No. 39, September 25. Madrid.

DÍAZ RONCERO, FRANCISCO

1930. "España gasta más de medio millón de pesetas en palmas para el Domingo de Ramos," *Estampa,* No. 117, April 8, Madrid.

Díaz Ungria, Carlos
1952. "Los diablos danzantes de San Francisco de Yare," Sociedad de Ciencias Naturales La Salle, Memoir, 12(32):95-106. Caracas.
Díaz de Villegas, José
1936. "Otra fiesta de 'moros y cristianos,' el ataque de Ochali a Sóller en 1561," *Africa*, September. Ceuta.
Diego Cuscoy, Luis
1943. *Folklore infantil*. Tradiciones Populares II, Consejo de Investigaciones Científicas, Instituto de Estudios Canarios. La Laguna de Tenerife.
Diego y González, J. Natividad de, and Africa León Salmerón
1915. *Compendio de indumentaria española*. Madrid.
Dobby, E. H. G.
1936. "Galicia: a Little-Known Corner of Spain," *The Geographical Review*, 26:555-580.
Drucker, Philip
1958. *The Native Brotherhoods: Modern Intertribal Organizations on the Northwest Coast*. Bureau of American Ethnology, Bulletin 168. Smithsonian Institution, Washington, D. C.
Dumont, Louis
1951. *La tarasque. Essai de description d'un fait local d'un point de vue ethnographique*. Abbéville.
Durán y Sanpere, A.
1943. *La fiesta del Corpus*. Barcelona.
Ebeling, Walter
1932. "Die landwirtschaftlichen Geräte im Osten der Provinz Lugo (Spanien)," *Volkstum und Kultur der Romanen*, 5:50-151. Hamburg.
Echagüe, José Ortíz
1947. *España, tipos y trajes*. Madrid.
Elen, R. P.
1950. *Advocaciones de la Virgen*. Barcelona.
Ellis, Havelock
1908. *The Soul of Spain*. London.
Emilio Jiménez, R.
1927. *Al amor del bohío (tradiciones y costumbres dominicanas)*. Santo Domingo.
Erminy Arismendi, Santos
n.d.   *Huellas folklóricas, tradiciones, leyendas, brujería y supersticiones*. Caracas.
Escobar Uribe, Arturo
1950. *Mitos de Antioquía*. Bogotá.
Espejo, Zoilo
1900. *Costumbres de derecho y economía rural consignadas en los contratos agrícolas usuales en las provincias de la península española, agrupadas según los antiguos reinos*. Memoir, Real Academia de Ciencias Morales y Políticas. Madrid.
Espinosa, Aurelio M.
1921. "A Folk-lore Expedition to Spain," *Journal of American Folklore*, 34:127-142.
1946-47. *Cuentos populares españoles recogidos de la tradición oral de España*. Consejo Superior de Investigaciones Científicas, Instituto Antonio de Nebrija. 3 vols. Madrid.
Fals-Borda, Orlando
1955. *Peasant Society in the Colombian Andes: a Sociological Study of Saucío*. Gainesville, Florida.
Fernández, José María
1949. "Un 'auto' popular de los Reyes Magos," RDTP, 5:551-621.
Fernández Costas, Manuel
1952. "Juegos infantiles en la comarca de Tuy," RDTP, 8:633-676.

FERNÁNDEZ MARTÍNEZ, F.
1931.   *Sierra Nevada.* Granada.
FERNÁNDEZ-NÚÑEZ, MANUEL F.
1914.   "Folklore bañezano," *Revista de Archivos, Bibliotecas y Museos,* 30:384-422.
        Madrid.
1931.   *Folk-lore leonés.* Madrid.
FERRANDIS, PILAR
1951.   *Nacimientos. Exposición celebrada en el Museo Nacional de Artes Decorativas.*
        Madrid.
FLECNIAKOSKA, JEAN-LOUIS
1954.   "Les fêtes du corpus a Ségovie (1594-1636)," *Bulletin Hispanique,* 56:14-37,
        225-248.
FLORES, ANTONIO
1877.   *Tipos y costumbres españolas.* Sevilla.
FLORES, LUIS
1959.   "De la vida y el habla popular en la costa atlántica de Colombia," *Revista
        Colombiana de Folklor,* 3(Segunda Epoca):127-135.
FLORES GONZÁLEZ-GRANO DE ORO, MIGUEL
1936.   "Fiesta de 'moros y cristianos' en la villa de Carboneras (Almería)," *Africa*
        (April), pp. 74-76. Ceuta.
FLOREST AN SAMANES, ALFREDO
1951.   *La ribera tuledana de Navarra.* Consejo Superior de Investigaciones Científi-
        cas, Instituto Juan Sebastián Elcano. Zaragoza.
Folk-lore Andalúz, El
1882-1883.   Sevilla.
Folk-lore frexnense y bético-extremeño, El
1883-1884.   Fregenal de la Sierra (Badajoz).
FONTAVELLA, V.
1951.   "La transhumancia y la evolución ganaderolanar en la provincia de Valencia,"
        Estudios Geográficos, 12:773-805.
FORD, RICHARD
1845.   *A. Handbook for Travellers in Spain and Readers at Home.* 2 vols. London.
1846.   *Gatherings from Spain.* London.
FORNET, EMILIO
1935.   "Boda en Valencia," *Estampa,* No. 381, May 4. Madrid.
FOSTER, GEORGE M.
1942.   *A Primitive Mexican Economy.* Monographs of the American Ethnological
        Society, V. New York.
1948a. *Empire's Children: the People of Tzintzuntzan.* Smithsonian Institution, In-
        stitute of Social Anthropology Publication No. 6, Washington, D. C.
1948b. "Some Implications of Modern Mexican Mold-Made Pottery," *Southwestern
        Journal of Anthropology* 4:356-370.
1951.   "Report on an Ethnographical Reconnaissance of Spain," *American Anthro-
        pologist,* 53:311-325.
1952a. "The Feixes of Ibiza," *The Geographical Review,* 42:227-237.
1952b. "The Significance to Anthropological Studies of the Places of Origin of Span-
        ish Emigrants to the New World." In *Acculturation in the Americas* (Sol
        Tax, ed.), Proceedings of the 29th International Congress of Americanists,
        2:292-298. Chicago.
1953a. "Cofradía and Compadrazgo in Spain and Spanish America," *Southwestern
        Journal of Anthropology,* 9:1-28.
1953b. "Relationships between Spanish and Spanish-American Folk Medicine," *Jour-
        nal of American Folklore,* 66:201-217.
1953c. "What is Folk Culture?", *American Anthropologist,* 55:159-173.

1954. "Aspectos antropológicos de la conquista española de América," *Estudios Americanos*, Revista de la Escuela de Estudios Hispano-Americanos, Sevilla, 8:155-170.

1955. "The Fire Walkers of San Pedro Manrique, Soria, Spain," *Journal of American Folklore*, 68:325-332.

FRAGUAS FRAGUAS, ANTONIO

1946. "Máscaras y sermones de carnaval en Cotobad," RDTP, 2:435-457.

1947. "Contribución al estudio de la Navidad en Galicia. Nadales, Aninovos, Xaneiras y Reyes." RDTP, 3:401-446.

FRIEDE, JUAN

1952. "Algunas observaciones sobre la realidad de la emigración española a América en la primera mitad del siglo XVI," *Revista de Indias*, 12(49):467-496.

FROTHINGHAM, ALICE WILSON

1944. *Talavera Pottery, with a Catalogue of the Hispanic Society of America*. The Hispanic Society of America. New York.

1951. *Lustreware of Spain*. The Hispanic Society of America. New York.

FUENTE ARRIMADAS, NICOLÁS DE LA

1925. *Fisiografía e historia del Barco de Avila*, Vol. 1. Avila.

FUENTE Y PERTEGAZ, PEDRO DE LA

1921. *Los heredamientos capitulares en Cataluña*. Memoir, Real Academia de Ciencias Morales y Políticas. Madrid.

F[UENTE], V[ICENTE] DE LA

1841. "La bajada del ángel," *Semanario Pintoresco Español*, 4:116-118. Madrid.

GALLARDO DE ALVÁREZ, ISABEL

1944. "La Navidad en Extremadura," *Revista del Centro de Estudios Extremeños*, 18:89-105, 117-138. Badajoz.

1949. "El culto de la santa cruz," *Revista de Estudios Extremeños*, 5:153-170. Badajoz.

GALVÁN DEL RÍO, CARMEN

1942. "Costumbres y fiestas de la natividad de la Virgen en Putla, Oax.," *Anuario de la Sociedad Folklórica de México*, 1:145-153, 1938-1940.

GAMIO, MANUEL

1922. *La población del valle de Teotihuacán*. 2 vols. México, D.F.

GARCÍA BOIZA, ANTONIO, AND JUAN DOMÍNGUEZ BERRUETA

1940. *El traje regional salmantino*. Madrid.

GARCÍA FERNÁNDEZ, JESÚS

1948. "Colmenar de Oreja: la industria de las tinajas y la explotación de canteras," *Estudios Geográficos*, 9:649-665.

GARCÍA FIGUERAS, TOMÁS

1933. "La fiesta de 'moros y cristianos' en Benamahoma (Cádiz)," *Africa* (June), pp. 110-113. Ceuta.

1939. *Notas sobre las fiestas de moros y cristianos en Benadolid (Málaga)*. Instituto General Franco para Investigación Hispano-Arabe. Larache.

1940a. *Las fiestas de San Jorge, en Alcoy*. Instituto General Franco para la Investigación Hispano-Arabe. Larache.

1940b. *Las fiestas de Ntra. Sra. de Gracia en Caudete*. Instituto General Franco para Investigación Hispano-Arabe. Larache.

GARCÍA ICAZBALCETA, JOAQUÍN

1899. *Vocabulario de Mexicanismos*. México, D.F.

GARCÍA-LOMAS, G. ADRIANO

1949. *El lenguaje popular de las montañas de Santander*. Santander.

GARCÍA MATOS, M.

1948. "Curiosa historia del 'toro de San Marcos' en un pueblo de la alta Extremadura," RDTP, 4:600-610.

GARCÍA MERCADAL, J.
   1928.   "Semana Santa en Aragón," *Estampa*, No. 14, April 3. Madrid.
GARCÍA RAMOS, ALFREDO
   1909.   *Estilos consuetudinarios y prácticas económico-familiares y marítimas de Galicia*. Memoir, Real Academia de Ciencias Morales y Políticas. Madrid.
   1912.   *Arqueología jurídico-consuetudinaria-económica de la región gallega*. Memoir, Real Academia de Ciencias Morales y Políticas. Madrid.
GARCÍA SANZ, S.
   1948.   "La quema de Judas en la provincia de Guadalajara," RDTP, 4:619-625.
   1951.   "Notas sobre el traje popular en la provincia de Guadalajara," RDTP, 7:141-151.
GARCÍA SUÁREZ, ALFREDO
   1950.   "Contribución al léxico del asturiano occidental," RDTP, 6:264-300.
GARRIDO ATIENZA, MIGUEL
   1889.   *Antiguallas granadinas. Las fiestas del Corpus*. Granada.
GARRUT, JOSÉ MARIÁ
   1950.   *Ramón Amadeu y la maravilla de sus belenes*. Barcelona.
GASCÓN DE GOTOR, ANSELMO
   1916.   *El Corpus Christi y las custodias procesionales de España*. Barcelona.
GIESE, WILHELM
   1934.   "Volkskundliches aus Ost-Granada," *Volkstum und Kultur der Romanen*, 7:25-54. Hamburg.
   1937.   *Nordost-Cádiz. Ein Kulturwissenschaftlicher Beitrag zur Erforschung Andalusiens*. Beiheft zur Zeitschrift für romanische Philologie. Vol. 89. Halle/Saale.
   1949.   "Notas sobre abejas y apicultura en el país vasco," *Eusko-Jakintza* (Revue d'Etudes Basques), 3:373-378.
   1951.   "Los tipos de casa de la península ibérica," RDTP, 7:563-601.
   1955.   "Telares de Astorga," RDTP, 11:3-14.
GIL MUÑIZ, ALFREDO
   1926.   "El valle de los Pedroches. El país y sus habitantes," *Boletín de la Real Sociedad Geográfica*, 66:45-76.
GILLET, JOSEPH E.
   1933.   "An Easter-Play by Juan de Pedraza (1549)," *Revue Hispanique*, 81(Pt. 1): 550-606.
GILLIN, JOHN
   1947a. *Moche: a Peruvian Coastal Community*. Smithsonian Institution, Institute of Social Anthropology Publication No. 3. Washington, D. C.
   1947b. "Modern Latin American Culture," *Social Forces*, 25:243-248.
   1955.   "Ethos Components in Modern Latin American Culture," *American Anthropologist*, 57:488-500.
GIMÉNEZ DE AGUILAR, JUAN
   1928.   "Los 'mayos' de Cuenca," *Estampa*, No. 24, June 12. Madrid.
GINER ARIVAU, L.
   1886.   "Folk-lore de Proaza," *Biblioteca de las Tradiciones Populares Españolas*, 8:101-308. Madrid.
GÓMEZ-TABANERA, JOSÉ M.
   1950.   *Trajes populares y costumbres tradicionales*. Madrid.
GONZÁLEZ IGLESIAS, LORENZO
   1945a. *La casa albercana*. Salamanca.
   1945b. "Nota sobre las gorras de rastrojera en la provincia de Salamanca," RDTP, 1:136-138.
GONZÁLEZ MARTÍ, MANUEL
   1933.   *Cerámica española*. Colección Labor, Sección IV, Artes Plásticas, No. 338. Barcelona.

1944. *Cerámica del Levante español. Siglos medievales.* Barcelona.

GONZÁLEZ PALENCIA, ANGEL, AND EUGENIO MELE
1944. *La maya. Notas para su estudio en España.* Consejo Superior de Investigaciones Científicas, Instituto Antonio de Nebrija. Madrid.

GONZÁLEZ SOL, RAFAEL
1947. *Fiestas cívicas, religiosas y exhibiciones populares de El Salvador.* San Salvador.

GOZALO BLANCO, ELENA
1921. "El traje y las costumbres en las provincias de La Coruña y Lugo." Unpublished manuscript, Museo del Pueblo Español, Madrid.

GUICHOT Y SIERRA, ALEJANDRO
1882-1883. "Supersticiones populares andaluces," *El Folk-lore Andalúz*, 1:21-27, 59-64, 199-203, 293-298, 337-341, 411-418.

GUTIERREZ DE PINEDA, VIRGINIA
1955. "Causas culturales de la mortalidad infantil," *Revista Colombiana de Antropología*, 4:11-85.

G., E.
1839. "Los Pasiegos," *Semanario Pintoresco Español*, 1:201-203. Madrid.

HAMY, E. T.
1900. "Note sur le plaustellum poenicum," *Académie des Inscriptions & Belles-Lettres, Comptes Rendus* 1:22-26. Paris.

HERNÁNDEZ DE SOTO, SERGIO
1883-1884. "La cruz de mayo," *El folk-lore frexnense y bético-extremeño*, pp. 280-295. Fregenal.
1884. "Juegos infantiles de Extremadura," *Biblioteca de las Tradiciones Populares Españolas*, 2:101-195; 3:85-205. Sevilla.

HERRERA, ADOLFO
1896. "Excursión á Elche," *Sociedad Española de Excursiones, Boletín*, 4:129-136.

HERSKOVITS, MELVILLE J.
1941. *The Myth of the Negro Past.* New York and London.
1948. *Man and His Works.* New York.

HISPANIC SOCIETY OF AMERICA, THE
1930. Eight folders illustrating modern Spanish pottery. No author. New York.
1931a. Series of nine folders showing Salamanca costume. No author. New York.
1931b. Three folders illustrating modern Spanish pottery. No author. New York.
n.d.(a). *Spain, Costume Details: Women's Coiffure, Jewelry.* (2 envelopes of pictures.) New York.
n.d.(b). *Extremadura Costume: Women's Festival Dress at Montehermoso, Caceres.* Envelope with pictures. New York.

HOYOS SÁINZ, LUIS DE
1922. "Medios naturales o primitivos de transporte en las diversas regiones de España," *Sociedad Española de Antropología, Etnografía y Prehistoria, Actas y Memorias*, 1:108-118.
1945. "Folklore español del culto a los muertos," RDTP, 1:30-53.

HOYOS SÁINZ, LUIS DE, AND NIEVES DE HOYOS SANCHO
1947. *Manual de folklore: la vida popular tradicional.* Madrid.
1953. "Zonas de la ornamentación en los trajes populares de España," RDTP, 9:126-139.

HOYOS SANCHO, NIEVES DE
1935. "Tocados y peinados femeninos regionales en España," *Anales del Museo del Pueblo Español*, 1:175-186.
1945. "Folklore indumental de España," RDTP, 1:139-157.
1948a. "Costumbres referentes al noviazgo y la boda en la Mancha," RDTP, 4:454-469.
1948b. "La vida pastoril en La Mancha," *Estudios Geográficos*, 9:623-636.

1951. "Fiestas en honor de Santa Agueda, patrona de las mujeres," RDTP, 7:446-456.
1952. *La casa tradicional en España.* Temas Españoles, No. 20. Madrid.
1953a. "Las fiestas del fuego." In *Antología ibérica y americana del folklore* (F. Coluccio, editor), pp. 145-149. Buenos Aires.
1953b. "Sobre las fiestas populares malagueñas," *Las Ciencias,* 18:163-171. Madrid.
1954. *El traje regional en España.* Temas Españoles, No. 123. Madrid.
1955. "El traje regional de Extremadura," RDTP, 11:155-177, 353-385.

HUNTER, MONICA
1936. *Reaction to Conquest.* London.

IBARRA Y RUIZ, PEDRO
1895. *Historia de Elche.* Alicante.

IRAVEDRA, LUISA, AND ESPERANZA RUBIO
1949. *Leyendas y tradiciones de la Rioja.* Logroño.

IRIBARREN, JOSÉ MARÍA
1946. *De Pascuas a Ramos.* Pamplona.
[1948]. *Retablo de curiosidades.* Pamplona.
1949. *Historia y costumbres.* Pamplona.

IZQUIERDO MOYA, JULIANA
1946. "Cofradías típicas en Pedroñera (Cuenca)," RDTP, 2:493-495.

JENSEN, OTTO
1946. "La Mancha (contribución al estudio geográfico de Castilla la Nueva)," *Estudios Geográficos,* 7:269-312, 479-524.

JIMÉNEZ DE GREGORIO, FERNANDO
1950. "La población en la Jara toledana," *Estudios Geográficos,* 11:201-250; also 12:527-581 (1951); 13:489-558 (1952); 15:209-245 (1954).

JIMÉNEZ SÁNCHEZ, SEBASTIÁN
1954. "Del folklore canario. El mes de San Juan y sus fiestas populares," RDTP, 10:176-189.

JOHNSON, ADA MARSHALL
1941. "*Custodias* for the Processions of Corpus Christi," *Notes Hispanic,* pp. 63-91. The Hispanic Society of America. New York.

KANY, CHARLES E.
1929. *Fiestas y costumbres españolas.* New York.
1932. *Life and Manners in Madrid, 1750-1800.* Berkeley.

KELLY, ISABEL, HÉCTOR GARCÍA MANZANEDO, AND CATALINA GÁRATE DE GARCÍA
1956. *Santiago Tuxtla, Veracruz. Culture and Health.* Institute of Inter-American Affairs and Dirección de Estudios Experimentales, Secretaría de Salubridad y Asistencia, México, D.F. (Mimeographed).

KLEIN, JULIUS
1920. *The Mesta: a Study in Spanish Economic History.* Harvard Economic Studies, Vol. 20. Cambridge.

KLEMM, GUSTAV
1869. "Aus dem Leben des Landvolkes in Südspanien," *Globus,* 15:88-91, 113-115.

KROEBER, A. L.
1948. *Anthropology.* New York.

KRÜGER, FRITZ
1925. *Die Gegenstandskultur Sanabrias und seiner Nachbargebiete.* Abhandlungen aus dem Gebeit der Auslandskunde, Vol. 20. Hamburgische Universität, Hamburg.
1927. "Die nordwestiberische Volkskultur," *Wörter und Sachen,* 10:45-137.
1929. "Sach- und Wortkundliches vom Wasser in den Pyrenäen," *Volkstum und Kultur der Romanen,* 2:139-243.
1935a. "Die Hochpyrenäen. B. Hirtenkultur," *Volkstum und Kultur der Romanen,* 8:1-103.

1935b. "Die Hochpyrenäen. D. Hausindustrie–Tracht–Gewerbe," *Volkstum und Kultur der Romanen*, 8:211-328.

1936a. *Die Hochpyrenäen. A. Landschaften, Haus und Hof.* Band I. Abhandlungen aus dem Gebiet der Auslandskunde, Vol. 44. Hänsische Universität. Hamburg.

1936b. *Die Hochpyrenäen. C. Ländlichen Arbeit.* Band I. *Transport und Transportgeräte.* Institut d'Estudis Catalans. Barcelona.

1936c. "Die Hochpyrenäen. D. Hausindustrie–Tracht–Gewerbe" (Schluss), *Volkstum und Kultur der Romanen*, 9:1-106.

1939a. *Die Hochpyrenäen. C. Ländliche Arbeit.* Band II: *Getreide-Heuernte-Bienenwohnung-Wein- und Ölbereitung.* Hamburger Studien zu Volkstum und Kultur der Romanen, Vol. 32. Hamburg.

1939b. *Die Hochpyrenäen. A. Landschaften, Haus und Hof.* Band II. Abhandlungen aus dem Gebiet der Auslandskunde, Vol. 47. Hänsische Universität, Hamburg.

1944. "Las brañas. Ein Beitrag zur Geschichte der Rundbauten im austurisch-galicisch-portugiesischen Raum," *Volkstum und Kultur der Romanen*, 16: 158-203.

1947. *El léxico rural del noroeste ibérico*, Consejo Superior de Investigaciones Científicas, Instituto Antonio de Nebrija, Madrid. (Translation of Krüger, 1927.)

KURATH, GERTRUDE PROKOSCH
1949. "Mexican Moriscas: a Problem in Dance Acculturation," *Journal of American Folklore*, 62:87-106.

LARREA PALACÍN, ARCADIO DE
1952. *El dance aragonés y las representaciones de moros y cristianos.* Instituto General Franco de Estudios e Investigación Hispano-Arabe. Tetuan.

LASAGA Y LARRETA, GREGORIO
1934. "Un entierro montañés–las caridades luces–ofrendas–otros sufragios," *Altamira*, 1:170-192. Santander.

LEWIS, NORMAN
1956. "Letter from Ibiza," *The New Yorker* (March 10), pp. 90-110.

LEWIS, OSCAR
1951. *Life in a Mexican Village: Tepoztlán Restudied.* Urbana.
1952. "Urbanization without Breakdown; a Case Study," *The Scientific Monthly*, 75:31-41.

LEZÓN, MANUEL
1903. *El derecho consuetudinario de Galicia.* Memoir, Real Academia de Ciencias Morales y Políticas. Madrid.

LINARES PALMA, JOSÉ
1952. "Villancicos para las misas del aguinaldo y nochebuena de Juviles (Las Alpujarras)," RDTP, 8:686-700.

LINNÉ, S.
1937. "Hunting and Fishing in the Valley of Mexico in the Middle of the 16th Century," *Ethnos*, 2:56-64.
1940. "Bird-Nets of Lake Texcoco, Mexico Valley," *Ethnos*, 5:122-130.

LINTON, RALPH
1940. *Acculturation in Seven American Indian Tribes.* New York and London.

LISCANO, JUAN
1950. *Folklore y cultura.* Caracas.

LIS QUIBÉN, VÍCTOR
1945. "Medicina popular gallega," RDTP, 1:253-331, 694-722.
1947. "Los pastequeiros de Santa Comba y San Cibrán, RDTP, 3:491-523.
1949a. *La medicina popular en Galicia.* Pontevedra.
1949b. "Medicina popular gallega," RDTP, 5:309-332, 471-506.

López Morán, Elías
1900. *Derecho consuetudinario y economía popular de la provincia de León.* Memoir, Real Academia de Ciencias Morales y Políticas. Madrid.

López-Tapia Laplana, Tomas, and Eduardo Naval-Galindo Garcés
1929. "Contribución al estudio del folklore en España y con preferencia en Aragón." Sociedad Española de Antropología, Etnografía y Prehistoria, Memoir 73, pp. 247-257. Madrid.

Lorenzo Fernández, Joaquín
1938. "Die Bremse am galizischen Wagen," *Volkstum und Kultur der Romanen,* 11:282-289.
1949. "Los silos de Villacañas (Toledo)," RDTP, 5:420-434. Madrid.

Lowie, Robert H.
1945. *The German People: a Social Portrait to 1914.* New York.

Llano Rosa de Ampudia, Aurelio de
1919. *El libro de Caravía.* Oviedo.
1922. *Del folklore asturiano: mitos, supersticiones, costumbres.* Madrid.
1925. *Cuentos asturianos recogidos de la tradición popular.* Madrid.

Llopis, Rodolfo
1928a. "El misterio de Elche," *Estampa,* No. 35, August 28. Madrid.
1928b. "Moros y Cristianos," *Estampa,* No. 40, October 2. Madrid.

Llorca, Francisco de
1930. "Las procesiones de los 'picaos' en San Vicente de la Sonsierra," *Estampa,* No. 117, April 8. Madrid.

Madoz, Pascual
1845-1850 *Diccionario geográfico-estadístico-histórico de España y sus posesiones de ultramar.* 16 vols. Madrid.

Magán, N.
1841. "Procesión del Corpus y custodia de Toledo," *Semanario Pintoresco Español,* 3:177-179. Madrid.

Malinowski, Bronislaw
1945. *The Dynamics of Culture Change.* New Haven.

Manrique, Gervasio
1950. "La casa popular del alto Duero," RDTP, 6:574-582. Madrid.
1952. "San Pedro Manrique. Cultura popular pastoril," RDTP, 8:494-525; 563-595.

Marcos de Sande, Moisés
1945. "Del folklore garrovillano. Usos y costumbres," *Revista de Estudios Extremeños,* 1:447-460. Badajoz.
1950. "Costumbres funerarias," RDTP, 6:139-143.

María de Azkue, Resurrección
1935. *Euskaleriaren yakintza (Literatura popular del país vasco).* Vol. 1, "Costumbres y supersticiones." Madrid.
1947. *Euskaleriaren yakintza (Literatura popular del país vasco).* Vol. 4. Madrid.

Martín Echeverría, Leonardo
1940. *España. El país y los habitantes.* México, D.F.

Martín Granizo, León
1922. "Paisaje, hombres y costumbres de la provincia de León," *Boletín de la Real Sociedad Geográfica,* 63:352-402.
1929. *La provincia de León. Paisajes, hombres, costumbres y canciones.* Madrid.

Martínez, Matías R.
1883-1884. "Folk-lore de Burgillos. El paso de la santa cruz," *El Folk-lore Frexnense y Bético-Extremeño,* pp. 24-33. Fregenal.
1884. *Apuntes para un mapa topográfico-tradicional de la Villa de Burguillos.* Biblioteca de las Tradiciones Populares, Vol. 6. Sevilla.

MARTÍNEZ ALCALDE, E. AMALIA
1930. "Estudio de la cordillera central de España y sus sierras principales: Guadarrama y Gredos." Unpublished manuscript, Museo del Pueblo Español, Madrid.

MARTÍNEZ CORBALAN, F.
1930. "Los panes benditos de San Blas," Estampa, No. 113, March 11. Madrid.
1931. "La procesión del silencio, las cadenas y las cruces," Estampa, No. 168, March 28. Madrid.

MASON, LEONARD
1955. "The Characterization of American Culture in Studies of Acculturation," American Anthropologist, 57:1264-1279.

MÉNDEZ PLAZA, SANTIAGO
1900. Costumbres Comunales de Aliste. Memoir, Real Academia de Ciencias Morales y Políticas. Madrid.

MENDIZÁBAL, DOMINGO
1905. "Una boda en Oropesa," Boletín de la Sociedad Española de Excursiones, 13:13-16. Madrid.

MENDOZA, VICENTE T.
1955. "El alumbramiento en el México de antaño y hogano," Anuario de la Sociedad Folklórica de México, 10:79-94. México, D.F.
1957. "La danza durante la colonia en México," Tradición, 7(19-20):12-24. Cuzco.

MENDOZA, VICENTE T., AND VIRGINIA R. R. DE MENDOZA
1952. Folklore de San Piedra Gorda, Zacatecas. México, D.F.

MENÉNDEZ PIDAL, RAMÓN
1950. The Spaniards in Their History. Translated by Walter Starkie. London.

MESONERO ROMANOS, RAMÓN DE
1851. Escenas matritenses, por el curioso parlante. 5th edition. Madrid.

MILIÁN, MARÍA VICTORIA
1948. "Nombres de la tarabilla," RDTP, 4:312-315.

MIÑANO, SEBASTIÁN DE
1826-29. Diccionario geográfico-estadístico de España y Portugal. 11 vols. Madrid.

MINTZ, SIDNEY W., AND ERIC H. WOLF
1950. "An Analysis of Ritual Co-Parenthood (compadrazgo)," Southwestern Journal of Anthropology, 6:341-368.

MIRALBES BEDERA, MARÍA ROSARIO
1954. "La transhumancia soriana en el momento actual," Estudios Geográficos, 15:337-377.

MONGE, RAFAEL
1847. "Una boda en Carrascalejo," Semanario Pintoresco Español, 12:25-28; 35-38. Madrid.

MONTOTO, LUIS
1883. "Costumbres populares andaluzas," Biblioteca de las Tradiciones Populares Españolas, 1:1-99. (Chaps. 1-9.) Sevilla.
1884. "Costumbres populares andaluzas," Biblioteca de las Tradiciones Populares Españolas, 4:281-314. (Chaps. 10-14.) Sevilla.

MORÁN, CÉSAR
1931. "Datos etnográficos," Sociedad Española de Antropología, Etnología y Prehistoria, Memoir 88, pp. 197-215.
1945. "Folklore de Rosales, León," RDTP, 1:598-608.
1948. "Notas folklóricas leonesas," RDTP, 4:62-78.
1950. "Los 'casorios'," RDTP, 6:232-242.

MOROTE BEST, EFRAÍN
1953. "Dios, la virgen y los santos (en los relatos populares)," Tradición, 5(12-14):76-104. Cuzco.

MURPHY, ROBERT CUSHMAN
1925. *Bird Islands of Peru.* New York and London.

NARANJO PORRAS, PABLO
1948. "Costumbres de ayer y de hoy," *Revista de Estudios Extremeños,* 4:147-158. Badajoz.

NATIONAL RESEARCH COUNCIL
1949. Committee on Latin American Anthropology, Memorandum, "Research Needs in the Field of Latin American Culture," *American Anthropologist,* 51:149-154.

NAVARRO, VÍCTOR
1901. *Costumbres en las Pithiusas.* Memoir, Real Academia de Ciencias Morales y Políticas. Madrid.

NIEMEIR, GEORG
1937. *Die Deutschen Kolonien in Südspanien.* Ibero-Amerikanische Studien des Ibero-Amerikanischen Instituts Hamburg. Hamburg.

OLAVARRÍA Y HUARTE, EUGENIO DE
1884. "El folk-lore de Madrid," *Biblioteca de las Tradiciones Populares Españolas,* 2:5-100. Sevilla.

OLIVARES FIGUEROA, R.
1946. "Particularidades y evolución del carnaval venezolano," *Revista Nacional de Cultura* 7 (55):121-139. Caracas.
1949. *Diversiones pascuales en Oriente y otros ensayos.* Caracas.

OLMO, VICENTE DEL
1928. "La romería de hoy: San Isidro Labrador de Madrid," *Estampa,* No. 20, May 15. Madrid.

ORTIZ, FERNANDO
1956. "La zambomba, su carácter social y su etimología," in *Estudios antropológicos publicados en homenaje al doctor Manuel Gamio,* pp. 409-423. México, D.F.

OTAÑÓN, EDUARDO DE
1928. "El Corpus en Burgos," *Estampa,* No. 23, June 5. Madrid.
1934. "El 'colacho': la Máscara del Corpus," *Estampa,* No. 334, June 2. Madrid.

PALENCIA, ISABEL DE
1926. *El traje regional de España.* Madrid.

PALM, ERWIN WALTER
1951. "Los orígenes del urbanismo imperial en América," in *Contribuciones a la historia municipal de America* (Rafael Altamira y Crevea *et al.*), Instituto Panamericana de Geografía e Historia, México, D.F., pp. 239-268.

PAN, ISMAEL DEL
1932. *Folklore toledano.* Toledo.

PARSONS, ELSIE CLEWS
1927. "Witchcraft among the Pueblos, Indian or Spanish?" *Man,* 27:106-112; 125-128.
1930. "Spanish Elements in the Kachina Cult of the Pueblos," *Proceedings of the Twenty-third International Congress of Americanists* (New York), pp. 582-603.
1936. *Mitla, Town of the Souls.* Chicago.

PÉREZ BUSTAMANTE, C.
1941. "Las regiones españolas y la población de América (1509-1534)," *Revista de Indias,* 2(6):81-120.

PÉREZ-CUADRADO, JUAN
1948. *El piadoso arte de los belenes.* Barcelona.

PÉREZ VIDAL, JOSÉ
1945. *La fiesta de S. Juan en Canarias,* Tradiciones Populares 3, Instituto de Estudios Canarios, Consejo Superior de Investigaciones Científicas. La Laguna de Tenerife.
1951. "Tradiciones marineras; el castillo y la nave," RDTP, 7:697-703.

PFANDL, LUDWIG
1942. *Introducción al estudio del siglo de oro. Cultura y costumbres del pueblo español de los siglos XVI y XVII.* Barcelona.

PITT-RIVERS, JULIAN
1954. *The People of the Sierra.* London.

PLA CARGOL, JOAQUÍN
1947. *Tradiciones, santuarios y tipismo de las comarcas gerundenses.* Gerona-Madrid.
1948. *Gerona popular.* Gerona.

PONIATOWSKA, ELENA
1958. "Carnaval en San Juan de Aragón," *Magazine de Novedades* (Feb. 23), pp. 8-9, 16. México, D.F.

PONZ, ANTONIO
1947. *Viaje de España seguida de los dos tomos del viaje fuera de España.* Madrid.

PORRAS MÁRQUEZ, ANTONIO
1916. *Prácticas de derecho y de economía popular observadas en la villa de Añora.* Memoir, Real Academia de Ciencias Morales y Políticas. Madrid.

PRIETO RODRÍGUEZ, LAUREANO
1947. "Vida del individuo, tierra de la Gudiña (Orense)," RDTP, 3:558-578.

PUCHE, E.
1928. "La Semana Santa en Levante," *Estampa,* No. 14, April 3. Madrid.

PUENTE, JUAN
1935. "Boda en Cataluña," *Estampa,* No. 381, May 4. Madrid.

PUIGGARÍ Y LLOBET, JOSÉ
1857. "Festividad del Corpus-Christi," *El Museo Universal,* 1(11):81-86. Madrid.

PURSCHE, ANNA
1944. "Scenes of Lima attributed to Pancho Fierro," *Notes Hispanic,* 4:93-132. The Hispanic Society of America, New York.

QUILÉZ VICENTE, JOSÉ
1935. "Bodas en Aragón," *Estampa,* No. 381, May 4. Madrid.

RACKHAM, BERNARD
1927. "Renaissance and Modern Pottery." In *Spanish Art* (Burlington Magazine Monograph II), pp. 80-85. New York.

RADEMACHER, C.
1919. "Carnival," in *Encyclopaedia of Religion and Ethics* (James Hastings, ed.), 3:225-229. New York.

RAMÓN Y FERNÁNDEZ, JOSÉ
1945a. "El folklore sobre los niños, en Cariño (Coruña)," RDTP, 1:158-161.
1945b. "Jueves de comadres en Escurial (Cáceres)," RDTP, 1:211-215.
1945c. "Combate entre moros y cristianos en la Sainza (Orense)," RDTP, 1:554-560.
1948. "Fiestas en Torrejón el Rubio (Cáceres)," RDTP, 4:470-474.
1950. "Costumbres cacereñas," RDTP, 6:78-103.
1952. "Amuletos lunares, en Cáceres," RDTP, 8:407-424.

RAMOS, JOSÉ R.
1935. "Boda en Galicia," *Estampa,* No. 381, May 4. Madrid.

REDFIELD, ROBERT
1930. *Tepoztlán, a Mexican Village.* Chicago.

REDFIELD, ROBERT, RALPH LINTON, AND MELVILLE J. HERSKOVITS
1936. "A Memorandum for the Study of Acculturation," *American Anthropologist,* 38:149-152.

RÉPIDE, PEDRO DE
1914. *Costumbres y devociones madrileñas.* Madrid.

RICARD, ROBERT
1933. *La "conquête spirituelle" du Mexique,* Université de Paris, Travaux et Mémoires de l'Institut d'Ethnologie. Vol. 20, Paris.

1938. "Notes pour un inventaire des fêtes de 'moros y cristianos' en Espagne," *Bulletin Hispanique*, 40:311-312.

1940. Review of Tomás García Figueras, *Notas sobre las fiestas de moros y cristianos en Benadalid (Málaga)*. In *Bulletin Hispanique*, 42:166.

1945. "Encore les fêtes de 'moros y cristianos' en espagne," *Bulletin Hispanique*, 47:123, 147.

1946. "Les fêtes de 'moros y cristianos' à Juviles, prov. de Grenade," *Bulletin Hispanique*, 48:263-264.

1950. "La plaza mayor en España y en América," *Estudios Geográficos*, 11:321-329. Madrid.

1952. "Encore les 'moros y cristianos,'" *Bulletin Hispanique*, 54:205-207.

1953. Review of Ramón Touceda Fontenla, *La fiesta de moros y cristianos de la Sainza en la provincia de Orense*. In *Bulletin Hispanique*, 55:219.

RIGOBERTO PAREDES, M.

1920. *Mitos, supersticiones y supervivencias populares de Bolivia*. La Paz.

RINCÓN RAMOS, VICTORIANO

1945. "La indumentaria lagarterana," RDTP, 1:131-135.

1958. "Costumbres de Boda. En Lagartera (Toledo)," RDTP, 14:187-192.

RISCO, VICENTE

1946. "Creéncias gallegas. La procesión de las ánimas y las premoniciones de muerte," RDTP, 2:380-429.

1948. "Notas sobre las fiestas de carnaval en Galicia," RDTP, 4:163-196, 339-364.

RIVERA, ABELARDO

1945. *Geografía de España*. Madrid.

RODRÍGUEZ ELÍAS, AVELINO

1934. "El Corpus en Galicia: la 'Coca' y las 'Penliñas' de Redondela," *Estampa*, No. 334, June 2. Madrid.

RODRÍGUEZ LÓPEZ, JESÚS

1948. *Supersticiones de Galicia y preocupaciones vulgares*. 3rd edition. Madrid.

RODRÍGUEZ MARÍN, FRANCISCO

1926. *Más de 21,000 refranes castellanos, no contenidos en la copiosa colección del maestro Gonzalo Correas*. Madrid.

RODRÍGUEZ SANTAMARÍA, BENIGNO

1923. *Diccionario de artes de pesca de España y sus posesiones*. Madrid.

ROSA, CÉSAR DE LA

1935. "Dos mil Judíos tocan el tambor," *Estampa*, No. 382, May 11. Madrid.

ROSA Y LÓPEZ, SIMÓN DE LA

1904. *Los seises de la catedral de Sevilla*. Sevilla.

ROYO VILLANOVA, RICARDO

1936. "El folklore médico aragonés," *Revista Española de Medicina y Cirugía*, 19:128-140.

RUBIO, GERMÁN

1926. *Historia de Ntra. Sra. de Guadalupe*. Barcelona.

RUIZ-FUNES GARCÍA, MARIANO

1916. *Derecho consuetudinario y economía popular de la provincia de Murcia*. Memoir, Real Academia de Ciencias Morales y Políticas. Madrid.

RUMEU DE ARMAS, ANTONIO

1944. *Historia de la previsión social en España. Cofradías-gremios-hermandades-montepíos*. Madrid.

SÁNCHEZ, ANTONIO O.

1935. "Los fantasmas de Arcos: idilios por las gateras," *Estampa*, No. 381, May 4. Madrid.

SÁNCHEZ DE ALBA, ANTONIO

1845. "Semana Santa, función del santo sepulcro en Lebrija," *Semanario Pintoresco Español*, 10:89-91. Madrid.

SÁNCHEZ-OCAÑA, VICENTE
1933. "Cristo en la provincia de Barcelona," *Estampa*, No. 275, April 15. Madrid.
SÁNCHEZ-OCAÑA, JAVIER
1935. "Moros y cristianos en Alcoy," *Estampa*, No. 383, May 18. Madrid.
SÁNCHEZ PÉREZ, JOSÉ A.
1948. *Supersticiones españolas.* Madrid.
SÁNCHEZ ROIG, MARIO AND FEDERICO GÓMEZ DE LA MAZA
1952. *La pesca en Cuba.* La Habana.
SANFELIU, LORENZO
1944. *La cofradía de San Martín de Hijosdalgo navegantes y mareantes de Laredo.*
Consejo Superior de Investigaciones Científicas, Instituto Histórico de
Marina. Madrid.
SANTA MARÍA, MARGARITA
1925. "Memoria sobre Badajoz, Siberia extremeño y Tierra de Barros." Unpublished
manuscript, Museo del Pueblo Español. Madrid.
SANTUGINI, JOSÉ
1929. "Las fiestas de San Juan y de Santa Quitería en Huete," *Estampa*, No. 69,
May 7. Madrid.
SÁÑEZ REGUART, ANTONIO
1791-1795. *Diccionario histórico de las artes de la pesca nacional.* 4 vols. Madrid.
SARTHOU CARRERES, CARLOS
1930. "Los calvarios de Levante," *Estampa*, No. 116, Madrid.
SCHOLES, FRANCE V.
1937. "The Beginnings of Hispano-Indian Society in Yucatan," *Scientific Monthly*,
44:530-538.
SCHROEDER, W.
1937. "Die Fischerboote von Finisterre," *Volkstum und Kultur der Romanen*, 10:
157-211.
SERRA BOLDÚ, VALERIO
1946. "Costumbres religiosas." In *Folklore y costumbres de España* (F. Carreras y
Candi, Director), 3:503-662. 3rd edition. Barcelona.
SERRA RÁFOLS, ELÍAS
1950. "De la covada en Tenerife. Un caso concreto." In *Homenaje a Don Luis de
Hoyos Sáinz*, 2:388-390. Madrid.
SERVICE, ELMAN R., AND HELEN S. SERVICE
1954. *Tobatí: Paraguayan Town.* Chicago.
SOCIAL SCIENCE RESEARCH COUNCIL
1954. "Acculturation: an Explanatory Formulation," *American Anthropologist*, 56:
973-1002.
STANISLAWSKI, DAN
1946. "The Origin and Spread of the Grid-Pattern Town," *The Geographical Review*, 36:105-120.
1947. "Early Town Planning in the New World," *The Geographical Review*, 37:95-
105.
STAPLEY, MILDRED
1924. *Popular Weaving and Embroidery in Spain.* Madrid.
STARR, FREDERICK
1899. *Catalogue of a Collection of Objects Illustrating the Folklore of Mexico.* The
Folk-Lore Society, London.
STEININGER, G. RUSSEL, AND PAUL VAN DE VELDE
1935. *Three Dollars a Year.* New York.
STEWARD, JULIAN H.
1943. "Acculturation Studies in Latin America: Some Needs and Problems,"
American Anthropologist, 45:198-204.

Subías Galter, Juan
    1941. *Imágenes españolas de la virgen.* Barcelona.
    1943. *Imágenes españolas de Cristo.* Barcelona.
    1948. *El arte popular en España.* Barcelona.
S., N. B.
    1839. "Costumbres valencianas. Moros y cristianos," *Semanario Pintoresco Español,*
        1:140-142. Madrid.
Taboada, Jesús
    1947. "La medicina popular en el Valle de Monterrey (Orense)," RDTP, 3:31-57.
    1952. "La noche de San Juan en Galicia," RDTP, 8:600-632.
    1955. "Moros y cristianos en tierras de Laza (Orense)," RDTP, 11:334-352.
Tal, Fulana de
    1899. *Recuerdos de Cádiz y Puerto-Real.* Paris.
Teijón Laso, Evelio
    1948. "Los modos de vida en la dehesa salmantina," *Estudios Geográficos,* 9:421-441.
Tenoria, Nicolás
    1914. *La aldea gallega.* Cádiz.
Teresa León, Tomás
    1947. "Auto de los Reyes Magos," RDTP, 3:579-589.
Thalamas Labandíbar, Juan
    1931. "Estudio etnográfico del pueblo vasco continental," *Anuario de Eusko-Folklore,*
        11:1-120.
Thayer Ojeda, Luis
    1919. *Elementos étnicos que han intervenido en la población de Chile.* Santiago.
Thede, Max
    1933. "Die Albufera von Valencia," *Volkstum und Kultur der Romanen,* 6:210-273,
        317-383.
Toor, Frances
    1947. *A Treasury of Mexican Folkways.* New York.
    1949. *Three Worlds of Peru.* New York.
Torres Balbás, Leopoldo
    1946. "La vivienda popular en España." In *Folklore y costumbres de España* (F.
        Carreras y Candi, Director), 3:139-502. 3rd edition. Barcelona.
Torres Balbás, L., L. Cervera, F. Chueca, and P. Bidagor
    1954. *Resumen histórico del urbanismo en España.* Instituto de Estudios de Admin-
        istración Local. Madrid.
Touceda Fontenla, Ramón
    1952. *La fiesta de moros y cristianos de la Sainza en la provincia de Orense.* Tetuan.
Tout, T. F.
    1934. *Mediaeval Town Planning.* Manchester.
Townsend, Joseph
    1791. *A Journey through Spain in the Years 1786 and 1787.* 3 vols. London.
Vaca González, Diodoro, and Juan Ruíz de Luna Rojas
    1943. *Historia de la cerámica de Talavera de la Reina y algunos datos sobre la de
        Puente del Arzobispo.* Madrid.
Valdizán, Hermilio, and Angel Maldonado
    1922. *La medicina popular peruana.* Vol. 1. Lima.
Valladares, Marcial
    1884. "El folk-lore gallego: meiguesías ó supersticiones," *Biblioteca de las Tradi-
        ciones Populares,* 4:118-119.
Van de Put, A.
    1927. "Hispano-Moresque Pottery." In *Spanish Art* (Burlington Magazine Mono-
        graph II), pp. 71-85. New York.
    1938. *The Valencian Styles of Hispano-Moresque Pottery.* The Hispanic Society of
        America. New York.

VAREY, J. E., AND N. D. SHERGOLD
1953. "La tarasca de Madrid," *Clavileño*, 4(20):19-26. Madrid.
VÁZQUEZ DE PARGA, LUIS, JOSÉ MARÍA LACARRA, AND JUAN URÍA RÍU
1949. *Las peregrinaciones a Santiago de Campostela*. 3 vols. Madrid.
VÁZQUEZ SANTANA, HIGINIO, AND J. IGNACIO DÁVILA GARIBI
1931. *El carnaval*. México, D.F.
VELA ESPILLA, FRANCISCA
1935. "El traje de pastor en España," *Anales del Museo del Pueblo Español*, 1:168-174. Madrid.
VELÁSQUEZ, ROGERIO
1957. "La medicina popular en la costa colombiana del Pacífico," *Revista Columbiana de Antropología*, 6:193-241.
VERGARA Y MARTÍN, GABRIEL MARÍA
1909. *Derecho consuetudinario y economía popular de la provincia de Segovia*. Memoir, Real Academia de Ciencias Morales y Políticas. Madrid.
1917. "Divisiones tradicionales del territorio español," *Boletín de la Real Sociedad Geográfica*, 59:110-118.
1936. *Refranero geográfico español*. Madrid.
VICARIO DE LA PEÑA, NICOLÁS
1901. *Derecho consuetudinario de Vizcaya*. Memoria, Real Academia de Ciencias Morales y Políticas. Madrid.
VIOLANT Y SIMORRA, RAMÓN
1949. *El pirineo español*. *Vida, usos, costumbres, creéncias y tradiciones de una cultura milenaria que desaparece*. Madrid.
1950. "Características tradicionales, antiguas y evolucionadas, del hogar doméstico popular en Cataluña," *RDTP*, 6:430-495.
1953. *El arte popular español a través del Museo de Industrias y Artes Populares*. Barcelona.
1954. "Instrumentos músicos de construcción infantil y pastoril en Cataluña," *RDTP*, 10:331-399, 548-590.
VOIGT, PAUL
1937. *Die Sierra Nevada*. Hamburger Studien zu Volkstum und Kultur der Romanen, Vol. 23.
WEST, ROBERT C.
1948. *Cultural Geography of the Modern Tarascan Area*. Smithsonian Institution, Institute of Social Anthropology Publication No. 7, Washington, D. C.
WHITEFORD, ANDREW H.
1954. "Holy Week in Popayán," *Américas*, 6:6-8, 42-43.
WILHELMY, HERBERT
1952. *Südamerika im Spiegel seiner Städte*. Hamburger Romanistische Studien. B. Ibero-Amerikanische Reihe, Vol. 23. Hamburg.
YABEN Y YABEN, HILARIO
1916. *Los contratos matrimoniales en Navarra y su influencia en la estabilidad de la familia*. Memoir, Real Academia de Ciencias Morales y Políticas. Madrid.

PLATES

EXPLANATION OF PLATES

Plate 1. *Top*, Plaza of Medinaceli, Soria. *Bottom*, Threshing floors, Guadalajara.

Plate 2. *Top*, Threshing sledge (tribulum). *Bottom*, Threshing cart (plostellum).

Plate 3. *Left*, Windmill-noria pump, La Unión, Murcia. *Right*, La Mancha grain-grinding windmill, Madridejos, Ciudad Real.

Plate 4. *Top*, Persian water wheel (aceña), Río Segura, Murcia. *Bottom*, Shaved rump of mule, Madrid.

Plate 5. *Left*, Woman of Alosno, Huelva, wearing woolen shawl. *Right*, Woman fish-net mender, Grove, Pontevedra.

Plate 6. *Left*, Market plaza de la Verdura, Ugijar, Granada. *Right*, Alcaldesas, Zamarramala, Segovia.

Plate 7. *Left*, The Virgen de la Peña. *Right*, Devil dancer, Almonacid del Marquesado, Cuenca.

Plate 8. The Shrine of the Virgen de la Peña, Puebla de Guzmán, Huelva.

Plate 9. *Left*, Beehive seller, Puebla de Guzmán, Huelva. *Right*, Musician with flute and drum, Province of Huelva.

Plaza of Medinaceli, Soria

Threshing Floors, Guadalajara

THRESHING SLEDGE (TRIBULUM)

THRESHING CART (PLOSTELLUM)

La Mancha Grain-grinding Windmill

Windmill-noria Pump, Murcia

Persian Water Wheel, Murcia

Shaved Rump of Mule, Madrid

Woman Fish-net Mender, Pontevedra

Woman Wearing Woolen Shawl, Huelva

ALCALDESAS OF ZAMARRAMALA

MARKET PLAZA, UGIJAR, GRANADA

Devil Dancer, Cuenca

The Virgen de la Peña, Puebla de Guzmán

The Shrine of the Virgen de la Peña, Puebla de Guzmán, Huelva

Musician with Flute and Drum, Huelva

Beehive Seller, Huelva

INDEX

Acculturation, v, 1, 6-9, 12, 13, 17-18, 20, 21, 30, 50, 95, 103, 164, 227-234 *passim*

Aceña, 50, 62, 63

Acequia, 27, 50, 62

Agriculture, 24, 26, 27, 50-65; in acculturation, 228, 230; tools, 54-55; plows, 16, 50, 52-54, 230, 234; hoes, 54; threshing techniques, 4, 16, 50, 51, 55-56, 230; terracing, 57; irrigation, 24, 56, 57, 58, 62-64; superstitions, 60-62

Alcaldesas, in fiesta of Santa Agueda, 15, 171-172, 206, 212, 213

Alforja, 99, 102

All Saints' Day, 15, 150, 165, 167, 198, 201-203

All Souls' Day, 15, 144, 150, 165, 167, 198, 201-203

Angelito, 146; baile del, 143, 147, 155, 156, 231, in America, 157n

Animal husbandry, 70-76; prestige value of horses, 72, 217-218, 220; in acculturation, 228-229

Antojos, 112, 114

Ascension Day, 161

Assumption Day, 161, 167; in America, 208n; dance of seises, 197, 199-201; agricultural contracts expire, 65

Atarraya, 4, 16, 81; in America, 77, 85

Autos sacramentales, 15, 163, 169-170, 192, 193, 196

Bagpipes, in Galician Mass, 160

Baptism, 112, 114, 120-122, 162; compadrazgo, 122-123

Barrios, 6, 34; of a cortijo, 60

Basketry, 93-95, 102

Bastide, 39, 44, 46

Batanes, 100-101

Bears, simulated in Carnival, 173, 175-176; in America, 187n

Bees, 73-74; transhumance of, 74; advised at death, 74, 151

Bells, 159; death tolling, 143, 145; names, 159; replaced by matraca, 159, 179, 188n; tolling for All Souls' Day, 201, 202; Christmas carolers, 203; in America, 208n. *See* Cowbells

Birth, 112; afterbirth disposition, 112, 117; couvade, 119-120; cuarentena, 5, 112, 119, 170

Boliche, 16, 78, 82, 230; in America, 85

Bread, ceremonial importance of, 138, 149, 150, 155, 201

Broad beans, Epiphany king of, 169

Burial, orientation of bodies, 148

Cabañuelas, 50, 61, 169; in America, 69n, 168

Cabildo, to work communal lands, 66; of fishing cofradía, 83

Calendar, Christian ceremonial, 15, 160-161, 165, 167

Campanilismo, 34

Candlemas, 15, 61, 160, 161, 165, 167, 170-171, 206, 231; in America, 187n; ornamental candles of, 170, 187n; in Almonacid, 210, 212

Carnival, 15, 126, 172-177, 206; in America, 187n

Carro chirrión, 105-106, 228; in America, 110

Cemeteries, 144, 148, 149, 150, 152, 201, 202; used as markets, 47

Charro costume, 97, 98, 99

Chinchorro, 4, 16, 78, 230; in America, 77, 85

Christmas, 15, 161, 165, 203-205; shepherds attending Misa del Gallo, 75-76, 205; seises dancing, 197

Christmas carols, 203; in America 208n

Churches, architectural features of, 158-160

Circum-Mediterranean culture, 25-26, 51

Cities and towns: appearance, 38, 214; barrios, 6, 34; grid-plan, 3, 16, 34, 38-49 *passim;* planning, 38-47; rivalries between, 34, 36-37; sizes of, 35; street names, 34, 37-38

Climate of Spain, 22-23, 24

Clubs, bachelors, 36, 126-127, 139, 141, 231

Cock-baiting, 172, 176, 177; in America, 188